MINISTER'S ANNUAL

MINISTER'S ANNUAL

PREACHING IN 1988

Compiled and Edited by

Jim & Doris Morentz

ABINGDON PRESS
NASHVILLE

Minister's Annual
Preaching in 1988

This book is printed on acid-free paper.

Library of Congress Cataloging-in-Publication Data

Minister's annual.

1. Sermons, American. 2. Bible—Liturgical lessons, English. I. Morentz, Jim. II. Morentz, Doris, 1929–
BV4241.M563 1987 252.6 87-1789
ISBN 0-687-2699-1 (alk. paper)

MANUFACTURED BY THE PARTHENON PRESS AT
NASHVILLE, TENNESSEE, UNITED STATES OF AMERICA

To Paul I. Morentz, my father, who was born of Orthodox Jewish parents in Russia in 1888. Converted to Christianity in 1902, he then served as a Lutheran minister until his death in 1937. This year, 1988, is the one hundredth anniversary of his birth.

> "Jesus then said to the Jews who had believed in Him, 'If you continue in my word, you are truly my disciples, and you will know the truth, and the truth will set you free.' "
>
> (John 8:31-32)

IN APPRECIATION

of all those pastors who so generously permitted the use of their sermons to make this book possible.

PREFACE

SECTION I

There are fifty-two sermons with suggested scripture lessons, calls to worship, offertory scriptures and prayers, invocations, and prayers for the day. This book also includes three hymns for each day; one of which is featured as the Hymn of the Day, with a short history of the hymn included. As with the previous *Minister's Annual,* in addition to the service material there is the bulletin announcement for next Sunday's sermon, and the joke of the week.

SECTION II

This section is, in turn, divided into three parts:

- Special Seasons: Ash Wednesday, Maundy Thursday, Good Friday, World Day of Prayer, Thanksgiving, Christmas Eve
- Special Occasions: Confirmation, Weddings, Funerals, Stewardship, Communion, Incarnation
- Special Series: A three sermon series on the Holy Spirit—Receiving the Holy Spirit; Experiencing the Holy Spirit in Your Life; and Living the Holy Spirit in the Church.

SECTION III

This section contains information you can use, including:

Highlight dates of the church year; colors of the church seasons; Bible selections; and ideas you can use: Your church building talks! How to wake up your Sunday school.

SECTION IV

This section contains indexes, divided into three parts:

- Index of Scripture References
- Index of Names, Titles, and Hymns
- Index of Sermon Topics.

HOW TO USE THIS BOOK

The primary goal of this book is to offer you fifty-two Sunday sermons with additional helps to make your life as a pastor a little easier. Here's what we offer:

A dated sermon for every Sunday of the year, recognizing the highlights of the church and the national calendars.

Suggestions for building a service around the theme of the sermon. For each Sunday you will find a:

Call to Worship
Processional Hymn
Invocation
Sermon Scripture
*Hymn of the Day
Offertory Scripture
Offertory Prayer
Prayer of the Day
Benediction
Recessional Hymn

Using the above suggestions, you should have no trouble building your service.

In addition, each Sunday contains the lectionary lessons for the day as well as our *special feature for 1988, the history of the Hymn of the Day. There is also the announcement for next week's sermon and the ever-popular funny story of the week.

Those of you who used *Minister's Annual: Preaching in 1987,* will recognize that additional materials for each Sunday have been added in the 1988 edition. These additions are at the request of pastors who actually tested the *Minister's Annual.*

It is the intention of the editors to insert additional material each year as they recognize the need.

CONTENTS

SECTION I:

FIFTY-TWO SUNDAY SERMONS

SECTION II: SPECIAL SEASONS, SPECIAL SERMONS, SPECIAL SERIES

Special Seasons

Special Sermons

Special Series

SECTION III: APPENDIXES

INFORMATION YOU CAN USE, IDEAS YOU CAN USE

A. Information You Can Use

B. Ideas You Can Use

SECTION IV: INDEXES

SECTION I:

FIFTY-TWO SUNDAY SERMONS

Sunday
January Third

Call to Worship: Therefore, if any one is in Christ, he is a new creation; the old has passed away, behold, the new has come. *II Corinthians 5:17*

Processional Hymn: "O Jesus Thou Art Standing"

Invocation: Happy New Year, Lord. Here we are at the start of another new year. What will we do with this year? We can sadden or gladden your heart by the way we like and love one another. Let us make it a good year in your name. *Amen.*

Sermon Scripture: II Corinthians 13:5-9

Sermon Presentation: "The Gospel and Marley's Ghost: A New Year's Carol"

Hymn of the Day: "Break Thou the Bread of Life"

Offertory Scripture: [God, our Savior] saved us, not because of deeds done by us in righteousness, but in virtue of his own mercy, by the washing of regeneration and renewal in the Holy Spirit. *Titus 3:5*

Offertory Prayer: Let me make a new year's resolution. I want to serve my God better and return those gifts that are due him all year long. *Amen.*

Prayer of the Day

Lord, is it true that there is nothing new under the sun? You stood by the Father as he moved his Holy Spirit across the chaos and brought forth the creation we call home. Since the dawn of that first day, you have seen so many things done and undone, so many things come and go. Unfortunately, too many things stay the same—conflict between people and wars between nations caused by centuries old prejudices and fear of the unknown, the different, and the new; relationships strained and then broken by selfishness and mistrust.

It almost seems as if we are wrapped up in chains, held in bondage by our past mistakes, uncertain about the present, confused about our future.

The biggest obstacle we face is an age-old condition we call *original sin,* our rebellious tendency to go against your will, to do our own thing, to trust our own judgment, to be our own person.

But we must never forget that you, indeed, have made all things new. By the cross and the resurrection you have broken the hold that sin and death have on us. For the truth of your word, for the freedom of your gospel, we give you our most hearty thanks. *Amen.*

Benediction: But this I call to mind, and therefore I have hope: The steadfast love of the Lord never ceases, his mercies never come to an end; they are new every morning; great is thy faithfulness. *Lamentations 3:21-23*

Recessional Hymn: "Take My Life, and Let It Be Consecrated"

Lectionary Lessons: The Second Sunday after Christmas

Lesson 1—Jeremiah 31:7-14 or Ecclesiasticus 24:1-4, 12-16; Psalm 147:12-20
Lesson 2—Ephesians 1:3-6, 15-18
Gospel—John 1:1-18

History of the Hymn of the Day: "Break Thou the Bread of Life"

Mary A. Lathbury, talented artist and writer, became associated with the famous "Chautauqua Movement" in 1877, when she was hired as an assistant to Dr. John H. Vincent, secretary of the Methodist Sunday School Union. She spent the summer of her thirty-fifth year at the assembly grounds on the quiet shores of beautiful Lake Chautauqua in the Finger Lakes region of western New York. One day as she and Dr. Vincent were standing by the lake watching the sunset, the Methodist bishop asked her if she would write a hymn to be used by the Chautauqua Literary and Scientific Circle. Miss Lathbury agreed and began to think of a possible theme. As she meditated about the blessing that had been received at the summer conference, she related the thought to the multitude that had been fed with bread on the hillside by Galilee. Thus came to life the words which Christians have come to know and to love.

Announcement for Next Week's Sermon: How well does God know you? That question scares most people. You can run, but you can't hide. Let's face that question together next Sunday.

Story of the Week: An industrial consultant was making a study of the working habits of the men in a manufacturing plant.

Speaking to one of the foremen, he asked, "Do the men in your department drop their tools the moment the quitting whistle blows?"

"Some of them do," the foreman said, "but the neat and orderly ones always have theirs put away and locked up by that time."

THE GOSPEL AND MARLEY'S GHOST: A NEW YEAR'S CAROL

"What has been is what will be, and what has been done is what will be done; and there is nothing new under the sun." There are times when this observation, written by a forgotten preacher from long ago, seems to accurately assess the condition of human history. A passing glance at any of the year-end pictorial reviews, such as those published by *Time* and *Newsweek,* should demonstrate that, for all of our thousands of years on this poor, abused planet, we haven't learned very much.

Political assassinations, famine, drought, war in the Middle East, and tension between the super powers are all part of our daily headlines. So are ecological disasters, the escalation of terrorism, the arms race, poverty, and pornography. There is rarely a newscast that does not mention a rebellion of peasants against rich land owners, the rise of racial strife, or the continuing debate over the relationship between religion and government. While these are topics that are covered by our media almost every day, they could also describe just about any time in history. The Modern Era, the Middle Ages, the first century A.D. and the third century B.C., when Ecclesiastes was written, all have examples of humans treating one another in manners that are nothing less than inhumane. Even the threat of total annihilation is not new, for each society has feared for the survival of civilization as it was known at the time. No matter where we look in the past, we can find corruption, aggression, greed, and prejudice. Our record as stewards of God's creation is, in all honesty, rather poor.

This assessment flies in the face of the theory (or myth, depending upon your perspective) that humankind is advancing. Who was it that said Darwin had it backwards? It seems that despite all of our efforts to make things better, despite all of our technological developments and intellectual sophistication, we are not that much different from any people before us. True, our methods of waging war are more efficient; our means of subduing the earth are more permanent. Still, what has not changed are the impulses that drive us. We continue to be motivated largely by fear as much as anything else. Fear of change, fear of outsiders, fear of life, fear of death. "And there is nothing new under the sun."

This analysis may sound fatalistic or, at least, pessimistic. We all lapse into such moods every now and again. However, we are not the first to feel this way. The very same mood appears to have stricken the author of Ecclesiastes. He was not simply having a bad day at the office, which can usually account for occasional dark moments. Nor can his words be dismissed as the misunderstood remnants of an unfortunate amalgamation of ancient Greek and Hebrew philosophy. The author of Ecclesiastes was an astute observer of human history. What sounds fatalistic may, therefore, be realistic.

If Ecclesiastes is correct, if the belief that we can make a positive impact on our world is vanity, then we have to ask some difficult questions. We have to ask what point there is to all of our labor on behalf of the kingdom. If we cannot alter our course, if we can never make things better, then what point is there in having churches? What point is there in our benevolences, or in living beyond ourselves and our own desire for immediate comfort and pleasure? What point is there in gathering together in God's name as a community which seeks justice and righteousness? If there is in fact nothing new under the sun, why should we even bother to get up in the morning and go out into the new day? It comes down to this: If we see no chance that 1988 will be different from or better than 1987, we must protest that the upcoming new year is neither happy nor new. Happy New Year? Bah, humbug!

As I struggled with these thoughts, I found it impossible to ignore this dismal conclusion. I became so depressed and so frustrated that late one night, long after everyone else in the house had fallen asleep, I sat staring at a blank piece of paper. Unable to find as much as an uplifting, hopeful sentence to begin my New Year's sermon, I went to the couch in my study and awaited inspiration. I remember hearing the clock downstairs chime twelve times, signaling the arrival of midnight. As I lay there, I noticed lights flickering on the wall. I paid no attention to this occurrence, and assumed it was caused by a passing car. I then felt a small breeze, a cold draft of air which came up the stairs. A noise was discernible, a noise from deep down below, as if some person were dragging heavy chains over the casks in a wine merchant's cellar. I recalled a chilling thought: Ghosts in haunted houses are often described as dragging chains.

The basement door flew open with a booming sound, and then I heard the noise much louder on the floors below, then coming up the stairs, then coming straight toward the study where I was presently located.

Without pause, a figure came through the closed door and entered the room. I immediately knew him to be Marley's ghost, the very one and same who appeared to Ebenezer Scrooge in Dickens' classic *A Christmas Carol.* I knew it was he, though around his waist were not the cash boxes, padlocks, and ledgers that Dickens described. Rather, wound around him like a tail and attached to a long chain was a series of empty boxes, each bearing its own distinct label. One was marked "Meaning." Another read "Hope." Another yet read "Dreams." A fourth was labeled "Future."

Though I looked at the specter through and through and saw it standing before me, though I felt the chilling influence of its death-cold eyes and marked the very texture of the folded kerchief wound about its head and chin, I was still incredulous and fought against my senses.

"What's this?" I asked. "What do you want with me?"

"Much," said the ghost.

"But you are Marley's ghost, are you not? You were sent to haunt Scrooge—what have you to do with me? How is it that you have escaped the confines of literature to come into reality and appear before me this night?"

The figure did not answer these questions. Instead, it replied, "Ask me who I am."

"All right, who are you?" I responded obligingly.

"I am your partner in life."

"No!" I shouted. "You are the ghost of Jacob Marley, the partner of Ebenezer Scrooge, a fictitious character from a story written in the last century. You're not my partner! You're not even real!"

The ghost bellowed a huge laugh. "Ha! You think that I belong only to one person, in one place and one time? You think that I am the product of an author's imagination? Let me tell you, I existed long before Charles Dickens. In fact, I have been in existence for as long as mortals have walked upon this earth. I am not the ghost of Jacob Marley alone; I am the partner who travels through life with each and every person."

"This cannot be happening," I protested. "You are nothing but the sounds of a creaking old house at night. You are shadows on the wall brought by a passing car. Or you are a dream, a nightmare from which I shall soon awake and then laugh at myself for being so thoroughly deceived by my own unconscious thoughts."

At this, the ghost raised a frightful cry, and shook its chain with a terrible noise.

"Dreadful apparition," I cried, "why do you trouble me? Why do spirits walk the earth; and why do they come to me?"

"I was sent to offer you a warning," the ghost answered. "I am here to tell you that each person has an unseen partner who is about them in every moment. Your partner is your vision of life itself. It is the vision which sees meaning in existence or which, on the other hand, blinds you to all that is worthwhile about being alive. You possess one or the other, and the difference is great. Those who understand that life is good can withstand the greatest trials with determination and hope. Those who believe that life is a futile enterprise know only despair and defeat. Which of these two partners do you claim as your own?"

I told the ghost about my recent impressions of Ecclesiastes. I said that I was prompted to conclude that no individual has the ability to reduce the sufferings of the world. I went on to say that I was feeling as though our lives ought to be spent seeking nothing other than our own personal gratification in the present, as there seems to be no hope for the future.

The ghost bid me silence and then spoke. "If your partner is not soon exchanged for the other, you will be doomed to wander this earth and witness what you cannot share, but might have had. I wear this chain, a chain you are now forging in life; it is made link by link, yard by yard. Fastened to it are these boxes you now see: empty boxes, representing the emptiness you find in life. Oh! Captive, bound and chained! Never to find the peace which comes with the knowledge that life is filled with meaning and purpose, even when we cannot see it so!"

"Hear this," the ghost continued, "belief that the future cannot be altered, or that we must remain the way we are for all time, with no hope for the improvement of our common lot, will mean that this chain will be yours. Once on it cannot be easily removed. For with this chain tied around you, it will be exceedingly difficult to stretch out your hands to others. It will be nearly impossible to perform deeds of love and selflessness. This chain will cause you to seek a hollow happiness, a temporary illusion which, like the end of a rainbow, will disappear the moment you believe it has been acquired. Your life will be a constant search for something that does not exist. And your boxes, containing your hopes and dreams for the future, will remain empty."

These words, coming from one who had obviously been directed to confront me with the perilous course my life was set upon, were quite disturbing. They were also somewhat comforting, for they suggested that my fate was not yet sealed and that there was adequate time for me to change partners before the warning would become true.

"Does this mean that I may not have to wear this chain or drag these empty boxes with me through eternity?" I nervously inquired.

"Hear me and do not interrupt!" thundered the ghost. "My time is nearly gone!"

I meekly responded, "I will listen, but don't be hard on me, for I am only a humble preacher badly in need of a sermon."

The ghost resumed his message, saying, "Involvement in the welfare of humankind is an obligation, not a choice. If we refuse this obligation, we will discover that, rather than being fulfilled, our boxes will remain empty. Charity, mercy, forebearance, and benevolence are what make us important to others and what make our existence significant in the grand scheme of life. These are the values that endure the test of time. All else is but a facade, a pretense. Why, then, do mortals persist in walking through crowds of their fellow beings with their eyes turned down and never raise them to that blessed star which led wise men to the abode of Christ, who taught that it is in dying that we live abundantly?"

"How," I interrupted again, "do I begin lifting my eyes to the star?"

The ghost answered, "You lift your eyes to the star not by raising them to the heavens above, but to the world in front of you. In order to do this, you must live in the past, the present, and the future. You must see yourself as connected to all people who have ever lived in days gone by and in all who will ever have life in days yet to come.

"There have been many who have contributed to your life's history. There is a long stream of family, friends, preachers, and others who have helped you to know that your life is meaningful. You are linked to them as well as to those who, over the course of the centuries, have shaped the community of faith of which you are a part. You are linked to all those who have lived before you. Thus, you live in the past.

"By this creed you can live in the future: That you share yourself with others and reflect the importance of their lives upon your own and upon existence itself. Doing so will mean that your life will have an impact upon those around you and upon those who will come after you. In this way, you can live in the past, the present, and the future . . . but there is something else."

I demanded that my visitor tell me what else he had to say. He proceeded to do so with little encouragement.

"You must realize that you are, in Christ, a new creation. As I have told you already, you are connected to the past, just as I am to these boxes. The past is an inexorable part of who you are and who you can be. However, it is wrong to believe that your fate is determined only by what was. It is possible, and in some instances most desirable, to break the grip of yesterday upon tomorrow.

"You are not compelled to repeat the mistakes of those who came before you. Instead, you are called upon to cease their repetition. Neither are you justified in blaming the woes of the present on previous generations. It is the duty of those in each era to enact the means of achieving God's kingdom without finding excuses for the delay in its arrival. You are responsible for the world of the present. You are not forced to maintain the world of the past.

"Today is another opportunity to do what God desires. Do not let this opportunity pass! The process of creation did not end with the formation of the physical universe. Creation goes on and on in each person in each moment of life. We are able to declare in all confidence that the old has passed away and the new has come!"

The ghost fell silent and walked backward from me, and at every step it took, the window raised a little, so that when the ghost reached it, the window was wide open. The ghost beckoned me to approach, and I did. When we were within two paces of each other, the ghost held up its hand, ordering me to come no further. I stopped not so much in obedience, as in surprise and fear, for on the raising of the hand I became sensible of confused noises in the air, incoherent sounds of lamentation and regret, wailing inexpressively sorrowful. The ghost, after listening for a moment, joined in the mournful dirge and floated out upon the bleak night sky. I called after it, "I will live in the past, the present, and the future! The spirit of all three shall strive within me!"

At that precise instant the clock downstairs chimed once, informing me that an entire hour had elapsed since my visit began. I found myself lying on the couch, unaware how I might have arrived there after standing beside the window, which was now shut and locked. I am sure that many of you will think that this was a dream. Perhaps it was. Perhaps not. I am, though, certain of this: In Christ we are new creations, connected, but not shackled, to the past, and always hopeful about the future.

Happy New Year, and the Lord be with you, everyone! *Amen.*

Todd M. Wyrick

Magnolia United Church of Christ
Seattle, Washington

Sunday
January Tenth

Call to Worship: Rend your hearts and not your garments. Return to the Lord your God, for he is gracious and merciful, slow to anger, and abounding in steadfast love, and repents of evil. *Joel 2:13*

Processional Hymn: "Crown Him with Many Crowns"

Invocation: O Lord, do you know me? All too well! You know me so well I should be scared to death. I am not, because I know you well, too. You love me, and you died for me. That fills me with hope, not fear. *Amen.*

Sermon Scripture: Psalm 139:1-24

Sermon Presentation: "First, Last, and Always"

Hymn of the Day: "Once to Every Man and Nation"

Offertory Scripture: Without having seen him you love him; though you do not now see him you believe in him and rejoice with unutterable and exalted joy. *I Peter 1:8*

Offertory Prayer: Lord, search my soul and find me acceptable of your love. Accept me and my humble gifts as an offering to you. *Amen.*

Prayer of the Day

Lord, there are no secrets between us, are there? You know me better than I know myself. "You have searched me" and know my deepest secrets and thoughts. You know what really makes me tick. You know and understand me. You accept me, warts and all. Sometimes that is a comfort to me, Lord. Knowing that, despite my rebellious nature, my arrogance and pride and my disobedience, you still call me your child.

How do you do it, Lord? There are days when I can't even accept myself. I disappoint myself with the way I act, with the way I treat other people, with the words that come out of my mouth, and with the thoughts that flash through my mind. There are days when I am hostile, selfish, and disrespectful, but you love me still. It is a love that truly is beyond understanding, a love that is patient and kind, a love that endures all things and hopes all things, a love that endures forever.

Thank you for your patience, for your understanding, for your acceptance, but most of all, for your never-ending love. *Amen.*

Benediction: So whatever you wish that men would do to you, do so to them; for this is the law and the prophets.

Matthew 7:12

Recessional Hymn: "When We Walk with the Lord" ("Trust and Obey")

Lectionary Lessons: The First Sunday after Epiphany (Baptism of the Lord)

Lesson 1—Genesis 1:1-5; Psalm 29
Lesson 2—Acts 19:1-7
Gospel—Mark 1:4-11

History of the Hymn of the Day: "Once to Every Man and Nation"

In 1845, at the same time Abraham Lincoln was opposing in Congress the agitators for a war with Mexico, the famed poet James Russell Lowell was using his talent to speak out against what he thought was the plan of the slave-holding states to gain more territory. It was a ninety-line poem, later reduced to thirty-two lines, which became one of the strongest hymns challenging national righteousness ever printed:

Once to every man and nation
Comes the moment to decide,
In the strife of truth with falsehood,
For the good or evil side.

Legend says that the tune used for his hymn can be traced back to its discovery in a bottle washed up on the shores of Wales.

Announcement for Next Week's Sermon: For God so loved the world. . . . We have said that so often perhaps it has lost some of its meaning. Next week, who is God's world?

Story of the Week: A minister was being entertained at dinner and the other guests were praising his sermon. One of them turned to his host's young son, who was at the table, and asked, "Young man, what did you think of the sermon?"

"Oh, it was all right," he said, "except he passed up three real good places where he could have stopped."

FIRST, LAST, AND ALWAYS

Psalm 139, like many of the psalms, is a prayer. It is a very personal prayer of one deeply impressed with the depths of God's knowledge, of God's presence, and of God's wisdom, and it is in the face of these facts that the psalm writer commits himself afresh to this all knowing, ever present, all wise God. This psalm is divided into four sections and answers three very important questions: How well does God know me? How near is God to me? How can I get to know God better?

How Well Does God Know Me?

This is, by far, one of the most important questions that any of us can ever ask about the character of God, for if God doesn't know me, then God is some impersonal force at best; he is uninvolved with people; God doesn't care. So the question has many implications. But if God does know me, then I can know God in some degree and relationship can be established. Our lives will take one of two directions depending upon how we answer that fundamental question. The psalmist answers that question in the first verse: "O Lord, thou hast searched me and known me!" Now the word translated *searched* in the scripture is the Hebrew word that means *dig*. That same word is used in Proverbs 2:4-5. The writer is saying to the son, "If you seek [wisdom] like silver and search for it as for hidden treasures; then you will understand the fear of the Lord and find the knowledge of God." So the term *search* means to investigate, to dig, to delve into, to understand. It is not surprising that in modern English, we use the word *dig* to mean understand. So verse 1 in modern English is, "Lord, you dig me, you understand me below the surface. You have a way of getting down to my real self. I can escape from some people and hide from most, but you know me fully—inside out and backwards." Then the psalmist goes on to talk of the ways God knows him: "Thou knowest when I sit down and when I rise up; thou discernest my thoughts from afar" (verse 2). I see two things here. God knows my conscious life, when I sit and when I rise up; that is when I am passive and quiet and when I am active and inactive. God understands my thoughts even before they come to the surface. He knows how I think and what I think. Verses in modern English might be: "Lord, you know my habits, my vocabulary, my favorite activities, my favorite haunts; you know it all. You would recognize me a million miles away; you read me like a book. You understand me completely. You know my language better than even I do. When I speak, you know exactly what I mean, and you understand even when I don't have the words." The psalmist is overwhelmed, and so am I at the realization of how well God knows us. He knows us better than any other person, including ourselves. How well does God know me? He knows me fully and perfectly.

How Near Is God to Me?

The psalmist answers this question with a question: Where can I go from your Spirit? Where can I flee from your presence? Because of God's omnipresence, *I am never alone.* I am always guarded, always loved, always known—how wonderful. But of course, God's omnipresence can be taken another way: Where can I go from your spirit? Where can I flee from your presence? There are no secrets, no privacy. I am always accountable. How awkward. How exposing. How threatening. The psalmist realizes that there is no hiding place from the eyes of God. God found Adam and Eve in the bushes. He found Moses in the desert, Peter in the boat, Matthew at the cash register, and God has found you. Here you sit in a congregation this Sunday morning, and God has found you. Is that good or bad? Is that a comfort or a discomfort? Does it bring gladness or embarrassment? The scripture says that God is all around me. He is the hound of heaven, and he will pursue us out of his perfect love forever and everywhere until we do one of two things: Until we either realize that evading God is not only impossible but silly and surrender to God, who hunts for us, and begin to discover the fullness of a life lived in his presence, or we tell God to back off, to leave, until we say "I don't want to be bothered right now with your claims—I realize they are legitimate, but I have more important things to do and when I am fifty-five or sixty or sick or whatever, then I'll come." We may tell God that, and even then we'll have a hard time convincing him that we mean it, but if we tell him long enough, he will finally let us have our way. Well, how near is God? The scripture tells us this God is as close as our breath, as near to us as our own heart, to the psalmist, that's good news. In verse 14, the psalmist gets all excited and breaks into praise because of the fantastic and intricate body that God has given to him and the wonderful intimate thought God has toward him. In verses 17-18, the psalmist rehearses some of those thoughts: "How precious to me are thy thoughts, O God! How vast is the sum of them! If I would count them, they are more than the sand. When I awake, I am still with thee." I think the psalm writer just about runs out of words in telling the gladness in his heart over the closeness and the knowledge of God. How well does God know me? Completely. How near is God to me? God can't get closer.

Then there is a great change in the tone of the psalm. He is enjoying his very close relationship with God and, like many of us in a close relationship with God, makes a request: "O that thou wouldst stay the wicked, O God!" He then goes on through three verses pleading that God should solve the problem of evil people and even suggests how God might do it. Slay them, wipe them out. I suppose he figures God never thought of that; so he makes that suggestion. Can you undertand that request of the psalm writer? I can empathize with him, and I imagine most of you can, too. We've all felt that way at times—you get a call from the police at four o'clock on a Sunday morning that your office was broken into. You find a rock on your desk and your files are ruffled through. You remember verses 19-22, "destroy the wicked." Or maybe if you hear children crying outside, and you discover your son or daughter has been teased by others. It hurts and you want God to do something about the evil. "Dear God, since you and I are so close, wipe them out." Fortunately God doesn't answer that prayer, because once in a while all of us are numbered among the wicked. God's way of dealing with the wicked is totally different. God doesn't wipe them out; he loves them in. That's how God deals with the wicked. God's loving ways become clear at Christmastime when, in love, God sent his Son not to punish, but to love. We all deserved punishment. It's hardly what we expected, God's love. We deserve just the opposite. Romans 5:8 summarizes God's actions in giving his love to us while we were still sinners by sending his Son to die for us. This is God's way of dealing with the wicked, not wiping them out, but loving them in. Finally, there is the third question the psalmist addresses in the last two verses of the psalm.

How Can I Come Near to God?

God knows me completely. He couldn't come closer to me. How can I come closer to God? Here are the two verses that many of us have memorized and songs have been written about: "Search me, O God, and know my heart! Try me and know my thoughts! And see if there be any wicked way in me, and lead me in the way everlasting!" The psalmist suddenly realizes that when he is pointing his finger at evil people, the others are pointing back at him. You have heard that. "Lord, take care of me and I will let you take care of them." From knowing God's infinite knowledge about us, we see that he is the perfect one to search and to test and to lead. And like a patient asking the doctor for the truth about sickness and then telling the surgeon to cut as deeply as necessary to purge, to dig, to investigate, to cut away, to remove, to refine, that we may be led. For it is only God who knows me so well, and God who is so close to me, that he is able to do those necessary operations deep down inside my heart. We are not talking about something we can do by ourselves. We are declaring our dependence upon God. It is for us to ask that the Lord be gracious and merciful, and for us to submit to his inspection and care. One of the ways we draw near to God, and one of the results when we do draw near, is confession—search me, try me, use me—and that's the necessary attitude as we approach the table. *Amen.*

Richard A. Weisenbach
First Parish Congregational Church
Wakefield, Massachusetts

Sunday
January Seventeenth

Call to Worship: Worthy is the Lamb who was slain, to receive power and wealth and wisdom and might and honor and glory and blessing! *Revelation 5:12*

Processional Hymn: "Love Divine, All Loves Excelling"

Invocation: As God becomes a real presence in our lives, make us worthy to be a temple of our Lord. Make our actions and our love shine through our lives so that people may see and say, "Surely this is one of God's people." *Amen.*

Sermon Scripture: Romans 8:35-39

Sermon Presentation: "The Perfect Economy"

Hymn of the Day: "Abide with Me"

Offertory Scripture: Before they call I will answer, while they are yet speaking I will hear. *Isaiah 65:24*

Offertory Prayer: Lord, you are always ready to give us answers to our problems and to hear our prayers. Let these gifts we offer now be our response to your love. *Amen.*

Prayer of the Day

Lord, you taught "love your neighbor" and we asked, "but who is my neighbor?" You taught that our neighbors aren't just those who are like us, but even those we don't know or those with whom we are angry. We begin to think to ourselves, "Can I really love my neighbor as I should?"

You taught us that justice is your expectation for our world. We are to treat one another with respect and humility and genuine concern for one another's well-being. But the past hurts, and present suspicion makes the prospect for a more just future dim.

Don't let us shrug our shoulders and give up. Give us the commitment and the courage to work for the justice you demand. Use us as your instruments to change the world to reflect your love and your will.

Loving involves risk! But you know that, Lord. You took the risk, and you ended up on the cross. But your resurrection showed that love can conquer hate; light will overcome the darkness, and life is stronger than death. *Amen.*

Benediction: And now, little children, abide in him, so that when he appears we may have confidence and not shrink from him in shame at his coming. *I John 2:28*

Recessional Hymn: "Jesus, Lover of My Soul"

Lectionary Lessons: The Second Sunday after Epiphany
Lesson 1—I Samuel 3:1-10, (11-20); Psalm 63:1-8
Lesson 2—I Corinthians 6:12-20
Gospel—John 1:35-42

History of the Hymn of the Day: "Abide with Me"
This famous hymn, written September 4, 1847, by Henry Francis Lyte, almost was not written at all. Life had not been easy for him, and at the age of fifty-four, this famed English clergyman, serving as vicar of Lower Brixham in Devonshire, was advised by his doctor to save his health by wintering in Italy. He was determined to administer Holy Communion once more to his congregation. And on the first Sunday of September in 1847 he did exactly that, even though the ravages of tuberculosis left him weak and exhausted. After the service he strolled by the sea until sunset thinking of the abiding presence of God and working on a hymn poem started many years before in the early days of his ministry. He was really too tired to complete the poem and thought of putting it aside until his return from Italy. However, some inner compulsion pressed him to finish the last line. That evening he placed the completed line "Abide with Me" in the hands of his family. He never returned from Italy, dying two months later on November 20. If he had waited until he returned, one of the world's most famous hymns would not have been written.

Announcement for Next Week's Sermon: What would you do to save your life or the life of someone you love? I am sure you would pay any price. Next Sunday I will tell you how much it will cost.

Story of the Week: It had started to rain during the meeting, so the speaker felt he should cut his talk short. "And now," he said, "I shall conclude my talk for this evening. In fact, I'm afraid I've already kept you too long."

"Oh, keep right on," said a voice from the rear. "It's still raining and most of us didn't bring umbrellas."

THE PERFECT ECONOMY

Epiphany is the season of showings in the Church Year. During this period, the presence of God in the life of Jesus becomes manifest. The lessons are chosen to show the dawning of awareness on the part of the church that Jesus is the Christ of God, or, to put this somewhat differently, that the divine nature is represented in the life and teachings of Jesus of Nazareth. In him, the love of God has become explicit and has been brought to light.

It is my intention to speak to you of the presence of God in our midst, of the ways in which God's love is implicitly present to all persons, Christian and non-Christian, and of how that love has been made explicit in Jesus. Jesus shows us that it is God who has been loving us through our neighbors, in the beauty of the order of nature, and in the religious practices of people. I shall be using the thought of Simone Weil to guide me in these reflections. This woman has a great deal to say about the workings of God, and this is a good opportunity to make use of some of her insights in regard to the way God's love makes contact with us. Today I shall speak to you about the love of God that is present in relations with our neighbors.

One need not be more than casually acquainted with the Christian faith to know that Christians are called by their faith to love their neighbors. Moreover, according to Jesus' teachings, all people are neighbors—not just those who live in close proximity, not just those with whom one shares common interests or common custom, not just friends, but strangers and outcasts and even enemies—all are to be loved. But what sort of love is it that has such a wide embrace, that can be extended to friends and enemies, foreigners and compatriots? How does one love equally a black South African victim of apartheid and Prime Minister Botha, the leader of the government that defends and enforces apartheid? What sense is to be made of a love that proposes to be universal in scope?

The first thing to be said is that the gospel makes no distinction between the love of neighbor and justice. We are, according to the gospel, to labor to create the conditions of justice, to bring about equality where there is none. That is why it is possible to love the oppressor and the oppressed at the same time without that love dissolving into the most insipid of trivialities. An example will, perhaps, help to make this clear.

Nobel Peace Prize winner Bishop Desmond Tutu of South Africa is committed to loving all his neighbors, not just the victims of the cruelties of apartheid, but Prime Minister Botha, the arbiter of the policy of apartheid, as well. How is the bishop to do it? There is only one way: He must work to bring justice to the situation. He must do what is necessary to end the racist policies of apartheid which prevent the balance of justice from being struck. To love the black South African means elevating his or her position; to love the prime minister means lowering his position as a white man in that society. Obviously the love of Bishop Tutu means something different for each of the parties involved, for they are in different positions with respect to the balance of justice. But the bishop brings the same love to both, the love of neighbor which the Christian gospel calls for from those who follow Christ.

But there is more to be said here. For the supernatural virtue of justice to be achieved, it is not enough simply to turn the tables, to put the lowly on top and to lay the mighty low. What is required is for the stronger to act in every way as if there were equality between himself or herself and the person in an inferior position, and for the person who has been in the inferior position to be grateful to the other for generosity for giving up the position of superiority. I trust you can see why I have called this sort of justice supernatural. Just imagine what it would take to bring the present supporters of apartheid to the point at which they would do everything necessary to live as complete equals with the people they are presently oppressing on the grounds of racial inferiority! And just imagine what it would take for black South Africans, who have suffered every indignity and cruelty at the hands of white supremacists, to be grateful to those who have given up their undeserved positions of superiority in order that justice be done! Think further of what it would take to bring both sides to the point in which such justice would even be possible. There is very little hope that something like that would happen. It is more likely that black South Africans will resort to force to achieve equality in their society and that they will be resisted by force; though a better balance might thereby be achieved, it will be a far cry from the justice that is a supernatural virtue.

The Christian can never be satisfied with anything less than this perfect justice; yet the Christian must, for love of neighbor, constantly struggle to do what is presently possible to create a more just situation for all of his or her neighbors. The Christian has a role to play on behalf of justice wherever one neighbor is "lording it" over another. The Christian is invariably the partisan of the poor and the oppressed until poverty and oppression are ended, until justice is realized. This is the Christian's vocation, the Christian's calling in the world. Whatever job one chooses to earn one's income must either serve this calling or be condemned for preventing the love of neighbor from coming to fruition. That is why the Christian cannot work at just anything at all; it is why the Christian cannot simply sell out to the highest bidder. These are difficult matters that require careful consideration.

For now, however, let us say that a person, Christian or non-Christian, works tirelessly for justice in the world. Let us say that he or she is wholeheartedly devoted to his or her neighbors and committed to loving them into a condition of greater equality than they presently enjoy. To be sure, this person is concerned about those neighbors, those persons encountered directly—persons with names and histories and lives of their own, rich or poor, kind or cruel—persons with distinctive faces who are to be loved for what they themselves are going through, loved for themselves alone. But now we come to the point that Christ reveals to us, for when we love our neighbors truly, when we love them simply because they are our neighbors, God is present. In such instances of love, God is present at the point where the eyes of those who give and those who receive meet. If one is looking for the love of God in loving one's neighbor, one will find neither God nor neighbor. But in truly loving one's neighbor, regardless of what one thinks of God, one meets God there, for God is implicitly present wherever there is such love.

There were two men in an isolated setting. One of the men was sick, and though essentially a stranger to him, the other gave him his coat to warm him. But this was not enough; the sick man was chilled through by fever, and he asked the other man to lie against him to share some of the warmth of his body. The other man did so, noticing as he did that the sick man had broken out in vile open sores. Still the sick man shivered terribly, and he could hardly breathe. He begged the other to breathe his breath into his mouth, which by this time was itself a stinking, leprous sore. The well man was appalled, but he could not refuse, and he pressed his mouth to that of the sick man.

Suddenly there was a transformation, or perhaps I should say, an *epiphany*, for he found himself pressed up against Christ, whose body was healthy and whose breath was sweet. He had never thought that this afflicted neighbor was anyone but an afflicted neighbor . . . and then Christ appeared.

Of course, this is just a romanticized version of Jesus' announcement that what we do to the least of our sisters and brothers we do also to him. Moreover, according to our faith, Jesus is the very incarnation of God's Holy Spirit. So Jesus makes explicit to us that God is implicitly present in all genuine instances of love of neighbor. We think we are only loving our neighbors: Jesus shows us that in so doing we have been touched by God. This love is the very movement of God in us, "a ray merged in the light of God." The love Christians have for their neighbors is not, then, merely a moral obligation that God has placed upon them. It is actually the place where we meet God. In the compassion and gratitude that characterize Christian love of neighbor, we encounter the love of God, the love by which the universe is made and sustained. God comes to us there. God dwells in the giving and receiving of this love.

I can imagine someone hearing what I have just said and asking, "But is that all? Is there no more explicit showing of God than this? Is there no more graphic show of God's love and presence?" I can only assume that this person is looking for some other God than the one revealed in Christ, perhaps some booming-voiced giant thundering from the clouds. How could God love us more fully than in the lives of our neighbors? What clearer showing can one reasonably expect than this? Does the person want miracles or spectacular events? Well, there is no greater miracle, no more spectacular event than the love Christ taught us to have for one another. But one can only know that love by loving. And so Christ reveals the perfect economy of God's love, that we might love better and recognize the presence of God in our midst. *Amen.*

Jeffrey C. Eaton
Chaplain, Hamilton College
Clinton, New York

Sunday
January Twenty-fourth

Call to Worship: Jesus answered him, "If a man loves me, he will keep my word, and my Father will love him, and we will come to him and make our home with him." *John 14:23*

Processional Hymn: "As with Gladness Men of Old"

Invocation: Lord, you offer us the good life, not without suffering or pain, but filled with the joy of serving you. Help us to accept the testing of our faith as a giant step to understanding your love for us and your care for us through our whole life. *Amen.*

Sermon Scripture: Luke 9:23-27

Sermon Presentation: "The Christian Challenge"

Hymn of the Day: "Be Still, My Soul"

Offertory Scripture: Everyone to whom much is given, of him will much be required; and of him to whom men commit much they will demand the more. *Luke 12:48*

Offertory Prayer: Lord, all of us love a challenge. That is the way we live in this competitive world. Let us accept the challenge to give our gifts in response to your great gift of your Son. *Amen.*

Prayer of the Day

Lord, our faith in you is indeed a challenge. You tell us that we must be willing to die if we are to experience eternal life. You teach us that the greatest among us must be the servant of all, that we should be willing to give up everything we have in order to live the "abundant" life.

You challenge us to believe that by dying on a cross you have opened the way to eternal life for all who trust in you. You challenge us to build our lives on the belief that the shame of the cross endured by you will ensure everlasting glory for us.

We know that being a follower of yours and a partner with you in ministry is not for everyone. In each generation there are those who will turn their backs on you and say, "It's just too hard. You ask too much; your expectations are too high. Your challenge is too great."

Help us to be among those who, like Peter, follow where you lead, do your will, and take up their own cross. Like Peter, we, too, know that when it comes to the words of eternal life, where else can we go?

We accept your grace—your love and your challenge. *Amen.*

Benediction: And by your descendants shall all the nations of the earth bless themselves, because you have obeyed my voice. *Genesis 22:18*

Recessional Hymn: "Go, Tell It on the Mountain"

Lectionary Lessons: The Third Sunday after Epiphany
Lesson 1—Jonah 3:1-5, 10; Psalm 62:5-12
Lesson 2—I Corinthians 7:29-31, (32-35)
Gospel—Mark 1:14-20

History of the Hymn of the Day: "Be Still, My Soul"
Katharina von Schlegel, born in Germany in 1697, was the author of this hymn of Christian experience. Very little is known of its origin or of its author save that it was discovered and translated by Jane L. Borthwick (1813–1897). It is thought that Katharina von Schlegel was head of a Woman's House of the Evangelical Lutheran Church at Gothen, Germany. No doubt one of the reasons for the great popularity of this hymn is its music. It is set to the famous melody of Sibelius, "Finlandia," one of the most stirring and beautiful melodies ever written.

Announcement for Next Week's Sermon: Are you happy in your marriage? I am not going to argue with you one way or the other. Next week we are going to do some serious talking about it.

Story of the Week: A kindergarten teacher was standing in front of a class of 5-year-olds during their exercise period. As she waved her arms and tapped out the rhythm with her foot, she kept saying, "Hurry up and wear yourselves out—wear yourselves out. Hurry up and wear yourselves out."

THE CHRISTIAN CHALLENGE

Are you up to a challenge? Friend, if you do not know where you will spend eternity, let me challenge you to consider Jesus of Nazareth, God's only Son, the Savior of the world.

Christian friend, the challenge is to live according to the gospel of Jesus Christ, who lived a sinless life and died a cruel death so you and I might live, really live, as committed disciples of a risen Lord! My desire for each of you is found in the words of the chorus, "I have decided to follow Jesus . . . no turning back, no turning back." Jesus went the full distance for us. I pray that we may do no less than go the full distance with him.

As we look at the ninth chapter of Luke's Gospel, we will notice three elements that present to us the Christian challenge: first, the cross of death; second, the course of life; and finally, the choice before us.

The Cross of Death

A strange paradox exists in life—out of death comes life. The farmer plants some seed. It dies and brings forth a life-yielding plant. What God created in the beginning still exists today. The age-old question is still asked, "If a man dies, will he live again?" The answer is: Only if he has that life-yielding seed within him. "What seed is this," you ask. A selfless life, an emptied ego, and a surrendered spirit! Jesus said, "What shall a man give in return for his life?" (Matthew 16:26). Do you think there is anything in this worldly existence that could purchase and guarantee eternal salvation? The search will lead you straight to the cross of Jesus Christ. Jesus also said, "For whoever would save his life will lose it; but whoever loses his life for my sake [and the gospel's], he will save it" (Luke 9:24). Don't be deceived; there is no other way to heaven, to a life filled with the beauties prepared for a chosen people, than through the shed blood of Jesus. He was determined to go, because he knew this was God's will for his life, and he was committed to that cross of death. The why of the cross is hard to explain, but we do know how Jesus moved toward it—unflinchingly, unwaveringly, and unashamedly. Have you been to the cross lately? Do you know the way of suffering, because you dare to remain true to that high calling we have in Jesus? Jesus said, "If any man would come after me, let him deny himself and take up his cross daily and follow me" (Luke 9:23). This cross of death for Jesus was a literal, once and for all, cross, upon which he died for you and me. The cross he asks us to take up is the one on which the self is figuratively hung daily, as we deny the self and seek to live for Christ each day. How resolved are we about going toward that holy city, the new Jerusalem, whose builder and maker is God? It is not made with hands, but is eternal in the heavens. Friend, are you ready to make this journey now? If not, I pray that you will not delay any longer, but allow Jesus to come into your life right now!

How can this be done? Because death could not keep Jesus captive, and neither will he allow you to be held captive. Turn your life over to Jesus, for he knows what you need and when you need it. Now is the acceptable time. Today is the day of salvation. Come to Jesus, who died so that you might live, really live, and enjoy life to the fullest!

Now that we come by the way of the cross, we need to linger a moment and note how we are to face this new life in Christ.

The Course of Life

The death of Jesus upon the cross of Calvary led to his glorification as the risen Christ and Lord of all life. What awaited Jesus in Jerusalem is represented in the incident that took place in his rejection in the Samaritan village. Why? It was not because he claimed to be the Son of God, but rather because he was a Jew on his way to Jerusalem.

There was enmity between the Jews and the Samaritans. It all began after the Babylonian exile, when the Jews returned to their native soil to find it being inhabited by half-breeds, whom they considered defiled pagans. The Samaritans offered a helping hand in rebuilding the Temple, but the Jews would not allow it. In 128 B.C., during the time of the Maccabean revolt, John Hyrcanus, high priest and king, destroyed the Samaritan temple, which was built on Mt. Gerizim. The hostility toward the Jews began to be intensified, and friendship with Rome commenced.

Here we find a pitiful condition that extends even to the present time. The Arab countries surrounding Israel today will not allow entrance to a person who has a passport showing Jerusalem as a destination. What atrocities have been done in the name of a religion that views God as its Father.

Yet, the Christian way does not promise us an easy life of ready acceptance. Ireland, Africa, Central America, Southeast Asia, the Middle East, even "the land of the free and the home of the brave" show signs of rejection. People do not wish to be bothered today, especially when you begin talking about your faith. People are quite satisfied with their life as it is, even though it might be as empty as a street person's bottle.

If we are true to God, we will face rejection. Jesus did and so will we, if we are following in Jesus' steps. We must not give in or give up! We must be determined to stay with it, no matter how bad the situation becomes. We should be confident in our faith as we seek to serve the Lord Jesus. I am determined to continue on no matter what comes; I believe God will show me the way, and his grace will see me through.

No, it is not easy in today's world; there seem to be many lopsided versions of the truth, and it is difficult to be confronted with the gospel. People cannot make up their minds but rather admit nonchalantly, "That's all right for you, but as for me, no way, Jose!" Jesus shows us that there will be rejection, whether we like it or not. We must accept it and go on, still believing in him and allowing the gospel to have its effect on those who are willing to receive, to learn, and to grow from it. Sometimes, we feel like the "sons of thunder," James and John. They wanted to bring an awful curse upon the people because they refused to believe God's witness and accept the person of his Son, Jesus Christ. But we should never try to live out this life with Christ in the flesh. It will certainly prove to be unlike anything that God produces, which is full of love and kindness, even when wronged. It is not surprising to hear these words from Jesus, "Love your enemies and pray for those who persecute you, so that you may be sons of your Father who is in heaven" (Matthew 5:44-45*a*). Let us be thankful that we have been chosen to spread God's message of love and salvation to the ends of the earth. It is for us to decide how we choose to live this life, which has been purchased with Jesus' blood and sealed with the promise of God's Spirit. We need only to give God first place in our lives, and we will be able to bear up under the rejection we find when we are witnesses for him.

The Choice Before Us

Jesus stated clearly, that the Son of Man came not to destroy people's lives but to save them. That is why Jesus resolved to go to Jerusalem, even among all the hostility and rejection that awaited him there. The reason he was willing to go is that it would mean redemption for everyone who accepted the claims of Christ for their life. Here is the principle lying behind the cross of death, as Jesus' name implies: "He will save his people from their sins" (Matthew 1:21). It is up to us, who call ourselves Christians, to make this a better place in which to live. We must continue in the way of Christ—which means suffering in his name and being rejected of men, but at the same time, it is loving Jesus with all our mind, heart, and soul; it is loving our neighbor, that person in need, as ourselves. This is the Christian challenge today! It has not changed in the slightest since Jesus first showed us the way to live. It was conceived of the Holy Spirit and recorded for our instruction in righteousness. We are to live out our lives redemptively! We are to be tolerant of others who do not understand the ways of God. We are to continue to be faithful as we carry out the Great Commission of our Lord when he said, "Go therefore and make disciples of all nations, baptizing them in the name of the Father and of the Son and of the Holy Spirit, teaching them to observe all that I have commanded you; and lo, I am with you always to the close of the age" (Matthew 28:19-20). The choice before us is clear and simple. We need to make it plain for all the world to see, hear, and know as we seek to live for Jesus daily, and make him real to those who seemingly are wandering around lost and undone without any purpose or direction in life. Let us show them the better way that will open up new adventures and present exciting challenges for them as we travel the road that leads to the new Jerusalem.

I trust you have been waiting for such a time as this, when you may come to Jesus and accept for yourself the claims of the gospel. Jesus is coming again. It may be today, or it may be tomorrow. Are you ready and prepared to meet him, when he does return? I hope that you will not let this moment pass you by; rather, I pray, that you will come to him just now. *Amen.*

Nicholas Kobek
Chapel Heights Baptist Church
Decatur, Georgia

Sunday
January Thirty-first

Call to Worship: We know that in everything God works for good with those who love him, who are called according to his purpose. *Romans 8:28*

Processional Hymn: "Savior, Like a Shepherd Lead Us"

Invocation: Lord, it is so hard to love one another all the time. Grant that in times of greatest stress we might pause and kneel together and ask for your healing love to bind us together again forever. *Amen.*

Sermon Scripture: Ephesians 5:21-33

Sermon Presentation: "Together Forever: Holy Deadlock"

Hymn of the Day: "Blest Be the Tie That Binds"

Offertory Scripture: He who has my commandments and keeps them, he it is who loves me; and he who loves me will be loved of my Father, and I will love him and will manifest myself to him. *John 14:21*

Offertory Prayer: Lord, we know that we cannot love without giving. Let us give freely of our love and our treasure as you have called us to do. *Amen.*

Prayer of the Day

Lord, one of the greatest miracles in this world of yours is the miracle of marriage. We remember that marriage and the family are an integral part of your creation since the beginning of time. We remember that in your earthly ministry you performed your first miracle—the changing of water into wine—at a marriage ceremony.

Help us to realize that you are a part of all relationships. We are mindful that the troubles existing in marriages and the problems that occur in the family are the result of our sinfulness.

Let us reflect the love that you have for us. Let us forgive as we are forgiven. Let us seek the best interests of others before our own self-interests. Remove all selfishness, pride, arrogance, and anger from us and our relationships. Replace these things with patience, understanding, and love. *Amen.*

Benediction: Husbands, love your wives, as Christ loved the church and gave himself up for her. *Ephesians 5:25*

Recessional Hymn: "O Perfect Love"

Lectionary Lessons: The Fourth Sunday after Epiphany
Lesson 1—Deuteronomy 18:15-20; Psalm 111
Lesson 2—I Corinthians 8:1-13
Gospel—Mark 1:21-28

History of the Hymn of the Day: "Blest Be the Tie That Binds"

The drama of this famous hymn centers around a loving congregation, a woman who spoke her mind, and a Baptist minister who refused a call to one of the largest churches in England. In the summer of 1772, the Rev. John Fawcett, whose family had "increased faster than our income," was overjoyed with the receiving of a "call" to the famous Carter's Lane Baptist Church in London. Immediately, preparations were made to transfer to this greater opportunity. A great loyalty and devotion had developed between pastor and people, and although they gave their time and strength willingly to help him pack, they did not hide their reluctance about letting him go. When the final day of moving came, the wagons arrived early and loading of boxes and bundles began. Finally only one box remained, in the middle of the dining room. Rev. Fawcett noted that his wife stood near it in deep thought. "What's the matter?" he asked. Her reply was slow and thoughtful, "Do you think we are doing the right thing?" she asked. "Where will we find a congregation with more love and help than this?" The minister was silent a moment, then he replied, "I think you are right, dear. I have acted too hastily. I was so overjoyed to think that I would have a better home and a larger salary for you and the children that I did not really pray about it." Together they walked to the porch and explained to their people that they had decided to remain.

Announcement for Next Week's Sermon: Do you think that you are guilty of worshiping false gods today? Oh no, not me! I like money, and I like to live well, but I don't worship them, at least I don't think I do. Do I?

Story of the Week: The visitor at the jail asked the man in the cell, "And why are you locked up?"

"I suppose they think I'd go home if I wasn't," he said.

TOGETHER FOREVER: HOLY DEADLOCK

In a recent public opinion poll taken in New York City, two hundred people were asked the question, "If by some miracle you could press a button and find you had never been married to your husband or your wife, would you press the button?" One hundred forty-eight people said "no," twenty-eight said "yes," and twenty-four had no opinion on the matter, which in reality said a good bit about their marriages! This less than overwhelming affirmation is needed desperately at a time when almost half of our marriages end in divorce. Forty-six out of every one hundred marriages are dissolved through the courts. The intent of marriage, according to scripture, is to permanently bind two people in such a miraculous way that they become one and remain one throughout their lifetime! Our wedding vows affirm this same position by reminding us that only death should dissolve the union—not the courts. *Together forever!*

In the book of Genesis, we read of a rather isolated and lonely individual named Adam. Despite the creation story in the first chapter of Genesis, in which God evidently created man and woman simultaneously, chapter 2 portrays Adam as a single. Acknowledging that it was not good for man to live alone, God said, "I will make for him a companion." At that point all the animals were created to fill the void in Adam's life—but to no avail. Then Adam took that now famous sleep during which he unknowingly participated in the creation of woman. God performed radical surgery and extracted one of Adam's ribs, from which he fashioned the "one and the only" who could satisfy Adam's craving and real need for companionship—a woman. When Adam awakened from that sleep his life would be forever different. He rejoiced and knew instantly that the one upon whom he looked was to be his life's companion! The narrator of the Genesis concludes this vignette by writing, "Therefore a man leaves his father and his mother and cleaves to his wife, and they become one flesh" (Genesis 2:24).

The opening statement of the traditional wedding service says that marriage is a holy estate, instituted by God. Undoubtedly many young couples, like Adam and Eve, have stood alongside each other with that same unsophisticated naïveté, thoroughly convinced that the needed one is found and that life together will be one long honeymoon. Unfortunately marriage does not unite two perfect people in idyllic circumstances where only marital bliss prevails in a continuous state of euphoria. Certainly Adam found Eve to be his greatest source of irritation and unhappiness. We need each other, but that need does not eliminate friction between the two who have chosen to be husband and wife. As one person has so aptly put it, "You can't live with them, and you can't live without them." Dagwood Bumstead of cartoon fame has said, "There is nothing like marriage—absolutely nothing!"

People continue to marry even though the mortality rate for marriages is a staggering 46 percent! Not many of us would undergo surgery if there were only a 54 percent chance of survival. Failure is not uncommon in marriage, as our statistics indicate. The solution is certainly not that of living together before marriage in a kind of apprenticeship or on the job training program. To do so is not a viable situation in the Christian faith. That which is wrong, all the rationalization in the world cannot make right. What is really frightening is the number of marriages that have failed but will never make it into the divorce courts. In these cases the marriage has died; it is only a symbol of what once was, but no longer is. Together forever—holy deadlock! A marriage looks like the real thing to most people, but it is only a caricature. We live in an age in which the unreal looks valid. People have to touch flowers to determine whether or not they are real.

Many marriages, like some flowers, look real. But they have become sterile and meaningless—a far cry from that which we originally intended. They only look real. So often it's the large aggregate of little things that destroy a marriage. We are proper, respectable, faithful, but—dead! We no longer use the generous word or the kind gesture; we ignore the thoughtful and considerate act.

> We flatter those we scarcely know,
> We please the fleeting guest,
> And deal full many a thoughtless blow
> To those who love us best.
>
> Ella Wheeler Wilcox

One marriage counselor likens this situation to the person who says, "When I think of all you've meant to me for all these years, sometimes it's more than I can stand not to tell you."

Many bumper stickers ask, "Have you hugged your child today?" Great! But why not ask, "Have you hugged your wife today?" or "Have you hugged your husband?" Marriage needs much tender loving care. Courtesy is the oil that prevents friction. Elton Trueblood, in his book entitled *The Vocation of the Family*, declares that a successful marriage is not one in which two beautifully matched people find each other and live happily ever after. Instead he states that it is a system by means of which sinful and contentious people are so caught by a dream bigger than themselves that they work, in spite of repeated disappointments, to make their dreams come true.

As goes the marriage, so goes the family! The family is important to us. It is basic to our Judeo-Christian heritage. Like marriages, however, the family itself is in a major crisis. In the *Communist Manifesto*, there is a deliberate attempt to destroy the family as we in our Western world ideally claim it to be. There are two annoying things about this manifesto: the openness with which the basic thesis to destroy the family is proclaimed and the way in which we who do not subscribe to the Communist philosophy are following it almost to the letter. The manifesto states that we must rid ourselves of the bourgeois notion of the sacredness of the family, especially about the hallowed relationship between husbands and wives and between parents and their children. The manifesto then proposes the methodology by which this goal is to be accomplished. The shifting of responsibility from family to social institutions is crucial. Militant feminism pervades the manifesto—men and women are to be treated identically in all respects (pregnancy being the exception), and women are to be emancipated from the home so that they may seek employment that gives status. Children, they believe, can be better educated in institutions than in families. Therefore, we must develop public nurseries, setting the mothers free from the burden of constant care of their young children and thus enabling these women to earn independent livelihoods—this is the germ cell of the Communist society.

Although we would not adhere to this basic Communist position, we have, nevertheless, pursued a course in recent years that has produced the highest divorce rate ever achieved in our country, and we have witnessed an unprecedented disintegration and breakdown of the family. The church is not free of blame. In our attempt to do good, we have created situations that contribute to family breakdown. Scrutinize any church calendar, and you can almost become convinced that programs are designed to separate husbands from wives and parents from children. Certainly Christians make good parents, but we must be realistic in acknowledging that not everyone involved in church and community activities has a meaningful faith. One can be a real success in such service while the marriage is steadily disintegrating. Howard Hendricks, in his book *Heaven Help the Home*, states that succeeding in the church and community can be a cop-out. A person may spend more and more time in his or her succesful activity and less and less time at home, where he or she is not making it. Many advertisers, in their usual simplistic and stupid style, suggest that if your family is drifting apart, you should buy a TV set. They offer "boob tube" induced hypnosis in a living room as an alternative to the futility of running around in circles, certainly a less than ideal approach. The danger is always two pronged: we idolize the home and let it keep us from the church, and we idolize the church and let it keep us from the family. Needless to say, we must have both, a balance! One of our hymns urges what must take place when it claims, "O Lord, May Church and Home Combine."

We must not forget the plight of the family! I am more concerned today, however, not with relationships between parents and children, but with those between husbands and wives. I am fully convinced that the best thing parents can do for their children is to love each other. Father Hershburgh of Notre Dame University, in speaking to a conference of men, once said, "The best thing you can do for your children is to love their mother." Adam found happiness and companionship in Eve. He did not look at her as the potential bearer of his children. It's little compliment to a woman to say, "I choose you from all others to be the mother of my children." There is nothing wrong with motherhood, but choose your wife because in her and her alone you can find fulfillment. Choose her because you love her. Be thankful she is the mother of your children, but choose her for herself—to be together forever!

If we have not found happiness and fulfillment in each other, if we have sacrificed being lovers and sweethearts for the role of parents, if we have allowed parental duties and responsibilities to sap our vigor for continuing the romance, if we have permitted our *together forever* to become a holy deadlock, then it will not be uncommon to see marriages of twenty to thirty years duration end in divorce. "We have remained together for the children! Now they are gone, there is no need to continue."

To strengthen the home, we must focus squarely on the fundamental marriage relationship. This relationship is a holy commitment of two people who have pledged themselves to live together forever. No step we take in this life is of greater significance. Unfortunately, many take that step long before they are prepared. The state has more stringent regulations for those seeking a driver's license than it does for those seeking a marriage license! Ministers attempt to alert potential brides and grooms to both the joys and the frustrations of marriage. But the spiritual aspect is oftentimes overshadowed by the social.

Divorce is always a failure, unless people did not mean what they said in their vows—together forever. When all love is gone, when there is no desire for reconciliation, the separation has already occurred, it seems almost merciful in those situations to legalize and recognize the demise of the marriage. If children are involved, that emotional separation and discontent can be of adverse affect to their growth. Contrary to the original intent, under extreme and irrevocable conditions it is best to end the continuing charade in court. We can stick it out because of social stigma (although there is presently little of that); we can endure hell in our marriage because of financial security; we can endure it because of an emotional dependence within ourselves; we can do it because of the children. We can endure being together forever in holy deadlock—but it's a miserable existence.

One can use the Bible to prove almost any position. In I Corinthians, the apostle Paul tells us that marriage is permissible in order to avoid fornication; a woman who has lost a husband may marry again, but it's better if she remains single; the unmarried are urged to remain single and the widows to avoid remarriage. The unmarried care for the things of the Lord and how they may please the Lord, but the married care for the things of the world and how they can please their mate. All this is from I Corinthians. In the nine years between the writing of his first letter to the church at Corinth and his letter to the Ephesians, Paul became convinced that the immediate advent of the second coming, which dominated his thinking when he wrote the letter to the Corinthians, was not to be as soon as he thought. From a rather temporary view of life on earth, Paul now concludes there is a real permanence to this life. First

Corinthians contains crisis and emergency regulations given at a time when Paul thought the world had only a short time to exist. Ephesians gives us Paul's view of marriage as part of the permanent situation of the Christian life.

Unfortunately, this beautiful passage from Ephesians is frequently misunderstood. Today the phrase stating that a wife is to be subject to her husband is looked upon with disdain by most "liberated" women. Generally speaking, it's not the scripture that fails to understand us; on the contrary, we fail to understand scripture. "Wives be subject to your husbands" should be preceded by the phrase "for example." The Greek construction of this passage insists that the text is best read as follows: "Be subject to each other out of reverence for Christ; for example, wives be subject to your husbands." This is but an example of what mutual subjection to each other means. In this passage, the husband is told three different times in three different ways to love his wife. Certainly we cannot conclude from the silence regarding instruction for the wife loving her husband that it is, therefore, not required.

The purpose of this passage is not control or subjection; it is love! Love means, and again we use the words "for example," to love your wife as Christ loved the church, as you love yourself! We look to Christ and his relationship to the church as the example of how spouses are to love each other.

Love can never be selfish. Christ loved the church not for what it could do for him, but for what he could do for it. Spouses are to love each other with a love that never exercises a tyranny of control, but with a love that is ready to make any sacrifice for the good of the other. One does not love to extract service, nor to ensure that physical comfort is attended to, nor for convenience. This kind of love is unbreakable. It unites us as (the various) members of the body are united to one another—in one flesh. Going back to Genesis, we see that we are urged to be together forever, to become one flesh. This does not mean, as many think, to have a child. I cannot think of separating my arm from my body, unless there is no possible way to make it better. Only under the most extreme conditions would I consent to such removal. I am a body—one flesh. In an analogous way, I am in one flesh with my spouse. To be separated would be unthinkable. If, however, as previously described, we are dead to each other and choose to remain that way, the oneness (the one flesh) is destroyed. In the Christian marriage, there are not two partners, but three—the husband, the wife, and Christ. He is the ever-remembered, although unseen, guest in the Christian home. Loving as Christ would have us love ensures that we can achieve in our marriage what God wants us to achieve and what we want to achieve—"Together Forever: Holy Wedlock." *Amen.*

Thomas R. Jarrell
St. Luke United Methodist Church
Sheboygan, Wisconsin

Sunday
February Seventh

Call to Worship: This is the day which the Lord has made; let us rejoice and be glad in it. *Psalm 118:24*

Processional Hymn: "How Sweet the Name of Jesus Sounds"

Invocation: Lord, hear us as we call on you today. We are surrounded by a world that calls us to an easy life. Don't let us be seduced to this way. Let us stand firm for your way in all that we do. Keep us in your name, we pray. *Amen.*

Sermon Scripture: Acts 17:16-34

Sermon Presentation: "Our Modern Idolatries"

Hymn of the Day: "Glorious Things of Thee Are Spoken"

Offertory Scripture: Deal bountifully with thy servant, that I may live and observe thy word. Open my eyes, that I may behold wondrous things out of thy law. *Psalm 119:17-18*

Offertory Prayer: Lord, you have called us to be your own. Let us praise you as we should. Do not let us be led away from your side; when temptation comes let us be strong. May these gifts draw us closer to you as your great gift saved us forever. *Amen.*

Prayer of the Day

Lord, you have commanded of us: "I am the Lord your God. You shall have no other gods before me." This is your expectation of us, if we wish to continue to be your people.

We seem to forget that we are created in your image. Too often we find ourselves busy creating a false picture of you, an image of God that we are comfortable with. A god that thinks like we do and finds our actions acceptable, if not always desirable.

We like to think that you are on our side—whatever we do, whatever we say. The greater, more important question for us should be: "Are we on God's side?"

We twist and turn your truth to fit our purposes. We pray, not asking that your will be done, but that you carry out our every whim. We divide our lives into the sacred and the secular. In one we talk about love and faith. In the other we "do our thing" with a dog-eat-dog philosophy.

Guide us, Lord, to find you, to listen to your word, to do your will as best we can. Help us to have faith in you—faith that is based on your truth, that reflects your love, and that leads us to live lives reflecting your will. *Amen.*

Benediction: Therefore be imitators of God, as beloved children. And walk in love, as Christ loved us and gave himself up for us, a fragrant offering and sacrifice to God.

Ephesians 5:1-2

Recessional Hymn: "Guide Me, O Thou Great Jehovah"

Lectionary Lessons: The Fifth Sunday after Epiphany
Lesson 1—Job 7:1-7; Psalm 147:1-11
Lesson 2—I Corinthians 9:16-23
Gospel—Mark 1:29-39

History of the Hymn of the Day: "Glorious Things of Thee Are Spoken"

This joyous hymn is considered to be the greatest ever to come from the pen of the Reverend John Newton, close friend of William Cowper. It was part of a collection by Newton and Cowper called "Olney Hymns" which included two hundred and eighty of Newton's and sixty-eight of Cowper's, and was in use in England at about the time of the American Revolution.

Announcement for Next Week's Sermon: Next week we deal with the law as sanctioned in both the Old and the New Testaments. Does the law really condemn us? Be in church next Sunday; that's the law!

Story of the Week: An elderly fellow who had trouble remembering important dates was leaving his house to go to town when his wife kissed him good-bye and said,"Don't you remember what day this is?"

He didn't remember whether it was her birthday or wedding anniversary or some other important date. So, he stopped by the drug store and had a two-pound box of candy sent over to the house. Then, when he had run his errands and headed home, he stopped in a shopping center and bought her a bottle of perfume and had it gift-wrapped.

When he came home and walked in the front door, he said, "Surprise, honey, look what I brought you to help celebrate this wonderful day."

She rushed into his arms and hugged him and kissed him and said, "My, how nice. This is the happiest Ground-Hog Day I can ever remember."

OUR MODERN IDOLATRIES

The story is told of a primitive tribesman who carried in his purse a little tin statue wrapped in a soft cloth. Most of the time this tribesman went about his daily business, ignoring this little statue. But then every so often, when things weren't going his way or when he wanted something he didn't have, this tribesman would suddenly stop everything he was doing to pull this little statue from his purse. After a few quick buffs with the cloth to restore its shine, the tribesman would set his little statue on the nearest flat surface—as a kind of "makeshift" altar. Bowing deeply before the statue, the tribesman would launch into deep, solemn prayers detailing all his desires. Then as soon as his pleas were ended, the tribesman would wrap his statue up, slip it back into his purse out of sight, and then confidently go on about his business.

Of course, the idea of a person carrying a little tin statue around to worship seems ludicrous in our modern day and age. Instead of the twentieth century, such an idea seems more reminiscent of the ancient Canaanites, who were always being condemned for their idolatry by the Old Testament Hebrew prophets. Of course, none of us in our modern day would be so primitive in our thinking as to imagine that God could be contained in any material object, for we know that God is a spiritual reality.

But consider this: As primitive as this tribesman's practice of worship is, are there not aspects of it that are altogether too similar to the way many Christians practice their faith today? Our modern idolatries have nothing to do with little tin statues. But they have a great deal to do with our conception of God and treatment of him.

The tribesman treated his god as though it were his own personal possession, to be pulled from his purse whenever he wanted to invoke its powers. Aren't many of us tempted to feel much the same way about God, almost as though it were we who had control over God and not vice versa? We are tempted to think of God in a very narrow way. More often than not, we expect God to be almost a mirror image of our own personal values, priorities, and prejudices. If we are Republicans, we tend to see a God who stalwartly espouses the "trickle down" theory of economics. If we are Democrats, we tend to see a God who is primarily concerned with extensive social programs for the needy. If you will, recall how often politicians from both parties have invoked visions of God's will for this country, which necessarily repudiate the visions of their opponents. At several points, the clergy even get into this game, anointing this or that candidate as "truly Christian," because of her or his political stand on even just one single campaign issue, such as abortion or military defense.

How very tempting it is to think of God as being merely an extension of ourselves. I recall a story that has often been told of Abraham Lincoln. During the Civil War, someone asked Lincoln if God was on the side of the Union. In his wisdom, Lincoln responded that the real issue was whether the Union was on God's side. The fact of the matter is that God is not merely an extension of our own personal hopes and desires. God is much greater than any personal image we might have of him. None of us possesses God. In fact, when any of us are tempted to think that we know God's will implicitly, without even a shadow of a doubt, then we are very likely to be off the mark. Despite our personal pretensions, there is always a hiddenness and a mystery about God and his will which eludes all our human attempts to pin him down and categorize him precisely. The prophet Isaiah realized this truth when he wrote: "For my thoughts are not your thoughts, neither are your ways my ways, says the Lord. For as the heavens are higher than the earth, so are my ways higher than your ways and my thoughts than your thoughts" (Isaiah 55:8-9).

We moderns don't believe in little tin statues that sit on makeshift altars. Yet, how easily do we fall into the belief that our own limited personal images of God are absolute. And how readily do we act as though God were created in our image, and not vice versa!

The tribesman treated his tin statue as though its only purpose was to satisfy his wishes, much like the proverbial magic genie in the lamp. We might laugh at this notion. But in reality, isn't that the way many people approach God—always expecting that he will grant them some special favor? Many people measure the strength of their Christian faith in direct proportion to the number of prayers they have had answered. As they say: "If you have enough faith, God will always reward you with the things you ask for." It is tempting to try to turn God into such a cosmic errand boy. It is tempting to imagine that he exists merely to provide for one's own pleasures. But the reality of God is far different from this. For his creative, loving purposes in our world go far beyond just responding in the affirmative to our individual wants.

God does care deeply for each and every one of us. But we turn this fundamental truth into sentimental mush if we imagine that his only purpose in this world is to make each of us happy all the time. As Jesus understood in the Garden of Gethsemane, there is much more to Christian faith than just having our own personal prayers answered. As Jesus prayed at this critical point of his ministry, "My Father, if it be possible, let this cup pass from me; nevertheless, not as I will, but as thou wilt" (Matthew 26:39). Beyond our own personal desires, there are often weightier matters, such as righteousness, justice, peace, and love for the neighbor, which are essential to God's purpose for our world.

A mother heard her young son at prayer enumerating a long list of personal requests for God. Interrupting her son, she said, "In your prayers, don't try to tell God what to do; just report for duty!" For many Christians, their faith is really just a thinly veiled vehicle for their own selfishness. Their discipleship knows no sense of obedience to God and no sense of trusting the wisdom of God's purposes for both the world and their own lives. Instead of the great Lord of the universe, the god they seek to worship is more like a personal talisman that they can pull out of their pockets at any time to do their bidding, and only their bidding.

Aside from his occasional efforts at prayer, the tribesman kept his little tin statue out of sight. The statue really had very little to do with the ongoing business of his life. It was only brought out for use and given a quick polish on certain special occasions. Isn't it a fact that many of us are tempted to treat our Christian faith in much the same way? And isn't this one of the foremost problems of our religion today? Even more than the primitive tribesman, we moderns live lives that are rigidly compartmentalized. There is our life at home, our life at the office, our life with our friends, our life in community affairs, and so on. The easy tendency for all of us is to separate these areas of our lives from one another, even to the point at which we act almost like a different person, with a different standard of values in each of these areas. For example, the way we act at home and the way we act in the office may be light-years apart. The thoughtful, sensitive individual at home may become the hard-driving, no-holds-barred competitor in the office. To a degree, this lack of personal consistency is to be expected, because different circumstances call forth different aspects of our personalities. But here is the problem: This tendency toward compartmentalization becomes a serious defect when it is allowed to shape our religious life.

Christians have often been criticized for living one kind of life in church on Sundays and a completely different kind the other six days of the week. I'm sure we have all heard this criticism from those who are outside the faith. Usually we reject this criticism out of hand. But probably more often than any of us would care to admit, there is at least a modicum of truth in this observation. Too often, the noble sentiments we espouse in our worship are not carried over and applied to the other areas of our lives. In many cases, this discrepancy is not due to any inherent perversity in our moral will. In many cases, it is, rather, a matter of our not even recognizing that such a discrepancy exists. Our lives are already so compartmentalized, that we rarely even notice when we treat our religion in the same way.

Perhaps the classic example of compartmentalization of one's religion can be seen in the life of John Newton, an eighteenth-century Englishman who created such famous Christian hymns as "Glorious Things of Thee Are Spoken," "How Sweet the Name of Jesus Sounds," and "Amazing Grace." Newton was a seaman who underwent a dramatic conversion to Christ after he survived a terrible ocean storm that nearly sank his ship and left the survivors without provisions for a full month. After his conversion, Newton became the captain of a slave ship. Very devout, Newton would lead his crew in worship services twice a week. He prided himself on his piety; yet, for a long time he saw no connection between his Christian faith and the black Africans bound for the slave market, whom he kept miserably chained together in the hold of his ship. We can imagine the terrible irony in Newton's solemnly preaching Christian love on the deck of his ship, while at the same time he was totally oblivious to the mass of humanity suffering and dying beneath his feet. Fortunately, Newton eventually did make the connection. He allowed his religious life to break free of the compartment in which he had it confined. In so doing, he felt compelled to repudiate slavery. Renouncing his slave ship captaincy, Newton not only became a minister in the Church of England, but also became responsible for the conversion and inspiration of William Wilberforce, who succeeded in convincing Parliament to abolish slavery forever from the British Empire.

John Newton's gravestone reads as follows: "John Newton, Clerk, once an infidel and libertine, was by the rich mercy of our Lord and Saviour, Jesus Christ, preserved, restored, pardoned and appointed to preach the faith he had long labored to destroy."

How easy it is to relegate our faith to its own separate compartment in our lives. How easy it is to enshrine our faith behind rigid walls of self-contentment and purity, which have little access or influence upon our daily existence. Yet how thoroughly does such artificial separation undermine and destroy that very faith we claim to cherish. The beliefs we espouse on Sunday need to be applied to our lives in the office, in the home, and wherever we might find ourselves. For more than just a tin statue that we bring out to polish and adore at certain special times, our faith requires full commitment at all times. As Jesus said, "You shall love the Lord your God with all your heart, and with all your soul, and with all your mind. . . . You shall love your neighbor as yourself" (Matthew 22:37, 39). As we might guess from Jesus' words, a compartmentalized faith is virtually no faith at all.

You will recall that Jesus was critical of certain Pharisees who prided themselves on their scrupulous observance of every last detail of their religious laws. Jesus came into conflict with these Pharisees over the issue of whether it was religiously proper to heal people on the sabbath. So compartmentalized was the religion of these Pharisees that they were blind to even the urgent demands of human compassion, which the true spirit of their faith would require. So Jesus rebuked these Pharisees harshly, saying that they were like white-washed tombs—all beautiful on the outside, but within filled with dead men's bones and all uncleanness.

Creating God in our own image, treating God like our own personal errand boy, confining our faith to certain special occasions—our modern idolatries have nothing to do with little tin statues. Yet in the actual practice of our Christian faith, how very close we often come to the primitive tribesman who worships that little figurine on a makeshift altar. *Amen.*

Douglas K. Showalter
The First Church in Belfast
(United Church of Christ)
Belfast, Maine

Sunday February Fourteenth

Call to Worship: Love does no wrong to a neighbor; therefore love is the fulfilling of the law. *Romans 13:10*

Processional Hymn: "The Son of God Goes Forth to War"

Invocation: Lord, we need your love every day of our lives. We need your law to keep order in our lives. Help us to balance your law and your love so that we may be with you for eternity. *Amen.*

Sermon Scripture: Matthew 5:20-37

Sermon Presentation: "Your Righteousness"

Hymn of the Day: "All Creatures of Our God and King"

Offertory Scripture: So if you are offering your gift at the altar, and there remember that your brother has something against you, leave your gift there before the altar and go; first be reconciled to your brother, and then come and offer your gift. *Matthew 5:23-24*

Offertory Prayer: Lord, your law says we should tithe. It is not easy when you have to live in this world. Help us. *Amen.*

Prayer of the Day

Lord, you warned us! You told us, "Behold I make all things new." We like to think that we are doing just fine when it comes to living up to your expectations. But you tell us that all too often we are content with merely "scratching the surface" when it comes to doing your will. We are content to meet the letter of the law and to do our best to avoid the spirit of the law. We pride ourselves in that we have never killed anyone; yet we gossip and destroy people's reputations. We brag that we have never committed adultery; yet we confuse sex and love. We are proud that we do not steal; yet when it comes to our time, talents, and treasures, we forget our response to you for your generosity. Our stewardship lacks commitment and meaning. We claim to love you, but we pray sporadically and worship only when it is convenient.

Help us to see the shallowness of our commitment. And then help us to grow in our discipleship so that we can truly "love you with all our heart, all our soul, and all our mind, and to love our neighbor as we love ourselves." *Amen.*

Benediction: But when the time had fully come, God sent forth his Son, born of woman, born under the law, to redeem those who were under the law, so that we might receive adoption as sons. *Galatians 4:4*

Recessional Hymn: "I Would Be True"

Lectionary Lessons: The Last Sunday after Epiphany (Transfiguration)

Lesson 1—II Kings 2:1-12*a*; Psalm 50:1-6
Lesson 2—II Corinthians 4:3-6
Gospel—Mark 9:2-9

History of the Hymn of the Day: "All Creatures of Our God and King"

In July 1225, one of the great Christians of all times, St. Francis, ill, blind, and lonely, came to a little group of buildings called St. Damian just outside the village of Assisi in Italy. Depressed and tired he found peace in this quiet little refuge with the sounds of birds and animals, which he always loved, and the kind care of a group of women called the Poor Clares. It was here, just one year before his death, St. Francis wrote a simple, beautiful hymn which has stood the test of ages. It praises the wonder of God's creation and reflects St. Francis' love of the simple things of life.

Announcement for Next Week's Sermon: I love you, although you are not what you could be. Love is accepting you as you are. Love is trying to make you better. I would love to talk to you about love next Sunday.

Story of the Week: The preacher had been talking for more than an hour. Finally, when he seemed to pause for breath, he said, "My friends, what more can I say?"

From the back of the church a weary-sounding voice said, "Amen."

YOUR RIGHTEOUSNESS

Jesus told his followers: "Unless your righteousness exceeds that of the scribes and Pharisees, you will never enter the kingdom of heaven" (Matthew 5:20). Then, in very specific examples, he showed just how this was to happen in their lives.

What was Jesus getting at? Did he really mean that we are to pluck out our eyes when we sin, or that we are damned to hell if we remarry after divorce? What do these strange, hard sayings mean for us today?

We get one clue from a few verses earlier, in which Jesus told his listeners: "Think not that I have come to abolish the Law and the prophets; I have come not to abolish them but to fulfill them" (5:17). The fulfillment of the law. That is what this passage is about. In order to fulfill it, the disciples were called to be more righteous than the Pharisees and the scribes, who were well-known for their scrupulous keeping of rules and regulations.

To make his point, Jesus argued in the style of the rabbis of his time. In four instances, he quotes Jewish Law with the words, *you have heard it said* or *it is said:*

"You have heard that it was said to the men of old, 'You shall not kill' " [Fifth Commandment] (Matthew 5:21).

"You have heard that it was said 'You shall not commit adultery' " [Sixth Commandment] (Matthew 5:27).

"It was also said, 'Whoever divorces his wife, let him give her a certificate of divorce' " [Law of Moses] (Matthew 5:31).

"Again, you have heard that it was said to the men of old, 'You shall not swear falsely' " [from the Holiness Code given to Moses] (Matthew 5:33).

These are all laws that a Jew would have known by heart. How did Jesus respond to these laws? He responded in a very unusual way. One would expect him to quote another famous rabbi, or to appeal to precedent—what others have decided these laws have meant in the past. Instead, Jesus said, "But I say to you. I, Jesus, am here to tell you what the Law means." Imagine the audacity of such a statement! No one is free to give his or her own interpretation of the Law unless that person is God!

And so, Jesus answered the Law against killing with, "But I say to you that every one who is angry with his brother shall be liable to judgment" (Matthew 5:22).

In speaking of the anti-adultery commandment, Jesus said, "But I say to you that every one who looks at a woman lustfully has already committed adultery with her in his heart" (Matthew 5:28).

In replying about divorce laws, Jesus said "But I say to you that every one who divorces his wife, except on the ground of unchastity makes her an adulteress" (Matthew 5:32).

And finally, in regard to swearing, Jesus said, "But I say to you, Do not swear at all" (Matthew 5:34).

Jesus' interpretations of God's will as revealed in the Law seem incredibly harsh to us, and almost impossible to keep.

In order to better understand what Jesus meant when he said that our righteousness must exceed that of the scribes and Pharisees, I'd like to focus on one of the stickiest of the laws—the law concerning divorce.

The original Mosaic Law stated that a man might divorce his wife if he found "some indecency in her." *Some indecency* came to have varying interpretations. One rabbinic school held that unchastity was the only ground for divorce. Another, more liberal, school had a broader interpretation: If a woman salted a man's food too much, spoiling his dinner, that was grounds for divorce. One bad meal and you could be out! If she went out in public view with her head uncovered, if she talked with men in the streets, all these were grounds for divorce. The process itself was very simple; a bill of divorce ran: "Let this be your writ of divorce and letter of dismissal and deed of liberation, that you may marry whatever man you wish." It had to be presented in front of two witnesses—and that was it.

A woman with no status or position in the Jewish world, apart from her husband, was left to fend for herself. At the time of Jesus, divorce had become so easy and common that many young women were afraid to marry because their lives were so insecure. The whole family system was on the verge of disintegration.

It's easy to see that the divorce law could be followed in a legal manner, yet not be humane. That is, the law could be followed with the result that a class of people—women without power or position in society—would be hopelessly exploited. Jesus said that's not the way it should be. There is more to it than that! "So whatever you wish that men would do to you, do so to them; for this is the law and the prophets" (Matthew 7:12). (You'll notice, too, that women were not free to divorce their husbands for unchastity or abuse or neglect.)

Jesus said that it isn't enough to obey the law, if you miss "its intent." The intent of the law is that life is preserved and protected. But the Pharisees and scribes prided themselves in keeping the law for the sake of keeping the law, and not for humanity's sake. Jesus says no to this.

Think of examples of this way of living in our lives. An extreme example is the S.S. men in Nazi Germany who killed millions of

Poles and Jews while "obeying orders." They were following the law and committing mass murder at the same time. Or think of Dickens' *A Christmas Carol*. Old Scrooge did pay Cratchit a salary. He cared for him in a legal sense, but where was Scrooge's humanity? His lack of it is the whole point of the story.

Law keeping applies also to stewardship of our time and talent and possessions. Several people have spoken to me of their stewardship as "paying their dues." When we think in those terms, we miss the point again that our whole lives and all that we are and have are gifts. "Paying our dues" does not witness to this fact. "Paying our dues" suggests that God is only active in a part of our lives, and that there is a part of us that we can withhold from God. Lot's wife is an example of such a person.

In stiffening the Law's demands on our lives, Jesus forces us to look at the intent of the Law. The intent of the Law is that our neighbor is cared for and that the earth is preserved and protected. This work, this calling, demands our entire being. "You, therefore, must be perfect, as your heavenly Father is perfect" (Matthew 5:48).

Perfect here does not mean "never making a mistake." Perfect means complete, single-minded devotion to the will of God. This means that the Law cannot be kept when someone is exploited, as in the divorce laws. This means that the Law cannot be kept while we watch our land erode away or blow up. This means that the Law cannot be kept if we hold back any part of ourselves from doing God's work in our world. And the great irony, the great secret of it all is that this calling to single-minded devotion is, at the same time, the way to real freedom in life. This is what Jesus meant when he declared, "Come to me, all who labor and are heavy laden, and I will give you rest. Take my yoke upon you, and learn from me; for I am gentle and lowly in heart, and you will find rest for your souls. For my yoke is easy, and my burden is light" (Matthew 11:28-30).

"Come to me," Jesus says to us in communion. Come to me, and I will forgive you your sins. Come to me and I will free you to turn to your neighbor. I will free you to live. Then your righteousness will exceed that of the scribes and the Pharisees. *Amen*.

Norene A. Smith
Christ Lutheran Church
Slayton, Minnesota

Sunday
February Twenty-first

Call to Worship: Greater love has no man than this, that a man lay down his life for his friends. *John 15:13*

Processional Hymn: "Let Us with a Gladsome Heart"

Invocation: I love you, I love you, I love you. You just can't say this too often if you love someone. We say it with our mouths, but we show our love by our actions. Help us to act as though we are in love with God and his people. *Amen.*

Sermon Scripture: I John 4:18-21

Sermon Presentation: "Everybody Can Have It"

Hymn of the Day: "All Glory, Laud, and Honor"

Offertory Scripture: The silver is mine, and the gold is mine, says the Lord of hosts. *Haggai 2:8*

Offertory Prayer: Lord, you showed us love by your death. We have to show our love by little things. The gift we place on the altar is one small way we prove our love. *Amen.*

Prayer of the Day

Lord, one day a man came to you and asked, "What is the greatest commandment?" You asked him what he thought it was. He responded, "To love the Lord your God with all your heart, all your soul, and all your mind, and to love your neighbor as you love yourself."

Even today it sounds so simple, yet it is such a great challenge. Too often we settle for a mere shadow of the real thing.

When we look to you, we see the perfect lover. You have accepted us just as we are. You have been hurt by us, but you have forgiven us as well. We have been disobedient, but when we ask for a new start you are willing to give it to us.

So often we are afraid to love others, because we are afraid to take the risk of letting others know us as we truly are. We are afraid that they will find us unlovable. But you know us best of all. Yet you who know—not only our actions, but our every motive and every thought—you love us still. You loved; you took the risk; you ended up on the cross. Yet the resurrection proved once and for all that love will conquer hate, forgiveness can overcome sin, reconciliation will overcome broken relationships, and life will overcome death.

Let us learn to love as you have loved us. *Amen.*

Benediction: And now, Israel, what does the Lord your God require of you, but to fear the Lord your God, to walk in all his ways, to love him, to serve the Lord your God with all your heart and with all your soul. *Deuteronomy* 10:12

Recessional Hymn: "The King of Love My Shepherd Is"

Lectionary Lessons: The First Sunday of Lent
Lesson 1—Genesis 9:8-17; Psalm 25:1-10
Lesson 2—I Peter 3:18-22
Gospel—Mark 1:9-15

History of the Hymn of the Day: "All Glory, Laud, and Honor"
"All Glory, Laud, and Honor" written by Theodulph, Bishop of Orléans, in the ninth century, one time freed its author from death in the dungeon. The story is told that on Palm Sunday, 821, King Louis the Pious, son of Charlemagne, while celebrating the day with his people, glimpsed the radiant face of Theodulph through the bars of the prison where he had been confined. The king had experienced trouble with his relatives and had suspected Theodulph of supporting them. Thus he had cast him into the dungeon. Now as he passed by, he saw the brave saint and heard his voice singing with joy "All Glory, Laud, and Honor," a song he had written himself. The king was so pleased at the evidence of religious devotion that he released Theodulph at once and restored him to his ecclesiastical position.

Announcement for Next Week's Sermon: How many times have you been right in the middle of a job and said, "There has got to be a better way"? Jesus asked that same question and answered it himself.

Story of the Week: A Texan was having a heart-to-heart talk with his little boy. "Son," the father said, "I just heard you ask that man if he was from Texas. You must never do that. If he is from Texas, he'll tell you. And if he isn't from Texas, you shouldn't embarrass him."

EVERYBODY CAN HAVE IT

Most of us have a rather vague and oftentimes too romantic concept of love. For example, look at the Valentine's Day we have recently observed. You know . . . the candy hearts being passed out in school. So very early in life we begin to teach the boy-girl relationship of "Be Mine," "I Love You," "I'm All Yours," and so on. Almost all of these sentiments are being expressed in a selfish and possessive style of love.

A friend of mine once visited Boston. Now for those of you who have been in Boston, you know what a deplorable situation it really is to try and get out of there and onto an expressway leading south. Four times my friend received directions on how to get out of the city, and four times he wound up hopelessly lost. I suppose his sheer frustration was communicated as he pulled into another gas station, for it was there that a complete stranger offered to take him out of the city and put him on the expressway leading to Plymouth. The stranger would even wait in the next block if the man following him missed the light. Finally, the man pointed to an entrance ramp, waved his arm, and that was the last he saw of my friend as he at last was on the right road. Why did the man do it? He did it because he wanted to. He didn't have to do it. He cared about his strange and hopelessly lost neighbors from out of state. So love is telling others what is deepest within our hearts. It is saying: I like you, because you like the Washington Redskins, the peace and the tranquility of the mountains, and the lush green fairways of the golf courses. I love you, although you do not care for the way George Allen coaches his team. I love the way you wear your hair, the style of life you seem to enjoy living. So love is, then, the process of my gently leading you back to yourself. Love is not always taught; it is caught. So many times in our person-to-person relationships with people, we ask beneath our breath. Well, what do they want from me this time?

So, I love you—although. I love you although we do not have the same tastes in our style of life. I love you because I recognize that you are a child of God, an inheritor of the kingdom of heaven, and that deep down inside you, you are full of the power and the glory and the majesty that is yours and yours alone—and I am waiting for you to release that power! However, we know that the world is still too full of lonely people, who are waiting for a sign of interest and an expression of love. What do I mean?

Let's go back to the time when we adults were in school. It was time for art class, and we couldn't wait! There we were with our art paper and our crayons on the desk ready to draw. In came the poor art teacher who already looked like she had taught a dozen classes that day. She gave her best cheery, "Good morning children. Today we are going to draw a tree." On her paper, she began drawing a big green thing with a brown stem and a few blades of grass. You muttered under you breath, "That's not a tree; that's a lollipop." But you also knew that if you wanted an "A" on your paper, you must draw her tree, not yours, and turn it in as quickly as possible. But Johnny was different, for he wanted to draw his own tree. He knew he had experienced in his young lifetime some things his teacher hadn't. He had climbed a tree, skinned his knees on a tree, fallen out of a tree, built a house in a tree, and listened to the wind singing through the leaves of a tree, so he drew his own tree. Out came the reds, the yellows, the browns, the greens—it was a really psychedelic tree! To Johnny it was real; so he turned in his paper to his teacher and said, "Here is my tree." The teacher took one glance at it and said, "Oh my goodness! Brain damage. This child should be in special education!" His style was not her style. She did not know the child, and the child did not know her. Love was an impossibility; neither could reach out and into the other person. Here is where we have one of our biggest hang-ups concerning love: We cannot pour out our innermost feelings, because we are afraid. We are afraid that what we reveal to that other person will seriously damage the image he or she has of us.

There is a misunderstanding about love; yet many people will argue over the fact that love is a natural thing, and that it is really easy to love if we can break through some of those hang-ups. Now, it's true that love is something all of us are starved for—we crave it; we scream for it; we play sick games to get a sick love, for it is better than no love at all. But it is pretty tough to give away something we don't have. We cannot really give love until we can find ways in which to get real love; you've got to get something going for you.

A young girl presented a sign to her pastor one day. It said: Because you are afraid to love, I am alone. He should have had a sign in his office which said: Because I am afraid to love, you are alone. I once saw a sign that said: Unless you love someone, nothing makes sense. Have we forgotten how to really love? Have we become so independent that we cannot say to people: I am dependent upon you and your love. I need you. I love you—when was the last time you said this to someone? When was the last time you really told a person that you loved her or him, with that certain kind of look in your eyes, the warm tone of your voice, the communicating clasp of your hand—when was it? Are you that hung up and strung out that you are afraid to let go? Is it so terribly silly to tell someone that you love him or her? Or do you feel that person would look upon you as some kind of "kook" for saying something like that?

Did you ever stop to think of what would happen if you suddenly grabbed your children and really told them that you loved them? And your children knew that you meant it, not through the buying of that love with things, but just seeing, feeling, and hearing that love. As a matter of fact, have you children ever done the same thing to your parents?

Now, suppose we had a storm like the one last summer. And suppose you were in the warning path of that deluge of water. You received a twenty-four hour notice to evacuate your home, but what would you take with you? Things? Your color television, your stereo, your golf clubs, Grandpa's brass spittoon—what would you take? Things? Oh, we place so much value and emphasis on things, when all we really have is ourselves. The only thing we have to take is ourselves. A man talked to me after a terrible storm. His house was in the way of the water. The next day, as he walked outside to survey the damage, the sun was shining, and there in his backyard was his flowering peach tree in full bloom. He said that it made him grow up right then and there as he looked at that tree. The world would go on in spite of him. It taught him that life, not things, is the most beautiful. Things cannot return anything to you, and that is what really counts, the returns you receive.

Each of us is the most beautiful part of God's vast creation; yet look at what we are trying to do to one another. We are saying: I don't dare tell you the truth about me; you don't deserve to hear the truth. Or, I want to keep on lying to myself about myself, despite your obvious need to know that I am a human being, too. So, what is there left to do? Look at it this way, there is still you, a beautiful person with tremendous capacities and potentials, all hung up and strung out with your little fears, anxieties, prejudices, and hates. You know, all things do come from you and what you can give to others. Everybody can have it. You can do it. You are a Christian! You are a child of God, precious in his sight; you've got to do it! He made real love possible! First John 4 tells us that we love because God first loved us. If we say "I love God," but hate our brother, we are liars, for we cannot love God, whom we have not seen, if we do not love our brother, whom we have seen. This, then, is the command that Christ gave us: "He who loves God should love his brother also" (I John 4:21).

Now let's return to that lovely you, not the lovely type that says: "Mirror, mirror on the wall, who is the fairest one of all?" but the type of person who loves himself in such a way that he feels compelled to give of what he has to others. Yes, to have it, enjoy it, to live it! I cannot really love you unless you allow me to know the real you. You cannot love me unless I allow you to know the real me. The more love you give away, the more love you will have to give away. This is the kind of loving I can understand, and it is a love that makes some semblance of order in this crazy world. It comes about only when you and I can really get to work on loving and work at it until we sweat real sweat. The more love there is, the more love comes out, literally oozing out of you! And in this kind of situation, there is more than enough for everybody, and everybody can have it!

Remember that the most loving thing we can do is to tell it like it is from deep down inside. Deep inside, where few people, if any, have ever trod, and oft times where you even fear to go yourself. But you still say: "I can't do that! If I tell it like it is, then they will run and tell everybody else. "Are you that afraid of yourself? I say, no. They won't run and tell everybody else like it is with you, for when they run and tell, it is a pretty sure sign that you really haven't gone deep down inside yourself. You've only touched the surface; you've partially faked it! So, the person who listens to you hears that fake. He feels that fake, and he says, "Friend, you are really not telling it like it is; therefore, I don't feel it necessary to respect your lack of confidence in me." Have you ever looked at it this way? Try it sometime!

Then I look elsewhere and find myself at the basic teaching center of life—the home—and what are we communicating there? Fears, prejudices, anxieties, mistrust, hate, things. Where is love? Mom and Dad, did your children ever see you in an argument? Did you apologize to each other, and then right before their eyes, tell your wife or your husband that you loved them? Did your children ever see this? They are no exception either. Have you ever gone to your parents, told them of what you did wrong, and asked for their forgiveness, with tears in your eyes? Well, it's a beginning, you know. Are we too sophisticated to tell our inner feelings to others, even members of our own family? Is the only time we feel we can tell them we love them when we are off in some dark corner where no one will see as we whisper into their ears? How long can we fake it? We've got to believe in what love really means, not in what others are trying to tell us what it should mean. Paul tells us that love is kind, patient, considerate, and beautiful!!! I agree, for to me it is the weak who are cruel, conniving, manipulating, forceful, and domineering. Gentleness can only be expected from those who are strong, and this is about as Christlike as we can become.

Listen to the words of a twenty-year-old girl, who was brilliant and creative. She tried to be real, and she tried to really love: "My happiness is me, not you, not only because you may be temporary, but also because you want me to be what I am not. I cannot change to merely satisfy your selfishness, nor can I feel content when you criticize me for not thinking your thoughts, or for seeing like you do. You call me a rebel, and yet each time I have rejected your ways and your beliefs, you have rebelled against mine. I do not try to mold your mind. I know you are trying hard enough to be just you, and I cannot allow you to tell me what to be, for I am concentrating on being me. You said that I was transparent and easily forgotten, but why did you try to use my lifetime to prove to yourself who you are?"

Let's do a little serious thinking about that, as parents, as pastors, as teachers, as community leaders, and as Christians, for it came from a girl who finally took her own life. She found it too hard to be just herself. She didn't like to draw those lollipops. She wanted to draw her own tree, but someone else always knew better. I like you because. I love you although—is this not what God is saying to us this Lenten season, that there from the Cross of Calvary was real love personified, his love in the process, that great and awesome forgiving process of his gently leading us back to ourselves and to him?

First John 4:7, 20-21: "Let us love one another; for love is of God. . . . If anyone says, "I love God," and hates his brother, he is a liar; For he who does not love his brother whom he has seen, cannot love God whom he has not seen. And this commandment we have from him, that he who loves God should love his brother also." *Amen.*

D. Timothy Robinson
Evangelical Lutheran Church in America
Calabash, North Carolina

Sunday
February Twenty-eighth

Call to Worship: You shall not take vengeance or bear any grudge against the sons of your own people, but you shall love your neighbor as yourself: I am the Lord. *Leviticus 19:18*

Processional Hymn: "Thine Is the Glory"

Invocation: Lord, as we look through this Lenten season to your suffering and death, keep our eyes ever on the cross. There is the real victory. There is the final triumph. *Amen.*

Sermon Scripture: Luke 4:1-13

Sermon Presentation: "Alternatives to the Cross"

Hymn of the Day: "Rejoice, the Lord Is King"

Offertory Scripture: The rendering of this service not only supplies the wants of the saints but also overflows in many thanksgivings to God. *II Corinthians 9:12*

Offertory Prayer: In this Lenten season we are not going to give up something; we will add something to our lives. Let it start here with this gift we place on your altar. *Amen.*

Prayer of the Day

Lord, why? Why a cross? It's so horrible, so brutal, and so difficult to understand. We wonder why the world would seek to kill the Son of God, whose only crime was bringing God's love and grace to our fallen world.

The cross is so difficult to understand. Satan gave Jesus an alternative. Peter found the idea of the cross unthinkable. Yet, the cross is the only way that God could reconcile the world to himself. The law had to be fulfilled. Punishment had to be meted out. Yet, you sent your Son to suffer in our place.

The cross shows us your power. You can take hate and overcome it with life. You can take hate and overshadow it with love. You can cast out the darkness of guilt with the light of your mercy. You showed us that your goodness is stronger than our wickedness. But most of all you showed us that your gift of life will overcome death.

This cross is a mystery. But your love for us is a reality. In that we trust. *Amen.*

Benediction: The creation itself will be set free from its bondage to decay and obtain the glorious liberty of the children of God. *Romans 8:21*

Recessional Hymn: "Rise Up, O Men of God"

Lectionary Lessons: The Second Sunday of Lent
Lesson 1—Genesis 17:1-10, 15-19; Psalm 105:1-11
Lesson 2—Romans 4:16-25
Gospel—Mark 8:31-38 *or* Mark 9:1-9

History of the Hymn of the Day: "Rejoice, the Lord Is King"
One of the six favorite hymns of Charles Wesley. The great Methodist hymn writer compiled thousands of hymns during his lifetime of eighty-one years and this one was written sometime in the vicinity of 1750. It is difficult to realize that one man could write such all-time favorites as "Jesus Lover of My Soul," "Love Divine All Loves Excelling," "O for a Thousand Tongues to Sing," "O Thou Who Comest from Above," "Ye Servants of God," and "Rejoice, the Lord Is King." But he did, and many, many others. Perhaps it suffices to say that here was a man so filled with the joy of the Spirit of God that it continuously manifested itself with the glad sound of music and psalm!

Announcement for Next Week's Sermon: Is religious faith wishful thinking? You may be surprised at the answer. Don't miss the answer next Sunday.

Story of the Week: As the opera singer was into her third number on a much publicized "television special," a woman said to her husband, "Isn't she wonderful? I hear that her singing has been responsible for the sale of thousands and thousands of television sets."

"I can understand that," her husband said. "After listening to her for another five minutes, I'll be ready to sell this one."

ALTERNATIVES TO THE CROSS

Lent follows so close on the heels of Christmas that it seems we barely get a glimpse of the babe in the manger before we must begin the prologue to agony on the cross. How we are to do this confronts us year after year; yet it is true that without the cross, the manger is a barren place, stripped of its meaning for any of us. Matthew and Luke knew this; so they dealt with the issue of the cross almost immediately after their beautiful telling of the Christmas story. They fairly jumped from the cradle to the story of the temptation of Jesus. You see, the temptation Jesus faced in the wilderness has a direct bearing on the crucifixion itself. The real issue in the wilderness temptation was the temptation of Jesus to avoid the cross.

From the moment he was born, the shadow of the cross covered Jesus. Even before he began his ministry, there was the temptation to find another path, to walk a less agonizing road than the Via Dolorosa, the Way of Sorrows.

It was an issue Jesus had to face from the start. He couldn't deal with the cross until he had first dealt with alternatives to the cross. God did not want Jesus to be a puppet, devoid of a will of his own, led to the cross like cattle are led to the slaughter. No, the way of the cross had to be a deliberate choice, made in the light of all of its alternatives. And so, we are told, Jesus "was led up by the Spirit into the wilderness to be tempted by the devil. . . . for forty days" (Matthew 4:1-2).

The temptation to seek alternatives to the cross had to be the first order of business, even before the formal ministry of Jesus could begin, and Jesus had to reject those alternatives if he was to see clearly the path down which he must go. Though he rejected the temptation during his month-long stay in the desert, the temptation to find another way never completely left him. In fact, the story of the temptation ends by saying, "When the Devil finished tempting Jesus in every way, he left him for a while" (Luke 4:13 TEV).

It was not to be the end. The temptation recurred many times throughout Jesus' ministry. Even in Gethsemane, when the cross seemed inevitable, Jesus cried out, "My Father, if it be possible, let this cup pass from me" (Matthew 26:39).

Isn't it striking, perhaps even a little frightening, that Jesus wanted (hoped beyond hope) to find another way? "Maybe, just maybe," his desire told him, "the cross is not the only way leading to the salvation of the world." But that's the nature of temptation. It is the desire to find alternatives to God's will. Many times alternatives look better to us than God's way. That's why they're tempting: "Hey! I've found the sure-fire road to success. And it hurts nobody. Isn't advancement and prosperity what God would want for me? Isn't success important?

What's wrong with a better life?" That sounds reasonable, doesn't it? Where's the temptation in that?

Evil, sin, and corruption are found not only in the dark alleys of big cities or the offices of politicians. They are found wherever people succumb to the desire to go another way, to take an alternative path, than the one God wants them to take. We learn that so clearly in the temptation of Jesus.

First of all, let's understand clearly that the main issue in the temptation of Jesus is not just turning stones into bread or having absolute authority in the world or showing the world miracles. Those were to be the end results. No, the real issue was: *If you are God's Son . . . .* The real issue was doubt, a haunting question, if you are God's Son. . . . "You were baptized by John in the Jordan, you had the Holy Spirit descend upon you in bodily form, like a dove, and you heard a voice from heaven saying, 'You are my own dear Son.' Can you believe it? Dare you believe it? What if it's not true? How do you know it's true? I'll give you a test—show you how to make sure—if you are God's Son." Tennyson once said, "There lives more faith in honest doubt,/Believe me, than in half the creeds" ("In Memoriam"). How true that is. To really believe, to have a faith that's more than a "head-trip," we must wrestle with our doubts and come to grips with truth until that truth is part of our very soul.

Jesus, before he could begin his ministry, had to wrestle with that doubt—doubt about who he really was, doubt that could raise so shocking a question, "If you are God's Son." Once that doubt was answered, the way would be clear to follow God's leading. The alternatives to God's way would be seen for what they are: evil (no matter how attractive), sin (no matter how beneficial), and corruption (no matter how justified).

So the temptation of Jesus was to lead him to disbelief: "If you are God's Son . . . you won't go to the cross. The cross is the last place for God's Son. Oh, no, I'll show you a better way. Order this stone to turn into bread. It's a simple matter for God's Son. Feed yourself, then feed the world. Put food in the stomachs of all the world's starving, and they'll believe and proclaim you Messiah . . . if you are God's Son."

That was an attractive alternative to the cross. Once the world's physical needs were met, the world would believe in him, and there would be no need for the cross.

The point was a strong one: It would crop up in Jesus'

ministry again. John tells us that once, after Jesus had blessed two barley loaves and a few fish and proceeded to feed five thousand men, plus women and children, with so meager an offering, the people rushed upon him to make him king! It was a mob scene, and Jesus had to push and shove to get through the thick of them.

So the temptation to order the stone to turn into bread was not far off the mark. People would believe, at least for a while, and maybe he could be spared the cross. But then again, maybe it wasn't God's way. So Jesus answered, "The scripture says, 'Man cannot live on bread alone' " (Matthew 4:4 TEV).

The next alternative to the cross was to exercise his authority and become spiritual ruler of the whole world. It would be a political shortcut to salvation. "If you are really God's Son, there can be no cross. You have the power to take control of things, become King of kings and Lord of lords, allow people to drag you to the cross? Never!"

That wasn't far off the mark either. Remember when Jesus stood before Pilate, about to be crucified? Pilate said, "I have the authority to set you free and also the authority to have you nailed to the cross." And Jesus answered, "You have no power over me!" And then, when Jesus was arrested, he said, "Don't you know that I could call on my Father for help and at once he would send me more than twelve armies of angels?" Notice how the temptations just kept cropping up in Jesus' life. He would never be free of them!

Power! He had the power all right; the world could be his. Why should he submit to the cross? Why? Because you can't take possession of the human spirit by force. That's tyranny. It is evil. It is bowing down and kneeling before the forces of evil. That is something Jesus would not do, could not do, and still be God's Son. So Jesus answered, "The scripture says, 'Worship the Lord your God and serve only him' " (Matthew 4:10 TEV).

The third alternative to the cross always hounded Jesus throughout his ministry. It was the temptation to be a miracle worker: "If you are God's Son, throw yourself down from the pinnacle of the temple. Turn an apparent suicide into a miracle. People will believe!"

Every time Jesus healed a person, this temptation came back to haunt him. "I can see! I can see!" the blind would cry out when they received their sight. The lame made to walk would leap for joy and spread the word. And Jesus would have to quiet them. "Don't tell anybody about this," he would plead with them. But it did no good. They wanted all the world to see what had happened to them, and the crowds around Jesus grew bigger and bigger.

The folks in Nazareth demanded, "Do the same kind of miracles here that you did in Capernaum!"

Other people asked, "What sign of power will you perform for us so that we might believe?"

Everyone, it seems, wanted a performance by the greatest traveling road show of them all—the "Magic Man from Nazareth"!

After Jesus raised Lazarus from the dead, the word spread like wildfire as he rode into Jerusalem on the back of a donkey. People cut branches from the trees and spread garments in his path and cried, "Hosanna. . . . Blessed is he who comes in the name of the Lord!" (Matthew 21:9).

"Throw yourself down from here," the temptation went. "Angels will bear you up! The people will believe—in miracles!" But fame and fortune are soon forgotten. Six days after Lazarus was raised from death, Jesus was nailed to the cross.

The hearts of people do not change because of miracles. Twenty centuries have come and gone since Jesus himself was raised from death, and people still do not believe. Avoiding the cross through miracles, as logical as that might seem, could not be God's way, and Jesus rejected it.

The alternatives to the cross, though attractive, and certainly tempting, could not lead to our salvation. There is only one way, God's way—unfortunately, it is the way of the cross.

I say it is unfortunate, because the cross is that tragic moment in history when we, the citizens of the world, wanted our way, and we took God's Son and we mocked him and we spit upon him and whipped him and shoved a crown of thorns on his head and drove spikes through his arms and feet and said, "There! You have no power over us!" And we thought then that we would be rid of him.

But, and this is the point, we're not rid of him. We're not rid of him, because the cross was the plan from the very beginning. Jesus had rejected every other way.

"For God so loved the world, that he gave his only son. . . ."

Amen.

Edward A. Beckstrom

Evangelical Lutheran Church in America
United States Air Force Chaplain, retired
Equality, Alabama

Sunday
March Sixth

Call to Worship: You will know the truth, and the truth will make you free. *John 8:32*

Processional Hymn: "My Faith Looks Up to Thee"

Invocation: Lord, make your life and death real to me. May this Lent be a time of discovery for me. Make me totally dependent on you and your grace. Never let me go. *Amen.*

Sermon Scripture: Matthew 17:1-7

Sermon Presentation: "Is Religious Faith Wishful Thinking?"

Hymn of the Day: "All Hail the Power of Jesus' Name"

Offertory Scripture: They gave according to their means, as I can testify, and beyond their means, of their own free will. *II Corinthians 8:3*

Offertory Prayer: Lord, make me a wishful thinker. Let me wish for every promise you made to your children. Let me respond to those promises with these, my gifts to you. *Amen.*

Prayer of the Day

Lord, can we share some of our wishes with you today?

In a world that is full of relationships that are often characterized by fading love and a growing lack of interest, we wish to be reassured of your unfailing love.

In a world of written lies and half truths that are spoken with an air of sincerity, we wish to know that your word truly is the truth, the whole truth, and nothing but the truth.

In a world that says, "Live for today," we know that when the future looks so uncertain, you are the same yesterday, today, and tomorrow. We wish to know the vision of glory that you promise for all who trust in you.

In a world haunted by the specters of decay and death, we wish to hear the good news of the resurrection, a good news that promises that, like you, we will live forever and know pain and suffering no more.

In this world, we wish to live with the certainty that love will conquer hate, truth will prevail over lies, and life is stronger than death.

Are these things too much to wish for? *Amen.*

Benediction: I have been crucified with Christ; it is no longer I who live, but Christ who lives in me; and the life I now live in the flesh I live by faith in the Son of God, who loved me and gave himself for me. *Galatians 2:20*

Recessional Hymn: "Pass Me Not, O Gentle Savior"

Lectionary Lessons: The Third Sunday of Lent

Lesson 1—Exodus 20:1-17; Psalm 19:7-14
Lesson 2—I Corinthians 1:22-25
Gospel—John 2:13-22

History of the Hymn of the Day: "All Hail the Power of Jesus' Name"

Edward Perronet, born in 1726 in the quaint village of Shoreham, was the son of a minister who served as vicar of this village. A giant cross stood facing the hill where Vincent Perronet enjoyed a long and holy ministry. Young Perronet received profound inner inspiration not only from his father, but also from John Wesley who frequently visited their parish. Perronet and Wesley remained friends, even though they differed in the question of lay administration of the Sacraments. Eventually he became a minister of an independent church in Canterbury. It was in 1779 while serving as vicar at the Canterbury Cathedral that "All Hail the Power of Jesus' Name" was written. The majesty of the words:

> "And Crown Him,
> Crown Him, Crown Him
> Crown Him Lord of all"

has reflected the power and glory of Christ to Christians the world over.

Announcement for Next Week's Sermon: I don't think a day ever passes that at some point everything seems to be going wrong. I give up! I give up! We don't usually mean it, but it is how we feel. Don't give up; come next Sunday and find out how to hang on.

Story of the Week: A minister's wife was suffering with a bad cold and stayed home one Sunday morning instead of going to church. When the minister came home, his wife asked him about the morning service. "What did you preach about this morning?"

"I talked about charity," he said. "I told them that it was a duty of the rich to give to the poor."

"How did it go over?" his wife asked.

"About 50-50," the minister said. "I convinced the poor."

IS RELIGIOUS FAITH WISHFUL THINKING?

Is religious faith wishful thinking? Now I suspect that you probably expect me to say, "No, religious faith is not wishful thinking." I hope I am able to be a little surprising when I say, "Yes, religious faith is wishful thinking." Who among us would not wish that the traditional Christian affirmation would be true? Is it true that there is behind all of reality a Divine intelligence out of which has come the creation of the world? Does this same Divine Spirit continue to be present with us, guiding our steps and sustaining us in our lives? And at the end of our journey when finally we breathe our last, is this same divine mystery there to embrace us and to give us a new life, a new existence in his kingdom which shall have no end? Now who among us would wish that it would be otherwise?

Unbelievers protest these wonderfully comforting and reassuring beliefs by calling them wishful thinking, as though by saying that these are only wishes, they thereby make them untrue. Oftentimes Christians respond by saying, "Well, if wishful thinking explains our hope for heaven, then how do you explain our fear of hell?" At first that seems to be a telling point. But, in fact, when psychologists have delved deeply into the fantasies and the imaginations of people, they have discovered that when people have much repressed hostility, they take great delight in fantasizing about their enemies, and those who oppose them, being cast into the fires of hell. So, actually, the fear of hell, as well as the hopes of heaven, can be explained in terms of wishful thinking! Sigmund Freud, the famous psychiatrist and pioneer in the understanding of human personality, was very clear that religious beliefs are rooted in these needs that all human beings seem to have. In fact, he said, even our conception of God the Father is rooted in our own earthly experience, that we take our images of our own earthly fathers and grandfathers and project those onto the Divine reality. Only Freud said there wasn't a Divine reality. We project those images onto the emptiness of space.

One of the observations made for many years is that it has never rained on a Harvard commencement. The explanation of that phenomenon is that God must be a Harvard man! During the nineteenth century, it was observed that God was a fine English gentleman. It's inevitable that we will conceptualize the Divine mystery in terms of our own human experience and project that experience onto God.

There is no point in denying that our religious beliefs are wishful thinking. But there is a tremendously important difference between the statement of Sigmund Freud and other unbelievers in regard to this issue. They say that religious beliefs are wishful thinking, and they are untrue. I submit to you that religious beliefs are wishful thinking, and they are true.

Our faith is something we know to be true, but it is not something we know to be true with certainty. The things we know with certainty are relatively unimportant; we say they are "dead certainties." We never know with certainty, for example, that someone we love will always be faithful or always care for us. We want people to have only positive feelings about us. We don't want people to have ambiguity toward us. We want them just to love us. And so we want to have certainty in those relationships. We long for that certainty. But, of course, the fact of the matter is that the more we demand such certainty, such guarantees from our relationships, the more we destroy the relationship and the more we live with uncertainty. The most we can hope for in human personal relationships is to develop a trust; we can trust the other person to stand by us and to be reliable, to be our constant friend. So it is in our relationship with God. We can never know with certainty, but we can develop a relationship of trust.

At one time in the history of the church, it was believed possible to prove the existence and the reality of God. But when we prove the reality of God through syllogistic logic, then we have only a dead certainty. But when we have a close, intimate, loving relationship with God, it has to be a relationship of trust, and not something we know for sure.

Surely there is reason not to believe in God. There are many people with great wisdom who do not believe that life has any final meaning. The great mathematician and philosopher Bertrand Russell declared that tragedy and death in the world amply demonstrate that the only reasonable foundation is, in his words, "unyielding despair."

There are also other witnesses and other reasons that make it possible for us to believe that the Christian story is not only wishful thinking, but it is also true. For example, it is always helpful to read scripture. I think many Christians, especially Protestant Christians, don't spend much time in reading the scripture. I find that every time I sit down and read the scripture, my faith is strengthened. My capacity for trust is strengthened. I find that is something which helps me to believe. I find that when I read about some of the scientific discoveries that have been made in recent years—the new understandings of quantum mechanics and the new physics—that also helps me to believe. When I read about the near-death experiences of people, especially when I meet and talk with someone who has had such an experience, I find that helps me to believe. Or extra-sensory perception; so many people have experiences of psychic phenomena that are just amazing. I find that when I hear those stories, that helps me to believe.

But most of all I am enabled to believe in the reality of God because of the religious experiences of other people and of my own life. There are moments when you have experienced the presence of God in your life. Every single human being has an instance in which he or she can say, "There. There was a point."

A man by the name of Karl Heim wrote a book a few years ago called *Christian Faith and Natural Science*. He tried to deal with some of the struggles and problems people have relating modern science with the Christian faith. He talked about a tribe of primitives on a Pacific island who were overwhelmed with the sense of a divine presence. There was a mysterious sense of a presence in their midst everywhere they went. And it was frightening to them. They tried to get away from it to avoid dealing with it. They would try to squeeze themselves into a little cave in the rocks in order to squeeze out this presence. But no matter where they went, there was the presence. They would dive into the ocean, down into the depths of the water, to get away from the presence. But there it was. No matter where they went, there was this presence. One is reminded of the great Psalm 139:

Whither shall I go from thy Spirit?
  Or whither shall I flee from thy presence?
If I ascend to heaven, thou art there!
  If I make my bed in Sheol, thou art there!
If I take the wings of the morning
  and dwell in the uttermost parts of the sea,
even there thy hand shall lead me,
  and thy right hand shall hold me. (7-10)

Have you ever climbed to the top of a high mountain and looked off and observed the vistas all around you and the magnificence of the world? Have you had an experience in which you just felt so full of this mysterious, overwhelming power? It's called a *mountaintop experience,* isn't it? Perhaps the archetypal mountaintop experience is that in the Gospel of Mark. Jesus went up to the Mount of Transfiguration with Peter, James, and John, his three favorite disciples. They were always going off with him to special places—to Gethsemane and now to the Mount of Transfiguration. They climbed to the top of this high mountain and an overwhelming religious experience took place. There are other mountaintop experiences: Paul, on the Damascus road, saw a light out of heaven. John Wesley felt his heart strangely warmed. But it was there, on the Mount of Transfiguration, that Peter, James, and John saw Moses and Elijah, standing alongside Jesus. His face was transformed, and it shone like the sun. A great cloud came over, and the voice of God spoke to them. After they had had this experience, what did they do? They said to Jesus, "Lord, this is wonderful. Let's build three booths right here, one for you, one for Elijah, and one for Moses." They wanted to build a monument, didn't they? They wanted to stop right there. That was going to be the end of it. They had been to the top of the mountain; they didn't want to go any further; they wanted to build a monument right there. But Jesus said no! He led them off the mountain, back down into human community where he went about his business of healing and teaching.

Let's just stop right here. This is all we need. Let's keep things just the way they are now. No more growth. No more changes. It's perfect. I love it just the way it is. Now that's always the temptation when our religious life has been especially meaningful, when we've been to the mountaintop. We want to build a monument. We want to stop all forward movements, stay where we are. Do you know what we call a place in which there are no visions of the future? There are lots of monuments, but no movement. It's a cemetery! That's not what Jesus wants us to do. That's not what Jesus permitted his disciples to do, was it?

Christians are continually invited to be a part of a revolution, a new vision, a new vision of the future, to have a vision of what life can be. Do you know what it means to have a vision of the future? It means to be engaged in wishful thinking. That's what Christians are all about—to be engaged in wishful thinking. Because wishful thinking is the meaning of the phrase to have a vision, a goal, a *wish dream*. The scripture says that where there is no vision, the people perish. The scripture also says that old men will dream dreams and young men will have visions. When a church or a community has a vision, they are able to move into the future with new hope and direction and power.

John, on the Isle of Patmos, in Revelation had a wish dream. He had a vision of "a new heaven and a new earth." Isaiah had a vision. He dreamed of a kingdom in which the lamb would lie down with the lion, in which we would beat our swords into plowshares and not learn war any more. That was the vision. And we are called to be people of vision, not to build monuments, but to be engaged in movements—movements for racial justice, for peace, for women's rights, for spiritual growth. Our world is desperately in need of more wishful thinking, more visionaries, people who have been to the mountaintop.

Martin Luther King, Jr., in Washington, D.C. in 1963 said, "I have a dream." It was a wish dream. Then, shortly before his death, he said, "I've been to the mountaintop." Jesus had been to the mountaintop. He went up there with Peter, James, and John. There they all had a vision. Elijah had a vision. He went to the top of Mount Carmel, and had a mountaintop experience in which he overcame the prophets of Baal. Moses went to the top of Mount Sinai, and God gave him the Ten Commandments. Talk about wishful thinking! God thought we'd obey those rules. At the end of his life, Moses went to Mount Horeb, and he looked out over into the Promised Land. You know what a mountaintop experience is for? It's to give us a vision, and that's what the religious life is about, because a religious experience is that point at which we get in touch with the Divine presence of God. It fills our imaginations with an idea, with a dream, with wishes. Wishful thinking—about how this whole world can be changed and how it ought to be, what it really ought to be like, what God wants it to be so that we can really pray, "Thy kingdom come, thy will be done on earth as it is in heaven."

Well, it's my prayer that our church will not only be a monument, but also a movement, a movement with lots of wishful thinking, dreaming, and visions about a new heaven and a new earth, and that we will grow in numbers and in our commitment to investing our resources—our money, our time, and our talents—to serving the kingdom of God, to put all of that which we have at the service of Christ to the glory of God. *Amen.*

James L. Kidd
Asylum Hill Congregational Church
Hartford, Connecticut

Sunday March Thirteenth

Call to Worship: Have you not read what was said to you by God, "I am the God of Abraham, and the God of Isaac, and the God of Jacob"? He is not God of the dead, but of the living. *Matthew 22:31b-32*

Processional Hymn: "Lead On, O King Eternal"

Invocation: O Lord, the beginning of our salvation is that time when we say "I surrender." That is the beginning of your controlling our lives. Take my life today. I surrender. *Amen.*

Sermon Scripture: Philippians 3:1-11

Sermon Presentation: "The Surrendered Life"

Hymn of the Day: "Beneath the Cross of Jesus"

Offertory Scripture: [God] who supplies seed to the sower and bread for food will supply and multiply your resources and increase the harvest of your righteousness.

II Corinthians 9:10

Offertory Prayer: Lent is a time for personal growth. May we draw closer to you, and may our gifts be a personal sacrifice to your honor and glory. *Amen.*

Prayer of the Day

Lord, we live in a world that values freedom and independence. We want to be able to do our own thing. But all too often we confuse freedom with irresponsibility. We confuse knowledge with truth, and power with glory. So often we measure greatness by the number of people whom we command or the titles we hold. Like the disciples, we need to learn that a follower of yours is the servant of all.

Help us to follow your example of humility and obedience to the will of God. Let us realize that in your kingdom there can be no blessings without suffering. There can be no crown without the cross. There can be no Easter without Good Friday.

You call on us to be willing to lay down our lives for others, to love our enemies and those who persecute us, to take up our cross and follow you.

Give us the faith and the courage to trust your call to discipleship in your name. Give us the strength to put aside our own ambitions. May we truly surrender our own selfish desires and seek your kingdom first, seek to do your will in all things. *Amen.*

Benediction: For we must all appear before the judgment seat of Christ, so that each one may receive good or evil, according to what he has done in the body. *II Corinthians 5:10*

Recessional Hymn: "Just as I Am, Without One Plea"

Lectionary Lessons: The Fourth Sunday of Lent
Lesson 1—II Chronicles 36:14-23; Psalm 137:1-6
Lesson 2—Ephesians 2:4-10
Gospel—John 3:14-21

History of the Hymn of the Day: "Beneath the Cross of Jesus"
This hymn of Christian experience, so popular as a solo for the male voice, was written by a woman. Elizabeth Cecilia Clephane was about thirty-five years old when she wrote the hymn near Scott's Abbotsford Abbey in England in 1865. Four years later she was dead. Although she lived only thirty-nine years, most people could live to be a hundred and not accomplish half what she did in the writing of two of the world's beloved hymns: "Beneath the Cross of Jesus" and "There Were Ninety and Nine."

Announcement for Next Week's Sermon: Loneliness is an awful thing to have to endure. All of us are lonely at one time or another. It is no fun, but we can get through it. Next Sunday—loneliness.

Story of the Week: A young actor was telling his father about his first part in an off-Broadway play. "It's going to be great," he said to his father, "I play the part of a man who has been married for 26 years."

"You've made a good start in show business, son," his father said. "Do a good job in that role and one of these days you'll get a speaking part."

THE SURRENDERED LIFE

It is said that Augustine wished to have seen three things before he died: Rome in its glory, Christ in the flesh, and Paul in his preaching. Men have seen Rome in all of its glory and have been no happier for having seen it. They have seen Christ in the flesh without being any happier for having seen him. Men have also heard Paul in his preaching, and yet were not converted by it.

Paul was, indeed, a great preacher, and one of his most profound statements is found in these words: "[I want to] know him and the power of his resurrection, and may share his sufferings, becoming like him in his death, that if possible I may attain the resurrection from the dead" (Philippians 3:10-11). These words were written in Rome during Paul's first Roman imprisonment. The Christians there were not as attentive to him as they should have been. He said of them that they all "look after their own interests, not those of Jesus Christ" (Philippians 2:21). In this imprisonment, Paul suffered many things for Christ, but he did not complain.

The letter to the Philippian church is full of love and joy. Some twenty times Paul uses the words *joy, rejoice, peace, contentment,* and *thanksgiving* in this short letter. The chief desire of his heart is that he might be true to his Lord. His words imply that Paul is rejoicing in these sufferings, because they are bringing him to a greater knowledge and appreciation of his Lord and Master. This is evidence of a completely surrendered life—to know Christ and the power of his resurrection; to share in his sufferings, becoming like him; and to attain the resurrection from the dead.

One with a surrendered life wishes to know Christ the Savior historically. Paul appreciated the value of knowledge, as he was a scholar and theologian. He knew, however, that to know Christ meant more than a mere intellectual knowledge of who he is. There are many who have heard of Christ and know him historically, but do not know him as their personal Savior. The greatest desire of one who is saved is to know his Savior. We should ask ourselves whether Christ is our Savior, whether we really know him. In a meeting once, a man said, "I have been a Christian a long time, but I never knew before that you could really know Jesus Christ."

The surrendered life wishes to know the power of Christ's resurrection. The word *power* makes all the difference between religion in the head and religion in the heart. One may have a knowledge of the fact of Christ's resurrection and never know the *power* of his resurrection. It was this power that drove the disciples out of their secret places to tell the story of the living Christ. It was through this power that Peter, who had denied his Lord, was able to stand up in the presence of the enemies of his Lord and defend the Christ whom he had once denied. It was also this power of resurrection that gave Paul the courage and strength, while yet in prison in Rome, to say, "But whatever gain I had, I counted as loss for the sake of Christ. Indeed I count everything as loss because of the surpassing worth of knowing Christ Jesus my Lord. For his sake I have suffered the loss of all things, and count them as refuse, in order that I may gain Christ" (Philippians 3:7-8). The surrendered life knows that Jesus is not dead. He is alive forevermore. The surrendered life knows this, not from hearsay, but by the power of the living Christ in his own life.

One who has a surrendered life wishes to know the fellowship of Christ's sufferings. The disciples had fellowship with Jesus in the flesh. There were times when this fellowship seemed wonderful: when he taught them to pray, when he healed the sick, and when he raised the dead. But there were times when they did not want his fellowship: when he prayed in the garden, when he raised the multitude of saints on the day of his crucifixion, and when he hung on the cross. They wanted the blessing without the sufferings, the crown without the cross, and the resurrection without the crucifixion.

Historically, the disciples found themselves incapable of entering into the fellowship of his sufferings, until touched by the power of his resurrection. Peter, James and John gathered with him around the supper table, they gazed into his sorrowful countenance, but they could not understand the mystery of his sufferings. They followed him to the garden and heard him say, "My soul is very sorrowful, even to death" (Mark 14:34). So little did they understand his sufferings that they went to sleep as he spoke these words that should have revealed the agony of his soul. How different it was when these same men saw things in the light of the glory that burst from the open tomb. Then they began to understand and to enter into the fellowship of his sufferings.

How many of us want to know the fellowship of Christ's sufferings? Paul knew something of this fellowship, but he wished to know more. He knew that there could be no resurrection without a crucifixion. He knew that there could be no crown without a cross. How many of us want to do something difficult for Christ? Oh, that we may enter into the fellowship of his sufferings, that we might *share* his sufferings! It was love that made Christ suffer for the world. "For God so loved the world . . ." (John 3:16). "For we have not a high priest who is unable to sympathize with our weaknesses . . ." (Hebrews 4:15). It is love that makes us suffer for our friends and for our Christ. We readily lay down our lives for those we love.

The surrendered life wishes to be made to comform to Christ's death, "becoming like him in his death" (Philippians 3:10), his atoning death and his sacrificing death. A Chinese convert, when trying to persuade his countrymen to give up their idols and believe in Christ, was ridiculed and scorned and at last pelted with mud and stones until his face was red with blood. The missionary said, "You have had bad treatment today." The convert smilingly said, "They may kill me if they will love Jesus." Shall we make the complete surrender of our lives to Jesus Christ?

This old world was lost in sin. The prophets had wept and prayed and proclaimed God's word, but still the hearts of people were hard and dull and dead. The priests had instituted all sorts of religious ceremonies, even to the sprinkling of the blood of bulls and goats, but even then the hearts of people did not ring with the music of heaven. Finally, on Calvary's cross, the Son of God was heard to say, " 'Father, into thy hands I commit my spirit!' And having said this, he breathed his last" (Luke 23:46). He made the complete surrender and poured his own precious blood into the crucible out of which was to come a glorious church, not having spot nor wrinkle, nor any such thing, but that it should be holy and without blemish. This one, who made such a surrender and such a sacrifice for us, demands the complete surrender of ourselves to him. Hear him as he says, "If any man would come after me, let him deny himself and take up his cross daily and follow me" (Luke 9:23).

When I survey the wondrous cross
On which the Prince of Glory died,
My richest gain I count but loss,
And pour contempt on all my pride.

Were the whole realm of nature mine,
That were an offering far too small;
Love so amazing, so divine,
Demands my soul, my life, my all.

"When I Survey the Wondrous Cross"

Amen.

Zion Robbins
Presbyterian Church, retired
Dayton, Ohio

Sunday
March Twentieth

Call to Worship: The sacrifice acceptable to God is a broken spirit; a broken and contrite heart, O God, thou wilt not despise. *Psalm 51:17*

Processional Hymn: "Children of the Heavenly Father"

Invocation: O how lonely we all are. We need to learn the secret of our Lord as he faced his hour of trial and loneliness. You must know that God is with you always, even to the end of the earth. Trust in the Lord. *Amen.*

Sermon Scripture: John 12:20-33

Sermon Presentation: "Jesus' Loneliness, and Ours"

Hymn of the Day: "Blessed Assurance, Jesus Is Mine"

Offertory Scripture: So each of us shall give account of himself to God. *Romans 14:12*

Offertory Prayer: Lord, help us to understand that all things come from you—our joys, our sorrows, and our loneliness. It is not a curse, but a blessing if we will only use these times to draw closer to you. Let us not curse the darkness, but rather praise God for the great light that shines in our lives. *Amen.*

Prayer of the Day

Lord, it must sound strange. There are so many people in the world; yet there are so many lonely people. We find people living in large apartment complexes, leading such lonely lives. They go to work, come home, and rarely, if ever, get to know, much less ever speak to, their neighbors. On crowded streets and highways, we find many individuals, each worried about arriving at his or her destination on time, each seeing the people that surround as mere obstacles to meeting a deadline.

We pass through crowded streets and malls, each of us with his or her own agenda. Loneliness is a part of our lives. But it is not what you intended for us. From the time of creation, you realized that none of us can find meaning and fulfillment in life. Yet you have promised that you will be with us always. Let us never forget that your presence is always with us. We are never without a friend, a companion, someone who loves us and accepts us as we truly are.

Guide us in all of our relationships so that we not take people for granted, but always treat the people we meet with the dignity and respect due a fellow child of God. *Amen.*

Benediction: These [signs] are written that you may believe that Jesus is the Christ, the Son of God, and that believing you may have life in his name. *John 20:31*

Recessional Hymn: "Come, Thou Almighty King"

Lectionary Lessons: The Fifth Sunday of Lent
Lesson 1—Jeremiah 31:31-34; Psalm 51:10-17
Lesson 2—Hebrews 5:7-10
Gospel—John 12:20-33

History of the Hymn of the Day: "Blessed Assurance, Jesus Is Mine"

Fanny Crosby's contribution to the Christian world through music is enhanced by another favorite, "Blessed Assurance, Jesus Is Mine," a song of true salvation. Her personal faith in Christ shines like a light in every verse. The stirring tune to this hymn which arouses many congregations to sing with great power and emotion was written by Phoebe P. Knapp.

Announcement for Next Week's Sermon: Palm Sunday is a great and happy day in the life of the church. What a day to talk about humility. Jesus taught humility on Palm Sunday; don't blame it on me.

Story of the Week: Once there was a little baby cabbage who said to his mother, "Mommy, I'm worried about something. As I sit in this row of cabbages and grow and grow and grow day after day, how will I know when to stop growing?"

"The rule to follow," the momma cabbage said, "Is to quit when you are a head."

JESUS' LONELINESS, AND OURS

All of us know what it means to be lonely. During those last days in the life of our Lord, he, too, must have experienced the same thing: "Now is my soul troubled. And what shall I say? 'Father, save me from this hour'? No, for this purpose I have come to this hour" (John 12:27). A New Testament scholar has said about this passage that the chief concern is the unfolding of the consciousness of Jesus in this dark hour.

However, it's in the sixteenth chapter of John that we discover Jesus' secret for living with loneliness. There he says, "The hour is coming, indeed it has come, when you will be scattered, every man to his home, and will leave me alone; yet I am not alone, for the Father is with me" (John 16:32). That's an eternal word for your life and mine as well as for his. *I am not alone, for the Father is with me.*

Look at the experience. Surely it's no respecter of persons, coming as it does to the rich and poor, to those who are leaders as well as to those who are the led. Tennyson said of the Queen of England at his time, "I felt for her, all alone on that height. It is dreadful." The president of a major corporation, comparing his present feelings with what they were when he was a chemist with the company, said, "I sit in executive committee meetings. I don't know for sure what they think of me, or what the larger organization thinks of me. How am I doing? You can't ask anybody. Nobody will tell you. Was that a really good speech I made, or was the audience just being polite to the president?" This is the loneliness of leadership.

But look, also, at the wide significance of human companionship as it touches our loneliness. To be sure, we need people. Even within the book of Genesis, it's written that "the Lord God said, 'It is not good that man should be alone' " (2:18). Consequently, according to this story of creation, God created woman from the body of Adam.

However, especially in our time, we tend to place on our intimate relationships a far greater burden than they were intended to bear. For example, in every intimate relationship there's a quality of incompleteness. In such relationships, no two people really touch each other completely. Even in our deepest moments of sharing, isn't there some reserve, some holding back that frustrates the intimacy for which we hunger?

Of course, when a loved one dies, this becomes especially poignant. We think of things we should have said, but didn't; things we should have done, but didn't; feelings and experiences we should have shared, but didn't. But, you know, even if we had done everything, the incompleteness would still be there. Therefore, what we all need is the grace of forgiveness for ourselves as well as for our loved ones. We need it, not only for the things that actually could have been different, but also for that estrangement which permeates our whole existence.

How, then, can we learn to live with loneliness? In more ways than we can examine in this brief time. But mainly by—learning to live from within. Obviously, our feelings of loneliness have several roots. But a mature person can people his solitude.

Of course, Thoreau pointed to this when he wrote, "I find it wholesome to be alone the greater part of the time. To be in company, even the best, is soon wearisome. . . . I never found a companion so companionable as solitude" *(Walden).*

Well, most of us would hardly go that far. But these statements make vivid that valid point: that, necessarily, we all have a world of solitude, apart from human companionship, that can be rich and full. Indeed, one of our basic ventures, as human beings and as Christians, is to learn how to live from within. It's not insignificant, at all, that our Lord himself, knowing he was going to be deserted by his friends, could yet affirm, "I am not alone, for the Father is with me."

Our second affirmation moves in another, and almost opposite, direction, much like the ebb and the flow of the sea. It is to take those times and those opportunities to get out of ourselves and live in the lives of others. Someone said it this way, "Until I loved, I was left alone."

The last affirmation, as we learn to live with loneliness, is that we come to a deep and vital faith in God. There's nothing quite like it to cure a deep and abiding loneliness. Surely this was the secret of our Lord in facing difficult times in his own life. When his enemies turned on him, when his friends deserted him, when the cross loomed up as a cruel possibility, he said, "I am not alone, for the Father is with me."

This simply means that there are those lonely times that can't be overcome by any human means; no matter what our outside interests, no matter how many friends we count within our friendship circle. It's in those crucial times that only a significant, lively faith in God will be sufficient. It is out of this conviction and rooted in this faith that the creed of the United Church of Canada leads us to affirm: "We are not alone; we live in God's world. We believe in God who has created and is creating."

No wonder, then, that one hundred thirty-ninth psalm still speaks its eternal word today. It continues to be that word wherever life is tough. A pastor stood at the bedside of a man in the coronary care unit of a hospital. The man wasn't well at all, and lived only because of life-support machinery. Before leaving, the pastor quoted from memory that section (verses 7-12) of the psalm, which was a favorite of young men in the second World War:

> Whither shall I go from thy Spirit?
>   Or whither shall I flee from thy presence?
> If I ascend to heaven, thou art there!
>   If I make my bed in Sheol, thou art there!
> If I take the wings of the morning
>   and dwell in the uttermost parts of the sea,
> even there thy hand shall lead me,
>   and thy right hand shall hold me.

Within the household of faith, this indeed is our conviction. And it is our privilege to appropriate the faith for ourselves. God makes us strong, when by ourselves we are weak. He gives us courage, where by ourselves we would be faint-hearted. He gives us a deep assurance, where by ourselves we would be lost in our loneliness.

I am not alone, the Father is with me. With this faith, we still confront problems. But with this faith, there comes a deep trust. At all times and in all places, we know we are "leaning on the everlasting arms." *Amen.*

Warren Nyberg
Excelsior United Methodist Church
Excelsior, Minnesota

Sunday
March Twenty-seventh

Call to Worship: Holy, holy, holy, is the Lord of hosts; the whole earth is full of his glory. *Isaiah 6:3*

Processional Hymn: "We've a Story to Tell to the Nations"

Invocation: Today is Palm Sunday. This is one of the happy days in the church; let us rejoice and be glad. Hosanna to God in the highest. Blessed be the Lamb of God. *Amen.*

Sermon Scripture: Mark 11:1-10

Sermon Presentation: "The Triumph of Humility"

Hymn of the Day: "Ride On, Ride On in Majesty"

Offertory Scripture: It is required of stewards that they be found trustworthy. *I Corinthians 4:2*

Offertory Prayer: Lord, let us wave our palms; let us cry our hosannas; let us shout for joy; let us give these gifts as part of that celebration. *Amen.*

Prayer of the Day

Lord, it's quite a choice to make! We want to be masters; yet you call us to servanthood. We want to be powerful, but you call us to be humble. We want to be aggressive, but you teach us that it is the meek who will be blessed by you. We would love to be invincible, but you call on us to follow your example and be vulnerable.

You are special, Lord. You don't just tell us what we should be doing. You show us the way by providing us with a strong example of the godly life we are called to live. Your claim on us and our lives is not one based on overwhelming might. Instead, it is based on the irresistible lure of humble love. You call us to trust you and believe that your light can cast out darkness, that love is stronger than hate, that death will never conquer life.

We listen for the still small voice in the midst of the whirlwind, and we hear you speak. We look for a king and we see a baby born in a manger. We look for a Savior and we see a crucified prophet. We look in the tomb for a dead hero, but we find a risen, resurrected Lord.

Help us do it your way, Lord. It really is the only way. *Amen.*

Benediction: But you are a chosen race, a royal priesthood, a holy nation, God's own people, that you may declare the wonderful deeds of him who called you out of darkness into his marvelous light. *I Peter 2:9*

Recessional Hymn: "In the Cross of Christ I Glory"

Lectionary Lessons: Palm Sunday
Lesson 1—Isaiah 50:4-9*a*; Psalm 118:19-29
Lesson 2—Philippians 2:5-11
Gospel—Mark 11:1-11 *or* John 12:12-16

History of the Hymn of the Day: "Ride On, Ride On in Majesty"

The hymn, "Ride On, Ride On in Majesty" is the most well-known of the Palm Sunday hymns. It was written by the Reverend Henry Hart Milman, dean of St. Paul's in London. Dean Milman, born in 1791, also won world acclaim as a historian. The Reverend John Bacchus Dykes wrote the music to this hymn and was famous in his own right for such favorites as "Lead, Kindly Light," and "Ten Thousand Times Ten Thousand."

Ride on, ride on in majesty!
Hark! all the tribes Hosanna cry;
O Savior meek, pursue thy road,
With palms and scattered garments strewed.

Announcement for Next Week's Sermon: No matter what it is in your life, you always get to the bottom line. If you want to buy something, you end up signing on the bottom line. There is a bottom line to your faith, too. Next Sunday see if you are ready to sign.

Story of the Week: When her husband returned home in the evening after making a speech at a civic club, his wife asked, "Well, how did it go? Did they like your speech?"

"They certainly did," her husband said. "When I finished and sat down, everybody said it was the best thing I'd ever done."

THE TRIUMPH OF HUMILITY

Almost everyone knows the ancient Greek legend of Achilles. He was supposed to have been the mightiest of the warriors at the seige of Troy. He was the hero of that epic poem "The Iliad" by Homer—many of us remember the agony of having to read that in high school or college literature classes.

Achilles was strong because when he was an infant his mother dipped him in the River Styx. Achilles' mother had been told to do this by the gods, and because of this he was to be invulnerable—except for one thing. At the spot where his mother held him, his heels, he would be vulnerable. From that omission comes the expression that any one's weak spot is his Achilles' heel. Achilles was told that if he went to Troy, he would be killed. But he was convinced he was invulnerable. And sure enough, he was killed—by a poisoned arrow shot into his heel.

Greek mythology is full of super heroes, and all of them have one weak spot: passion or lust, greed or avarice, vengeance or cruelty, malice or ambition. In fact, the gods of Greece and Rome are everything that humans are, only larger and worse.

The story of the God that we worship is the opposite. Jesus shows us that God's "weakness" is his love for us. Jesus knew that if he went to Jerusalem he would be killed. Yet the New Testament says that "he set his face to go to Jerusalem" (Luke 9:51). *The Living Bible* gives a stronger emphasis to the line; it says; "He determined to go to Jerusalem with an iron will."

The importance of Palm Sunday, just before Good Friday, is to emphasize the determination of God that he would conquer his enemies with his weapons, not theirs. In all likelihood there were children present that day. They may not have been certain of the significance of the palm branches, only aware that something special was happening. And there in the midst of it was that simple man on a simple beast, looking a bit disappointed, yet with a subdued regal bearing that set him apart and drew from the crowd a spontaneous acclaim.

Achilles went to Troy thinking he was invincible. Jesus rode into Jerusalem with the full knowledge that he was totally vulnerable. There is a line in Shakespeare's *Henry VIII* in which one of the courtiers laments that he is "naked to mine enemies."

The disciples were not able to perceive the importance of the situation. They were elated that at last the popular sentiment had rallied behind their Master. Now the kingdom would be established. How they must have cheered. How little could they have guessed that before five more days were ended, they would see Christ on a cross, with a different procession, a different hailing of him as king.

When we, in our faith, proclaim Christ as the Savior of the world, part of what that salvation means to us is portrayed in the events of Palm Sunday. We are reminded again how much of our faith is demonstrated by Jesus in his actions. Our God is a God who does things. Our faith is in the deeds of God, not just a string of ideas and philosophies. We follow Christ; we do not just sit at his feet and listen. Our Lord shows us his way and leads us in it; he does not just tell us about it.

Palm Sunday is the ultimate demonstration that God will accept nothing short of the complete triumph of his plan of salvation. He will not accept any hollow, pompous homage. He asks more of us than the waving of palms and the shouts of hosanna. It is the Herods and the Caesars, the kings and emperors, the dictators and the presidents of the world who are satisfied with hosannas and popular acclaim. Christ is looking for those who believe enough to remain faithful after the crowd has gone home, who will stand by him when he is scorned and ridiculed, who will wait beneath his cross, and who will at last come to an empty tomb and accept the gift of resurrection on faith alone.

Two things are taught by this Palm Sunday event, one about Jesus and one about ourselves.

First: When Paul looked back on the revelation of Jesus that had been his burning faith, he suddenly burst out in a mini-doxology about Christ. Speaking of Jesus, he said: "though he was in the form of God, did not count equality with God a thing to be grasped, but emptied himself, taking the form of a servant, being born in the likeness of men. And being found in human form he humbled himself and became obedient unto death, even death on a cross" (Philippians 2:6-8).

The world in which we live is so twisted and filled with pride that we have difficulty dealing with true humility. Almost every day, we can clip our newspapers and divide the stories into a series of pride and power. We read of White Supremacy and Black Power, of economic or industrial clout, and of military muscle. Society can be paralyzed by labor's or management's intransigence.

How many of television's highest rated programs are about power—to be gained or preserved—or about its loss? Even "Fantasy Island" and "The Love Boat" interpret dreams, aspirations, and human relationships in terms of power. Love is not a relationship; it is a maneuver to hold another person in an embrace that controls, or at least holds, the one loved in a state of belonging or ownership. But have you ever heard of Donkey Power? Jesus uses the most irresistible force of pure and absolute love.

Jerusalem is a strange place for God to choose for this event to take place. It's different from all other cities. There are no broad esplanades down which triumphant armies can surge, no Champs Élysées, no Unter den Linden, no Pall Mall, not even a Pennsylvania Avenue. The streets are crooked and crowded. They even go up and down steps, so that automobiles in our day cannot drive through the old city. The gates of the city are low, so that anyone on horseback has to bend down to go through some of them.

The Caesars built Rome, with its Forum, through which their chariots could clatter in victory parades. No so, Jerusalem. Yet, through her streets had paraded those who had conquered her—Nebuchadnezzar's armies, Syrian invaders, Philistine conquerors, and most recently, Rome's legions. Squeezing down those crowded streets had come their soldiers in armor, their banners, their rulers.

But God's entry into that city and into human hearts comes as a king in humility. How ironic it is that this simple ride should, in the end, prove more enduring than all the armies that stormed Jerusalem's gate. How wonderful that the peace he commanded has outlasted all the weapons of war ever wrought.

God demonstrates to us that the ultimate battle for human loyalty is won in the humility of Jesus. We come to him and accept him as our Savior, not because he overwhelms us with his might. We are, instead, drawn by that irresistible lure of humble love.

Had God sent Jesus as a king upon a throne, we might have crawled to him in shameful obeisance. Had he enslaved us in the chains of a moral bond, we might have obeyed him out of fear. Instead, he demonstrated a humility that is binding because of its liberating freedom. He chose to abandon his might and power. He set us free to reject him. The first time was in Eden, when he gave man the freedom to eat the forbidden fruit of the tree of the knowledge of good and evil. It wasn't that Adam and Eve were naughty and ate of what they were forbidden. Rather, they wanted to be God. They wanted the pride of being God.

Now the choice is offered again. Choose the humility of Jesus. Choose his way of peace and love. Walk in the pathway of humble service.

But once again, man chose to cry, "Crucify him! . . . We have no king but Caesar" (John 19:15).

We have failed to see that his love from such a lowly beast of burden is not the victim of the cross. He is the triumph over it.

And then the second lesson Palm Sunday teaches us is found in a single line in the Gospel of Mark. Jesus says, "Go into the village . . . you will find a colt" (11:2). The other Gospel accounts make it clear that the beast was an ass—about the lowliest and least likely animals to be used for a triumphal entry!

Jesus says: "If anyone says to you, 'Why are you doing this?' say, 'The Lord has need of it' " (Mark 11:3). He still says it of you and me. Our lives seem as unlikely a beast to carry the love of God as that other on which he rode into Jerusalem. We wonder why he should call us—demand of us—use us. But he does. We belong to him.

A man who grew up in Nova Scotia tells of his childhood when young boys carved model ships and sailed them on the waterways among the islands. He worked long hours. His boat was the finest. His pride in his workmanship was boundless. One day while sailing it, he ignored the turning tide. As it ebbed, his craft was taken away from him.

Many months later, in a neighboring town he saw it in a shop window; it was unmistakably his. A wise mother told him he could not merely claim it. The shop owner had invested in it, and was entitled to his claim.

So the boy worked the summer long to earn enough to make it his own again. Said he. "It's really mine now. I made it. I lost it. I bought it back."

So God says of our lives: "I made you. I lost you. I bought you back."

When the Great Wall of China was built, it stretched for thousands of miles. Its builders believed it was impregnable against all attackers—too high to be scaled, too thick to be breached, too long to circumvent. But it was defeated three times in its history, not by scaling, not by battering down. It was breached by bribing the gatekeepers. The wall was no stronger than the character of the person who kept its gates.

Palm Sunday carries all the overtones of the betrayal of Judas, the denial of Peter, the abandonment of the disciples, and the smugness of the priests. God's mighty fortress of love was breached by human sin. But his love prevails. It prevails because his humility is impervious to all threats. You and I, and any of his followers, may fail him. But he never fails. He still says of our lives: *The Lord has need of thee.* Our faith seems an unlikely vehicle of his love. Yet he calls us, uses us, and transforms us to be the carriers of his gospel.

In a high school Sunday school class recently, the devoted teacher gave each student the sign of the zodiac under which he or she was born. The teacher tried to show them the foolishness of believing in such hopeless and false notions of their destiny. The teacher wanted them to know that they were not born under the sign of distant stars; they are under the sign of the cross.

That's why we preach Christ. We proclaim his crucifixion, and we trust him to take our lives and make us more invincible than Achilles. Not even death will prevail against us. And in the end we will appear before him in thanksgiving and say: "O God, thank you for wanting us enough to come to us—and needing us enough to use us." *Amen.*

Kenneth E. Hartzheim
St. Paul's Lutheran Church in Sunny Hills
Fullerton, California

Sunday
April Third

Call to Worship: The hour is coming, and now is, when the true worshipers will worship the Father in spirit and truth, for such the Father seeks to worship him. *John 4:23*

Processional Hymn: "Christ the Lord Is Risen Today"

Invocation: Christ the Lord is risen today; he is risen, indeed. On this happy day, we greet the risen, living God; that is what makes us different. He is risen. He is risen, indeed. *Amen.*

Sermon Scripture: I Corinthians 15:1-4, 12-20

Sermon Presentation: "The Bottom Line of the Christian Faith"

Hymn of the Day: "There Is a Green Hill Far Away"

Offertory Scripture: And he said to all, "If any man would come after me, let him deny himself and take up his cross daily and follow me. *Luke 9:23*

Offertory Prayer: Father, as we gather here to celebrate the resurrection, we cannot forget the trials and suffering that led to this happy day. Help us to remember, when our trials and testing come, that you have won the victory and that we are part of that victory. You died that we might have life eternal with you. *Amen.*

Prayer of the Day

Lord, we look to you and we see so many things. We hear your parables. We listen to your Sermon on the Mount. Like the people of your day, we know that you speak with authority. Your teachings are without parallel. Your wisdom and truth are clearly evident to all who hear your words.

In looking at your life, we see that your actions match your teachings. Your deeds support your words. You have provided us with a model of godly living—a life of service, sacrifice, and obedience to the will of God. Even your death shows us that you were willing to lay down your life for all humanity.

But the bottom line, the most important, the most crucial aspect of our faith is our belief in your resurrection. The empty tomb on Easter morning has shown us the validity of your teachings. It shows us that God indeed is more powerful than the forces of evil in our world. We know that death is not the end of our days, but the beginning of eternal life. We know that, because you live we shall live, also. *Amen.*

Benediction: Go therefore and make disciples of all nations, baptizing them in the name of the Father and of the Son and of the Holy Spirit, teaching them to observe all that I have commanded you; and lo, I am with you always, to the close of the age. *Matthew 28:19-20*

Recessional Hymn: "I Know That My Redeemer Lives"

Lectionary Lessons: Easter Sunday

Lesson 1—Acts 10:34-43 *or* Isaiah 25:6-9; Psalm 118:14-24
Lesson 2—I Corinthians 15:1-11 *or* Acts 10:34-43
Gospel—John 20:1-18 *or* Mark 16:1-8

History of the Hymn of the Day: "There Is a Green Hill Far Away"

This hymn, picturing the crucifixion of Jesus, was written in 1848 by Mrs. Cecil Frances Alexander, wife of the Reverend W. Alexander, D.D., bishop of Derry, Ireland. Written for children with the purpose of making the Scripture more understandable, Mrs. Alexander conceived the idea for the song while driving on a shopping expedition to Derry. Outside the city walls there was a little green-covered hill which always made her think of Calvary. Therefore, when she explained the meaning of the death and resurrection of Christ, this little hill came into mind and she wrote:

There is a green hill far away
Without a city wall.

Announcement for Next Week's Sermon: If you think we had a happy day this week, wait until next week. If will be a day filled with joy.

Story of the Week: For five years, the stockroom man had been coming to work late. Finally, the boss called him in and said, "Look, Joe, instead of waiting until you have worked for us 25 years to give you a wristwatch, we are giving you this alarm clock—now!"

April Third

THE BOTTOM LINE OF THE CHRISTIAN FAITH

Paul tells Christians that, without the resurrection, their faith is of no value.

The bottom line. This is an expression originally from the business world that's getting more and more use today in our overly complex society. An automobile salesperson can talk for hours on end about options, accessories, performance, discounts, rebates, deals, promises, and so on. But when it's all said and done, only one thing is really important—the bottom line. The bottom line tells you exactly how much you're going to have to pay out for the car you want. Our current United States president has a great gift for gab in front of the cameras. Many times I've sat in front of the television, listening to him explain over and under, up and down, the details of all the "whys" and "wherefores" of an issue. Most of these times, I find myself saying, at least silently, "That's all very interesting, but what are you really saying? What are you going to do in this situation? *What's the bottom line?*"

Our church tries to meet the needs of many people. We're big, broad based, mainline. We try to serve just about everybody. We try to communicate God's love to all sorts of humans, being on the one hand faithful to the gospel of Jesus Christ, on the other flexible enough to accommodate the individual faith-needs of many millions of diverse persons without forcing anybody into a neatly molded box.

You here today constitute a cross-section of the wonderful diversity that can be found in the Christian church. There are more of you here today than at most other times of the year, and that's a typical attribute, too. But each of you is special, unique, distinct in your perspective of the Christian faith. Even so, we share a great deal in common as Christians, whatever stripe, shade, or label we may choose for ourselves.

My experience as a pastor and my study of the experiences of other Christians have convinced me that, while every individual's faith is somewhat unique, most persons come to know and accept Jesus Christ in four generalized ways. I've come to think of these as four steps, or stages, of entry into the Christian life.

The first level of entry into the Christian life, the one at which the majority of persons begin their journey with Jesus, is through the teachings of our Lord—the Golden Rule, the Sermon on the Mount, the parables and stories Jesus told. *As you wish that men would do to you, do so to them*—this kind of statement has an appeal in and of itself. It "feels right" to most people. *Blessed are the peacemakers, for they shall be called sons of God.* This is the way things ought to be; there's an inherent ring of basic truth there. On hearing the parable of the Good Samaritan, without ever being told out-right, we know what kind of neighbors we ought to be, one to another. The teachings of Jesus are powerful, truthful, and appealing. Many people have gained faith in Christ through belief in his teachings. Some of you here have probably received Christ via this point of entry—his teachings.

Many other people approach the Christian life from a point of belief in the exemplary life that Jesus, himself, led. Some start out here, others, after hearing and believing in his teachings, want to know more of the life of the one who could teach such wisdom and truth. His demonstrated love, his power, his purity of heart, his open, forgiving nature—the life of Jesus is a magnetic example to millions. He is calling us to "come, and live likewise." Little children are beckoned to sit on his knees and hear of the love of God. He gives a word of pardon to a tax-collector whose sins and wrongs were infamous far and wide. He offers a soft answer to turn away the wrath of those who sought to make a fool of him in public. The life of a convicted adulteress is saved by an insightful, penetrating response to her would-be executioners. The life of Jesus has no equal among humans. It draws us: "Come! Follow me!" Again, some of you have probably come to Christ via this, the second point of entry—his life.

Still other persons enter into the Christian faith through the fundamental appeal of the death of Jesus. If his life was exemplary among men, his death was even more so. It was a sacrificial death, inspiring, as are all truly sacrificial deaths. There are other, human, examples of such sacrificial deaths: A soldier falls on an exploding grenade to save his buddies in a foxhole. A woman runs into the street to push a small child out of the way of a speeding car, losing her own life in the rescue. However, the death of Jesus went far beyond the usual bounds of even sacrificial death. Examples of offering up one's life for a friend are few, for a stranger even fewer. But to die for the good of one's sworn enemies is unheard of. To forgive one's murderers in the act of carrying out their vile deeds is almost unimaginable. The death of Jesus becomes the unique example for all time of death with honor, dignity, and mastery. His death, too, like the teachings and the life of Jesus, has a quality that draws men and women to follow after him. Perhaps you've been drawn to Christ by the attraction of his unique, sacrificial death.

By now, however, I hope you're saying to yourself: "I wonder how the pastor plans to end this sermon? This is all fine for the preliminaries, Preacher, but let's get on with what you really want to say this morning. What's the bottom line?" All right. The bottom line, the fourth, final, and deepest level of entry into the Christian faith is exactly what we're here to celebrate today—the resurrection of Jesus Christ. Without the resurrection, any who would dare to call themselves Christians are fools. Without the resurrection, all other bases for faith in Christ crumble into rubble. As a teacher, Jesus becomes a liar, for he clearly taught that he, and those who followed him, would rise from death. The exemplary life of Jesus becomes a sham, a devious plot designed to win fame and notoriety through reverse psychology. And the inspiring death of Jesus becomes a dead end, a life needlessly wasted, thrown away at far too early an age. If you cannot believe that Christ rose from the dead, you're wasting your time sitting here this morning.

But if you can affirm that Christ has risen, as I proclaim to you on this beautiful Easter morning, then you are in possession of the greatest hope that any human can ever know—the hope of immortality. The resurrection of Jesus Christ is the bottom line of the Christian faith. The message of Easter is simple and straightforward: Christ has risen from the dead! Christ has risen from the dead! I offer you that message, and that hope, and I pray that you will accept it as the basis of your faith in Jesus Christ, who conquered death on the first Easter morning! *Amen.*

David Z. Ring, III
St. Mark's United Methodist Church
El Paso, Texas

Sunday
April Tenth

Call to Worship: I was glad when they said to me, "Let us go to the house of the Lord!" *Psalm 122:1*

Processional Hymn: "Jesus, Keep Me Near the Cross"

Invocation: Lord, we are back to worship, still tingling from the excitement of another Easter experience. Help us to keep that high pitch of enthusiasm throughout the whole year. *Amen.*

Sermon Scripture: John 20:24-29

Sermon Presentation: "Filled With Joy"

Hymn of the Day: "When I Survey the Wondrous Cross"

Offertory Scripture: It is required of stewards that they be found trustworthy. *I Corinthians 4:2*

Offertory Prayer: It is good to be back here with you again today. We come to respond to your love and the great gift of life. Accept these gifts as a token of our effort to return your love. *Amen.*

Prayer of the Day

Lord, to be honest with you, there is a great deal of the doubting Thomas in each of us. There are times when we are confused by it all. We doubt the truth of the "goodness," of the freedom from the power and sting of death, of the forgiveness of our sins, of a new beginning, of eternal life. These are the things we long for, the things we hope for. You have promised them to us, if we follow your way and strive to live by your word.

Yet your love, your grace, and your goodness are awesome, sometimes too awesome for us. We wonder: Can it be true, that God loves me just as I am? Can it be true that if I surrender myself to your will, I will be truly free? Can it be that we will live forever in your glorious kingdom?

Yes, it is true. Your word is the truth for our lives. Your love is the only foundation we need. We are your children. You are our Father, and you have promised to love us despite our fears, our doubts, our uncertainties, and our lack of trusting you. It is true—it is. *Amen.*

Benediction: I am the vine, you are the branches. He who abides in me, and I in him, he it is that bears much fruit, for apart from me you can do nothing. . . . As the Father has loved me, so have I loved you; abide in my love. *John 15:5, 9*

Recessional Hymn: "Were You There"

Lectionary Lessons: The Second Sunday of Easter

Lesson 1—Acts 4:32-35; Psalm 133
Lesson 2—I John 1:1–2:2
Gospel—John 20:19-31

History of the Hymn of the Day: "When I Survey the Wondrous Cross"

The noted critic Matthew Arnold said of the two-and-a-half-century-old Christian hymn "When I Survey the Wondrous Cross" that it was "the greatest hymn in the English language." He had such admiration for it that he sang and quoted it on his deathbed. Written in 1707 by Isaac Watts, the hymn was inspired by the words of Paul as recorded in Galatians 6:14, "God forbid that I should glory, save in the cross of our Lord Jesus Christ, by whom the world is crucified unto me, and I unto the world."

Announcement for Next Week's Sermon: Do you have religion? If you do, you are wrong. No one should have religion. If you don't agree with that, you'd better not miss next Sunday.

Story of the Week: The speaker had been giving a long-winded and boring talk about his travels out West. After an hour, he launched into a description of the Grand Canyon. "There I stood," he said, "standing on the rim of one of the natural wonders of the world. I was overcome with awe as I gazed into that huge abyss yawning before me."

A voice in the back called out, "Tell us. Was it yawning before you arrived on the scene?"

FILLED WITH JOY

The story went like this: Mary Magdalene discovered the tomb was empty. She met Jesus alive in the garden and ran to the disciples to tell them what had happened. That same night, Jesus appeared to those same disciples back in the room where they had again gathered out of fear and bewilderment.

The Gospel writer John continues this way: "Jesus came and stood among them and said to them, 'Peace be with you.' When he had said this, he showed them his hands and his side. Then the disciples were glad when they saw the Lord" (John 20:19-20).

The interesting character in the scripture today is Thomas, of whom John says, "Thomas, one of the twelve, called the Twin, was not with them when Jesus came" (John 20:24).

Thomas made some serious mistakes. There are times when we are hurt, or someone has disappointed us and we just want to be left alone. This was such a time for Thomas. He had such high hopes for Jesus and his cause. The arrest, trial, and crucifixion were a terrible embarrassment. Besides, Thomas felt guilty for having turned tail and deserted Jesus when things got tough. He just wasn't very proud of his behavior, and was not sure what the others in the group of twelve would think of him.

The rest of the disciples returned to the home of John Mark's mother on Mount Zion, where they often gathered. Thomas did not go there to be with them. That was a serious mistake. He needed to be with the others, especially now.

It's our mistake also. We often absent ourselves from church and the gathering of believers when we need their affirmation the most. That's true especially when doubts creep in. It is true when we have been hurt or get angry, when we are disappointed or feel we have been let down. So at the time when we most need the church, we often stay away.

Thomas has become the patron saint of a long line of Christians who have "lost face" in the family of believers. He stayed away at a time he needed to be there to be assured that he was okay, even though his former behavior wasn't the best.

The most risky time to miss worship in the company of our congregation is when we feel doubts, our faith seems weak, we have had our toes tramped on, we didn't get our way, or the pastor or someone in the congregation disappointed us.

Interesting Christian, this Thomas! Perhaps his twin is here worshiping with us today.

Perhaps the disciples wanted to take a special offering for the burial of Jesus and Thomas was offended because it was his money they were spending. Maybe Jesus had talked about the zealots' political party and the oppression of the poor in Jerusalem by the Romans, maybe Thomas quit because of these social issues being discussed. Maybe the twelve voted on where to hold the Passover, and Thomas didn't get his way. Perhaps they didn't sing his favorite hymn before they went out to the Mount of Olives. Maybe the money changers Jesus drove out of the Temple were related to Thomas.

You see, the very nature of the fellowship of Easter people is that, whenever we come together, all we imperfect sinners get to start over. We can experience beautiful forgiveness and be healed by the presence of others who believe and care.

Thomas wasn't there, so when Jesus came, he missed out on the "joy at seeing the Lord." That same joy the disciples experienced is available here as well. We can have the same joy here that those disciples had back then. The joy of having our faith affirmed is available. We need that kind of reminder of what we believe and how many of us believe it. There is this dimension to the fellowship of believers, that when we get together, it helps us to be sure. There is much strength and encouragement available here in our gathering. It's what Thomas needed and what we need as well.

According to statistics, more teenagers have committed suicide than ever before. Nationally, it's an epidemic. What in the world is happening? Why is it that a young person can become so desperate in life and be at a place where there seems to be no hope at all?

We have hope here, when we assemble in this place. But without the risen Christ and his church, things do seem nearly hopeless. Because we are humans, we need frequent reassurance and affirmation and reminders that we belong and have a safe place and a safe fellowship where we are accepted and loved.

When we gather here, there is also much to be learned. There is a different way of life, a different way of viewing current events, a different set of priorities, and a different way of dealing with enemies and with the world.

We live in a time in which the world coaches us to get all we can for ourselves. We hear from the sergeant on *Hill Street Blues*, "Let's go out there and do it to them before they do it to us." We are told that the best way to treat enemies is to point deadly weapons at them and make sure we have more weapons pointed than they do. We live in a time in which an effort is made to erase the cause of poor and the elderly from our budgets. Ours is an age that has counseled the young to do anything that gratifies and feels good. We are taught that if it makes a profit, it's okay to cheat and gamble and tell little white lies. Soap operas tell us it's okay to go from one bedroom to another. In many television programs, we are given examples of great wealth and how to earn it for ourselves.

Here, where the risen Christ and his people gather, there is a different life-style held before us. We are taught and encouraged to love our enemies. We hold up concern for justice and mercy. We talk about compassion for the poor and disabled. We call for a self-discipline of our lives and a sharing of the gifts given us.

The Bible is full of good advice, inspiration, and motivation to enrich our existence. It's also jam-packed full of hope and encouragement. When we face our doubts and questions honestly, like Thomas, we can grow and mature. The lives of other people around us are so much better for it. One of my preaching partners writes, "At least Thomas had the courage to honestly question and when presented with the truth, to firmly believe." So, when we are down, depressed, simply low, that is the best time of all to come and join the fellowship. Here there is joy to be found and experienced right in this upper room. It is a joy that is not the absence of trouble to be faced out there in the world; rather it is a joy that comes from being in the very presence of the Almighty and his family.

Notice what filled the disciples with joy. "The disciples were filled with joy at seeing the Lord" (John 20:20). For Thomas, joy had gone out of his life as he tried to live on his own without the fellowship of believers. The Bible tells us that when he did return to the upper room, Thomas' doubts were eliminated, his depression removed, and he experienced joy. Jesus gave him the Holy Spirit, and so once more he went away encouraged, and equipped and full of joy.

The saddest thing that can happen to us is to attend church and still not experience joy. Notice again that the disciples got this joy because they "saw the Lord." If we come here to see the pastor, the choir, to hear the hymns we used to sing, the familiar territory, to hear our old prejudices further enforced, we'll miss the joy! Or if we are here to prove a point or to get even or to embarrass someone or to relive the old days, we'll miss the joy! If we have come to pass judgment on whether we like or dislike the way things are done now, we've missed the joy. In such instances, we have become wrapped up in the incidentals and have missed the joy of being a part of God's family. It's the risen Lord we have come to see and worship and take home with us.

Dr. F. Eppling Reinartz, a former president of the Southern Lutheran Seminary in Columbia, South Carolina, used to say that people would often speak to him about their churches. They would point out how they had a tireless pastor or an outstanding pastor or a beautiful building or a great choir. But Dr. Reinartz said the most moving word he ever heard said about the church came from an elderly lady who told him, "I love this church, for when a person joins it, from that moment on they never have to bear another burden alone."

On this Sunday, we need examine our own visits to the upper room to be with the rest of the disciples. Are we tapping this fellowship for the right reason and taking from it all the joy that believing and worshiping and being in his presence can give us? Large doses of joy are available here, for joy is the opposite of unbelief.

Perhaps it won't be hand clapping, rolling in the aisles, belly-laughing, joy, but joy that comes from seeing the risen Christ face to face and in the eyes of the others around us. It is a joy that comes from being sure that we are safe at our death, that we are loved during our life, and that we are always in the company of God's family and friends who also know the joy.

It's still Easter, and we're again in the upper room. Thomas has finally come. *The disciples were filled with joy at seeing the Lord. Amen.*

Jerry L. Schmalenberger
Saint John's Lutheran Church
Des Moines, Iowa

Sunday
April Seventeenth

Call to Worship: How beautiful upon the mountains are the feet of him who brings good tidings, who publishes peace, who brings good tidings of good, who publishes salvation, who says to Zion, "Your God reigns." *Isaiah 52:7*

Processional Hymn: "My Hope Is Built"

Invocation: Lord, let us love you; let us worship you; let us follow you all the days of our lives. Lord, show us how to do all these things. Show us how you would have us love and obey your word. Grant us true religion. *Amen.*

Sermon Scripture: Acts 17:22-34

Sermon Presentation: "No One Should Have Religion"

Hymn of the Day: "Trust and Obey"

Offertory Scripture: Every good endowment and every perfect gift is from above, coming down from the Father of lights with whom there is no variation or shadow due to change. *James 1:17*

Offertory Prayer: Teach us how to truly give of ourselves and our goods to you. We need to give gifts that are pleasing to you, not to satisfy our own needs. Take my life first, and my gifts will be worthy. *Amen.*

Prayer of the Day

Lord, we are a religious nation. But the important question is, "Are we a faithful people?" We find that we are surrounded by many different religions. Many of them claim to be representatives of you. But we find that too often these religions are not what you had in mind when you established your church.

Many of them are based on feelings and opinions, and not on your truth. Some appeal to our emotions. These "feel good faiths" appeal to our desire for comfort and security. They have little interest in the sacrifice, obedience, and discipline that you demand of your disciples.

Others are religions of the mind and not of the heart. They are built on logic and rational thought. Those things that do not fit into their system or philosophy are ignored or discarded.

Then there are those approaches to God that stress and teach that our fulfillment and happiness are to be found in ourselves.

Guide us to find a true faith that responds to your love for us. Guide us that we may truly follow your way to the kingdom of heaven and eternal life. *Amen.*

Benediction: Trust in the Lord, and do good; so you will dwell in the land, and enjoy security. Take delight in the Lord, and he will give you the desires of your heart. Commit your way to the Lord; trust in him, and he will act. *Psalm 37:3-5*

Recessional Hymn: "Standing on the Promises"

Lectionary Lessons: The Third Sunday of Easter
Lesson 1—Acts 3:12-19; Psalm 4
Lesson 2—I John 3:1-7
Gospel—Luke 24:35-48

History of the Hymn of the Day: "Trust and Obey"

During a series of meetings conducted by the famous D. L. Moody in Brockton, Massachusetts, a young man rose in the congregation and said, "I am going to trust, and I am going to obey." Present in the group that evening was a professor of music by the name of D. B. Towner. The young man's statement appealed to the professor and he wrote it down and sent it together with the story to a Presbyterian minister, J. H. Sammis. Sammis, recognizing the appeal of the young man's sentence, wrote the well-known chorus which has been a favorite through the years:

Trust and obey
For there's no other way
To be happy in Jesus
But to trust and obey.

Announcement for Next Week's Sermon: Did you ever want to climb mountains? Next week we will talk about God's sure-footed people. You are never too old to learn.

Story of the Week: The man was in the middle of the river, drowning. Suddenly, from the center span of the high bridge the hero came to the rescue. He hit the water with a mighty splash and within moments had begun to tread water and hold the drowning man's head out of water. Moments later a rescue boat picked both of them up and headed for shore.

Immediately, the hero was surrounded by well-wishers and members of the news media. "Congratulations," a TV reporter cried out. "You're a hero for jumping from the bridge to save this man's life. Do you have anything you'd like to say?"

"Yes," the hero said, "I'd like to know who pushed me."

NO ONE SHOULD HAVE RELIGION

Taking a cab across West Berlin, a tourist came to the Kaiser Wilhelm Church, what's left of it. It was bombed out and only the steeple was left. It is now maintained as a memorial. The tourist said to a young cab driver, who was a native Berliner, "Tell me, the Kaiser Wilhelm Church, was it Protestant or Catholic?" To which the driver answered, "I don't know. I don't believe in God." I'm grateful that God believes in that young Berliner.

Here is a paradox: Alongside our growing secularism, in this country and in western Europe, there is also a growing interest in religion. We are unlike the people to whom Paul preached in Athens. Recall again that vivid scene at the cultural center of the ancient world. The Athenians were brilliant. Their mathematics, their understanding of physics, their philosophy were so brilliant that they considered all the other people in the world barbarians, people who went around saying, "Bar, bar, bar."

To this cultural center of the world, Paul went with the gospel of the crucified and risen Christ. At Areopagus, Mars Hill, where the philosophers met, he went to declare the Christ. Paul shaped his text as he walked through the Agora, the marketplace. Among all the temples and shrines, he came upon an altar dedicated to the unknown God.

That's what you might call hedging your bets in the midst of polytheism—just in case there is some god overlooked, we should build an altar to him, too. Paul picked up on that with a real genius and said, "What therefore you worship as unknown, this I proclaim to you" (Acts 17:23). The people listened as Paul talked about this God's being the Creator of all the world. They listened as Paul quoted two of their pagan poets, saying God is the author of all races. They listened until Paul spoke about the resurrection. That turned them off.

The point is that Paul said, "I perceive that in every way you are very religious" (Acts 17:22). They were. The same can be said about our day as well. While we, on the one hand, are increasingly secular, we are also very religious.

The Encyclopedia of American Religions identifies twelve hundred different religions in the United States. That reflects our pluralism, doesn't it? Did you know that there is a Church of John F. Kennedy where people meet to worship Kennedy and claim miraculous healings in his name? Wouldn't he be surprised, since he couldn't heal his own body. The Church of Universal Wisdom believes in flying saucers. There is actually a church called the Church of What's Happening Now. There is a Cathedral of Tomorrow. There is a twenty-five-hundred-year-old religion that has been in America for only a few years. It is from the Far East and is called Jainism. This cult came into this country in 1971. The reason they were so long in coming is their rule that no church member is allowed to cross water except on foot. I haven't yet found out who walked across the Pacific. Some churches are built around the use of drugs. There is a church called Adam's Apple Church.

I was surprised to learn that there are nine denominations of Episcopalians in America. There are seventy-two different denominations of Baptists in the United States, including the Two Seed in the Spirit Predestinarian Baptists and Seventh Day Baptists.

Paul would say today what he said on Mars Hill, "I perceive that you are very religious." But much of that religion is not based on the Bible. Much of it is folk religion. People want a religion they can understand, one that is as systematic as the chemistry charts. The only problem with that is that the Bible and life are not systematic, but ambiguous. Why is it that good people suffer? Shouldn't good people be blessed? Why is it that evil men prosper? How did Hitler come to have such evil power if there is a good God in heaven? There is mystery here, things we cannot explain on this side of the veil.

Folk religion also wants a faith without great cost. It wants to avoid the commitment of the faith. It wants Christianity without a cross, without tears, without sacrifice. It wants what is called "cheap grace." The whole world wants that, and you can get a crowd by preaching it.

It is a religion of easy answers to complex problems. It is a religion that looks for quick results. It is a religion of formulas—simplistic, rationalistic folk religion.

The Bible, itself, recognizes that there are different religions. In I Corinthians, chapter 13, Paul describes these different religions. He describes emotional religion, those who "speak in the tongues of men and of angels" (13:1), who want their religion to make them feel good. Their religion is little more than emotional froth. There are others whose faith is purely intellectual. They understand all mysteries and have the gift of prophecy; they're in the know, like the Gnostics: "If you join us, we will initiate you and let you in on the secret."

Paul describes those who were activists, who had "faith, so as to remove mountains" (13:2). He also describes humanitarian religion, those who "give away all [they] have." And he described aesthetic religion, those who "deliver [their bodies] to be burned" (13:3). Paul is not putting down these different types of religion. The point he makes is that none of these are valid if they are lacking in *love*. Love is the supreme mark of the gospel—radical love which prays for its enemies. This love is contrary to the secular world and its self-seeking attitude.

Edward Gibbon, a rationalist, wrote *The Rise and Fall of the Roman Empire*. He had little use for religion. In fact, Gibbon thought that Christianity contributed to the fall of the Roman Empire because, he argued, it weakened the aggressive policy of power politics.

Gibbon wrote a damning thing about religion. He wrote that the people of ancient Rome considered all religions as equally true. The philosophers considered all religions as equally false, and the politicians considered all religions equally useful. That describes our day as well. Not all religions are equally true. Jesus said, "You will know them by their fruits" (Matthew 7:16). Not all religions are of equal value, but the man on the street believes that one religion is as good as another.

The philosophers, said Gibbon, believe that all religions are equally false. That's not right, either. The intelligentsia, the thinking man, tends to be indifferent to religion. Secular universities often have this spirit. They view religion as a superstition. They believe that answers to our deepest need will be found in science, technology, and politics.

A psychiatrist at Duke University was profoundly converted. He had real problems reconciling what he had taught about the scientific method as a psychiatrist with what he had discovered in his experience of the life-changing power of Christ. He finally succeeded in reconciling them, but it was not easy or automatic.

The last thing Gibbon said about religion in Rome is that the politicians considered all religions equally useful. Karl Marx labeled religion as "the opiate of the people." It keeps them in their places and puts them to sleep. If you don't believe the politicians consider all religions useful, listen carefully in any election year.

I vote, and I will help people to register and vote. However, the church must be above partisan politics. It dare not endorse a partisan candidate.

Remember the Falkland Islands War? Remember seeing the military ruler of Argentina kneeling in prayer? When the Argentines had an election and turned those military rulers out, they discovered that the militaristic rulers had killed forty thousand of their fellow citizens and had buried them secretly in mass graves. The politicians consider all religions equally useful.

When in this malaise do we find an authentic faith? We find it in Micah 6:8. The prophet tells us what God requires: Justice—do what is right; Mercy—kindness toward others; Faith—walk humbly with your God. It is hard to improve on that.

The Christ of the New Testament is not the Christ of our culture, the pale Galilean, the gentle Jesus, meek and mild. He is not the revolutionary of liberation theology in South America. He is not the parochial, pygmy Christ we Christians tend to preach. The Christ of the Gospels taught radical love. The Christ of the Gospels does not fit into our cultural molds, but breaks them. He shapes our culture and reshapes us, if we let him. He gives spiritual power: "To all who received him, who believed in his name, he gave power to become children of God" (John 1:12).

Personal conversion and the transformation of society happened in the first century with the apostle Paul. It happened in the fourth century with Augustine of Hippo, and it happens still for those who publicly profess their faith in the Lord Jesus Christ. People's lives are transformed by the power of the gospel and the living Christ.

I contend that no man ought to have religion, because to have religion means you possess something. You may do with it as you will. Instead of having religion, our faith should have us. We should become the slaves of Christ and his will.

Be honest with yourself for a moment. Do you have a convenient, cultural religion, or does Christ have you? Is Christ in you the hope of glory? Only you and God can answer these probing questions. *Amen.*

Alton H. McEachern
First Baptist Church
Greensboro, North Carolina

Sunday
April Twenty-fourth

Call to Worship: The sacrifice acceptable to God is a broken spirit; a broken and contrite heart, O God, thou wilt not despise. *Psalm 51:17*

Processional Hymn: "How Firm a Foundation"

Invocation: Lord, as we climb the mountains of life, we are concerned for our safety. You can make us secure. You can guide our feet so that we are safe and secure in your loving care. *Amen.*

Sermon Scripture: Matthew 17:1-8

Sermon Presentation: "Surefooted on the Heights"

Hymn of the Day: "He Leadeth Me: O Blessed Thought"

Offertory Scripture: Walk in love, as Christ also hath loved us and hath given himself for us an offering and a sacrifice to God for a sweet-smelling savor. *Ephesians 5:2 KJV*

Offertory Prayer: Lord, we dare to follow you. Lead us, and we will follow. Teach us to give of ourselves as you would have us do. *Amen.*

Prayer of the Day

Lord, it has been said that an encounter with our God is truly "a mountaintop experience." Moses received the Ten Commandments, Jesus often went to pray on the tops of the highest mountains; it is the place where the human spirit aspires; it is the mountaintop.

You have encouraged us to lift up our eyes. You want us to rise above the humdrum routine and realize the high calling you have given us as your children. But so often we find that the trail is steep; sometimes it is very narrow; sometimes the route is faintly marked. Traveling to the mountaintop is not a task for the lazy, the weak of will, the easily distracted, the spiritually poor. But you are our guide, our strength, and our companion for the journey.

You comfort us when we are fearful. You strengthen us when we are weak. You show us the way when we are lost. You hold our hands throughout the entire journey. Take us higher Lord; take us higher. *Amen.*

Benediction: No temptation has overtaken you that is not common to man. God is faithful, and he will not let you be tempted beyond your strength, but with the temptation will also provide the way of escape, that you may be able to endure it.

I Corinthians 10:13

Recessional Hymn: "What a Friend We Have in Jesus"

Lectionary Lessons: The Fourth Sunday of Easter

Lesson 1—Acts 4:8-12; Psalm 23
Lesson 2—I John 3:18-24
Gospel—John 10:11-18

History of the Hymn of the Day: "He Leadeth Me: O Blessed Thought"

In March 1862, during the Civil War, twenty-eight-year-old Reverend Joseph H. Gilmore, son of a New Hampshire governor, was supplying in a historic old Philadelphia church, the First Baptist Church at Broad and Arch Streets. Because of the dark depression of the war between the states, Gilmore selected as a theme the Twenty-third Psalm, emphasizing God's leadership during dark days. Over and over again he repeated the phrase, "He Leadeth Me." Later at the home of one of the deacons, Gilmore was so filled with the thought of his theme that he was unable to contain himself. Seizing a piece of paper, he jotted down these lines: "He leadeth me! O blessed thought; O words with heavenly comfort fraught." When he finished there were four stanzas and a chorus. Gilmore promptly forgot all about what he had written; but his wife, recognizing something good, sent a copy to a Boston periodical. It was here that William Bradbury, famous composer and publisher of church music, discovered it and set it to music.

Announcement for Next Week's Sermon: Have you ever been afraid? Not a little afraid, but scared to death. How do you handle fear? Get the answers next Sunday.

Story of the Week: The office manager of a bank had been complaining to his wife about being overly tired at night and with having terrible pains in his back. Then, one day when he came home from work he said, "I've found out what's been causing my back trouble. As I told you, an interior decorator has just redesigned the office and furnished it with some of that ultramodern Scandinavian furniture. And I discovered today that for the past two weeks I have been sitting in my wastebasket."

SUREFOOTED ON THE HEIGHTS

God, the Lord, is my strength; he makes my feet like hinds' feet, he makes me tread upon my high places. (Habakkuk 3:19)

Mountains are prominent in both the landscape and the imagery of the Bible. To climb a mountain is to go through changes of climate that would take place in hundreds of miles of northward travel. From the streaming, shady forests at the mountain's base, one moves up onto a shoulder of the mountain. Rocks show through the soil, and in an hour or so, roaring cascades are heard below on either side. As one continues to climb, the trees become smaller and gnarled, until they are like shrubs growing horizontally from protected pockets of soil. The climber emerges from the crevice that provided foot and handholds. The sky opens, and alpine meadows alive with special flowers and rare birds spread out to invite relaxation. A spring offers clear refreshment at the summit's skirt. Ice and snow continue in the summer shadows.

Rested, one pushes on and up. Clouds float by, churning in the wind. At the summit, if clouds and atmosphere permit, one sees the world spread out a hundred miles on every side, and looking down, the climber sees that there are other approaches to the summit, and people slowly coming from many directions to a common destination. Years and years later, the memory stays with the climber, sharp and unfading, of a total horizon, of clouds looked out at and down upon, or, perhaps, of lightning striking around the next peak and thunder echoing among the crags.

No wonder that in the Bible the mountain symbolizes the encounter of the human with the divine. God revealed his commandments to Moses on the mountain. Elijah was commissioned on a mountain. As Luke tells it, Jesus prayed all night upon a mountain and then selected his disciples. And it was on a mountan that Peter, James, and John saw Jesus transfigured before them and conversing with Moses and Elijah. Thus they realized that their rabbi was a mighty successor to the great wilderness and mountain holy men of old. The mountain was where one, in his solitude, met God. The mountain was where the God-beset person selected his closest followers, and the mountain was the test of their devotion. The mountain was the place and symbol of decisive choices. The mountain was, and is, a symbol of human aspiration.

Dag Hammarskjold in *Markings* responded to mountains in this way:

> I am being driven forward
> Into an unknown land.
> The pass grows steeper,
> The air colder and sharper.
> A wind from my unknown goal
> Stirs the strings
> Of expectation.
> Still the question;
> Shall I ever get there?
> There where life resounds,
> A clear pure note
> In the silence.
>
> "Thus It Was"

Certainly, Hammarskjold was in tune with the prophet Habakkuk's saying: "God, the Lord, is my strength; he makes my feet like hinds' feet, he makes me tread upon my high places" (3:19).

He makes my feet like hinds' feet. Hind is an old English term for doe, or female deer. The fallow deer was common in Palestine, running through the woods and across the hilltops. So deftly could they run across the rock-strewn mountains there that the Bible more than once refers to their surefootedness. The tiny hoofs of animals who live in high places are wonderfully adapted for climbing on the rocks. These deer have sharp edges on the front of the hoof that dig in like cleats and soft, non-skid pads on the dew claws back of the hooves that hold the animal firm when a sudden stop must be made while running down a steep hill.

God . . .makes me tread upon my high places. Is a striking image of high spiritual experience understood as an achievement by grace; it is given, not earned or won. The prophet says to us that there are high places of spiritual experience, and that God equips us to venture there and to continue there longer than we thought possible. Such a high place is the out-of-doors, with all its creatures, all its beauty, and all its many moods. A golden sunset or a rosy-fingered dawn; wind-sculptured snow or the soft green of early spring; the vesper hymn of a thrush or a burst of daisies in a meadow—these can raise our spirits high. But, on our own, we are too clumsy to walk the heights for long. We begin to watch our feet and think about our walking. We stumble and come down to where dawn means breakfast time and getting into traffic, to where snow is something to be shoveled, and the green of springtime something to be mowed and clipped, and where birds and animals are to be dealt with according to whether they will feed us, clothe us, damage our crops, or not affect us practically.

The arts—painting, sculpture, music, drama, writing—are the heights upon which the surefooted of the Lord can walk far without stumbling, for here is ordered beauty, called out of nature and given shape and position by the human mind and hand. God gives us ears to hear and eyes to see and hearts with which to rejoice on the heights. But to walk well on these heights we must walk frequently. Often, people fear they may be laughed at for the awkwardness of first steps in performance or appreciation. So, they stay down off the heights and poke fun at those who venture up, away from the practical and the obvious.

Meditation—sustained attention to what is taking place in the recesses of one's own mind, creative brooding on a single theme, wrestling with an idea until it confers a blessing—is a high place to climb, from which we can see great vistas of truth. But the trail is steep and narrow and sometimes faintly marked. Lazy minds give up, get distracted, and head downward to pick over the trivia that others have tossed out as they sped along the valley highway.

Conversation can reach high peaks, too. If one who meditates can find others of like mind who will accompany the seeking and share the finding. But all must be surefooted, holding to the heights a while, and not too soon let the talk slip down to the commonplace chatter about house and automobile maintenance, and of who wore what, and who has how much of what, and why.

Many people tell us that after searching for a long time to find God in the things that surrounded them, they discovered him at last within themselves. Meditate deeply upon these words, for they are of great profit for anyone who has difficulty in recollecting oneself to understand this truth; to know that it is not necessary to raise oneself to Heaven in order to converse with the Divine Father and find happiness with him, nor to elevate the voice so as to be heard. God is so near that he hears the lightest whisper from our lips and the most secret thought. We have no need of wings to go in search of him. Let us enter into the solitude and look within ourselves; it is there that he is.

Let us talk with him in great humility, but also with love, like children talking with their Father, confidently telling him our troubles and begging him to help us and recognizing, above all, that we are not worthy to bear the name of his children.

These words remind us that we reach the high places by God's grace, not by our striving. It is God who makes our feet like hinds' feet and enables us to walk on the heights, which may be inward and invisible to many eyes.

Worship can be a high place of Christian experience; a time when we approach God in prayer and hymn; a time when God can speak through scripture, song, and sermon; and a time when we can respond with uplifted hearts, giving our very selves as an offering. But this means accepting the gift of worship and not allowing it to slip because our thoughts are not steadfast and our affections are not kindled, because our minds wander and our hearts are cold, and we are not prepared to let anything happen to us.

> The Lord God is my strength;
> he makes my feet like hinds' feet,
> He makes me tread upon my high places.

We must be assured that there are high places that by the grace of God, are accessible to us. There are moments that stand out from the hours and hours that stand out from the days and days that stand out from the years. And the intense and lovely moments, hours, and days can have the strength to make the longer span of time be sweet and meaningful. There are high places, and the memory of them sustains us through our wandering in the lowlands.

Be assured that God, the Lord, is our strength. God is the giver. Whatever strength we have of body, mind, or spirit is from God. From God comes eyes that can see loveliness in a sunset, ears that can hear beauty in the song of a thrush, and hands that can shape objects of beauty for ourselves and others to enjoy. It is God who gives us minds that can seek truth and lips and ears with which we share our thoughts with one another. From God comes our ability to reach upward, or inward, to meet God's outstretched hand. We do have high places in our lives. Let us allow God to equip us, to let us be strong in the strength of the Lord and walk on those high places to which he leads us. *Amen.*

Loring D. Chase
Westmoreland Congregational Church
Washington, D.C.

Sunday
May First

Call to Worship: And they were filled with awe, and said to one another, "Who then is this, that even wind and sea obey him?" *Mark 4:41*

Processional Hymn: "Jesus Shall Reign"

Invocation: Lord, teach us to be calm in the midst of turmoil. Let love conquer our fear. Let your grace be sufficient for all our needs. Grant us your peace. *Amen.*

Sermon Scripture: Mark 4:35-41

Sermon Presentation: "Fear in the Midst of Calm"

Hymn of the Day: "Jesus Calls Us O'er the Tumult"

Offertory Scripture: Honor the Lord with your substance and with the first fruits of all your produce. *Proverbs 3:9*

Offertory Prayer: Prayer is our great defense against fear. Keep us in close communion with you. Accept these gifts as an act of love, not fear. *Amen.*

Prayer of the Day

Lord, we're scared! Our boat is so small. The sea is so big. The storms seem so great. Lying in the port of our own minds, in settings that are comfortable, we are brave and secure. When we set sail, we find that all too often the calm of the harbor is replaced by the storms of the open sea.

Help us to realize that you, who created the wind and the waves, are the same Lord who cared so much for us that you were willing to lay down your life for us and to die on the cross so that we could receive the forgiveness of our sins and the promise of eternal life.

In the midst of the waves of doubt, bring us the stillness of your presence. In the midst of the storms of life, help us to know the calm of your presence that gives us hope, strength, and courage. Be our strong rudder, guiding us toward the place that you have prepared for us in your eternal kingdom. Be our anchor, holding us fast to the course that you have chosen for our lives. *Amen.*

Benediction: But in your hearts reverence Christ as Lord. Always be prepared to make a defence to any one who calls you to account for the hope that is in you, yet do it with gentleness and reverence. *I Peter 3:15*

Recessional Hymn: "Jesus, Savior, Pilot Me"

Lectionary Lessons: The Fifth Sunday of Easter
Lesson 1—Acts 8:26-40; Psalm 22:25-31
Lesson 2—I John 4:7-12
Gospel—John 15:1-8

History of the Hymn of the Day: "Jesus Calls Us O'er the Tumult"
This beautiful gospel hymn was written in 1852 by Mrs. C. Frances Alexander. Based on Matthew 4:18-19, which contains the verse, "Follow me and I will make you fishers of men," this hymn is written in the simple, unadorned, emotional but refined style so typical of Mrs. Alexander. Used by some denominations as a hymn for St. Andrew's day, "Jesus Calls Us O'er the Tumult" is a favorite in the hymnal of every church.

Announcement for Next Week's Sermon: Don't forget to get a Mother's Day card. Next Sunday, bring Mother to church. We will celebrate Mothers!

Story of the Week: The Congressman had spoken to the political science students at a large university and was in the midst of a question-and-answer period.

One student raised his hand and asked, "Sir, how do I get started in politics?"

"You're already started," the Congressman said, "every day you are in the university, you are spending somebody else's money."

FEAR IN THE MIDST OF CALM

When storms descend upon us, surrounding us with all their fury, they are not always seen and felt in terms of the elements. They come in many varieties and degrees of intensity, from minor irritations to major calamities. Being caught in a rainstorm with no umbrella is a minor irritation, depending on whether you have on new clothes, or if you are carrying a load of books to the car. Being caught in an ice storm can be more fearful and difficult to cope with. Being caught in the midst of life's emotional storms can be just as irritating, fearful, or just plain terrifying, depending on the severity of the storm.

Throughout the history of Israel, story after story of God's deliverance from one kind of a storm after another is told. One of the most familiar to us is the story of Jonah, who ran from God and ended up being cast off a ship, calling to his God for help in the midst of his storm. Jonah experienced fear both within and without.

Mark tells us the story of another storm in another time in history. Jesus and his disciples set sail to the other side of the Genessaret Sea from where he had been teaching in parables all day. The crowds had been very large, so large that Jesus had taught from the fishing boat while the people sat on the shore. As Jesus taught the people in parables, he explained carefully to the disciples what he meant. They left the place just as they had come. They did not take time to make reservations or buy provisions. They just left.

Jesus made his way to the stern of the ship where there was a small clearing with a carpet and a pillow, kept especially for guests. He was soon in a deep, restful, peace-filled sleep. Like Jonah, he was so sure of his safety that he could sleep.

As the storm arose, the experienced boatmen fought and heaved and shouted orders until they were hoarse. Those less experienced, some of the disciples were not fishermen, followed orders and with much fear and trembling tried to keep the boat from filling with water.

Still Jesus slept, until, finally, the disciples became a little annoyed that he could sleep when it seemed that they were going down for the third time!

"Teacher, wake up! We are going to perish! Don't you care? How can you sleep when we are perishing? How can you be so relaxed and calm when things are in such a turmoil?" We don't like to see others remaining calm when we are upset. If we are really fighting for a worthy cause, we cannot understand why everyone else doesn't think it is so worthy a cause.

This was a major calamity as far as the disciples were concerned. To Jesus it was a minor incident. "Peace! Be still!" and the winds stopped and the waves withdrew. No big deal! No major problem! Why should they wake him for this?

The disciples really had not expected Jesus to do what he did. They just wanted him to be with him in their hour of death—and, presumably, his death as well. They wanted him to maybe pray with them, maybe help them through the storm. They really were not ready for the results that Jesus produced! They had asked, "Lord, don't you care?" But they really did not expect an answer, at least not one so dramatic!

As the reality of what had happened began to sink in and dawn upon them, real fear set in, starting at the tips of their toes, going right on up their trembling knees and shaking hands to the cold sweat breaking out on their brows. "Why are you afraid? Have you no faith even now? Even after I have taught you all day the meaning of all those parables, even after all the miracles you have witnessed, even after all we have been through together? You see these things, and yet you have no faith? Blessed are those who have not seen and yet believe!" The disciples were filled with awe. "Who is this that even the wind and the waves obey him?"

Echoes of their early teaching raced through them, causing them to tremble in his presence. "By the word of the Lord the heavens were made. . . . He gathered the waters of the sea as in a bottle. . . . Let all the earth fear the Lord. . . . For he spoke, and it came to be; he commanded, and it stood forth" (Psalm 33:6-9). "Be still, and know that I am God" (Psalm 46:10). These verses and many more must have raced through their minds as they stood there before him, not knowing how to answer him.

They stood in awe realizing that Jesus had given them much more than they had expected. Had he also expected more than they had given? The storm that the disciples weathered with Jesus was a violent, sudden, devastating storm that throws fear into the hearts of sailors of all generations. We often joke about the weather's being unpredictable and our not being able to do anything about it, but I wonder if sometimes the inner storms we experience are not more difficult and frightening to deal with. We can see the lightning, hear the thunder, and feel the rain and wind beat upon us. We can experience all of those aspects of the elements together. When one sees lightning, others see lightning. When one hears the thunder, others hear the thunder. When one feels the sting of the rain, others also feel the sting of rain.

Our inner storms are different. We often experience them alone, at least we feel alone. No one else feels the sting within us. No one else hears the roar of thunder or sees the flash of lightning. It is then that we most want to reach out for someone who can share our burden and feel our pain; yet this is the time that is the hardest for us to reach out!

If anyone went through the stormy turmoil of life, it was Job. Job lost everything—family, friends, health, wealth. His closest friends, and even his wife, did not really experience his storm. His "helpful" friends heaped guilt on top of guilt in an effort to find out what he had done wrong that God would punish him so. His wife, believing the greatest sin that he could commit would be to curse God, pleaded with Job to do so and die, to be out of his misery and hers. She must have suffered with him even though she did not understand what was happening.

Job, believing that he had done nothing to deserve this treatment, from the midst of his storm cried out, "Where are you, God? Don't you care that I'm perishing?" When the calm came and Job confronted God, he began to question with fear and trembling, "Who is this that controls the universe?" He could say, "I have uttered what I did not understand, things too wonderful for me."

When he called out to God in his anguish, he really did not expect the answer he got. He knew he had done nothing to deserve his fate, but he did not realize God's complete care for him. With awe he could come to the point of saying, "I don't understand, but I believe!" He did not expect God's response. Did God expect a response from Job?

Sixteen-year-old Mary waited with fear and anguish as her beloved father was being taken to the hospital. Praying as only a babe in Christ can, she cried out to God, "Take care of him. Let everything be all right." She waited, expecting God to give her what she had asked for. Soon she was awakened from her light sleep by the closing of a car door. Her mother was home, so Dad must be all right. The minister brought her mother into the house. Mary would never be able to talk or sing with her father again. "Where are you God? Don't you care?" Why? Why? That storm was not so easily or quickly stilled. Echoes of thunder and lightning still flash on occasion. Storms continue to break out upon life, and we must cry out in pain and anguish, "Where are you God? Don't you care?"

When the calm comes and we face Christ, it is then that we will realize our real fear. It is not that we cannot face life without our loved ones. It is not that we cannot face friends and family when our children do not live up to our standards. It is not that we are afraid of failing. No, it is not the fear of the storm that causes us to tremble. It is the words of Jesus, "Are you still afraid? Where is your faith?"

When we call upon the Lord for his help, he gives us far more than we ask. He calms the wind and the sea, when only his presence would be necessary. Surprised? We should not be! Are you fearful when you realize that he has given you much more than you ever expected and the question burns within, "Does he expect more of me than I have given?"

Mark does not really give us the answer that the disciples made to this burning question; yet the story does not end there. God did give the children of Israel more than they ever deserved, and yes, he did expect more from them than they ever gave. But his love and mercy continued beyond all they could ever give.

Yes, even in Job's questioning and anger toward his Creator, there was love and acceptance and willingness to do more for Job.

Yes, the disciples who had been with Jesus throughout his ministry, who had seen his miracles, and who had listened intently to his teaching still did not understand and show the faith that they should have had—but that was only one point in their lives. We know there were many more times of doubt and fear, but we know what Jesus expected and what they became.

Yes, we've had doubts and fears. We have experienced the fear of knowing we are expected to do more, and somehow we have the feeling that we will again experience those doubts and fears. We will never really be able to fulfill all that is expected of us, but that's all right. Even though we may tremble in his presence, it is not all fear. It is awe—it is excitement—it is love. It is knowing that Jesus is at the heart of the storm, and if he is there all is well.

It is knowing that even though we fear and doubt and fail to live up to our capabilities, God is still there in all his love and mercy and grace giving us the strength to ride out the storm with him, bringing us to the place of calm, to a place where we can say:

> The storms of life may surround me,
> The waves my soul wash o'er;
> I may wake the sleeping Master,
> And look for a calmer shore.

He stills the storms within me,
His word calms the sea.
"Why are you afraid, now?"
He is looking straight at me.

It's not the storms I fear,
Or even that death must be.
I realize who this Christ is
And what he asks of me!

But even in his askings
Is mercy deeper than the sea;
He remembers who I was,
And he knows who I will be.
Mary Lu Warstler

Mary Lu Warstler
Kenmore United Methodist Church
Akron, Ohio

Sunday
May Eighth

Call to Worship: Let the words of my mouth and the meditation of my heart be acceptable in thy sight, O Lord, my rock and my redeemer. *Psalm 19:14*

Processional Hymn: "Savior, Again to Thy Dear Name"

Invocation: On this day, Lord, when we come to honor all mothers, help us to see the sacrifices that they have made for us. This is truly a part of Christian service, to raise up the children that they may know and love you. *Amen.*

Sermon Scripture: John 14:23-29

Sermon Presentation: "The Gift of Roots and Wings: The Greatest Parental Challenge"

Hymn of the Day: "Fairest Lord Jesus"

Offertory Scripture: Honor the Lord with your substance and with the first fruits of all your produce; then your barns will be filled with plenty, and your vats will be bursting with wine. *Proverbs 3:9-10*

Offertory Prayer: Let the example of the unselfish giving of our mothers be an inspiration to our own giving to you. Let us give the best as a symbol of the love we have learned and know. *Amen.*

Prayer of the Day

Master, Lord Jesus, on this day we focus our attention on a most valuable gift—the family. We know that you shared the experience of being a member of a human family with us. You know from your own earthly life how important a good family is to each of us. But you also know how much work and responsibility a good family life can be.

Help us to build trust in all of our relationships, especially with those with whom we have the closest bond. Help us to build channels of open, honest, and meaningful communication between us and our family members. Let us take time to listen carefully, to choose our words wisely, to seek healing instead of anger, and to express loving concern at all times.

May our families be the places in which we learn to be faithful followers of yours; the places in which we learn to deal honestly and openly with all people; the setting in which we work toward becoming co-operative and productive members of society. *Amen.*

Benediction: You did not choose me, but I chose you and appointed you that you should go and bear fruit and that your fruit should abide. *John 15:16a*

Recessional Hymn: "How Great Thou Art"

Lectionary Lessons: The Sixth Sunday of Easter
Lesson 1—Acts 10:44-48; Psalm 98
Lesson 2—I John 5:1-6
Gospel—John 15:9-17

History of the Hymn of the Day: "Fairest Lord Jesus"
This famous hymn had its origin in Germany in the seventeenth century, and was discovered in America in 1850 by Richard Storrs Willis, a musician and newspaperman, who wrote books on church music and other musical subjects. The tune is an ancient Silesian folk song derived from legend and story, which is a ballad picturing common life with its interests and enthusiasm. It was said to have been sung by the German Knight Crusaders on their way to Jerusalem in the twelfth century and is still referred to as the Crusaders' hymn, although no proof of this has been established. This hymn telling of the beauty of nature is often called "The marching song of the out-of-doors" and is a favorite of young people. It is also interesting to note that pianist Franz Liszt used this tune in his oratorio "St. Elizabeth."

Announcement for Next Week's Sermon: Who was the first astronaut? You may be surprised when you find out. Join the space program right here next Sunday.

Story of the Week: The church board had voted to give the minister a lifetime contract. The announcement was made at a big family-night dinner in the church social hall. Everyone there cheered and clapped and assured the minister that they wanted him to stay as long as he lived.

Later, a friend said to the minister, "You didn't seem very excited about being given a lifetime contract. You ought to be the happiest man in town. Why, you are fixed for life."

"The reason I'm not too excited about it," the minister said, "is because I know another minister who was given a lifetime contract. Then several years later, after all of the old board members had retired and a new board was running things, they called him in, declared him dead, and fired him."

THE GIFT OF ROOTS AND WINGS: THE GREATEST PARENTAL CHALLENGE

This is the second Sunday of May, the date that is traditionally known as Mother's Day. Instead of just preaching a sermon to mothers or about mothers, let us speak to and about the Christian family. Good parenting can be defined as preparing a child to live outside the bounds of the home in a productive way, and our faith can teach us how to be good parents.

There are some definite parallels between what Jesus did for his disciples and what parents do for their children. Jesus had been with his disciples for about three years. He knew he could not always be there with them. The day for them to begin a ministry of their own was coming quickly. He tried to prepare them for his death and for the fact that he could no longer be physically present with them. He had accomplished his goals with them, and now he must prepare them for his leaving. As parents, we know that we cannot always remain with our children. We know that the day will come when they will have to leave our homes and go out into the world or off to college. The day must come when they will move away and find a job and perhaps get married to another person. It is our task to prepare them for that time in their lives.

An effective, functioning family is one in which the members are prepared to live outside the bounds of the family. Parents teach children to walk, to feed themselves, and to talk so that they may function well outside the home environment. One of the ways we do that is by teaching them that they are worth a great deal to us. How do we do that? Do we buy them expensive toys? Do we give them their every want? Do we say, "Yes, it costs a lot of money, but you are worth it, honey."

The one gift that enhances the self-esteem of the child is the parents' time. Spending time with children is like saying to them, "You are important to me." In Jesus' dealings with his disciples, we see from the scripture accounts that he was with them all the time. He was there to tell them how important a link they were in the plan of God. He did not treat them as if they were common fishermen with little or no religious training. He treated them as if they were valuable people. He used those three years to build their confidence in God's plan for them as well as their confidence in themselves.

We need to use the years we have with our children under our roofs to build their confidence in themselves, so that they will be able to make the right decisions when we are not with them. Our children face decisions every day in all aspects of their lives. They must choose whether they are going to use drugs, whether to be responsible enough to do their homework, or whether they will tell a lie because it will get them out of trouble quicker or tell the truth and take the consequences. Children can look at the disciples and see that they tried to do their best to be faithful to the trust Jesus had in them. Young people should be faithful to the process of building their parents' trust in them.

People who are not trusted have usually proven themselves as untrustworthy. Once we have lost the trust of our parents, it is very difficult to regain it. Trust is most important in family relationships. We have to be able to trust one another with the love we give, and we must be constantly on our guard that nothing destroys that trust. Family members who cannot trust one another cannot be families; they cannot effectively prepare to live in the outside world. Husbands and wives who do not trust each other are not seriously considering their marriage promises. We build self-esteem in one another when we can trust and be trusted. Jesus knew he could trust his disciples to continue his work even after he was gone. The disciples knew they could trust Jesus to keep his promises. They believed in one another. Family members who believe in one another will have self-esteem. Seeing the others as worthwhile and trustworthy helps us to put down roots; it helps us to view our homes as places to be restored and strengthened, an oasis for both the body and the spirit.

Jesus and his disciples communicated well with one another, and that communication grew out of their trust for one another. Jesus could talk to the disciples. He could tell them of his hopes and dreams; he could tell them secrets and share his feelings with them. They could go to Jesus and ask questions without being called stupid or treated as though they were in the way.

The homes in which people are allowed to ask questions about any subject, from birth to death, and are paid attention to and answered are those people who will do the best in the outside world. They are taught by example the meaning of patience; they are taught the rewards of finding answers to their questions; and they feel cared for, worthwhile.

Children who are told, "Ask me some other time," "Go ask your mother," or given some excuse are those who experience great frustration in their growing process. How can any of us learn if we do not ask questions? Good communication techniques must be practiced on a daily basis. If we can communicate well on minor subjects, when the major topics of discussion arise we will have a better chance of communicating effectively on that level. Perhaps the most important tool we have in communicating effectively is our ability to listen. The disciples of Jesus knew how important it was to listen to him. They knew he would not always be there to guide them. Jesus knew how important it was to listen to the disciples and to help them prepare to continue the ministry.

We are made with two ears and one mouth, which means we are to listen twice as much as we talk. Listening to one another is very important if we are to help prepare one another for living in the outside world. Good communication helps us to put down roots. It teaches us about other people as we talk and listen. Trust and communication were two important factors in the relationship between Jesus and his disciples. They are just as important among family members.

Another parallel between the effective family and the relationship of our Lord and his disciples is the need for rules. The disciples knew that there was an acceptable code of behavior for them. There were rules that Jesus expected them all to live by. These were rules that were fitting for their calling. These were rules based on honesty and fair play. They were rules based on an ethical standard like no other of its day. They were rules based on love for the people and for the good of the people involved. Now, the Pharisees had rules, but they taught that people existed for the good of the rules. The rules, and not the people, were the central priority. With Jesus, the rules were to make the lives and the witness of the disciples more effective; the rules were to enhance their work.

In every effective family, there must be rules that are tailor-made to fit the needs of the individuals, yet within the over-all belief system of the family unit. The question or the test the disciples should apply to situations in which they had doubts as to what they should do or how they should respond is: "How does what I am doing represent the love of God?" They were to be the representatives of God's love in all they did. As families, we are called to no less a code of behavior. In our dealings with one another, we should ask ourselves that same question: "How does what I am doing represent the love I have for my parents, my children, and God?" Does staying out all night and getting drunk represent the love I have for my parents? Does it represent the love I have for myself? Does it represent the love of God? Does cheating on my spouse represent the love of God? Does stealing money from a purse or an apple from the grocery store represent the love of God? If what we do does not represent the love we have for one another as people and the love of God to his world, then the rule should be that we don't do those things.

Rules in a family, rules that are flexible, rules that are made with people in mind, to serve people and enhance their relationships with one another, help family members to have roots. They help us understand what we are all about, what we value, what is right and wrong.

A final parallel between Jesus and his disciples and our relationships within families is our link to the world outside the bounds of those relationships. Families who have consciously made efforts to enhance one another's self-esteem or self-worth, families who have tried to communicate effectively—both speaking and listening—families who have lived within the rules governed by the overall concepts of love for one another and love for God, have definite roots. In such a family, even though death may take one or more of its members, even if all the children grow up and move away, even if in-laws come into the family and grandchildren are born, even if the parents grow old and die, the family will always have its roots. Families whose members have their roots firmly planted in what they believe about themselves, who have established good patterns of communication, and in which the rules are flexible, but the ethic consistent, will find that they have given one another the greatest gift family members can give, the gift of wings. This is the gift of being able to go outside the bounds of the family and function effectively in society as independent persons.

When those people leave the home, they are well prepared to be productive citizens of the community. When Jesus could no longer be with his disciples, he was confident that they were prepared to continue his work. Jesus left his disciples with part of himself. He told them he would send the Holy Spirit to remind them of his teachings and guide them in their lives.

As parents, we often try our best in preparing our children to be assets to the world outside our homes, and we spend time worrying about their successes and giving our advice and criticism, claiming that we love them and want the best for them. Jesus trusted the disciples; he had done his work well, and now he was entrusting them to the guidance of the Holy Spirit.

Parents who have brought up their children to know God, to receive Jesus Christ as their Savior, and to respect the rights of other people have done well in preparing their children to live outside the bounds of the home. We can be confident that those children who know Jesus Christ as their Savior have been given the Holy Spirit. The Holy Spirit will guide them and help them remember the principles they have been taught. Parents should continue to be available to their children for consultation, when needed, and for listening, even when the children are grown and have moved away from the bounds of the family home. In so doing, we help strengthen their abilities to continue to function effectively in the world, and we continue to give them wings which free them to be productive. It is in giving them the proper roots, the proper beginning in the home, that we have given them wings to be free to live outside the bounds of our families and be productive citizens contributing to the kingdom of God and the betterment of the world. Parents, you are the major contributors to this task. Thank God for all parents. *Amen.*

Dennis E. Morey
The Presbyterian Church
New London, Iowa

Sunday
May Fifteenth

Call to Worship: "Holy, holy, holy, is the Lord of hosts; the whole earth is full of his glory." *Isaiah 6:3*

Processional Hymn: "All Hail the Power of Jesus' Name"

Invocation: Lord, make us committed to you as the main goal in our lives. As the astronauts found God in space, so let us find him here on earth. Give us your gift of assurance that eternal life is ours today. *Amen.*

Sermon Scripture: Acts 1:1-14

Sermon Presentation: "The First Astronaut"

Hymn of the Day: "For the Beauty of the Earth"

Offertory Scripture: Every man shall give as he is able, according to the blessing of the Lord your God which he has given you. *Deuteronomy 16:17*

Offertory Prayer: Let us give with a dedication to your work as we are able and then some more. Let us go the second mile in giving. *Amen.*

Prayer of the Day

Lord, we live in a world that places a great deal of emphasis on power. We measure the power of this world in terms of horsepower, missiles with nuclear warheads, firepower, the size of our bank accounts, and the number of people we know who are in high places. Yet, you have promised to provide us with a different kind of power—the power of the Holy Spirit. It is a power that calls us to serve rather than be served, to seek out the lost, to care for a neighbor in need, to seek to lift people up instead of putting them down. It is a power that calls us to a life of humility and obedience to you, the power that you share with all of us who are called by your name.

Help us to avoid the seduction of relying on the power of this world, a power that is often measured in its ability to destroy and not create. Instead, make us content to live under your influence and power. Remind us that your power created the world. Your power saved the three young men from the fiery furnace. Your power crushed the mighty pharaoh as you saved your chosen people. It was your power that created the world and the universe. It was through your power alone that your beloved Son rose from the cross and conquered sin and death. It is this same power you promise to share with us now and forever. *Amen.*

Benediction: And it shall come to pass afterward, that I will pour out my spirit on all flesh; your sons and your daughters shall prophesy, your old men shall dream dreams, and your young men shall see visions. *Joel 2:28*

Recessional Hymn: "Are Ye Able"

Lectionary Lessons: The Seventh Sunday of Easter

Lesson 1—Acts 1:15-17, 21-26; Psalm 1
Lesson 2—I John 5:9-13
Gospel—John 17:11*b*-19

History of the Hymn of the Day: "For the Beauty of the Earth"

Folliott Sanford Pierpoint was twenty-nine years old when he sat on the green hillside late in the spring of 1864 outside his native city of Bath, England. The violets and primroses were in full bloom and the world was a beautiful place to see. As he sat down to rest and meditate he could not help feeling the wonder and glory of God around him. His glad fingers had wings of joy as he wrote word after word, inspired by the spreading springtime beauty:

For the beauty of the earth,
For the glory of the skies,
For the love which from our birth
Over and around us lies;
Lord of all, to Thee we raise
This our hymn of grateful praise.

Announcement for Next Week's Sermon: Pentecost calls for a new spirit. If you are afraid of spirits, you have a problem. Come find the spirit next week.

Story of the Week: Early one morning a man called for a taxi to take him to the airport. Half an hour later he called to say it had not arrived, and the dispatcher said it was on the way. After another half-hour he called again. "I need that taxi in a hurry," he said. "I've got to make that flight to the West Coast that is due to leave in 30 minutes."

The young lady at the taxi company said, "I'm sorry for the delay. But your cab should be there any minute now. But don't worry. I'm sure you won't miss your plane because that flight is always late taking off."

"Well, one thing is for sure," the man said. "It will be late taking off this morning because I'm the pilot."

THE FIRST ASTRONAUT

Some Americans in 1961 were quite disturbed when Russia launched the first human being into space. In April of that year, a major in the Soviet Air Force orbited the earth once. Less than a month later, Alan B. Shepard, Jr., became the first American to go into space, but he did not orbit the earth. About nine months later, John Glenn did succeed in flying the first orbital mission for our country.

I want to talk about the One who really can claim to be the world's first astronaut. A record of his feat appears in the first chapter of the Acts of the Apostles. There it states, "He was lifted up, and a cloud took him out of their sight" (Acts 1:10).

Now, right at the beginning let me point out an essential distinction. To compare the space feats of 1961 to the Ascension of Jesus may seem to be improper. In one, we quote fairly reliable recorded history. In the other, we draw from the memories of man's spiritual experience. The accounts of faith cannot be considered in the same way we do the records of history. We read about an event's taking place on the Mount of Olives forty days after the first Easter. That cannot be understood in the same way we recall John Glenn's blast off from Cape Canaveral the morning of February 20, 1962. But we can draw parallels between the two events. Both incidents have something to say about power. Both incidents tell us something about the character of a person. And both events must be interpreted in terms of goals or objectives.

Power, character, goals. Take the first, the idea of power. Today's astronaut or cosmonaut depends upon tremendous speed. You and I, restricted to fifty-five miles per hour or less, simply cannot imagine the force exerted in propelling John Glenn 17,400 miles per hour. He went around the world three times in four hours and fifty-five minutes.

Even youngsters today know about thrust. A little boy's father read his son nursery rhymes. The lad listened attentively until the father came to the story of the cow jumping over the moon. Obviously impressed, the boy spoke up, "That's interesting. Now tell me how the cow developed that much thrust."

Astronauts depend upon power. The ascension of Jesus Christ also involved power, but now we have to think of an energy vastly different from that generated by rocket fuel. We deal now with the invisible force that men for centuries have known, yet cannot really describe. The Hebrews knew they had been saved from the pursuing Egyptians. In the hour of deliverance Moses and the Israelites sang to their God: "Thy right hand, O Lord, glorious in power, thy right hand, O Lord, shatters the enemy" (Exodus 15:6). Or take the three Jews in Babylon, condemned to the fiery furnace. This trio told King Nebuchadnezzar, "Our God whom we serve is able to deliver us from the burning fiery furnace; and he will deliver us out of your hand, O king" (Daniel 3:17).

Throughout their long history of suffering and frustration, the Hebrews knew they could rely on their God. So the psalmist could declare, "Ascribe power to God, whose majesty is over Israel, and his power is in the skies. Terrible is God in his sanctuary, the God of Israel, he gives power and strength to his people" (Psalm 68:34-35).

Jesus, however, came to give a new understanding of power. We see this event in the ascension account. Christ gathered the eleven together for the last time on the Mount of Olives. They asked him there, "Lord, will you at this time restore the kingdom to Israel?" By that question, the disciples revealed that they clung to the old idea of things. To be powerful in the world meant the unchallenged right of control. In those days of the Roman Empire, the Romans had a saying about kings having long arms—royalty ruled with a rod of iron—and most Jews dreamed of the day when Israel once again would be a force to contend with in the world.

In his reply to the disciples, Jesus used the word *power* in a new sense. "You shall receive power when the Holy Spirit has come upon you" (Acts 1:8). By this, Christ did not refer to the authority and political dominion the Jews craved. He referred, instead, to the constructive energy that ennobles and elevates life, that changes character. The Master had only recently given his followers an object lesson in that kind of power. In the Upper Room, Jesus washed the feet of his comrades. In ancient societies, a host or a leader did not demean himself by performing such a menial service for others. Kneeling down and washing feet remained the task of a slave. But Christ came as a servant, and he called his followers to that style of life. The Lord told them, "If I then, your Lord and Teacher, have washed your feet, you also ought to wash one another's feet. For I have given you an example, that you also should do as I have done to you" (John 13:14-15).

Christianity at its best has been a religion of service as well as of salvation. Wherever the gospel has gone, it has met people's needs. Thus churches have organized to help feed the hungry in the city; followers of Christ can never do too much for the underprivileged. We can never forget the Master's vivid description of the Last Judgment. The souls who inherited the kingdom had given food and drink to the hungry and the thirsty. They had welcomed the stranger, clothed the naked, and visited the sick and the prisoner. Now, human beings do not instinctively reach out to others. We are not born caring and unselfish. Those habits and qualities of character arise only as our spirits grow. We serve others only as we overcome our own self-centeredness.

In 1931 the Nobel Peace Prize was awarded to two Americans; one of them was Jane Addams. She had devoted forty-two years of life to the poor of Chicago. Born into a wealthy home, Miss Addams, nevertheless, had a vision of helping the underprivileged. As a young woman, she entered the slums of Chicago, there to begin one of the most remarkable service careers in all history. Miss Addams pioneered the use of unpaid volunteers. "They are all Christians from evangelical churches," Jane Addams said of those workers. "I have a good many altruists try it, but I never knew any slum worker to stand the wear and tear of our work for over three weeks unless inspired by Christian love."

On the mount of his ascension Jesus promised the first Christians that they would receive power. That energy has continued to inspire believers in every era. Today it empowers men and women, young and old. But we must note a second parallel between the conquerors of space and the divine astronaut of nineteen centuries ago. They not only display power, but also character.

In our national space program, not everyone can be an astronaut. America selected the first spacemen twenty-six years ago. More than a hundred men volunteered. NASA interviewed and tested them, then selected thirty-two. Six finally made space flights. They stood out as individuals with a high degree of skill and courage. They also demonstrated the ability to resist stress, mental as well as physical.

Astronauts know they face great danger. They forever must risk their lives. Astronauts must be committed. When they go into the program, they put their lives on the line. They accept the possibility of sacrifice.

No hero in all of human experience has met that qualification more thoroughly than Jesus of Nazareth. Scripture clearly shows that Christ understood the need for sacrifice. When the Master disclosed this to the disciples, they could not believe him. They clung, of course, to a false pride of power and success. And when Jesus stood face to face with the sacrifice of his life, his companions all disappeared. They could not be baptized with his baptism nor drink the cup he drank.

But the Christian life continues to call for commitment. No longer, perhaps, do believers have to die in the jaws of lions in the amphitheater. No longer do they face the fiery stake. No longer are people hanged from gallows on the Boston Common for their faith. Perhaps the age of dungeon, fire and sword has passed, but Jesus Christ still expects faithfulness from his people.

In a godless society such as ours, commitment takes forms unimagined in Bible times. The early Christians belonged to a small closely knit fellowship, exercising daily influence over their lives. The believers had all things in common. Individuals sold their possessions and goods and distributed them to all, as any had need. In all your years have you belonged to a church like that? If you ever have, you have certainly learned the meaning of commitment.

Religion today frequently has become a voluntary pastime for people who have nothing more exciting to do. We share with our church whatever we have left over of our time and money. And when we do go to church, we don't want the scripture lesson to be the one including the words, "If any man would come after me, let him deny himself and take up his cross and follow me" (Matthew 16:24). We likewise don't care to sing:

Take my silver and my gold;
Not a mite would I withhold.
Take my intellect, and use
Every power as thou shalt choose.

Astronauts must be persons of committed character as well as of power. Finally, they must have goals. Back in the sixties, some Americans wondered why both Russia and the United States competed against each other in the space race. We could not wait until we had planted the "Stars and Stripes" on the moon. Whatever the reasons our government gave for its interest in the space program, its main motivation obviously had to be political. If there had to be two superpowers, America wanted to be the superior of the two.

We cannot help but recall the question Jesus asked: "What will it profit a man, if he gains the whole world and forfeits his life?" (Matthew 16:26). Perhaps Christ had in mind Alexander the Great. Everyone knew how the young Greek prince conquered the entire civilized world of his day. After subduing the Persian Empire, Alexander moved eastward, hoping to add India to his realm. He never made it, because in Babylon he came down with malaria and died. He was only thirty-two years of age.

We do not have to go as far back as Alexander the Great. The last two hundred years have seen leaders with Alexander's ambitions. What happened to them? They did not gain the whole world, and they forfeited their lives. We may speculate whether the space program feeds the goal of world domination. But whatever their countries seek, astronauts as persons follow one objective: to go out, perform their mission, and return safely to earth.

What about the goal Jesus pursued? We might say, perhaps flippantly, that he set out to perform his assignment and return safely to heaven. God sent Christ for one reason: to show men the divine love. The human family knew it had been placed here by an obviously intelligent God. It also understood this Creator to be a just, moral deity, and he expected his children to be just and moral. To help them, the Almighty provided the human race with a set of ten laws.

The Ten Commandments set limits on conduct. Everyone assumed that if people obeyed the ten rules, God would be happy with them, and they would be happy and wealthy. It did not take long to realize that obeying the rules did not keep human beings happy or rich. In spite of the law, people encountered all kinds of evil. Even the best soul suffered. In his vision on Patmos, John beheld four horsemen. Those riders represented conquest, war, famine, and death. For many in the world of antiquity, existence consisted of little more than those trials.

Into this apparent hopelessness came a Galilean teacher. He did not cancel out the Law of Moses; Jesus clearly believed in the Ten Commandments. But Christ taught that the secret of happiness on earth could be found only in love, the spirit that forgives and shares. Love grows out of gratitude. When an individual truly realizes and accepts the love of God, then he will be moved to love his neighbor.

This explains why God left his throne and his kingly crown to come to earth for you and me. He brought with him a living word to set his people free. But when he had delivered his message, he returned to heaven. Jesus had no intention of remaining here in the flesh. His purpose could be fulfilled only as he invaded peoples' minds and hearts.

It may be a puzzle to us as to why Christ came to earth only for a few years. That he, a divine person, should live to be only thirty-three may seem very strange. Yet we understand his reason when we distinguish between the spiritual and the natural or material. Thoughtful minds recognize that our experience includes not only physical things, but also unseen, invisible values.

Thus we should not be mystified that scripture tells us about the ascension. We can judge neither the resurrection nor the ascension as physical happenings, as scientific realities, or as episodes of history. We will never be able to explain why the Lord Jesus Christ left his earthly friends in the flesh that he might reign supreme in their hearts. He did not invade outer space. Rather, he entered the inner space that we call the soul or the spirit, there to command our wills and loyalties.

Did you know that the very first liquid drunk by human beings on the moon, and the first food eaten there were the elements of the Holy Communion? Let me conclude with a modern astronaut's story, and you can think about it in any way you like.

The copilot of the first lunar landing mission, Edwin Aldrin, the second man to walk on the moon, carried with him consecrated bread and wine from his home church in Texas.

That congregation planned to gather for the sacrament as close as possible to the same hour on Sunday that Aldrin expected to be on the moon. On July 20, 1969, Apollo XI made its historic landing. Very soon after the landing, Aldrin took Communion, using the elements he had brought from earth.

That incident may mean different things to different persons. To me it suggests the lordship of Christ, a sovereignty bound by no time, no place, no condition. Man can conquer space, but only God can conquer human beings, to make them truly free in love and peace and justice. *Amen.*

Charles W. Kern
First United Methodist Church
Raymond, New Hampshire

Sunday
May Twenty-second

Call to Worship: But the fruit of the Spirit is love, joy, peace, patience, kindness, goodness, faithfulness, gentleness, self-control; against such there is no law. *Galatians 5:22-23*

Processional Hymn: "Christ Is Made the Sure Foundation"

Invocation: Let your spirit pour forth on each of us today. Lord, grant that we might relax and let that spirit consume us so that it controls our every thought, word, and deed. *Amen.*

Sermon Scripture: John 3:5-8

Sermon Presentation: "The Renewing Spirit"

Hymn of the Day: "Faith of Our Fathers"

Offertory Scripture: But the Counselor, the Holy Spirit, whom the Father will send in my name, he will teach you all things, and bring to your remembrance all that I have said to you.
John 14:26

Offertory Prayer: Lord, grant that we might study your word, remember your word, and do your will. These offerings are in accordance to your will and command. *Amen.*

Prayer of the Day

God, we know you as the loving Father who creates, the sacrificing Savior, the renewing Spirit. It was your Spirit that moved across the chaos and created the world. It was that same Spirit that you promised would guide your followers as a counselor, so that they might know your truth. Your Spirit gathered your people, the church, together to be a community of faith and a fellowship of saints. It is your Spirit that continues to be a driving force in our world and in our church, renewing, recreating, reforming, always bringing us closer to being the people you desire us to be.

Make us sensitive to the guidance of the Spirit even when your will is that the foundations of our lives be shaken. Help us to trust you and to know that you are always leading your people to greater faith, greater commitment, and greater understanding. Allow us to be born anew so that we might be worthy to be called children of God. *Amen.*

Benediction: A new heart I will give you, and a new spirit I will put within you; and I will take out of your flesh the heart of stone and give you a heart of flesh. And I will put my spirit within you, and cause you to walk in my statutes and be careful to observe my ordinances. *Ezekiel 36:26-27*

Recessional Hymn: "My Faith Looks Up to Thee"

Lectionary Lessons: Pentecost
Lesson 1—Acts 2:1-21 *or* Ezekiel 37:1-14; Psalm 104:24-34
Lesson 2—Romans 8:22-27 *or* Acts 2:1-21
Gospel—John 15:26-27; 16:4*b*-15

History of the Hymn of the Day: "Faith of Our Fathers"
There is no Christian hymn that lifts the soul or stirs the imagination more than "Faith of Our Fathers," written in approximately 1850, by Frederick W. Faber, an Anglican clergyman of England. Yet the strange fact is that very few people realize the reason for his writing the hymn. Record shows that all his hymns were written after he was received into the Roman Catholic Church in 1846. One of Faber's views was that the true Church of England was continued through the Roman Catholic Church. This is what he meant when he spoke of the "faith of our fathers." However, this was a case of what he had written far exceeding the boundaries of what he had intended; and thus, Protestants sang the hymn with equal meaning and fervor as Catholics. It proves, once again, that the mass singing of hymns is one of the strongest expressions of faith in Christendom.

Announcement for Next Week's Sermon: One thing we all learn at an early age is to say no and to dislike authority. We just don't like to be told what to do. You always need some authority in your life. If you need some help, start next Sunday.

Story of the Week: A man noticed a young lady edging her car back and forth in a tight parking space. Being a helpful fellow, he stopped to help her. He signaled how she should turn the wheel and when to go forward and when to back. After a few minutes, under his expert directing, the car was nestled tightly against the curb.

"There you are," he said. "Snug as a bug in a rug."

"I know," she said, "and I appreciate your help. But, I wasn't trying to park it. I was trying to get out."

May Twenty-second

THE RENEWING SPIRIT

Unless one is born of water and the Spirit, he cannot enter the Kingdom of God. (John 3:5)

Scripture tells us that when Peter preached the first Pentecost sermon almost two millennia ago, three thousand people were converted to the faith. This has always been a pretty tough act to follow; I doubt that anyone has ever surpassed that record in one sermon, even the redoubtable Billy Graham. I know that I've never even come close. Come to think of it, all my preaching over the years has been to the already converted, so the best I could ever hope for was an occasional renewal of the faith. But renewal is also an important function of the Holy Spirit, and that's what I would like us to think about for a few minutes today, spiritual renewal, its occasions and its consequences. We'll begin with a closer look at the first Pentecost, take note of some patterns that develop in both Testaments and in the history of the church, and then come to the meat of the matter, which is: What in the world is the Spirit up to in these days, in our lives?

Let's imagine for a moment that we are followers of Jesus in the year A.D. 33. Fifty days ago he was executed, and ever since then we have been wandering around in a daze, confused, leaderless, dispirited. We pray often, we have replaced Judas with Matthias, but mainly we are just waiting for something to happen, what we don't know. On this day, we are gathered in one place when we hear what sounds like the rush of a mighty wind. We see what appears to be tongues of fire hovering over us, and we are seized by an ecstasy that causes us to babble incoherently. Attracted by this strange behavior, a crowd gathers and accuses us of being drunk and disorderly. Peter seizes the opportunity to preach a sermon. Without getting bogged down in just what we heard, saw, and spoke, we can say that the bestowal of the Holy Spirit that Jesus promised brought about two things. One was the birth of the church; before, we were isolated individuals, now we are a community of faith, the Body of Christ. We have been molded, melded into a fellowship with faithful people of all ages, tongues, and races. It could also be noted that this was an act of renewal by the Spirit, a re-creation of the people of God, a new Israel, with the universal vision of the later prophets. Something radically new had come into being, but something that had connections with the past, like the birth of a baby. So what we have here is creation and/or renewal.

An immediate consequence of this creative act by the Holy Spirit was a certain amount of disorder. In the modern vernacular, we would say that those folks were spaced out, perhaps abusing some controlled substance; in fact, they were accused of drunkenness. Peter denies this, saying that they are high on the Spirit promised by the prophet Joel and Jesus. Can we understand that any act of creation is a jolt, a shock causing tremors in the old order of things? We parents know full well that the arrival of babies causes no end of disorder in our households. We re-order our existence; we adapt, but things are never really the same again. Can it really be said that the creative power of the Holy Spirit also brings disorder in its train? Let's check that out with a look back into the Bible and forward into the history of the church since that first Pentecost.

The second sentence of the Bible says that "the Spirit of God was moving over the face of the waters," creating light and land, flora and fauna, and humans, turning the formless chaos represented by the deep into a natural order. With the flood of Noah's time, the primal disorder was allowed to prevail again for a time for the purpose of purification, but the rainbow sign after that assures us that those powers will not be unleashed again.

In Exodus, we hear of another mighty act of God; the creation of the people of Israel, hitherto a powerless group of Hebrew nomads, but now the chosen of Yahweh, delivered from slavery and given the Ten Commandments, the Promised Land, and a binding covenant. In order for this creative act to take place, Egyptian society had to be disordered to an extreme degree by plagues, economic disaster, and the destruction of an army in hot pursuit. One nation is born, but another's life is disrupted. Creation followed by disorder.

Hundreds of years later, the Jewish religion was a sham, the leadership corrupt, the people oppressed. Renewal was called for by the prophets, and it came when the Spirit of God was breathed into Ezekiel's valley of dry bones. But not before the Temple was destroyed, the land ravished, and the people taken into captivity in Babylon. Disorder and creation.

Five centuries later, religion had again gone bad, captured by culture, an empty, white sepulchre guided by the letter rather than by the spirit of the Law. The Holy Spirit came upon a woman named Mary, and a child was born for the redemption of Israel and the world. Jesus brought not peace, but division into his society; he was rejected, despised, beaten, and crucified; his followers were persecuted. Creation and disorder.

His servant Paul traveled all over the Mediterranean in the power of the Spirit, nurturing the infant church, creating and renewing faith communities. But wherever he went there was civil disorder. In Ephesus, he was attacked by a mob for being anti-business; his preaching of the gospel was seen as depriving them of their livelihood as artisans for the local god, Artemis. In Thessalonica, his people were accused of sedition and subversion; it is said that they wanted to turn the world upside down. Creation and disorder.

Fifteen hundred years later, the church was again in moral disrepute. Salvation was bought for money. The church was temporally powerful and wealthy, but spiritually weak and impoverished. A monk named Luther called the church to account, and a schism ensued. New churches come into being, including our own, and the Roman Catholic Church experienced a reactive renewal in spite of itself. The Reformation was surely a spiritual event of great significance; yet there followed almost total chaos in Europe, war upon war fought in the name of Christ. Creation and disorder.

To escape persecution, the Puritans came to North America, and hopes were high for a morally upright society, a city set on a hill, a New Jerusalem, a model for the world to copy. But the pace faltered. In 1740, Jonathan Edwards of Northhampton sparked the Great Awakening, a spiritual revival that spread up and down the East Coast like a brushfire. There has been nothing like it before or since in this country. In its questioning of any authority other than God, it sowed the seeds of a rebellion thirty years later, our Revolution, a guerilla war fought by ragtag freedom fighters from behind trees in Lexington and Concord. A war of attrition against superior forces was won, and a nation was born. There was another spiritual awakening in the 1800s, followed by the abolitionist movement and the Civil War. Another occurred in the 1960s with civil rights and Vietnam. Creation, spiritual renewal, disorder.

We seem to have established the existence of a pattern here, one that is somewhat disturbing. I must confess at this point that I much prefer order in my life. I do a lot of picking up around my house; my desk and bureau and beside table are neat. I may be compulsive, but I like to know where things are, what's going to happen, and when. Disorder is threatening; it makes me nervous, as does the unexpected. It may be human nature. So I ask myself the question: Is an orderly life, or house, or society, or world God's prime concern? The biblical answer is clearly, no. If we are to believe what we read in the Bible, we must admit that justice, not order, is what God wills for us. Certainly order is desirable, but only in a just society. The Hitlers, the caesars, the pharaohs provided order also, but where injustice prevails, the Spirit promotes disorder, not violence mind you, but disorder. Order is not synonymous with peace; there can be no peace without justice. The Apostle Paul wrote that "where the Spirit of the Lord is, there is freedom" (II Corinthians 3:17), and we can add that there is probably some disorder.

Now, what does all this mean to us at Pentecost? Sisters and brothers in Christ, I believe with all my heart that the Holy Spirit is mightily at work in this world today. Ever since the Second Vatican Council of 1965, when all the bishops were together in one place, the Spirit has been creating a new church that will cut across old barriers and dividing lines; a church that is inclusive and egalitarian in structure, rather than exclusive and hierarchical; a church that renounces violence in any form, especially war; a church that strives for justice for the wretched of the earth; that is willing to risk fame and fortune, life and limb for the sake of the gospel. The evidence is everywhere. In the Philippines, South Korea, South Africa, even the Soviet Union and Eastern Europe, this new church has had hundreds of martyrs; Christians are risking their lives for justice; they are enduring prison, torture, and death. But it is in Latin America that this new creation has become most clearly manifest. For twenty years, Christian base communities have been proliferating all over that continent, from Puebla to Patagonia, from Acapulco to Recife—one hundred thousand communities in Brazil alone. Oscar Romero of El Salvador and Camilo Torres of Columbia are the best known of the martyrs, but there have been thousands of priests, nuns, and Christian lay workers killed for taking up the cause of the poor and the powerless.

How will the North American church react to all this? Let me suggest an answer by paraphrasing the story of Nicodemus and Jesus. A wealthy and powerful church approached Jesus secretly for advice, saying, "We know that you are a teacher come from God, because you made the United States number one and helped the Celtics beat the Lakers."

But Jesus answered, "Never mind the miracles. If you want to make it into the kingdom, you must be born again."

"But how can we go back to the Reformation or the first Pentecost and be born again?" asked the church, playing it straight.

"You must be born of water and the Spirit," was the answer.

"How can this be?" asked the church.

"With all your emphasis on religious education, you still can't understand this?" replied Jesus.

We can reject, deny, and quench the Spirit by continuing to support, or at least tolerate, the killing of our brothers and sisters in Christ in Central America. We can opt for orderly lives and business as usual. Or we can take the risk of opening our hearts and our churches to those tongues of purifying fire, that mighty rush of wind from heaven. We cannot know where this Spirit will take us, perhaps even into non-violent disorder, but we can know that disorder brought about by injustice is divinely inspired, and we need not be afraid, because God has promised to be with us in any affliction.

My friends, there is revolution in the air, not communist revolution, as it is termed by those who reject the Spirit, but spiritual revolution. And God is calling us to support it with our prayers, with our financial resources, and with our bodies. It comes none too soon, to save us from the threat of extinction. Do not be afraid; the Spirit will guide us. *Amen.*

Franklin A. Dorman
First Congregational Church
Cambridge, Massachusetts

Sunday
May Twenty-ninth

Call to Worship: Worthy is the Lamb who was slain, to receive power and wealth and wisdom and might and honor and glory and blessing! *Revelation 5:12*

Processional Hymn: "God the Omnipotent"

Invocation: On this Trinity Sunday, we celebrate the three-in-one God: God the Father, God the Son, and God the Holy Spirit. Let us worship you in your full majesty, Lord of lords forever. *Amen.*

Sermon Scripture: John 3:1:17

Sermon Presentation: "The Wind of the Spirit"

Hymn of the Day: "Holy, Holy, Holy! Lord God Almighty"

Offertory Scripture: For you know the grace of our Lord Jesus Christ, that though he was rich, yet for your sake he became poor, so that by his poverty you might become rich.

II Corinthians 8:9

Offertory Prayer: Lord, teach us to give as we should, not as our spirit moves us, but as your Spirit moves us. Let these gifts be a response to your love. *Amen.*

Prayer of the Day

Lord, the fact of the matter is very simple: without your Spirit, we are but empty shells, mere robots who move about not really alive. Your Spirit is the moving force in our lives. Just as your Spirit moved across the waters at creation and gave form to the universe, your Spirit creates in us the gift of faith that raises us from mere existence to life in a loving relationship with you.

We thank you for the gift of your Spirit that guides us to a greater understanding of your truth, for the Spirit that moves us to confess you as the Son of God and Savior of the world, for your Spirit that gives us the strength to overcome temptation, to walk in your way, and to be born anew—a new creation born of grace with the promise of the Resurrection and the gift of eternal life.

Keep the fire of your Spirit burning brightly in our hearts, O Lord, today, tomorrow, and forever. *Amen.*

Benediction: Take heed to yourselves and to all the flock, in which the Holy Spirit has made you overseers, to care for the church of God which he obtained with the blood of his own Son. *Acts 20:28*

Recessional Hymn: "Onward, Christian Soldiers"

Lectionary Lessons: Trinity Sunday
Lesson 1—Isaiah 6:1-8; Psalm 29
Lesson 2—Romans 8:12-17
Gospel—John 3:1-17

History of the Hymn of the Day: "Holy, Holy, Holy! Lord God Almighty"
One of the greatest hymns of all ages, "Holy, Holy, Holy" was written in 1826 by Bishop Reginald Heber. It was based on the meter of the Apocalypse as found in Revelation 4:8-11: "Holy, Holy, Holy, Lord God Almighty, which was, and is, and is to come." The famed English poet-bishop wrote the hymn especially for Trinity Sunday as a tribute to the Trinity. It is one of the few hymns written for a specific Sunday of the church year, yet equally adaptable for every other Sunday. It is said of this hymn that it is found in more hymnbooks than any other hymn written.

Announcement for Next Week's Sermon: Would you like to preach next Sunday? If you are going to preach, you had better have something to say, not what you want to say, but what God wants said. Are you ready to preach? See if I am.

Story of the Week: The minister arrived at church one Sunday morning wearing a tiny patch on his face to cover up a cut. "This morning while I was shaving," he explained as he began his sermon, "I was thinking about my sermon and cut my face."
After church was over, he found a note slipped under the door of his study which read, "Next week while you're shaving, why don't you think about your face and cut your sermon?"

THE WIND OF THE SPIRIT

What was the first word you ever learned? Probably it was the word *no*.
"No! Didn't I tell you not to touch that?"
"No! You can't go over to Timmy's."

"No! No! No!"

Little by little the authority of parents is established, most often by the word *no.* Authority is identified by the things we can't do. But then, as we grow older, we begin to learn that those old restrictions were often good for us. Our fingers might have been slapped because touching the stove would have burned us, or going to Timmy's house would have meant that we would miss dinner. Eventually, if our upbringing was a healthy one, we began to understand that "authority" does not only mean "restrictions," but it also means knowledge about something that we need to know.

The University of Southern California is a university of authorities. Its professors are the authorities other professors quote. That's because USC is, first and foremost, a research institution, making the latest discoveries in the fields of medicine, behavioral sciences, law, computer technology, and a host of other fields. USC strives to be the authority in many fields.

Nicodemus was an authority too. He was an authority on religion. He was trained in the finest schools; he was a certified religious leader—a Pharisee—and a scholar of the highest order in religious law. The people around Nicodemus could be pretty sure that when he analyzed a situation and then spoke, he would have his facts clear, and his judgment would be accurate. So when he approached Jesus, it was no small matter. He came and spoke, as a person of authority.

"Rabbi," he said, "we know that you are a teacher sent by God. No one could perform the miracles you are doing unless God were with him."

That was a high endorsement of Jesus' character. There was not a hint of ridicule in it—not like the ridicule Jesus received from some Pharisees. And, certainly, Nicodemus was no less an authority than the other Pharisees.

You would think, then, that Jesus would make some comment on this endorsement by Nicodemus. He readily commented on statements made about him by people at other times; yet he apparently ignored the compliment Nicodemus had given him. Why do you suppose that's true? Do you think perhaps it's because, although Nicodemus was an authority on religion, it was obvious to Jesus that he really didn't understand who Jesus was?

When Nicodemus said, "You are a teacher sent by God," all he was saying was that Jesus was a godly man. Down through history there have been millions, and perhaps billions, of godly people in the world, but Jesus was unique. There has only been one Jesus. No, Nicodemus didn't understand who Jesus was.

Compare Nicodemus' assessment of Jesus—"You are a teacher sent by God"—to Peter's confession of faith at Caesaria Philippi: "You are the Christ, the Son of the living God!"

According to Peter, there could only be one person like Jesus—the Christ—the Son of the living God. Because Nicodemus didn't really understand who Jesus was, Jesus ignored his compliment, but he did not ignore Peter. To Peter he said, "Blessed are you Simon, son of John!"

Poor Nicodemus. He meant well, but he just didn't understand. Yet Jesus wanted to help him understand. So he told Nicodemus what must first happen before he could understand: "I am telling you the truth," Jesus told him. "No one can see the kingdom of God unless he is born again." In other words, despite how religious you are, or how much authority you have, in order for you to understand, you must become a new being, a new creation. You must have the breath of spiritual life blown into you from the Spirit of God.

You see, being religious, or having authority, is not the criterion. You can attend church seven times a week. You can memorize every verse in the Bible. You can understand every Christian doctrine. You can be baptized, receive Communion, pray ten times a day—and it means nothing unless somehow the Spirit of God has grabbed you and made you a new creation.

In the movie *Oh, God* when the main character told "God" (George Burns) that he was not religious, God answered, "That's okay. I don't belong to any religion. I belong in the heart." That's an oversimplification of what it means to be born again, but it gets close to the matter.

It was rebirth by the Spirit that allowed Peter to blurt out, "You are the Christ, the Son of the living God!" But because Nicodemus had not yet experienced that rebirth, the best he could utter was, "You are a teacher sent by God."

However, just because Peter had experienced that rebirth didn't mean that all the vestiges of the old Peter were gone. He was no more pious, no more holier-than-thou, than anybody else. Peter still had his problems. It was the same old Peter who, a minute after he called Jesus "the Son of the Living God," tried to stop him from going to the cross, and whom Jesus called "the Devil." It was the same old Peter who, a short time later, would lie and swear that he had never known Jesus. Oh, yes, Peter was still Peter, but through God he was a new creature, and that's why he understood who Jesus was.

Nicodemus, on the other hand, had not been touched by the Spirit, not yet, so Jesus tried to explain it to him: "No one can enter the Kingdom of God unless he is born of water and the Spirit. . . . The wind blows wherever it wishes; you hear the sound it makes, but you do not know where it comes from or where it is going. It is like that with everyone who is born of the Spirit" (John 3:5, 8 TEV).

Nicodemus could understand this verse better than we can. The reason is that Jesus is using a rich play on words that is difficult for us to catch in English. In Greek, in Hebrew, and in Aramaic, only one word is used for *wind, spirit,* and *breath.* When Jesus spoke of being born of the Spirit, and then talked of the blowing of the wind, he used the same word. Also, in his language, the word for *sound* also means *voice.* So, he was telling Nicodemus that the Spirit blows into our lives like the wind, and the voice of the Spirit comes upon us like the sound of the wind. Do you see the play on words?

The same binding together of the concepts of wind, spirit, and breath occurs throughout Scripture. In the second chapter of Genesis, when God formed man from the soil of the ground, he blew into man the breath of life. He gave man a spirit. Then, of course, there is that marvelous passage from the book of Ezekiel that tells of the prophet Ezekiel's looking out over a valley filled with dry, disjointed bones—the symbol of a despondent, defeated, lifeless nation. God said to Ezekiel, "Mortal man, prophesy to the wind. Tell the wind that the Sovereign Lord commands it to come from every direction, to breathe into these dead bodies, and to bring them back to life" (Ezekiel 37:9 TEV). And so the wind gave breath to the dry bones and imparted life to them.

In the New Testament, following the resurrection, Jesus appeared to the disciples, and "he breathed on them and said, 'Receive the Holy Spirit' " (John 20:22 TEV). Last Sunday, when we celebrated the Festival of Pentecost, we heard these words: "All the believers were gathered together in one place. Suddenly there was a noise from the sky which sounded like a strong wind blowing, and it filled the whole house where they were sitting. . . . They were all filled with the Holy Spirit" (Acts 2:1-2, 4 TEV).

The Spirit of God moves through this world like the wind, and it is that Spirit that imparts life to us—new life. Is it any wonder that Jesus compared the Spirit's giving new life to the blowing of the wind?

Do you remember the popular song of a few years ago that proclaimed, "The answer, my friend, is blowing in the wind"? How true it is. The answer to the spiritual questions, perplexities, doubts, and fears is blowing in the wind. It is the work of the Spirit. This new life, this new creation, this rebirth, comes upon us and we do not know how or when or where it will happen. The wind, Jesus said, blows wherever it wishes. It comes upon us in this moment or that moment—we never know when.

Haven't there been times in your life when you knew, you just knew, that God's Spirit was speaking to you? Sometimes these moments come when we are in worship, when we are at prayer or in private meditation or in Bible study or in church. But there are other times when we don't expect it; when we hear him speaking, perhaps ever so softly, in a child's voice, in a friendly hello, in the tears of sorrow, in the pain of tragedy. We never know when the Spirit is going to blow into our lives.

The Spirit blew into the life of a chaplain at Sonderstrom Air Force Base, Greenland. One day a military airplane crashed, killing twenty-two people. The runway and fields were strewn with bodies and pieces of bodies everywhere. Being the only chaplain on the base, the entire burden was laid on him to try to bring comfort, and the Word of Christ, to a shocked community staggered by a seemingly senseless loss of life.

But there was little time to mourn that day. The grisly task of locating, gathering up, and identifying the bodies needed to be done before there could be any mourning. And so, the chaplain, along with a young lieutenant who had been assigned the duties of a mortuary officer, and a group of volunteers went about the business of picking up mutilated bodies, and pieces of bodies, and trying to identify the dead so that family and relatives back home could be notified.

It was a heart-rending and exhausting task, but it had to be done. Although their hands and clothes were covered with blood and bits of flesh, the people worked in shocked silence well into the night until they almost dropped from fatigue.

When every last remnant of death had been picked up, they each went silently to their individual rooms.

That night, after midnight, there was a knock on the chaplain's door. Outside stood the young lieutenant, the Mortuary Officer. He said nothing. He just stood there and wept. For a moment, the chaplain stood silent and let the young man have his tears, but then he broke into tears, too. They stood with their arms around each other, and together they cried the tears that they so desperately needed to release.

After some moments, the lieutenant finally spoke through his tears. "I realized," he said, "as we were picking up pieces of bodies today, that the only other people out there with us were the people who go to church here. I have always been an unbeliever, and I used to ridicule these same people who were out there with us. Yet they are the only ones who would, or perhaps could, do what we had to do today. It must have been a great act of faith that could help them see beyond the gore—to a hope."

That tragic day turned around the life of that young lieutenant. As he readily admitted, he had never been religious, had seldom gone to church except for weddings or funerals, but from that time on he was a new man. He took an active part in the Christian ministry of that base. He began attending church regularly, singing in the choir, and becoming totally involved. Then he did an unheard of thing: He extended his tour of duty at Sonderstrom for one year; he was the first person in the history of the base to do that. He did it because he wanted to be able to tell others the story of how the Spirit blew into his life that tragic day.

"The wind blows wherever it wishes. . . . It is like that with everyone who is born of the Spirit" (John 3:8 TEV). *Amen.*

Edward A. Beckstrom
Evangelical Lutheran Church in America
United States Air Force Chaplain, retired
Equality, Alabama

Sunday
June Fifth

Call to Worship: Great indeed, we confess, is the mystery of our religion: He was manifested in the flesh, vindicated in the Spirit, seen by angels, preached among the nations, believed on in the world, taken up in glory. *I Timothy 3:16*

Processional Hymn: "O Master, Let Me Walk with Thee"

Invocation: Let the words of my mouth be acceptable in your sight. Speak to us today through the spoken word as we seek new insights to your will and love for us. *Amen.*

Sermon Scripture: Romans 10:10-17

Sermon Presentation: "To Preach the Gospel"

Hymn of the Day: "Have Thine Own Way, Lord"

Offertory Scripture: Seek first his kingdom and his righteousness, and all these things shall be yours as well. *Matthew 6:33*

Offertory Prayer: Give me words to move hearts to respond to your great gift, your only Son. Let us make a sacrificial gift as a response to that love. *Amen.*

Prayer of the Day

Lord, I can't believe it. Every day I am surrounded by and bombarded with messages too numerous to count. In the newspaper, on the television and radio, I'm on the receiving end of words like *the best, tremendous, stupendous, incredible, amazing, extraordinary.* Pretty soon, these words become common and are so easy to ignore.

When I think about it, I just can't believe it. I can't believe that you have entrusted me and people just like me with the "good news," the most important news that God has ever shared with his people.

I'm not sure why, but you have chosen me to tell others about the "good news" of God's love; love that accepts us just as we are and grace that reconciles us to him when we are repentant over our disobedience. You have selected me to share the "good news" of God which heals our divisions and brings light to our often dark world. Ours is a priceless gift, a pearl of the greatest value, a treasure in a field, worth sacrificing everything for in order for us to possess, a lamp to light the world, the salt of the earth. Accept my thanks for this great gift.

I humbly ask just one more thing. Make me worthy of your calling. *Amen.*

Benediction: For if while we were enemies we were reconciled to God by the death of his Son, much more, now that we are reconciled, shall we be saved by his life. *Romans 5:10*

Recessional Hymn: "Once to Every Man and Nation"

Lectionary Lessons: The Second Sunday after Pentecost
Lesson 1—I Samuel 16:14-23; Psalm 57
Lesson 2—II Corinthians 4:13, 5:1
Gospel—Mark 3:20-35

History of the Hymn of the Day: "Have Thine Own Way, Lord"

"Have Thine Own Way, Lord" was written in 1902; the music, composed by George Cole Stebbins, was not written until five years later. Although Miss Pollard wrote many hymns and poems, "Have Thine Own Way" was the only one to survive the tests of time. However, this alone would justify her claim to fame, for this hymn became a favorite throughout all the Christian world.

Announcement for Next Week's Sermon: Think of a word that has changed millions of lives. Next week the sermon is about that word. I wonder what that word could be?

Story of the Week: The owner of the company was conducting a sales meeting. He thought he would get the attention of his audience and put them at ease by telling a few funny stories. After each joke, everyone laughed uproariously—except one man sitting on the front row. He never cracked a smile. After the fourth or fifth joke, the boss looked at him and said, "What's the matter with you? Don't you have a sense of humor?"

"I don't have to laugh," the man said. "I'm quitting at the end of the week to take another job."

TO PREACH THE GOSPEL

When a new minister comes into a community to serve a new church, it is like a boy and girl on their first date. The questions in the minds of all are: "Will everything go right? Will he or she like me? Will he or she like my family? What of the future? How are things going to work out between us? Is this the beginning of a long, pleasant, and lasting relationship? Or will it not be so?" There is a sense of thrill, of adventure, and the pull of just plain curiosity as we confront new experiences of life. There is the fascination of the unknown, a force pulling us toward the unknown, and at the same time a force pulling us away from it.

Why does a minister come? Well, we might say he or she is appointed and has to be accepted, or we might say that he or she comes to serve the needs of the people of the community, that he or she is the servant of God and of the people.

But what did Jesus say was the purpose of his preaching? It is not too much to assume that, by looking to Jesus, we may find a pattern for our own lives. Jesus, when he stood up to preach his first sermon in his home town of Nazareth, quoted the book of Isaiah, in which it is said that he had come to "preach good news to the poor . . . release to the captives . . . recovering of sight to the blind, to set at liberty those who are oppressed, to proclaim the acceptable year of the Lord" (Luke 4:18-19).

Thus, Jesus came to preach the good news of God's reconciling love, the fact that God was reaching out in the world into the lives of people, to bring them together in fellowship with him and with one another. This is why preachers come, to do this same task of proclaiming the reconciling love of God. Our task is to follow in the footsteps of Jesus, to do what he did, to proclaim what he proclaimed, to tell of the God he represented.

Just why do we believe in what Jesus preached and attempt to follow his example? Why are we attempting to be ambassadors of Christ, to do what he would do, and to do it as well as a mere mortal is able to do it?

First of all, we do so because Jesus is real. Jesus is the most real man who ever lived. He has a touch of reality about his life. He was acquainted with real life. He knew real people and real situations. He was a carpenter, and we can almost imagine his calloused hands that had gotten that way from handling wood and tools.

He was a man who had gone through the sorrowing experiences of life. He wept at the grave of Lazarus, and apparently his own father had died when he was but a lad.

He was a man who loved little children. He loved to have them around him, and he said that the kingdom of God must come to us as to little children, if we are to receive it at all. There is something about Jesus, when we think of his relationship to children, that pulls us toward him, that makes us think that truly here is one who is a representative of God. Here is one who is really concerned about all of God's creatures.

He was a man who loved parties. He was no long-faced, sour person. He was a man of joy, despite all the hardships and tragedies of his life. He looked upon these experiences as having value and worth in God's plan.

He was a person who became angry with people and situations that did not improve. Thus, his humanness is something which commends him to us. He is one who has walked this life with us, one who has shared our burdens, one who knows what our life is like; therefore, he can deal with it with us.

His life, as we have said, has the note of reality about it. This reality comes out especially when we see him shocking the self-righteous and the complacent, and when we see him in difficult situations because of his plain speech.

I seek to follow Jesus because his life inspires me to a level of higher achievement. While we may try to set up our own goals and try to follow and achieve them, there is something about the Master that keeps pulling us onward and upward to greater things in life. The hymn "Dear Master, in Whose Life I See" expresses these thoughts so well:

> Dear Master, in whose life I see
> All that I would, but fail to be,
> Let thy clear light forever shine,
> To shame and guide this life of mine.
>
> Though what I dream and what I do
> In my weak days are always two,
> Help me, oppressed by things undone,
> O thou, whose deeds and dreams were one!

We believe in Jesus because he taught a kingdom of God that was coming into being in his own person. God's kingdom meant something more for Jesus than just an idea; it was not just a teaching, not just a thought, not just something good that one day might come to be. It was actually coming into being in his own work of teaching and proclaiming the kingdom of God. The reconciling power of God's love was already at work in the world, because Jesus had come. In Jesus, something of God had come into the world.

We believe in Jesus because he loved. Love is a word that has been seriously distorted and almost destroyed of its meaning by Hollywood. Love, there, is something less than love in the Christian sense. But love is a mature, strong emotion, not something weak and sentimental. Love requires mature persons to experience it in its fullness. Love is bearing one another's burdens. Love helps us to see another's point of view; love helps us not to insist on our own way.

What does this gospel that we preach mean to our lives, this gospel that must be related to our everyday lives if it is to have any meaning at all? This gospel is not just an idea or thought, but something that came into actual being through the work of Christ, something that we may become a part of and that may transform us.

This gospel means, first of all, judgment. Judgment is not a pleasant word; it is not a comfortable word. It is not pleasant to anticipate the thought that God has anything against us; yet this aspect of the gospel is necessary. Christianity is no "contented cow" religion; we're not called to be so peaceful that all we want to do is wander through deep green grass and sit about chewing our cuds. Our faith requires something more of us.

The judgment of the gospel is a challenge to our self-sufficiency. Judgment makes us aware of the fact that we do not and cannot save ourselves. Love always implies judgment, because there is something about the nature of love that cannot let wrong go unchallenged. To be loved by another is to come into a relationship with that other person. We cannot then treat that person as an object, but must treat him or her as a person. To rebel against a tyrant is valor, bravery, but to rebel against God, who is good, is to sin, for God is love. To rebel against love is to commit sin. Our sinful state makes us hate the good and love the evil. Is this why we have so many problems and difficulties in the world? The good comes, and we would rather have the less good. This is what the Bible proclaims, light came into the world, and men loved darkness instead, and so Jesus was crucified. Yes, the gospel is judgment, because it calls us to account for the way we have lived.

Yet, the gospel is more than this. It is the good news of God's love and reconciliation. The gospel is for left-out people. It is for people who, in one area of their lives or another, are aware of need.

The good news is peacemaking. It heals the divisions within ourselves that keep us from being whole personalities, those cross purposes within our lives that take up our energies and keep us from being what we ought to be. The good news is peacemaking between persons, and in result individuals come to share and appreciate one another. The gospel is peacemaking in society and the world at large. The leaven of the gospel infuses the world, and little by little, bit by bit, transforms the relationships of people into the way of Christ. As Christians, we become peacemakers and share in the task of Christ. We become, as heretical as it may sound, "Christs" to our neighbors. As someone has said, "our lives are the only Bibles that many people will ever read."

The prayer of St. Francis expresses this peacemaking quality that is the Christian's in a fine way:

> Lord, make me an instrument of Thy peace.
> Where there is hate may I bring love;
> Where offense, may I bring pardon;
> May I bring union in place of discord;
> Truth, replacing error;
> Faith where once there was doubt;
> Hope, for despair;
> Light, where was darkness;
> Joy to replace sadness.
> Make me not to so crave to be loved as to love.
> Help me to learn that in giving I may receive;
> In forgetting self, I may find life eternal.

Jesus expressed this thought in the Beatitudes: "Blessed are the peacemakers, for they shall be called sons of God." (Matthew 5:9). The peacemakers shall be called the *sons* of God. No other quality has this reward attached to it, that if we are peacemakers we shall be as sons and daughters of God. What a goal; what a promise this is, that if we share in the task of reconciling the world to itself and to its God, we shall become children of God.

To be a peacemaker means to put love into action. It means offering love to the unlovely, again and again and again, not just once or twice, but time and time again. To love is to put faith into action. People "who never saw love in action have to test it a long time before they can believe it."

The first task of the church is not self-preservation, but to be the Body of Christ set in the middle of the world. The church gives its life away that men might know the good news of the God who loves them. This is our purpose; this is our reason for being Christians, not just to build a greater and more beautiful church, but to give our lives, through our church, to the task of reconciling people to one another and to their God. We are called to give that love, because God has first loved us.

Why have I come? Why do I stand in this pulpit today? I have come to proclaim that while we were yet sinners, Christ died for us, to reconcile us to God, to bring us to himself, and so to help us expand that love into the lives of others. I have come, in the best way that I can and to the extent of my abilities, with the help of God's grace, to help you find God and his will for your life. I have come to share in the growth of all our lives as children of God, not in any sense of superiority, but in the recognition that we are all growing in *sonship* to God. *Amen.*

Richard A. Chrisman

First United Methodist Church
Mason City, Illinois

Sunday
June Twelfth

Call to Worship: Oh, send out thy light and thy truth; let them lead me, let them bring me to thy holy hill and to thy dwelling!
Psalm 43:3

Processional Hymn: "There's a Wideness in God's Mercy"

Invocation: O God, we come so close to being worthy of your grace. We keep on trying for perfection, but we know it cannot be. Only through your grace will we ever achieve your eternal reward. Help us to keep on trying. *Amen.*

Sermon Scripture: Acts 26:1-20

Sermon Presentation: "Almost"

Hymn of the Day: "I Am Thine, O Lord"

Offertory Scripture: I beseech you therefore, brethren, by the mercies of God, that ye present your bodies a living sacrifice, holy, acceptable unto God, which is your reasonable service.
Romans 12:1 KJV

Offertory Prayer: Here is my gift to you. I want to do more, but I just can't seem to make it. Don't accept my almost; help me to do it for you. *Amen.*

Prayer of the Day

Lord, it's a word that expresses so much. It soothes our failure. It masks our defeat. It covers our shortcomings. Yet there is no hiding the fact that *almost* means we came close, but in the final analysis we have been unsuccessful.

To say we *almost* did it helps us to cope with our feelings of not succeeding. Yet in our relationship with you, we find that your grace covers our shortcomings. Your mercy accepts our failures. Your love seeks out the sinner, the lost, the outcast.

But you warn us not to take our relationship with you for granted. We are to "love you with all of our heart, all of our soul, and all of our mind." You expect us to seek your kingdom first. You will not accept anything less than our total commitment to your way. To say we *almost* followed you is not enough. To say we *almost* sought to do your will is unacceptable in your sight.

To be called a child of God is the greatest of honors. To hear your Word is one of our greatest pleasures. To receive your sacraments is our greatest blessing. Strengthen our commitment to do your will, to follow your way, to live by your truth. Let us never forget that you have called us not to be successful, but to be faithful. *Amen.*

Benediction: Blessed is the man who endures trial, for when he has stood the test he will receive the crown of life which God has promised to those who love him. *James 1:12*

Recessional Hymn: "O God, Our Help in Ages Past"

Lectionary Lessons: The Third Sunday after Pentecost
Lesson 1—II Samuel 1:1, 17-27; Psalm 46
Lesson 2—II Corinthians 5:6-10, 14-17
Gospel—Mark 4:24-36

History of the Hymn of the Day: "I Am Thine, O Lord"
This gospel hymn written by Fanny Crosby has been a favorite of Christian Endeavor societies the world over. It was written on an occasion of the famed blind poetess' visit to Cincinnati, Ohio, at the home of W. H. Doane, who had composed scores of popular gospel songs. They were sitting together in the still hush of the evening twilight hour talking about the nearness of God. The close fellowship of these two great Christians so impressed Miss Crosby that before retiring she had written the complete hymn. The next morning Mr. Doane fitted the music to the words and thus was born a special favorite of gospel hymn lovers wherever gospel hymns are sung.

I am Thine, O Lord, I have heard Thy voice,
And it told thy love to me;
But I long to rise in the arms of faith,
And be closer drawn to Thee.

Announcement for Next Week's Sermon: Let's give old Dad a break. Next Sunday is Father's Day, and we have a very special message for the whole family.

Story of the Week: The speaker for the big banquet was checking into the hotel. The desk clerk said, "Yes, we have a reservation for you but you didn't say what price room you want. Would you like one with a tub or a shower?"

"What's the difference?" the speaker asked.

"You have to stand up in the shower," the desk clerk said.

ALMOST

Then Agrippa said unto Paul, Almost thou persuadest me to be a Christian. (Acts 26:28 KJV)

Some years ago in the U.S. Open Golf Tournament held in Oakmont, Pennsylvania, Arnold Palmer almost won the championship of that prestigious tournament instead of Jack Nicklaus. One of Arnold Palmer's putts hung right on the edge of the cup. Palmer stood there for three and a half minutes waiting for the putt to drop in. But it didn't, and so he had to tap it in. It cost him not only the championship, but also thousands of dollars. The putt almost went in the cup. But almost is not good enough.

The word *almost* covers a multitude of situations in life. It has often been said that football is a game of inches, and we all know of occasions in which our favorite team *almost* made a first down in a crucial series of plays, or they *almost* made a touchdown. There was the year the Dallas Cowboys played Pittsburgh in the Super Bowl, and on a blitz, the Cowboys almost got the quarterback. But he threw a touchdown pass that won the game for Pittsburgh. Almost wasn't good enough.

We could all make our own personal list of almosts, some of them important, some not so important. Many of them we have forgotten, and that's probably just as well, because worrying or fretting over the past "almosts" of life really doesn't do any good.

This morning, I want you to think about the word *almost* in a slightly different context. I want you to look again at Acts 26:28. Some people think the Bible is a boring book. If so, then they have never really given an honest reading to the Acts of the Apostles, the full title of this book. It lives and breathes with drama and excitement, because those early apostles did indeed do some mighty acts as the Christian church began to live and to grow.

In the passage for today, the Apostle Paul is under arrest. He had been preaching in Jerusalem, and some people excited a mob and accused Paul of teaching the Jews to forsake Moses.

When the authorities realized that Paul was a Roman citizen, they felt he should be given a fair trial. He was taken to a place called Caesarea, and there he was tried before King Agrippa. His speech before the king is a moving one. The Scripture tells us that he began by giving his own background in the Jewish faith, that as a strict Pharisee he opposed Jesus. He told how he had persecuted the Christians and had put many of them in prison. Then he told about that momentous day when, on his way to Damascus, he suddenly was struck by a light from heaven and fell to the ground. He heard the Lord Jesus saying to him: "Saul, [as he was called before his conversion] Saul, why are you persecuting me?" And Paul said: "Who are you, Lord?" And Jesus said: "I am Jesus, whom you are persecuting. But now I want you to stand up, because I am sending you to the Jews and Gentiles to open their eyes, that they may turn from darkness to light and from the power of Satan to God, that they may receive forgiveness of sins." Paul gives a moving Christian witness. And at the end, King Agrippa says, "Paul, you almost persuade me to be a Christian."

You *almost* persuade me to be a Christian. Now, Bible scholars are not certain whether Agrippa actually said this because he was really almost persuaded to be a Christian, or whether he said this as a form of sarcasm. But we do know that Agrippa is never heard of again. You can't help but wonder how much different his life might have been if he had become an altogether Christian instead of an almost Christian.

We try to make certain that those who visit this church feel that someone cares, that we are glad they have come. When we visit with these newcomers, we try to encourage them to keep their interest in the church whether they eventually join ours or some other church. Some become almost church members, almost followers of Christ who drift away and, like Agrippa, are never heard of again. The fact of life is that only those who make a tremendous effort to be complete and altogether Christians are the only ones who make a success of it.

Paul made his speech to King Agrippa. He said that Jesus told him to go and be a witness to the people, so that they would turn from the power of Satan to God and so that they would receive forgiveness of sins. And then Paul said: "Wherefore, O King Agrippa, I was not disobedient to the heavenly vision, but declared first to those at Damascus, then at Jerusalem and throughout all the country of Judea, and also to the Gentiles, that they should repent and turn to God and perform deeds worthy of their repentance" (Acts 26:19-20).

Paul said that he was not disobedient to the heavenly vision. What is your vision of your Christian life? What is your vision of your place in the church? The question that needs to be asked of the life of all of us is: Have we been faithful to our vision, to our destiny as God's man or God's woman?

Paul stands among those who were obedient to the end. He knew how to run the race. He knew how to keep his eye on the goal and then press onward to it with all his energy. And so it was that Paul, standing before King Agrippa as a prisoner, wound up wearing the crown of life that never fades away. And Agrippa, the King, wound up with nothing.

A pastor had a wedding for a young couple. He talked with them one night before the wedding about the importance of the Christian faith and the church in their marriage. The night of the rehearsal, the bride mentioned how enthusiastic they were about the church's being a part of their marriage. After the couple got married, they didn't attend church for several Sundays, so the pastor called to ask how things were going and to tell them they had been missed. The wife said. "Well, we've just gotten busy with other things." The vision that was there at one time was now apparently gone. Almost Christians, almost church members—but almost isn't good enough for them or for Christ or for the church.

Well, it's good for us all to ask ourselves: How nearly are we Christians? Is it just almost? Is it a kind of trivial thing? Are we offended and quit church over the least little thing that happens?

None of us can afford to be content with being almost Christians; rather the goal has got to be toward becoming altogether Christians, following after the Lord Christ. There are men who are not almost Christian, but altogether Christians. And they say, "I pray that God will forgive me, because I fail so often." But they are in there every day, trying to become the Christians that God would have them be. That should be the goal of each of us. How nearly all out are we as Christians? How nearly all out are we as members of the church?

In the book of Hebrews, there occurs this magnificent passage:

> Therefore, since we are surrounded by so great a cloud of witnesses [of Paul and many other people who have gone before us in the church], let us also lay aside every weight, and sin which clings so closely, and let us run with perseverance the race that is set before us, looking to Jesus the pioneer and perfecter of our faith, who for the joy that was set before him endured the cross, despising the shame, and is seated at the right hand of the throne of God. (12:1-2)

My Christian friends, that's for us. If we could only see the joy of success, of completion, of getting the job done, of being a Christian not only in word, but in deed. Let us commit ourselves to that goal, to that vision for our good, for his glory, and for the joy that comes only to those who commit themselves to being altogether Christian. *Amen.*

Thomas G. Wilbanks
First Presbyterian Church
Mesquite, Texas

Sunday
June Nineteenth

Call to Worship: Therefore God has highly exalted him and bestowed on him the name which is above every name.

Philippians 2:9

Processional Hymn: "Nearer, My God, to Thee"

Invocation: Today, Lord, we ask thy special blessing on the families of this church, with a special blessing for the fathers whom we honor today. Grant that by their example they may show their love for you. *Amen.*

Sermon Scripture: II Samuel 18:24-33

Sermon Presentation: "O Absalom, Absalom!"

Hymn of the Day: "Amazing Grace!"

Offertory Scripture: Whatsoever ye do in word or deed, do all in the name of the Lord Jesus, giving thanks to God and the Father by him. *Colossians 3:17 KJV*

Offertory Prayer: We thank you for the gifts that you daily provide, especially for the love that is the family. Accept these offerings as a token of this love. *Amen.*

Prayer of the Day

God, you have given us the great privilege of calling you "Father." It is a great honor to be counted among your children.

In your plan for creation, you intended that our relationships be marked by love and concern for those around us. But our rebellion, our disobedience, and our sinfulness have disrupted and sometimes destroyed what you have planned for us. We have become selfish and uncompromising. We have tried to buy the love of those around us by giving them everything they want. Our love has often been misguided. It's motives have been questionable. The effects of this love have often been devastating to all involved. Yet in your love for us, you have promised us the chance to have a new beginning, to change our course, to do things the right way—your way.

Help us to further your example of parenthood. May we be loving and fair, disciplining when necessary, but always loving. *Amen.*

Benediction: In him you also, who have heard the word of truth, the gospel of your salvation, and have believed in him, were sealed with the promised Holy Spirit, which is the guarantee of our inheritance until we acquire possession of it, to the praise of his glory. *Ephesians 1:13-14*

Recessional Hymn: "Dear Lord and Father of Mankind"

Lectionary Lessons: The Fourth Sunday after Pentecost
Lesson 1—II Samuel 5:1-12; Psalm 48
Lesson 2—II Corinthians 5:18–6:2
Gospel—Mark 4:35-41

History of the Hymn of the Day: "Amazing Grace!"
John Newton wrote "Amazing Grace" in 1779; and only he could write this hymn with such meaning. "Amazing Grace" was the story of his life. Every word was pulled with pain from the dark days and the treacherous times of his early sea-faring youth to the wondrous joy of his discovery of the love of God. His epitaph, written by his own hand, tells more eloquently than any other words the extent of depth and height he experienced: "John Newton, clerk, once an infidel and libertine, was by the rich mercy of our Lord and Savior, Jesus Christ, preserved, restored, pardoned and appointed to preach the faith he had long labored to destroy." Every line of his hymn is filled with tears of remorse because of the greatness of his sin, and expressions of joy because of the discovery of God's grace:

Amazing grace, how sweet the sound,
That saved a wretch like me;
I once was lost but now am found,
Was blind but now I see.

Announcement for Next Week's Sermon: Do you think evil is real? If it is real, how do we protect ourselves against evil? Answers will be given next Sunday.

Story of the Week: "This morning," the minister said, "I'm going to speak on the relationship between fact and faith. It is a fact that you are sitting here in the sanctuary. It also is a fact that I am standing here speaking. But it is faith that makes me believe that you might be listening to what I have to say."

O ABSALOM, ABSALOM!

On this Father's Day, I want to share with you a story, one direct from the Bible. The Bible contains many great stories about fathers—and their children. I'm sure you can all call to mind at least one such, the parable of the prodigal son and the forgiving father. The narrative I want to focus our thoughts upon this morning is probably less familiar to you. It's the story of King David of ancient Israel and his son, Absalom. It's a rather lengthy story, encompassing all of chapters thirteen through eighteen of the Old Testament book of Second Samuel. We can't possibly read it verbatim this morning in the sermon time, so I'll try to narrate the high points of it to you. In recent years, the television networks have been dramatizing quite a few Bible stories, making them into specials and movies, and I think this story would make a dandy. It has all the essential elements for modern appeal—sex, violence, family quarreling, conspiracy, duplicity—it's practically a natural plot line for a soap opera. I hope you'll be interested enough to read it in its entirety later for yourself. Before we begin the story, however, let's pause for a word with our sponsor; in other words, let's seek our Lord in prayer: Father, may I present your Word correctly at this time, and may we each receive it as you will, Amen.

King David, in his prime, was the greatest of God's anointed leaders. David had, as was the custom of his day for those who could afford such, many wives—and many, many children. Among his children by one wife were a daughter, Tamar, and her brother, Absalom. By another wife, David had a son, Amnon. As these children grew toward adulthood, troubles began. Of all the possible women he could have picked, being the king's son, the young man Amnon developed a desire for his half-sister, Tamar. By hook and crook, he managed to lure her to his bedside one day, and you can anticipate the rest of that incident, I'm sure. When he was done with her, having taken his pleasure, Amnon threw Tamar out of his house. Afterward, Amnon was hated, quite naturally, by Tamar and her brother Absalom, and, in turn, Amnon hated them. Eventually, Absalom's hatred grew so strong that he set up a little plot, wherein he murdered Amnon. Surmising that his father wouldn't be happy about all this, Absalom headed for the hills, hiding outside the country to escape his father's wrath.

Eventually, though, King David ceased grieving for his dead son, Amnon, and, not wishing to lose two sons, decided to forgive Absalom's crime and invited him to come back home.

That was a mistake. When Absalom recognized how soft-hearted his father was, he felt only contempt for him, and he began to conceive a plot against his father. The Bible says that Absalom was a handsome young man, with a fine, brilliant mind, gifted in many ways. Slowly, but surely, by cunning political maneuvering, Absalom won the hearts of the people of Israel away from his father. After six years of conspiring, Absalom had enough support that one day he simply gave his father notice to "get out of town." David, realizing too late how cunningly he had been tricked, decided not to make a stand at that time, but to accede to Absalom's demand and leave Jerusalem. Thus six years after he forgave Absalom and urged him to come back out of exile, David, himself, was forced, in disgrace, to go into exile at the hands of Absalom. Absalom became king, and David was left to hide in the wilderness with only a handful of loyal followers.

But that's not the end of the story. David didn't get to be king by accident. Absalom's intelligence and cunning were largely inherited from his father. And David had a few tricks left up his sleeve, too. A few carefully placed spies kept him informed of every move that Absalom was about to make; David even managed to get one of his own men appointed as Absalom's most trusted advisor. After a few unwise atrocities by the rash young king, public opinion began to swing back toward David. He gradually mustered an army of those disaffected with Absalom, and, when he had acquired sufficient strength, brought his forces back to do battle with his son's army. Even then, though, he could not bring himself to order the rebellious boy killed. David's military commanders were given specific orders not to harm Absalom, but only to capture him. David's chief general, Joab, disobeyed that order, however, and Absalom was killed in the final battle for control of Jerusalem. This rather long and involved story concludes with David's learning of the outcome of the battle:

> Now David was sitting between the two gates; and the watchman went up to the roof of the gate by the wall, and when he lifted up his eyes and looked, he saw a man running alone. And the watchman called out and told the king. And the king said, "If he is alone, there are tidings in his mouth." And he came

apace, and drew near. And the watchman saw another man running; and the watchman called to the gate and said, "See, another man running alone!" The king said, "He also brings tidings." And the watchman said, "I think the running of the foremost is like the running of Ahimaaz the son of Zadok." And the king said, "He is a good man, and comes with good tidings." Then Ahimaaz cried out to the king, "All is well." And he bowed before the king with his face to the earth, and said, "Blessed be the Lord your God, who has delivered up the men who raised their hand against my lord the king." And the king said, "Is it well with the young man Absalom?" Ahimaaz answered, "When Joab sent your servant, I saw a great tumult, but I do not know what it was." And the king said, "Turn aside, and stand here." So he turned aside, and stood still. And behold, the Cushite came; and the Cushite said, "Good tidings for my lord the king! For the Lord has delivered you this day from the power of all who rose up against you." The king said to the Cushite, "Is it well with the young man Absalom?" And the Cushite answered, "May the enemies of my lord the king, and all who rise up against you for evil, be like that young man." And the king was deeply moved, and went up to the chamber over the gate and wept; and as he went, he said, "O my son Absalom, my son, my son Absalom! Would I had died instead of you, O Absalom, my son, my son!"

The biblical story of King David and his son Absalom is a long, intricate narrative, with a somewhat unusual, rather tragic ending. It is appropriate for Father's Day, because it contains several important lessons for fathers and sons and all of us, even in this modern day so far removed from ancient Israel. Three of those lessons from God's word might be: First, the story of David and his son, Absalom, reveals to us that human nature, and, more specifically, the nature of family relationships, aren't changing for the worse. Somehow or other, every generation has the mistaken belief that the next generation—our children—is worse than their parents were. Recently I listened to some men who were serving as counselors at a junior high church camp, men decrying the laziness, indolence, and delinquency of youth today. "It wasn't that way when we were kids," they almost all agreed. David and Absalom lived three thousand years ago, and they had a rather serious father-son generation gap. It would be an understatement to say that Absalom was a spoiled, no-good, bratty kid. By the standards Absalom set, the very worst of our sons and daughters would qualify as near angels. We cannot blame all the problems of our world on the young. Our children aren't all that bad, not if we're honest with ourselves.

Second, the other side of the same matter is that over-indulgence of one's children is not "love." It is harmful, not helpful, and especially when the over-indulged become adults. Absalom murdered his brother, Amnon, and after a relatively brief period of anger, David ignored the crime completely. In no way was Absalom ever called to account for murder. Now, there may be a number of cases right here at this church in which fathers and mothers are continually pulling adult children and even grandchildren out of scrapes—advancing sums of money; bailing sons and daughters out of legal, financial, and marital difficulties; even encouraging, or at least condoning, grossly immoral and, in some cases, illegal practices—all in the name of love. A ten-year-old boy was once caught throwing rocks at church windows. After the fourth time he was seen doing this, his father, who was a city policeman was approached. "You're wrong!" he said angrily. "It wasn't my boy! My boy is a good boy. He didn't do it!" What had been seen didn't matter. The father's mind was made up. In the name of parental love, he would ignore the facts of his boy's actions. King David would tolerate anything from his children, because he thought he was loving them. But all his "love" led to was tragedy, for him and for his children. Our children aren't all good, just because they're our children.

The last point, and perhaps, the most positive one in this whole story is: Where does God fit into this rather involved family chronicle? In the Old Testament, we can read many chapters without a single specific mention of God, and this is one such place. Yet, God is present in this story, especially at the very end. King David had been a very foolish parent. In the name of misguided love, he had raised a selfish, no-good son. It had cost him much heartache; Absalom had rebelled and even tried to kill his father. But now Absalom was dead, the victim of his own evil schemes. It was a death well-deserved; justice was served. David should be relieved to have defeated this twisted child, who had turned so completely against his father. But instead, he cried: "O my son Absalom! My son, my son Absalom! If only I had died instead of you, O Absalom, my son, my son!" Was David taking things too far to wish to die in the place of the one who wished to kill him, this rebellious creation of his loins, who had gone so completely wrong? It didn't make sense. Yet, there would one day be a God, father of all mankind, who would come down to earth and volunteer to die in place of his rebellious, wanton, misguided children. That wouldn't be logical, either, but he would do it. And thanks be to God that he did! *Amen*.

David Z. Ring, III
St. Mark's United Methodist Church
El Paso, Texas

Sunday
June Twenty-sixth

Call to Worship: Thanks be to God, who gives us the victory through our Lord Jesus Christ. *I Corinthians 15:57*

Processional Hymn: "In the Hour of Trial"

Invocation: O Lord, you came into this world to overcome the powers of evil. Help us to attain that victory in your name. Let us follow your example by overcoming evil with good. *Amen.*

Sermon Scripture: Romans 12:14-21

Sermon Presentation: "How to Live in an Evil World"

Hymn of the Day: "This Is My Father's World"

Offertory Scripture: I will freely sacrifice unto thee: I will praise thy name, O Lord; for it is good. *Psalm 54:6 KJV*

Offertory Prayer: You know, Lord, we try to be good. We do our best to follow your law of love. We try to treat others justly. We know we will fail unless we do all this in your name and to your honor and glory. Make us right with you. *Amen.*

Prayer of the Day

Lord, it gets a little scary in this world of ours. But you knew and experienced the horror and evil that surrounds us firsthand.

The forces of evil and the children of darkness seem very powerful and relentless. You tell us that we should be as "wise as serpents." That is, we should be alert and take the necessary steps to protect ourselves and our families. You warn us not to be overcome by the evil that surrounds us. Keep us from sinking into the swamp of revenge, anger, hostility and one-upmanship that surrounds us.

We know that the one who led Adam and Eve astray, the one who tempted you in the wilderness, the one who killed you on the cross, is the same one who would love nothing more than to steal our faith and replace it with doubt, despair, and the loss of all hope.

You tell us that we should strive to overcome evil with good. Remind us that you have shown us the way. In your life, death, and glorious resurrection we have seen that love can overcome hate, that faith can overcome doubt, that certainty can overcome despair, that joy can overcome sadness, and that life can overcome death.

We know that, thanks to you, the war is won; yet the battle rages on. Give us the strength, the courage, and the faith to do it your way. *Amen.*

Benediction: And the peace of God, which passes all understanding, will keep your hearts and your minds in Christ Jesus.
Philippians 4:7

Recessional Hymn: "O Love That Wilt Not Let Me Go"

Lectionary Lessons: The Fifth Sunday after Pentecost
Lesson 1—II Samuel 6:1-15
Lesson 2—II Corinthians 8:7-15
Gospel—Mark 5:21-43

History of the Hymn of the Day: "This Is My Father's World"
One of hymnody's most beautiful nature poems, this hymn was written by the Reverend Maltbie D. Babcock, prominent Presbyterian minister, during his first pastorate in Lockport, New York. Filled with a deep devotion to his calling, the learned clergyman would often say to his people, "I am going out to see my Father's world." Whereupon he would run to the summit of a hill about two miles outside the city and gaze upon the panorama of the combination of Lake Ontario, natural life, and a bird sanctuary where there were forty different varieties of birds. Speaking of the birds, he would say, "I like to hear them raise their carols in praise to God." Upon the return from one of his morning pilgrimages he wrote down his feelings with these lines:

This is my Father's world,
And to my listening ears
All nature sings, and round me rings
The music of the spheres.

Announcement for Next Week's Sermon: If you think freedom is free, you have a lot to learn. Next Sunday would be a good time to start.

Story of the Week: The used car salesman was taking his prospect for a ride in a rather questionable car. Each time he would put it into gear, it would buck and jerk.

"What makes it jerk so whenever it starts up?" the prospect asked.

"Oh, that just shows how much enthusiasm it has. It's anxious to get going," the salesman said.

HOW TO LIVE IN AN EVIL WORLD

The victory is with God, and we do not have to join the forces of evil in order to overcome evil.

There are wolves all around. There are hijackers. There are child molesters. There are drug pushers. There are people in the corporate jungle who are out to get you, stepping over your body. And there are songs actually being played on the radio today that are filled with the spirit of suicide. Did you know that? There are wolves out there, no question about it. Jesus' warning is to "be wise as serpents" (Matthew 10:16). We must be wise, sensible, and thoughtful. We have to take seriously the evil of the world and take steps to protect ourselves. We need to screen the television programs our children watch. We need to check out the families to whose homes they go to play. We need to be alert all the time about the wolves out there. I don't know how one survives in the corporate jungle, but perhaps one needs to keep records of things, perhaps one needs a third person when saying certain things. I don't know. But the Christian religion, which the world dismisses as being unrealistic, is the only realistic way of looking at life, because we believe in the reality of evil in the world. And we believe in sanctified common sense, in taking steps to protect ourselves against the evil. The evil out there is real and we do have to take steps to protect ourselves.

"Do not be overcome by evil" (Romans 12:21). This is the point at which the enemy gets us again and again and again. Someone comes at us in a nasty spirit and we succumb. We answer in kind. We descend to his or her level. We use his or her techniques. And we have already lost the battle, because the battle wasn't with that person. The battle was with the spirit in which he or she approached us.

Paul wrote to the Ephesians, "For we wrestle not against flesh and blood, but against principalities, against powers, against the rulers of the darkness of this world, against spiritual wickedness in high places" (6:12 KJV). The enemy is spiritual;

that we Christians know and believe. The world doesn't want to believe that evil is spiritual, but it is. The enemy is a spiritual foe, not one of flesh and blood. The battle of life is a spiritual battle between the power of evil and the power of good. It is very unfortunate that in our English tradition we do not say the Lord's Prayer the way it is said in most countries: "Lead us not into temptation, but deliver us from the evil one." In the Greek, the noun for "the evil one" is masculine, not neuter. In French, it's "le Malin." In many languages, the word is translated as "the evil one." And that's what it really means, our spiritual enemy. The week before the hostage crisis in Beirut occurred, the United States Supreme Court overturned a Connecticut law. When the Connecticut legislature opened up the Sabbath Day to commerce, they passed a law that if any employee who, for reasons of conscience, did not want to work on the Sabbath, he or she had to be excused. By a vote of eight to one the Supreme Court overturned that law.

If nothing is sacred, nothing is sacred. Our liberties are mere pieces of paper, if those who have power over those pieces of paper have no fear of God in their hearts. When we read in the newspaper about such injustices as that above, we hit the ceiling. And we are out to get those justices of the Supreme Court and so on and so on. Then there are hijackings and we all hit the ceiling. We want blood. Well, we can get blood, but usually it is the wrong blood. When American troops were withdrawn from Beirut, we didn't want to appear to be weak so we ordered a naval bombardment, and since we thought that the Shiites were responsible for the death of the Marines, we aimed at their shanty towns. They are the bottom people in the social scale in Lebanon. The one who did the dirty work at the Marine barracks was killed during the bombing, so we didn't get him. Someone who had worked at the American University in Beirut wrote an account of the times. Students were awakened one morning by an explosion in the building across the street. The reason the building was being bombed is that there was a bar in the building. Shiites are very pious Moslems. To them liquor is an evil; therefore, you must blow up bars.

That's the temptation for religious people, to destroy the evil. But you destroy people in the process and add to the evil. The enemy is not people. The enemy is the Devil, the spirit of evil, the spirit of vindictiveness in this world. The Bible says that it's all right to be angry: "Be angry but do not sin; do not let the sun go down on your anger" (Ephesians 4:26). But nowhere does the Bible say that vengeance, vindictiveness, and retaliation are right. They are never right; scripture is very clear on this. And when we descend to the level of vindictiveness and getting back, we have left our Christian faith and have gone the way of the world. We have to choose which way we want to go in this life.

"Do not be overcome by evil, but overcome evil with good," wrote Paul in Romans 12:21. Jesus said, "Be . . . innocent as doves" (Matthew 10:16). We take steps to defend ourselves the best we can. We set up a legal system so that criminals will be punished, not to get back at them, but to protect society and deter crime. The desire to get back at people—even the joy we have in seeing the bully taken care of—is from Satan. We cannot rejoice in any man's death if we're Christians.

Only by God's grace can we enter into the heart of Jesus. When the guards were mistreating Corrie ten Boom's sister in the concentration camp, Corrie picked up a shovel and started to hit one of them. But her sister said, "No, show them Jesus." And when the guards beat a retarded girl to death for wetting her pants, Corrie's sister said, "These poor people, we must do something for them after the war." She was talking about the guards. Her heart went out to them, because she knew the hell they would face. That's not the way my mind works. It's not the way your mind works, but that is the way of God. And that is the only hope of the world. Lebanon is in the condition it is in today because of retaliation. The philosophy of retaliation creates a jungle in which the innocent suffer and the guilty escape. It only exacerbates the situation, makes it worse. It deepens the hatred. We have in our country a whole frontier, our northern frontier, with peace. And that is not because of our atom bombs or our powerful military forces. It's because of good will. The only power in this world that is real is the power of love. Military power is powerless, as we see in Lebanon right now. Financial power is powerless when we see what can happen to the children of the wealthy. We see intellectual brilliance wasted every day. The power is in Jesus. All the power of the television networks and the broadcast media is organized to keep God from getting glory. And in this whole hostage crisis God has gotten the glory again and again in the lives of ordinary people caught up in the crisis. There was a young man who said, "I have never been out of control before in my life, and this has really made me start thinking about God." We had that wonderful picture of the pilot of the TWA plane, leaning out of the window of the plane with a big smile on his face and speaking about his confidence in God and right next to his ear was a pistol held by one of the terrorists. God is going to get his glory anyway. God is going to win anyway. There is no victory apart from him. If we give in to vindictive revenge, then we are joining the way of the world and choosing the way of the jungle. God will use others to do his will in this world if we refuse. The fourth psalm ends on this note: "Thou alone, O Lord, makest me dwell in safety." There is no safety if we choose the way of retaliation, because "those who take the sword will perish by the sword" (Matthew 26:52). If we think God is on the side of America, we must remember what happened to Judah and Jerusalem when the people would not listen to the prophets. *Amen.*

Nathan Adams
Stanwich Congregational Church
Greenwich, Connecticut

Sunday
July Third

Call to Worship: You did not choose me, but I chose you and appointed you that you should go and bear fruit and that your fruit should abide. *John 15:16*

Processional Hymn: "My Country, 'Tis of Thee"

Invocation: Lord, you have blessed this land with abundance in excess of our highest hopes. Grant that these things may never blind us to the greatest gift of all, the freedom to worship you without fear of interference. Bless this land with your grace and peace. *Amen.*

Sermon Scripture: Galatians 5:13-18

Sermon Presentation: "The Responsibility of Freedom"

Hymn of the Day: "America the Beautiful"

Offertory Scripture: Justice, and only justice, you shall follow, that you may live and inherit the land which the Lord your God gives you. *Deuteronomy 16:20*

Offertory Prayer: Lord, you have dealt with us justly throughout history. Now let us, through these gifts, show our love for justice and mercy. *Amen.*

Prayer of the Day

Lord, I want to be free. It is the one thing I want more than anything else in the world. You have told your people that it is only in knowing the truth that we will be free. By your grace, we will experience a freedom that helps us to rise above the tensions, fears, and anxieties that would enslave us. Today we remember that ours is a nation under God, built on the ideals of freedom and justice for all. But we know that true freedom can never be legislated by the laws we write.

Ignorance, superstition, prejudice, death, handicaps, crime, war, bitterness, anger—these are the things that hold us in bondage and would rob us of our humanity and restrict our growth. But you have promised to make us free.

Your death has given us the freedom that is beyond our ability to achieve by our own efforts. Thanks to you, we will know a freedom that the world cannot give, a freedom that, like your love, is often beyond our understanding, but without which life would be meaningless and hopeless. *Amen.*

Benediction: But the fruit of the Spirit is love, joy, peace, patience, kindness, goodness, faithfulness, gentleness, self-control; against such there is no law. *Galatians 5:22-23*

Recessional Hymn: "The Battle Hymn of the Republic"

Lectionary Lessons: The Sixth Sunday after Pentecost
Lesson 1—II Samuel 7:1-17; Psalm 89:20-37
Lesson 2—II Corinthians 12:1-10
Gospel—Mark 6:1-6

History of the Hymn of the Day: "America the Beautiful"
Katherine Lee Bates, author of "America the Beautiful," daughter of a clergyman, was born in Falmouth, Massachusetts, in 1859. After graduating from Wellesley College she became a full professor of English literature of that college in 1891. While on her way to Colorado Springs to teach in a summer school, she stopped in Chicago during the Columbian Exposition in 1893. The tremendous beauty of the Colorado fruited plains and the "alabaster city" of the World's Fair became the inspiration for writing this hymn. These words have been sung in every corner of the world substituting "Australia" for "America," or when sung in Canada, the refrain reads, "O Canada, O Canada"; even in Africa the missionaries sing, "O Africa, O Africa." But all nations can join and sing together:

God shed his grace on thee,
And crown thy good with brotherhood,
From sea to shining sea.

Announcement for Next Week's Sermon: Is there any romance in the world anymore? Is there any love? If those are your questions, too, you need next Sunday's sermon really bad.

Story of the Week: A businessman had flown in to the city to "go through" one of the nation's most famous medical clinics. After three days of tests and consultation with several doctors, he was told that he was in good shape but that his blood pressure and cholesterol count were a bit too high.

He was happy with the verdict and took a taxi to the airport. The taxi driver was the kind who likes to talk, and he said to the man, "I picked you up at the clinic. Were you there to see a doctor?"

"Yes," the man said, "I came for my annual checkup."

"Well," said the taxi driver, "you look like a healthy businessman except your blood pressure and cholesterol count are probably a bit too high."

THE RESPONSIBILITY OF FREEDOM

> For you were called to freedom, brethren; only do not use your freedom as an opportunity for the flesh, but through love be servants of one another. For the whole law is fulfilled in one word, "You shall love your neighbor as yourself." (Galatians 5:13-14)

One of the most precious words in our language is *freedom.* When we hear this word, our minds race back through history to dramas of persons chained in dungeons, small children tied to textile machines, to whole nations under the grip of a tyrant. On an even higher level, the bondage of the human mind under ignorance, superstition, or prejudice excites our horror. For the human body, the limitations of handicaps or the thralldom of disease bring deathly repression. The most devastating tragedy of all is the subjugation of the human spirit, itself. No wonder, then, that like a blazing light out of scripture comes the assurance: "You will know the truth, and the truth will make you free" (John 8:32).

On this annual observance of the signing of the Declaration of Independence, we naturally renew our gratitude for the proclamation that the laws of nature and of nature's God decree the freedom of both the person and the mind. The dimensions of this very precious word, *freedom,* are almost limitless. The possibilities of the free human soul, guided and disciplined only by the love of people, surpass the powers of imagination. I speak here not of the responsibility to secure freedom, nor of the responsibility to defend freedom, but of the responsibility of freedom itself.

Our text suggests a many-faceted splendor. First of all, in a characteristic phrase from Paul, it declares that all of us are called to freedom. For Paul, the word *called* is not a mere invitation, not an impersonal "to whom it may concern" communication. It is addressed to each person as if it were meant for him or her alone. Yet it reaches out to all. This is the conception underlying Paul's notion of God's call to us. Each is singled out. Each is called to the high road of freedom. In Christ the call of God is to all; yet the call is to each person as if he or she were the only recipient.

This call to freedom, to the spacious expansion of the human spirit, was indeed something new, something God in his sheer generosity had given to his children. Thus today in the midst of tensions, fears, and anxieties that concern the very meaning of human existence, we are again called to freedom.

In the second place, we are counseled as to the inner meaning of this freedom. When Paul says, "Only do not use your freedom as an opportunity for the flesh," he is pointing out that freedom fundamentally is positive, not negative, not a mere absence of restraints. There are really two opposing reasons why people want to be free from restraints. One is to escape discipline, so that in reality they are not corrected, guided, or challenged. The other reason is a higher aspiration to exceed mediocre norms, so that greater and greater challenges may be accepted, greater and greater responsibilities may be engaged. There is no question as to the kind of freedom that Paul has in mind. It is one that reaches out to the highest challenge. It underlies our entire conception of personal morality, social obligation, political democracy, or the full fruition of the spirit of God kindling the spirit of people. Christian freedom, therefore, turns out not to be less demanding, but more demanding than rigid and detailed prescriptions of behavior.

We may well inquire today how well we have been exhibiting the spacious possibilities of our freedom. For example, in education, freedom has laid great emphasis on the "development of growing persons"; in marriage our freedom prescribes that marriage is for love, that above all it should foster the growth of affection and mutuality; in government, freedom decrees that the preservation of rights, privileges, and opportunities of the individual member of society is the first duty of political society; in Christian faith freedom has stimulated us into a splendid preoccupation with every endeavor that fosters the development of the personality. Never in the history of the world has so much of both money and effort been invested in religious education. Never before have religious forces concentrated so much attention on the ways and means of changing environmental conditions inimical to human development. Never has there been such an array of church sponsored agencies—clinics, counseling centers, study groups on "understanding ourselves." Yet we have to confess in sorrow that all too often we lack the inner compulsion that requires us to invest this freedom in undiscourageable dedication to the purpose of God in us. Too many times we take refuge in the contention that, "My life is my own private affair."

In the third place, we have to ask if this elevated principle of freedom has, within itself, its own corrective. Paul affirms that it does. After taking the high stance that freedom is a call of God, but that it is no sanctuary for mediocrity or irresponsibility, he lays down the firm affirmative that for freedom to have its full sway it has to be boosted by the compulsive pull of God's love upon us and by the consequent love for our fellow associates. This is no mere moral action that simply says the highest good of society is for each person to be concerned about the welfare of others. It actually encompasses the whole growth of the human spirit to its newly discovered possibilities. We may point out that the story of evolution has been, stage by stage, the emergence of mind to take control of the body. In a similar way, the development of our faith and our relationship to God means the emergence of a new people under the control of the Spirit of God. Our greatest achievement of human worth can be gained only by the recognition of compelling higher authorities, not by the renunciation of discipline. To understand the immense complexities of the world within which we live and the world beyond our mental horizons, now challenges the greatest capacities of the human mind. No statute or constitution could compel such dedication and devotion to scientific inquiry on a cosmic level as now engages people the world over. No legal command can bring us to the devotion and faithfulness of one person to another equal to that which recognizes the inspiring obligation expressed in the hymn: "I would be true, for there are those who trust me."

In the last analysis, no law can possibly compel the inner spirit of a person to the dedication which his own inner sense of duty dictates. In John Masefield's play *Escape,* the principal character, Mat Dennet, is convicted of an offense for which he is imprisoned, but he and his friends affirm that he is not guilty and that justice has miscarried. The play concerns itself with Mat Dennet's escape from prison. Its scenes range over fields, through villages, through the homes of friends, and finally to a church whose rector remembers the case, feels that justice has been thwarted, and consents to give refuge to the escaped Dennet. When the police arrive, the rector, by subtle evasion, is able to divert the search elsewhere. Then the moment of drama emerges. Just when physically he is at last free, Dennet comes from hiding and gives himself up. He explains to the rector that "it is one's decent self one cannot escape."

Not until that same compelling discipline of compulsive love gives us a new vision of servanthood can we really bring to maturity our precious heritage of freedom. *Amen.*

Forrest C. Weir
United Church of Christ, retired
Pacific Palisades, California

Sunday July Tenth

Call to Worship: There are friends who pretend to be friends, but there is a friend who sticks closer than a brother.

Proverbs 18:24

Processional Hymn: "Love Divine, All Loves Excelling"

Invocation: Lord, we need some romance and some love in our lives. We can't go on from one drab day to another. Something has to happen once in a while to turn us on. Let it be your presence and your love. *Amen.*

Sermon Scripture: I Corinthians 13:1-13

Sermon Presentation: "Is There Any Romance?"

Hymn of the Day: "I Love to Tell the Story"

Offertory Scripture: Since, therefore, we are now justified by his blood, much more shall we be saved by him from the wrath of God. *Romans 5:9*

Offertory Prayer: Lord, grant that as you have saved us from sin and death, we may respond with these gifts to say thank you for your mercy. *Amen.*

Prayer of the Day

Lord, is there any love left in the world? Oh, we use the word *love* a great deal. Actually, we are misusing and abusing it a great deal.

We confuse love with infatuation. We equate love with sex. We tell people, "If you love me, you'll do it my way."

Ours is a world in which loneliness, alienation, and separation are all too often not the exception, but the rule. Even you, Lord, knew loneliness. Hanging on the cross, you felt that everyone, even your heavenly Father, had forsaken you.

To be a follower of yours, you said that we must love God with all of our heart, all of our soul, all of our mind, and we are to love our neighbor as much as we love ourselves. To be the kind of lover that you want us to be involves so much risk, Lord.

We would pray that you would make us receptive and open to your love, a love so great that God sent his Son into our world to die so that we could live. Then help us to reach out to others, loving them in a way that says, "I truly care for you. I want what is best for you."

Teach us to love, Lord, as you love us. *Amen.*

Benediction: Without having seen him you love him; though you do not now see him you believe in him and rejoice with unutterable and exalted joy. *I Peter 1:8*

Recessional Hymn: "I Love Thy Kingdom, Lord"

Lectionary Lessons: The Seventh Sunday after Pentecost
Lesson 1—II Samuel 7:18-29; Psalm 132:11-18
Lesson 2—Ephesians 1:1-10
Gospel—Mark 6:7-13

History of the Hymn of the Day: "I Love to Tell the Story"
Katherine Hankey was thirty-two years old when she wrote the hymn "I Love to Tell the Story." It arose out of a deep desire in her heart to tell the simple gospel story wherever she was in life. First, it was in the Sunday school of Clapham, England, where she became a devoted, refined consecrated woman. Then, it was in the heart of Africa, where she spent most of her life, giving the sales of all her writings to missions. Finally, it was in the hospitals of London, where she spent the last minutes of her life telling lonely patients of God's beautiful love. When Katherine Hankey wrote "I Love to Tell the Story" in 1866, she was doing more than expressing a feeling in her own being, she was projecting that same feeling into the minds of thousands of people through the years who would sing her song and receive the same challenge.

I love to tell the story, Of unseen things above,
Of Jesus and His glory, Of Jesus and His love,
I love to tell the story, Because I know 'tis true
It satisfies my longings, As nothing else can do.

Announcement for Next Week's Sermon: Did you ever get talked into a job at church that you really did not think you could do? You're not alone. Amos was made a prophet, and he did not want to do it. Next week you can sympathize with this reluctant prophet.

Story of the Week: The Congressman was addressing a group at a political rally and was quoting famous men right and left. "And as Daniel Webster says in his great unabridged dictionary . . . "

"Hold it," a voice in the audience called out, "Noah wrote the dictionary."

"I know what I'm talking about," the Congressman shouted. "Noah is the man who built the ark."

IS THERE ANY ROMANCE?

A pastor was serving in a hospital chaplain training program and assigned to the Intensive and Cardiac Care Unit. When he reported for work one day, the head nurse suggested he visit a new patient. Her name was Margaret. She was seventy-two years old, and she had attempted suicide by taking an overdose of pills.

Margaret was in a private section of the unit. The light in her room was off. The pastor paused at the door before entering her room, for he heard a hushed voice. She had seen his approach and was speaking. "Is there any romance? Is there any love?"

He was unprepared for this. He walked to the bedside. Margaret reached up and touched his face and hair. She spoke again, "Is there any romance in the world anymore? Is there any love?"

Margaret is an example of the truth that humans are relational creatures who suffer when they do not experience love from other humans. The absence of love, felt so deeply by an older woman, and the resultant loneliness represent grave problems in society.

Ours can be a very lonely world! Separation, estrangement, being without love are the terms defining loneliness. Suicide, drug addiction, alcoholism, sexual abuse, promiscuity, and human exploitation are serious matters with no simple causes. But loneliness is at or near the core of each of these problems.

Loneliness is not limited to those who have the easily identifiable problems. Everyone experiences this emotion in some degree, because loneliness is the result of sin. Thus understood, everyone, even those of us within the church, shares the universal experience of loneliness.

A solution to loneliness is not likely to come until there is an admission of its universality. Loneliness is not isolated in the outside world. Loneliness is alive in our midst.

But many of us are unwilling to admit our loneliness. It's unchristian, we say. Christians are strong. Christians are people of high calling. By so stating, we ignore the Christ of the cross, who yelled out, "My God, My God, why have you forsaken me?" By hiding our feelings, we pretend. By pretending, we shut off honest relationships with others and increase the loneliness.

So let us be honest with ourselves. There is a problem called loneliness, and all of us experience it! In pursuit of a solution, we discover that the answer to the loneliness of the world and of our own experience is the same. Margaret's lonely feelings were expressed when she said, "Is there any romance? Is there any love?" Yes, there is. Whenever someone enters into Margaret's life in a caring way, that person will have resolved Margaret's loneliness as well as his or her own. Loneliness wanes as love increases.

We who are the church are called to be a people of caring love. We follow the Christ of the cross, who shows us the vulnerability of the love of God and summons us to love in the same manner. The Christian style of life is summarized in two ideas: understanding the costly nature of God's love and then loving others in the same way God loves us.

To cure loneliness means to (in a caring way) love! To love, Christian style, is to be vulnerable. Vulnerability begins when you and I are ourselves, without pretense. Christ loves us as we are. We need not repress our feelings or change our personalities. We need only to care.

Since we are so loved, then our caring for others should be in the same fashion. We must care for people as they are, without any effort to change them. We should identify sympathetically or empathetically, because we, too, know the gamut of human emotions and pain.

There are Margarets all over this world. They seek love, and they are satisfied quite easily. Just let them know you care. Most of the time, that's sufficient.

An ancient parable describes the creation of mankind. Care took a bit of clay and began to shape it. Jupiter saw what was being done and gave spirit to the form. Then Care and Jupiter began to argue over a name. Soon Earth entered the disagreement, because the clay belonged to the Earth. Matters were getting out of hand when Saturn arrived with an offer of arbitration. "The issue is to whom does the creation belong," said Saturn. "Well, Jupiter gave it spirit and will receive the spirit at death. Earth gave the clay and will receive the body at death. But Care first shaped the creature and shall possess it as long as it loves." Life is given over to caring. The Margarets of the world plea for someone to care enough to share their pain. They are within and without the church. Help them!

Let your caring love be honest. Most people do not expect to receive answers to their problems. They merely want to know they are not alone, that some other human being has similar concerns.

Let your caring love be expressed by honest involvement. To be a Christian is to have the extraordinary freedom to share the burdens of the daily, common, ambiguous, transient, perishing existence of others, even to the point of actually taking the place of another, whether that person be powerful or weak, in health or in sickness, clothed or naked, educated or illiterate, secure or persecuted, complacent or despondent, proud or forgotten, housed or houseless, fed or hungry, at liberty or in prison, young or old, white or black, rich or poor.

If there is to be any love, any romance in this world, we Christians must become involved in a caring way. But do not think this is easy. Caring love is risky!

A minister tells of a woman he once met. She explained that her marriage was failing. She and her husband never quarreled, were never angry, they just had no relationship. The husband came home from work, ate dinner, watched television, read the paper, and went to bed. Every night for years this was the pattern.

Under questioning by the pastor, the woman related how she kept inviting her husband to a prayer group, and how she left religious books and pamphlets on the tables at home, hoping he would read them. Nothing worked. So the pastor suggested, "Why don't you try something radical and costly to you? This is what the cross is all about. You must be vulnerable for your husband in the same way that Christ on the cross was vulnerable for you. Some night (out of the blue) when he's watching television, why don't you put on your flimsiest lace nightie and your best perfume, jump into his lap and ruffle his hair and tell him you love him as much as ever. What do you think his response would be?"

She giggled.

"But what's the worst thing that might happen if you took this step in faith?"

She replied, "He might laugh at me. That would hurt more than anything I can think of."

"This is what faith in Christ is all about," said the minister, "lived out in the dimension of marriage . . . to do something like this gives him the chance to respond lovingly or with hostility. Is your faith in Christ sufficient to enable you to take such a risk?"

A few days passed, and a letter reached the pastor. It read, "Dear Pastor, I did what you suggested, and guess what? He didn't laugh." Remember, please, that he could have laughed. That's the risk of caring love.

The vulnerability we express is to be united with affirmation. Caring love is best illustrated by the cross on which Christ gave himself in an act that affirms the worth of humanity in the sight of God.

The entire ministry of Jesus was the same way. He affirmed the strength and the potential of twelve ordinary men. He affirmed the value of Zaccheus and Nicodemus and the woman caught in adulterous activity. His love showed others that they were important.

The same must be true of us. There is no love when we become indifferent toward others. There is no love when we flatter and manipulate. There is no love when we are critical without justification.

The principal of a school met the buses each morning and sent them off every afternoon. There were over four hundred children in the school, and that principal knew the first names of all of them. He spoke to them; he teased them; he helped them. His attitude had an effect on his staff, who became much like him. A young man who hated school became an excellent student. Why? This principal called him by name and affirmed his worth. The results were amazing!

Yes, if there is to be love in this world, we followers of Christ are called upon to give it. Love Christian style is found in affirming, vulnerable, caring actions toward other people. When someone loves that way, he or she runs a terrible risk. Jesus loved like that. He ended his life on a cross.

Margaret asked, "Is there any love?" Her loneliness led her to a suicide attempt. That's not only unfortunate, but also it is unnecessary. She needed the help of caring love that Christians should be giving.

July Tenth

A few days after his first meeting with Margaret, the pastor learned she had been moved to another room in the hospital. During this time, her two sisters and one brother had come to be with her. They had not visited for years.

He stood again at the doorway to her new room and heard her say to her family, "Oh, I didn't try to kill myself. . . . It was an accident." In disbelief, he looked at her. She was smiling. She looked lovely. She was happy. And why not? Her family had come to fill the void of loneliness with a caring love.

What a great ending to a possible sad story, unless that family returns to their normal ways once Margaret is home. Without love, she will be lonely once more. Without love, she will have another "accident."

There are scores of people named Margaret. Some are right here among us. They plead, "Is there any romance? Is there any love?" We have the answer! *Amen.*

Frederick L. Parish
Bethel United Methodist Church
Woodbridge, Virginia

Sunday
July Seventeenth

Call to Worship: So we are ambassadors for Christ, God making his appeal through us. We beseech you on behalf of Christ, be reconciled to God. For our sake he made him to be sin who knew no sin, so that in him we might become the righteousness of God. *II Corinthians 5:20-21*

Processional Hymn: "Lead On, O King Eternal"

Invocation: O God, too often we hear your call to go and do your will. We want to help, but we have very busy lives. Make us willing workers who say, "Here am I; send me." *Amen.*

Sermon Scripture: Amos 7:10-15

Sermon Presentation: "The Reluctant Prophet"

Hymn of the Day: "Just as I Am, Without One Plea"

Offertory Scripture: Let us hold fast the confession of our hope without wavering, for he who promised is faithful.

Hebrews 10:23

Offertory Prayer: We must be willing, and we must be faithful. Make us willing and faithful givers of all that we have to your glory. *Amen.*

Prayer of the Day

Lord, are you really calling me to be your disciple—your spokesperson—your representative—your partner in ministry? Do you really want me? I know you could find someone better. I'm not really prepared to take on the awesome responsibility of speaking your word, being your witness, bringing your message of hope and peace to those I meet. But you call us to a partnership in ministry. You stand by our sides, guiding our actions and inspiring our words.

We look to the past and see how you called some unlikely people to your service. Jonah was so reluctant. Moses could not speak clearly. Matthew was a tax collector and a social outcast. Paul was a persecutor of Christians.

Let us never forget that you take us as we are and make us worthy of our calling. Call us! Guide us! Inspire us! May ours be the calling, but yours the glory. *Amen.*

Benediction: I am the vine, you are the branches. He who abides in me, and I in him, he it is that bears much fruit, for apart from me you can do nothing. . . . As the Father has loved me, so have I loved you; abide in my love. *John 15:5, 9*

Recessional Hymn: "O Zion, Haste"

Lectionary Lessons: The Eighth Sunday after Pentecost
Lesson 1—II Samuel 11:1-15; Psalm 53
Lesson 2—Ephesians 2:11-22
Gospel—Mark 6:30-34

History of the Hymn of the Day: "Just as I Am, Without One Plea"
At the age of thirty-three, Charlotte Elliott, because of the pressure of a musical education, had become a helpless invalid. She developed a bitter and rebellious spirit. One evening at her home, while being visited by Dr. Cesar Malan, a noted Swiss minister and musician, the frustrated woman inquired of the noted clergyman with despair, "How do you become a Christian?" He replied, "You pray this prayer: O God, I come to you just as I am." Fourteen years later in 1836, Miss Elliott, reminiscing about the evening with Dr. Malan, wrote her famous seven-stanza poem which began:

Just as I am, without one plea,
But that thy blood was shed for me.

Announcement for Next Week's Sermon: Did it ever occur to you that you should enjoy God? I enjoy a good dinner or a good piece of candy, but enjoy God? I never thought of God in that way. I know I will next Sunday.

Story of the Week: A woman shopper went into a meat market and ordered two pounds of hamburger.
The clerk yelled at the butcher, "Two pounds of enthusiasm."
"Why do you call it enthusiasm?" the shopper asked.
"Because he puts everything he's got into it," the clerk said.

THE RELUCTANT PROPHET

The book of Amos might better be entitled "The Reluctant Prophet." But then again, most prophets are reluctant about their tasks.

There was a showdown between the court priest Amaziah and Amos. Amaziah was King Jeroboam's chief assistant. He was the mouthpiece of the king, who believed that he was also the mouthpiece of God. So you can understand why neither the king, nor Amaziah wanted the likes of this stranger from Judea. Amos was a threat to both Amaziah and Jeroboam, because Amos claimed to speak for the Lord. If, indeed, Amos was God's mouthpiece, then there were some very hard times ahead for the Northern Kingdom, Israel.

There were many itinerant false prophets in those days, going around making a living off the fears and superstitions of the people. Amaziah considered Amos a charlatan and ordered him to take his dog and pony show some place else. When Amaziah called Amos a prophet, he was using it in a pejorative sense.

Amos' response to Jeroboam and Amaziah was straightforward: "I am not a prophet, or one of the sons of the prophets. I am a herdsman and a dresser of sycamore trees." Amos was an ordinary sort of person, who was chosen to be God's messenger. And so Amos spoke God's word to those who would rather not hear it.

Jesus sent out those whom he had called. But Jesus sent them apparently frightfully unprepared. All they were given was authority "over the unclean spirits." That is to say, they were given authority over all the manifestations of evil of their day which they knew or which they might encounter. One theologian has suggested that those unclean spirits today could be likened to cancer and/or nuclear weapons. Words to speak, and One to witness to was about all the disciples were given. Jesus charged them to take no bag (that is a begging bag), no money, nor were they to wear shoes, only sandals. This is a spartan list for such a large task.

There is a story told about God's choosing the common, the ordinary, and making it extraordinary. It is also a story about trust, radical trust. When God commissions someone, he or she carries the promises and Word of God, but little more.

This story can be a "Once upon a time . . . " or "Just the other day . . . " story. However, we can be more involved and a part of the story if it begins:

A long time ago and far, far away, there lived a modest shoemaker named Damon. He was an ordinary sort of fellow. He made good shoes. They weren't the best, but then again they weren't the worst either. No one would have ever said his shoes were on the cutting edge of fashion, because they were not. His styles were very middle-of-the-road, which made him quite popular with all the other average people in his town.

Damon was not an adventurer. He traveled only once in a while to the neighboring fairs. He was always interested in what were the latest fashions in shoes. Occasionally, he would even sell his own middle-of-the-road wares at these fairs. But by and large, he went to them out of curiosity and was always happy to return home.

Damon made it a practice not to draw attention to himself. He was no different from you and me, for when we get right down to it, outside of our mind's eye, all of us are pretty much average as well. We, too, are curious about new and different things, but most of us truly do not want to call too much attention to ourselves either.

The quiet life-style of Damon was brought to an abrupt halt. One day, there he was, minding his own business when all of a sudden, wham! Things were never the same again.

Damon was out in front of his shop one day sweeping the walk. Now this was not unusual, because Damon swept the walk every morning before he opened. Damon was a very clean person. Now, he wasn't a fanatic or anything. It was just that he liked to have things neat and tidy, and that included the walk outside his little shop. Now, getting back to our story, on this particular day, he was sweeping the walk, when out of nowhere somebody with a very hurried look on his face walked right into Damon. This other guy just wasn't looking where he was going, and he bowled Damon right over.

"So there you are. I've been looking all over for you," the stranger said to Damon.

"I beg your pardon, are you talking to me, sir?" Damon asked.

"Why of course I'm talking to you. You don't see anyone else here on the walk, do you?"

"Well, no," replied Damon. "But you said you've been looking for me?"

"That's right, kid. I have an important message for you from the king and queen."

"How can that be?" asked Damon. "I don't even know the royal family."

"Well, they know you. And they think that you will be just perfect for the job!"

"You've got to be kidding. I'm not perfect for any job. There are lots of better shoemakers in town. Why don't you call on one of them?"

"No, kid. You've got it all wrong. The king and queen do not want you for a shoemaker. They want you to come and stay with them, and, are you ready for this, they want you to be the Royal Court Jester."

"Now there has got to be some kind of mistake. I'm no jester. I'm a shoemaker."

The man who bumped into Damon would not take no for an answer. So with a little more prodding and persuasion, he was able to get Damon to accompany him to meet the king and queen.

Now, the account of how Damon settled into the court and his first few days as jester, well, that is a complete story in itself. Suffice it to say that after a period of adjustment for Damon, he came to like his role in the royal court. He started to see truly how much the king and queen really did enjoy his company. Little did he realize that in this transition period, the king and queen were carefully instructing him and teaching him the ways of the realm. In time, Damon began to recognize how the king and queen carried out their business.

It was at this time, when Damon realized how things were handled, that another surprise announcement came. The royal couple called him into their chambers and announced to him that he was to become an ambassador. Well, you know how the conversation went. Damon pleaded that he was but a simple shoemaker. He said that he was not skilled in the affairs of state. And his main argument was that he, now a professional fool, could never be a representative of the king and queen. Who would respect such a lowly character sent off with such a lofty mission? Certainly they could find someone more suitable for the job.

Naturally, the royal family convinced Damon that he indeed was their choice. They wanted him to be an Earth Shaker, a Care Taker, a Life Saver, a Risk Taker, and a Joy Maker. Bolstered by the encouragement from the royal family, Damon departed as their ambassador. He left with nothing more than promises and memories. So equipped, he ventured boldly into his new task. Eventually, Damon trusted the king and queen's decision. He trusted their words, and he had faith in what he had been taught. And so equipped with those memories and promises, he set out as their ambassador.

Now, there were many who thought it odd of the king and queen to choose a fool, a shoemaker, to carry out their work, but that was their way. They called, chose, and commissioned the fool, the weakling, the unlikely one to do the surprising, the unexpected, the miraculous.

Friends, we, too, are being sent as ambassadors. Like Amos, like the twelve, and like Damon, we are sent. We go with a feeling of being unprepared. We set off feeling that surely there is someone, anyone, more qualified for the job. Yet we are the ones who have been chosen! And like Damon, we carry with us memories of the past and promises for the future. In our Christian faith, those memories of the past and promises of the future are very, very important to us. The memories remind us of who we are and of where we have been. The promises tell us where we are going. The memories and promises of the faith bind us to all other people of faith, those before us and those to come. And it is through worship and fellowship that our past and future come together in the present. Because of a cross and the promises made, we, too, are sent out to bear God's news, to be God's ambassadors. We are to share God's story, which has become our story, as we recount memories and remember promises.

Now, there are some who might think it odd of God to choose such people as you and me to bear that message and to carry out God's ministry. But that is grace—God calling, choosing, and commissioning the fool, the weakling, the shoemaker, the teacher, the mother, the architect, and the doctor to do the surprising, the miraculous, and the unexpected. God calling, choosing, and commissioning you and me to be ambassadors.

You have been called, chosen, and sent. Leave this worship and fellowship refreshed and ready to bear God's news, to tell the story of memories of a cross and empty grave and promises of crosses and empty graves to come. *Amen.*

Scot E. Sorensen
Mt. Carmel Lutheran Church
San Luis Obispo, California

Sunday
July Twenty-fourth

Call to Worship: He hath showed thee, O man, what is good; and what doth the Lord require of thee, but to do justly, and to love mercy, and to walk humbly with thy God. *Micah 6:8 KJV*

Processional Hymn: "Jesus Calls Us O'er the Tumult"

Invocation: What a great discovery! We are supposed to enjoy God forever. We can love him. We can serve him. We can work for him, but we are also supposed to enjoy him. Thank you, Lord, for your friendship. *Amen.*

Sermon Scripture: Luke 10:38-42

Sermon Presentation: "Enjoying God"

Hymn of the Day: "My Hope Is Built"

Offertory Scripture: I beseech you therefore, brethren, by the mercies of God, that ye present your bodies a living sacrifice, holy, acceptable unto God, which is your reasonable service. *Romans 12:1 KJV*

Offertory Prayer: We come before thee, Lord, filled with joy. We really need to feel your joy, not just fear, and love you. Accept these gifts as an outpouring of our joy. *Amen.*

Prayer of the Day

Lord, the greatest question in our world is: "Why?" *Why* do we walk upright? *Why* do we breathe air? *Why* are roses red and violets blue? *Why* were we made by you? What is our purpose? What is our ultimate goal?

Oh, we could simply use words that have been used so often before—words like glorify you, serve you—but enjoy you? That's something to think about. We are used to enjoying things—pizza, hot dogs, great music, our favorite television show. But enjoying you and your presence in our lives is something new to us.

We rush around at a frantic pace. We fuss about so many things. Sometimes we even become anxious about things that we don't understand or over which we have no control.

But, Lord, let us never forget that the most important thing we can ever have is our relationship with you. It is in trusting you with our lives that we can find real security. In doing your will, we can find the true meaning of our lives.

Open our hearts, our minds, and our lives to you and the fullness that you promise to each of us, your children. *Amen.*

Benediction: And be not conformed to this world: but be ye transformed by the renewing of your mind, that ye may prove what is that good, and acceptable, and perfect will of God.

Romans 12:2 KJV

Recessional Hymn: "O Jesus, I Have Promised"

Lectionary Lessons: The Ninth Sunday after Pentecost

Lesson 1—II Samuel 12:1-14; Psalm 32
Lesson 2—Ephesians 3:14-21
Gospel—John 6:1-15

History of the Hymn of the Day: "My Hope Is Built"

Before Edward Mote became a Baptist minister in England, he was an ordinary laborer in London. Here are his words regarding the writing of his hymn, "One morning as I went to work I thought I would write a hymn on the experience of being a Christian." Before the day was finished, he had not only completed his hymn, but had sung it at a neighbor's house where much spiritual comfort was received from its content. Later, in 1836, it was published in a volume called *Hymns of Praise.*

Announcement for Next Week's Sermon: Did you ever need to just get away from it all for a little while, just to be alone? How do you get away without feeling guilty?

Story of the Week: A church installed a set of electronic chimes, the kind that work from a tape and with speakers that have adjustable volume control. The plan was to mount the speakers in the tower of the church and play sacred music every Sunday afternoon. To make sure that they were not playing too loud, several teams from the church checked with the people in the neighborhood during the first concert. One of the deacons rang a doorbell and the lady of the house came to the door.

The deacon said, "I'm here from the . . ."

"What did you say?" the woman asked.

"I said I am here from the church, and . . ."

And the lady said, "I'm sorry but you'll have to talk louder. I can't hear a word you are saying on account of those darn chimes."

ENJOYING GOD

What is the chief end of man? This question begins the Westminster Confession of Faith. It's a great question, for it seems to sum up all the other questions anyone might ever have. Where are we going? What are we doing? What will I do with my life? All of our wants, needs, and desires are summed up in one question. What is our goal? What should we aim at? What is it that will make us happy?

The answer the confessional writers of the Reformed church offer is surprising, surprising, yet profound. It seems to suggest that there might be a whole new dimension to this age-old question. The chief end of man, they tell us, "is to glorify God and to enjoy him forever."

The idea of enjoying God is one that we just don't seem to think about. It doesn't seem to be in our natures to think of God as being enjoyable. On the one hand, we speak of the beatific vision, the idea that being in the presence of God brings us pleasures unmatched by anything that we will ever know. Yet, we seem to be lacking in expressions to convey the idea that we can experience God in the here and now, and that this presence can be just as beautiful, and just as enjoyable as any that is promised to come. It is almost as if we are afraid to admit that we do enjoy God.

The psalmist wasn't afraid when he proclaimed: "All the nations thou hast made shall come and bow down before thee, O Lord, and shall glorify thy name. For thou art great and doest wondrous things, thou alone art God. . . . I will give thanks to thee, O Lord my God, with my whole heart, and I will glorify thy name for ever" (Psalm 86:9-10, 12).

Neither was Paul the least bit afraid to urge the congregation at Rome: "That ye may with one mind and one mouth glorify God, even the Father of our Lord Jesus Christ. Wherefore receive ye one another, as Christ also received us, to the glory of God" (Romans 15:6-7 KJV).

Christ receives us "to the glory of God," and the episode with Mary and Martha sheds great light on this often troubling concept in a personal, revealing way.

All of us, I am sure, have been in situations in which hosts or hostesses have been like Martha. They so desperately desire to please that they seem to be unable to relax and enjoy themselves. They rush and fuss and cook. They ask countless times whether they can get us anything. And while our slightest wishes may be their commands, we always get the feeling that they are far more interested in the preparations than they are in us.

Martha went through quite a lot in preparation for Jesus' visit. It was a big deal to have their friend for dinner, and there is little doubt that the preparations were extensive. It was also an opportunity to have Jesus all to themselves, without the crowds, without the other disciples, without anything to deprive them of his company.

However, Martha's preparations continue on even after the honored guest arrived. One can almost feel her tension mount. Just watch how she buzzed about. She was torn between wanting to be with Jesus and trying to impress him with her culinary creativity.

Then there was her sister, Martha. She just sat and chatted, gossiping with her friend. The table still needed to be set; the wine still needed to be poured; even the vegetables needed stirring, and Martha's sister just went right on "chatting with Jesus."

All this became too much for Martha, and she asked Jesus to intervene. Perhaps she had already tried on her own to secure Mary's help and had failed. Now she requested her guest's help in getting her sister to do her fair share of the work.

Jesus showed the greatest concern for Martha, but not in the way she expected. Intead of chastising Mary, he lovingly invited Martha to "forget the veggies" and come and join them. He kindly reached out to her and told her to relax. "Martha, Martha," he lovingly said, "you are troubled by many things." He could see the stress and strain all the commotion had placed upon her. He saw and respected all the trouble she had gone through for him. But, for all her preparations, she had unintentionally done something else. She had deprived him of her presence.

Does that surprise you? You probably expected me to say that she deprived herself of his presence. Yes, that is so, but it is not all. You see, Jesus wanted to be with her, too, to speak with her, to listen to her as well as to have her listen to him. Their fellowship was to be a mutual one.

A friend of mine was invited to a girl's birthday party when he was about eight or nine. He was at that awkward stage that all boys go through when they are not sure whether they should like girls, and they don't know how the other guys on the block are going to react to doing something as "sissy" as going to a girl's birthday party. So, in order to avoid going he devised an elaborate plan: He bought a beautiful gift that took up his entire allowance and some savings. It was, by far, the most expensive gift at the party. He then sent the gift to the party with his sister. He was sure that he was off the hook.

The next day in school he ran into the birthday girl. She was angry, and he was puzzled. "What's the matter?" he asked. "didn't you like my present?"

"I didn't want your present," she replied. "I wanted you." She didn't want his present; she wanted his presence.

This is what Jesus is telling us about God through the persons of Mary and Martha. The "good portion" is ours through our relationship with God, which comes through our encounter with Jesus Christ. Here, in Christ, God has chosen to be with us. God has, by becoming one of us, chosen to sit at a human table. God enters into our lives in a real and personal way.

Christ brings us God's ministry of presence, God's presence with us in our joys, concerns, cares, and sorrows. It would be impossible to enjoy God if he were afar off, but in Christ we discover a God who draws near to us and to whom we can relate. The way we enjoy God is to simply follow the example of Mary—to draw close to God's presence so that God can give us what we need, the capacity to trust God with all that we do or say or have.

It is only when we totally trust God that we can enjoy God's glory, taking our problems, whatever they are, and presenting them, yielding them up, to the one who was nailed upon a cross and sharing our joys, great and small, with the one who was raised from the tomb on that "great getting-up morning." It is here that we feel God, through Jesus Christ, closer than anything we could ever hope to enjoy. God continually invites us into his presence, where we might "glorify God and enjoy him forever."

A pastor once told a story about his friend Agnes.

> After a long illness, her beloved husband, Frank, died. While she was recovering from that loss, her eyesight began to fail. The surgeon told her that he could not remedy the disability with further surgery. Added to that, she was hit with a deep concern for a loved one. Problems piled up.
>
> One day she sat down to write God a letter. In her customary

frankness, she told God what she thought about the whole mess and signed her name.

The next day Agnes saw her next-door neighbor. In response to a neighborly, "How's it going?" Agnes relayed some of her problems and that she had told God about them in very clear terms how she was feeling. She told her neighbor about her letter to God. A couple of days later, my friend received a letter. It said:

> Dear Agnes:
> You think you've got problems. I've got a whole universe to run, with people who have problems as big or bigger than yours. But I know and care about you. I will give you what you need to endure. You will have faith to trust Me!
> Love, God

God gives us exactly what we need to enjoy him if we will only draw near and trust him. Then God can open us up to an exciting faith that can proclaim with the psalmist: "Wait on the Lord: be of good courage, and he shall strengthen thine heart: wait, I say, on the Lord" (Psalm 27:14 KJV).

God will always be there, present for us, never too early and never too late. Wait, I say, on the Lord. *Amen.*

David C. Nelson
Mount Pleasant Lutheran Church
Racine, Wisconsin

Sunday
July Thirty-first

Call to Worship: Then they said to him, "What must we do, to be doing the works of God?" Jesus answered them, "This is the work of God, that you believe in him whom he has sent."
John 6:28-29

Processional Hymn: "I Need Thee Every Hour"

Invocation: Lord, let us work for you and your kingdom. We are your hands; we are your feet; we are your voice. Show us the work to be done, and we will do it to make your kingdom come. *Amen.*

Sermon Scripture: Mark 6:30-34

Sermon Presentation: "It's Your Day Off, But . . . "

Hymn of the Day: "Now the Day Is Over"

Offertory Scripture: What does it profit, my brethren, if a man says he has faith but has not works? Can his faith save him? . . . So faith by itself, if it has no works, is dead. But some one will say, "You have faith and I have works." Show me your faith apart from your works, and I by my works will show you my faith. *James 2:14, 17-18*

Offertory Prayer: Lord, are we saved by faith or works? You have told us that one without the other is dead. Accept these offerings as our faith at work. *Amen.*

Prayer of the Day

Lord, chaos! Uncertainty! Disorder! These things seem to be the characteristics of the world in which we live. We look for leaders to show us the "way" to peace, prosperity, and wholeness. But all too often we become disillusioned and discouraged by leaders who are inadequate, corrupt, or self-seeking. They are false prophets, fake messiahs, and unworthy shepherds.

But in you, Jesus, we find one who is worthy of the title the "Good Shepherd." You alone can bring truth to the confusion and ignorance that is so rampant in our world and causes us so much pain.

You alone provide meaning and purpose to our lives. You show us that we can live together without hostility. You even make peace for us with God, our heavenly Father. In the time of death you stay by our side and guide us through the "valley of the shadow of death" and lead us to the promised land of eternal life. Most important and comforting for us, you never take a day off. *Amen.*

Benediction: Therefore, my beloved brethren, be steadfast, immovable, always abounding in the work of the Lord, knowing that in the Lord your labor is not in vain.

I Corinthians 15:58

Recessional Hymn: "Be Not Dismayed" ("God Will Take Care of You")

Lectionary Lessons: The Tenth Sunday after Pentecost
Lesson 1—II Samuel 12:15*b*-24; Psalm 34:11-22
Lesson 2—Ephesians 4:1-6
Gospel—John 6:24-35

History of the Hymn of the Day: "Now the Day Is Over"
In the quaint village of Calder Valley of Yorkshire, Sabine Baring-Gould, a thirty-one-year-old curate, wrote this hymn especially for his own created "night school." The children of the valley would join in with their parents in asking Gould to tell them stories after their day's labor in the mill. Tirelessly he would tell stories and lead them in songs in his crowded two rooms. Through the chinks in the floor the voices of children would ring out the hymn written for them:

When the morning wakens,
Then may I arise
Pure, and fresh, and sinless
In Thy holy eyes.

Announcement for Next Week's Sermon: As a Christian, you have to grow! You can't stay the same. You can't stop children from growing, but you can stop them from becoming mature. If you stopped your Christian growth in Sunday school, you need next week's sermon.

Story of the Week: An old fellow had lived in the same house in a small southern town for 40 years. Then one day, he suddenly sold his place and moved into the house across the street. "What did you move for," a friend asked him.

"Oh," he said, "I suppose it's just my natural wanderlust coming out."

IT'S YOUR DAY OFF, BUT . . .

"Pastor, I know it's your day off," the voice on the other end of the telephone begins, and I take a deep breath. I'm standing there in our kitchen at home at 10:30 on a Monday morning, half-dressed, with a half-full cup of coffee in my hand and the half-read Sunday paper under my arm.

"Pastor, I know it's your day off, but . . ." the voice continues. There is always the "but." I wonder what's coming next. Will it be a request to buy tickets for a charitable benefit show? Will it be an eager young woman wanting to schedule a wedding eighteen months hence, who couldn't wait to tell me because she just got engaged last night? Or will it be somebody wanting to schedule the use of a room at the church for some civic group's meeting?

To hear those words, "Pastor, I know it's your day off, but . . . " usually causes me to utter a silent, but intense prayer that goes something like this: "Aw, come on, Lord! You command a day of rest. You know I have worked over sixty hours the past six days. Why do you do this to me?"

My usual reason for blaming God comes when I sense in the tone of the caller's voice a note of personal pain and a hint of crisis. "Pastor, I know it's your day off, but . . . we have been up all night arguing about our marriage. You see, my husband says he doesn't love me anymore." Or it may be the crisis of a teenager caught using drugs, or a member of the family in an auto accident, or a death in the family and funeral plans to be made. Sometimes it is a parent calling long distance, distraught over a child involved in a cult.

You see, I tend to hold God responsible for the calls from hurting persons, because I sense his presence in, with, and under the callers' pain and needs. And those hurting people need a pastor's attention. Sometimes I try to see what can be done today and what can be scheduled for Tuesday. I try to respond sensitively to their needs as well as salvage the only day of the week I have to catch my breath and cut the grass.

I know that many of you have such intrusions from your jobs into your off-duty time, too. I know because I hear your beepers go off during services, meetings, and classes, and I watch you try to leave as inconspicuously as possible as you try to do your duty faithfully.

In these situations, we are caught in the bind between our commitment to ourselves and our families on the one hand and on the other a world of job responsibilities to others that at times threatens to devour us. That seems to have been the situation that Jesus faced in the incident described in the sixth chapter of Mark.

Jesus' twelve disciples had just returned from their first trip of ministering on their own. Jesus had sent them forth to preach, teach, and demonstrate the power of the kingdom of God by healing. They returned tired and hungry. Jesus urged them to "come away by yourselves and rest." Mark relates that they had been so busy and the crowds so demanding that they had "no leisure even to eat."

To escape, they got into a small boat and headed across the Sea of Galilee, but the crowds wouldn't let them be alone. The crowds guessed where they were headed, perhaps from Tiberias to Capernaum, and raced around the lake to catch up. When Jesus and his disciples got off the boat, the eager crowds were waiting for them. That was the moment I call "I know it's your day off, but. . . ."

Jesus "had compassion on them, because they were like sheep without a shepherd; and he began to teach them many things" (Mark 6:34). Jesus set aside his fatigue and hunger, and that of his exhausted disciples, and gave himself to the needs of the people. The reports and debriefing from the disciples' trip would just have to wait. Jesus found the will of God indicated in the needs of the crowds, and he responded.

If you and I are looking to Jesus today for some practical help in coping with our day-off instrusions, we may be disappointed. If we are looking for Jesus' Seven Steps to Saying No Graciously, we won't find them in Mark 6. The only clue Jesus gives us comes in his ability to discern in the needs of persons what God wants him to do.

What this passage does tell us—far more than practical tips for successful living—is what God is like. Jesus' action in setting aside his own needs and those of the disciples is a parable in action. Jesus demonstrated two things: the compassion of his heavenly Father and identification of himself as the long-awaited Good Shepherd. He had compassion for the people because he knew himself to be the Good Shepherd.

Jesus' demonstration of the love of God stands in stark contrast to the false shepherds condemned by the Old Testament prophet Jeremiah in the first lesson " 'Woe to the shepherds who destroy and scatter the sheep of my pasture!' says the Lord" (Jeremiah 23:1). God does not look favorably on leaders of his people who do not exercise their responsibility. For Jeremiah, that was king and clergy alike, political leaders and priests. These bad shepherds abused the sheep and violated the trust God had given them. They punished and neglected the people. They exploited the people of God for their own pleasure and profit. They took care of the shepherd's needs, ignored the needs of the people, and ran for cover whenever danger approached.

The people of God have had good reason to despair of the kinds of human leaders they have experienced, for most of the human leaders in the Bible are described as far less than what was needed. And the history of the church since then continues the story of the shortcomings of the humans who have led the people of God.

Jesus became the Good Shepherd for whom the prophets hoped, because so many other kings and clergy had failed. Jesus, the Good Shepherd, fulfilled what Jeremiah had written, "I will raise up for David a righteous Branch" (Jeremiah 23:5). To people discouraged and disillusioned by human leaders who turn out to be inadequate at best and corrupt at worst, the Word of God comes to us today with the good news that there is, indeed, one leader who is worthy of our trust, one shepherd who, indeed, deserves the name "Good"—Jesus Christ.

Look around the world today and you see how many people are as desperate as those crowds that ran after Jesus around the Sea of Galilee. They are looking for a human leader to become their god. We have a booming number of aspirants for the job of being god for somebody else, cult leaders, gurus, and psychotherapeutic messiahs are coming out of the woodwork like the termite parasites they really are. Some of them even disguise themselves as Christian evangelists!

How many people are disillusioned when their pastors have been found guilty of alcohol abuse, of adultery, of embezzlement, of heresy, of the abuse of spouse and children, and of fraud and deceit. The painful violation of trust has turned many to cynicism and bitterness. Yet, in the midst of all the chaos, the Word of God is still being proclaimed. There is only one leader worthy of our worship and trust—Jesus Christ. The biblical message continually warns against expecting too much from human leaders, civic or ecclesiastic. They stand under God's judgment and his grace just like everybody else, because as the psalmist knew full well:

> The Lord is my shepherd; I shall not want. He maketh me to lie down in green pastures: he leadeth me beside the still waters. He restoreth my soul: he leadeth me in the paths of righteousness for his name's sake. (Psalm 23:1-3 KJV)

"As [Jesus] went ashore he saw a great throng, and he had compassion on them, because they were like sheep without a shepherd; and he began to teach them many things" (Mark 6:34). The Good Shepherd brings truth to this world's confusion and ignorance. The Good Shepherd brings meaning and purpose to this rat-race called human society. The Good Shepherd lays down his life for the flock, and by his blood breaks down the walls of hostility between humans and God, and he brings peace. The Good Shepherd gathers the people of God into a flock and cares for that flock. He feeds them and cares for their wounds.

> Yea, though I walk through the valley of the shadow of death, I will fear no evil: for thou art with me; thy rod and thy staff they comfort me. Thou preparest a table before me in the presence of mine enemies: thou anointest my head with oil; my cup runneth over. (Psalm 23:4-5 KJV)

It is what the Good Shepherd has done for us, the model Jesus has demonstrated, the pattern he has set, that looms in the background when I hear the telephone ring on Monday mornings. And I get ready for the intrusion into my day of rest that the ringing telephone may bring. "Oh, Jesus, Good Shepherd, what do you want me to do for this sheep of your flock?"

"Surely goodness and mercy shall follow me all the days of my life: and I will dwell in the house of the Lord for ever." (Psalm 23:6 KJV). *Amen.*

Richard L. Dowhower
Trinity Evangelical Lutheran Church
Camp Hill, Pennsylvania

Sunday
August Seventh

Call to Worship: The earth is the Lord's and the fulness therefore, the world and those who dwell therein. *Psalm 24:1*

Processional Hymn: "The Church's One Foundation"

Invocation: Lord, grant us a true and mature faith. Help us to grow as Christians through the study and living of your true Word. Let us accept our responsibilities for our deeds and draw closer to you every day of our lives. *Amen.*

Sermon Scripture: Matthew 11:16-19

Sermon Presentation: "The Courage to Grow"

Hymn of the Day: "Praise to the Lord, the Almighty"

Offertory Scripture: As each has received a gift, employ it for one another, as good stewards of God's varied grace.

I Peter 4:10

Offertory Prayer: Lord, open our hearts and minds to your Word. Faith will overcome all confusion. Let us give in proportion to our understanding of your Word. *Amen.*

Prayer of the Day

Lord, too often we get confused. We confuse being "child-like" with being "childish." But the confusion doesn't stop there. We often confuse religion with faith, rules with beliefs.

We are often close-minded and open-mouthed. We speak before we think, and we often act without thinking. Too many times our eyes are blind, our minds are closed, and our hearts are like stone. We think we know it all. We believe that we alone possess the truth. We assume that our way is the only way.

Paul told us that when he was a child, he spoke like a child. He thought like a child. He acted like a child. But when he became an adult, he put away childish things.

Help us to put away the childish things, such as anger, selfishness, and greed. They not only destroy our relationship with those around us, but also disrupt our relationship with you. Guide us as we grow to maturity in our relationships and in our faith in you. *Amen.*

Benediction: Therefore, brethren, be the more zealous to confirm your call and election, for if you do this you will never fall. *II Peter 1:10*

Recessional Hymn: "Faith of Our Fathers"

Lectionary Lessons: The Eleventh Sunday after Pentecost
Lesson 1—II Samuel 18:1, 5, 9-15; Psalm 143:1-8
Lesson 2—Ephesians 4:25–5:2
Gospel—John 6:35, 41-51

History of the Hymn of the Day: "Praise to the Lord, the Almighty"

This hymn of praise was written by Joachim Neander shortly before his death at thirty years of age in 1680, in Bremen, Germany, the city of his birth. It is said that the hymn developed out of a difficult situation experienced in Dusseldorf in the Rhineland, Germany, while he was schoolmaster there. When Neander refused to conform to the rules of the elders of the Reformed Church who controlled the school, he was forced to seek retreat in a wild cave where this and many other poems were written.

Praise to the Lord, the Almighty,
the King of creation!
O my soul, praise him,
for he is thy health and salvation! All ye who hear,
Now to his temple draw near;
Join me in glad adoration!

Announcement for Next Week's Sermon: What is this old world coming to? It sure seems to me that the Bible should have some answers to that question. Let's take a look next Sunday.

Story of the Week: The Congressman had a reputation for remembering names and faces. He was pretty good at it, but he also faked a lot. Once when he was campaigning in his own city, his tailor was in the audience. After his speech, and when people were gathering around him to shake his hand, the tailor shook his hand and said in a quiet voice, "Remember me? I made your pants."

"Why certainly," the Congressman said, "I would have known you anywhere. My old friend, Major Pantz."

THE COURAGE TO GROW

> We have piped unto you, and ye have not danced; we have mourned unto you, and ye have not lamented. (Matthew 11:17 KJV)

Jesus loved children. We catch glimpses of him, especially in the Gospel of Luke, gathering children about him and giving them his blessing. It is not so often that we catch a glimpse of his own childhood; yet there are sayings of his here and there that make us think that he is remembering things that happened when he, himself, was just a child. In the eleventh chapter of the Gospel of Matthew, we find, perhaps, one of these sayings. Jesus seems to be remembering the days when, as a boy, he played with other children in the marketplace.

Jesus was disheartened and discouraged with the Jewish leaders. He thought how much they were like some children he used to play with, or like some children he had seen recently playing in the marketplace. They were spoiled children who had never been taught by their parents to get along with other children. They wanted their own way. Their motto was "I want to be the captain, or I won't play." No matter what game was suggested by other children, they wanted to play something else.

The game Jesus had in mind is what recreational leaders call "informal dramatics." Children have a simpler name for it. They call it "make believe." "Let's play wedding," some one suggests, and spoiled children object. "No," they say, "we wanna play funeral." But if their game is suggested, spoiled children still object, saying, "No, we wanna play wedding." No matter what is suggested, it's wrong. They start a game all their own, and are surprised and chagrined when nobody follows them. They say, "We piped—that is, played the flute for the wedding—and you did not dance. We mourned—as for a funeral—and you have not lamented."

The Jewish leaders were like that, said Jesus. John the Baptist came, preaching repentance and the need of God's forgiveness. He told them they must give up their easy life. They must live sacrificially, do the hard things. They must give up the good things to eat and drink; in short, they must live the simple, rugged life that made their nation great. And what did the leaders say of him? They said he was out of his mind, that he was possessed by a devil. Life for John was a funeral, but the leaders wanted to have a wedding.

On the other hand, Jesus came emphasizing the things John had missed. Jesus went among people at their daily work and in their homes; he had dinner in the homes of friends and disciples. He taught them how joyous and happy God intended life to be. He tried to uplift the fallen, the weak, the oppressed classes, and the forgotten ones. He was the opposite of John, but did the leaders like him? They said he was a vicious man, associating with vicious men and sharing in their vice. They said, "Behold, a glutton and a drunkard, a friend of tax collectors and sinners!" (Luke 7:34). Life for Jesus was a wedding, but the leaders wanted it to be a funeral. How like children they were, playing in the marketplace and saying to their fellows, "We piped unto you and ye have not danced; we mourned and ye have not lamented."

The plain fact of the matter is that they did not really like anybody or anything except themselves. They had an artificial, unreal kind of religion, and they did not want to be disturbed by anything that might make them think, that might make them face life, that might make them try to solve some of the problems that beset humanity. Life for them had been reduced to a set of rules. When they came to a rule that did not work, instead of trying to change the rule or find a different basis for life, such as faith—the faith that Christianity found—they made another rule. There was no room in their lives for any great enthusiasm. Instead of giving their lives to a great faith, they spent their lives picking to pieces the lives of others, finding fault with those who did have some genuine enthusiasm. If someone was carried away by a great new idea and refused to conform to the Jewish leaders' narrow creed, they petulantly said, like children playing in the marketplace, "We piped unto you and ye have not danced. We mourned and ye have not lamented."

Much of our religion is like that. There is an interesting story, rather exaggerated to be sure, but one which illustrates nevertheless the formalism and legalism of much of our religion. The story is of a woman who was worshiping in a dignified liturgical church. She suddenly began to be rather noisy in her worship. She was approached by one of the church officers, who remonstrated, "My good woman, you can't do that." The woman explained that she was happy, that she had "gotten religion." To which the official replied, "I can't help that; you didn't get it here."

Someone has said that the difference between the actor and the preacher is that the actor talks about unreal things as if they were real, while the preacher talks about real things as if they were not real. As it is said of the minister, so it can too often be said of the church. If our world today has been carried away by so many false enthusiasms, it is so because the church has refused to be kindled with any true enthusiasm. We have books today by the hundreds, even by the thousands, that capture the popular imagination. Many contain glaring untruths, even absurdities, but they do show a great enthusiasm. The authors believe something with all their souls. We have so many false beliefs because the church has so often refused to express the truth with enthusiasm and earnestness. The church has proclaimed the same old things in the same old ways for ever and ever. When anyone suggests a new idea, church leaders retreat to their own little world, saying like the children in the marketplace, "We piped unto you and ye have not danced: we mourned and ye have not lamented."

There are sections of the church, and of the world, today that are very much like the Jewish church of Jesus' day. This is true not only of some of those who call themselves fundamentalists or conservatives, but also of some of those who call themselves modernist or liberal. Such segments of the church cannot be called in the deepest sense Christian. The church cannot be truly Christian, it cannot be worthy of Jesus unless it can find room in itself for great ideas, even if those ideas seem new and strange. The secret of success for the future, in the church as well as in the state, in the religious as well as in the economic, social, and political realm, in the interpretation of the Bible as well as in the ordering of our economic system and the adjustment of ourselves to new international relationships, is this, to hold fast the best traditions of the past, keeping our minds open to the best new things that God has to give us.

There is a striking fact about the Bible that we ought always to remember. Though the Bible is a textbook of religion, the word *religion* occurs in it only five times, and it is used only by two of the Bible writers. The word that is always used instead is *life*. The book of Deuteronomy records God as saying to the Hebrew people, "I have set before you life and death, blessing and curse; therefore choose life" (30:19). And Jesus said "I came that they may have life, and have it abundantly" (John 10:10). The world can only move forward as it thinks, with Jesus, not in terms of logic or science or machinery, but in terms of life, and only as it sees that life as a precious gift of God.

Secular historians tell us the story of how humanity moved out of the ages of ignorance and barbarism into the new world of modern times. That is true, but it is not all the truth. We Christians believe that the Spirit of God is moving in the history of nations as well as in the church. History, in the highest sense, is more than the study of human civilization. It is the story of a divine influence pouring out of an eternal world to mingle with human life. It is the story of humanity's moving toward a new world in which human civilization, as well as the church, shall be a "new creation in Christ Jesus."

We Christians above all people should be touched by that divine influence. When God speaks to us through the minds and lips of the great thinkers and writers and speakers of our day, let us not be like children playing in the marketplace, insisting upon our own way of thinking. *Amen.*

F. J. Yetter (deceased)
The United Methodist Church
Pitman, New Jersey

Sunday
August Fourteenth

Call to Worship: Blessed is the man who trusts in the Lord, whose trust is the Lord. *Jeremiah 17:7*

Processional Hymn: "Christ Is Made the Sure Foundation"

Invocation: Lord, today we pray for the church. Not just this church, but the whole church of God, where God is worshiped and the risen Christ is king. For all the people and churches, we pray. *Amen.*

Sermon Scripture: Ephesians 2:19-22

Sermon Presentation: "The Great Church"

Hymn of the Day: "When Morning Gilds the Skies"

Offertory Scripture: For I desire steadfast love and not sacrifice, the knowledge of God, rather than burnt offerings.

Hosea 6:6

Offertory Prayer: Lord, how could we know you except through the presence of your church. Let us say thank you to you and your church on earth by our gifts. *Amen.*

Prayer of the Day

Lord, we who are your church have been called "the body of Christ" in the world. We have also been called a "Communion of Saints, the Family of God, a Community of Faith."

You have given us the responsibilities, awesome responsibilities, of preaching your word, of witnessing to your gospel, of reconciliation, of sharing your love and forgiveness, and of administering your sacraments. Yet due to our sinfulness, your church falls short of your intentions. Even in the "good old days" we find that there were problems, disappointments, and frustrations. But as Paul tells us, we of the church are like "a treasure in earthen vessels." While we struggle with our sinfulness, you still allow us to do good works by the power of your grace. Your light shines so often through the darkness of your people.

You are one who called the world into being. You are the same God who corrects, guides, inspires, and leads your people, the church. Help us to rise to the new challenges that we face in the present and in the future. Help us to rely on your Holy Spirit to show us the way and your truth. Make us faithful to our calling, and help us to live up to our God-given potential. *Amen.*

Benediction: Thou dost keep him in perfect peace, whose mind is stayed on thee, because he trusts in thee.

Isaiah 26:3

Recessional Hymn: "How Firm a Foundation"

Lectionary Lessons: The Twelfth Sunday after Pentecost
Lesson 1—II Samuel 18:24-33; Psalm 102:1-12
Lesson 2—Ephesians 5:15-20
Gospel—John 6:51-58

History of the Hymn of the Day: "When Morning Gilds the Skies"
A famous old German folk song hymn translated into English by Edward Caswell in 1853. One of the first churches to use this hymn was St. Paul's Episcopal Church in London, England, where leaflets were printed and distributed so all the congregation could share in the singing of this beautiful music. One of England's eminent ministers of the nineteenth century, Canon Liddon, considered this one of the greatest of all the church hymns and requested that it be sung at his funeral service.

When morning gilds the skies,
My heart awaking cries,
May Jesus Christ be praised!

Announcement for Next Week's Sermon: If you have never had any doubts about your faith, you are a rare human being. Come join the rest of us next Sunday as we look at our doubts and how to live with them.

Story of the Week: A directive from the Department of Defense was sent to all Army units in the field. It read: "It is necessary for technical reasons that these warheads must be stored upside down, that is, with the top at the bottom and the bottom at the top. To prevent anyone making a mistake, and in order that there will be no doubt as to which is the bottom and which is the top, for storage purposes, it will be noted that the bottom of each warhead has been labeled with the word 'top.' "

THE GREAT CHURCH

You are no longer aliens in a foreign land, but fellow-citizens with God's people, members of God's household. You are built upon the foundation laid by the apostles and prophets, and Christ Jesus himself is the foundation-stone. In him the whole building is bonded together and grows into a holy temple in the Lord. In him you too are being built with all the rest into a spiritual dwelling for God. (Ephesians 2:19-22 NEB)

One man, invited to attend a particular church, replied, "I can't; I see too many hypocrites in it."

"Oh, don't let that bother you," his friend rejoined. "There is always room for one more."

These two views point up the singular contrast most often discussed when the value or influence of the church is under consideration. The biblical image of the church is clear; it is the body of Christ, a community of faith in him, commissioned by him to continue his work of reconciliation.

Paul proclaimed that view of the church in the above text. This image and character of the church has inspired our profession of faith through the centuries, from the time of the apostles until now. Yet, is it not equally true that for any one of us, at any given place or time, we have never seen an actual congregation that fit the picture?

Herein lies the incredible dilemma: The biblical image and our vision are authentic. The church, itself, is one of the acts of God in human experience, but the human reality does not correspond to the authentic vision. To resolve the dilemma, we often look backward to the "good old days."

Surely the early nineteenth century would furnish a model of the ideal church. Yet in 1800 only 5 percent of the population in the United States were participating members of churches, and the doleful comments of church leaders in the 1880s do not reflect an awareness of great churchly influence.

What then of the Middle Ages, when, unquestionably, the church dominated the scene? The thirteenth century, for example, was the period of great cathedral building throughout Europe. But a reading of Dante's writings will disclose a picture of weakness and ineffectiveness inside the church.

If any time would give us a gloriously triumphant church, it should be the apostolic age, when such towering figures as Paul penetrated the whole world of his time with the affirmation of the spiritual household of God. Yet his own description of the Corinthian church as a place of "quarreling, jealousy, anger, selfishness, slander, gossip, conceit, and disorder" (II Corinthians 12:20) does not confirm it. The epistle of James even suggests that there is, in the church, an undue favoritism toward the wealthy.

This backward look at church history is not reassuring. It reminds one of the response the editor of *Punch* made to a reader who complained that the magazine was not as good as it used to be. "It never was," said the editor. Thus the backward look does not resolve the dilemma; it only accents it.

Paul suggested an intriguing view: "We do not lose heart," he reminded the Corinthians. "But we have this treasure in earthen vessels." What a suggestive figure! The church as the community of faith, incorporating the redemptive ministry of Christ himself, is a rare treasure. We know from our own experience that we, its carriers, are indeed very much earthen.

The full backward look, however, discloses that the early church did plant totally new religious and social ideals into the soul of the caesars, fostering kindness and morality in the midst of cruelty and vice. One observer in the second century recorded that those Christians outlived, outthought, and outdied the people around them.

The church in the Middle Ages, for all its spiritual weakness, absorbed and refined the brutish pagans that overran western Europe. The church preserved, especially in the monasteries, the hard won cultural gains of ancient Greece and oriental antiquity, laid the foundations of civil law, and kept available the very materials used to quicken minds and fire the creative forces of the Renaissance and of the Reformation, which ushered in the modern world.

Furthermore, from the colonial pulpits of America poured forth the historic civic declarations that underpin our national structure. The visitor to Williamsburg, Virginia, can still today see the very pews in the Bruton Parish Church in which sat George Washington, Thomas Jefferson, Alexander Hamilton, and other powerful colonial leaders on the occasion of the parish rector's so dynamically phrasing the issues between the colonists and the mother country, England. This sermon was the inspiration for the Virginia Resolution in the Continental Congress, which sparked the American Revolution.

That such historic treasures should be carried in our faulty earthen vessels is an idea that proposes a great mystery: How can the human institution we know as the church be the residence of powerfully redemptive forces, which are capable of literally remaking both persons and nations? Paul unblinkingly accepted this mystery. God had, in Christ, revealed his divine purpose for the whole creation, which had been hidden for ages in the God who created all things. That same God has determined that "through the church the manifold wisdom of God . . . be made known to the principalities and powers. . . . This was according to the eternal purpose which he has realized in Christ Jesus our Lord, in whom we have boldness and confidence of access through our faith in him. So I ask you not to lose heart" (Ephesians 3:10-13). In that marvelous fusion of reality and faith, the apostle wrote the words of our text, picturing the actual human congregation as "a dwelling place of God in the Spirit." Surely only a divine process could survive the human frailty through which it has been transmitted through the centuries.

In this perspective, the church is literally a pilgrim people, the people of God, searching for ways to manifest more fully the sovereignty of Christ over us. At one and the same time it reveals our disorder and God's design for us.

J. B. Phillips, who has given us one of the more helpful modern translations of the Bible, once described his feelings in the process of translating meanings that are eternal into the phrases through which the contemporary mind could grasp them. He was, he felt, in the position of the electrician who had to rewire the house without turning off the main current. The church, therefore, must be seen as the "house," imperfect though it be, into which flows the kindling power and love of God. The cables and outlets must be repaired and occasionally replaced. Even the whole house must, at times, be remodeled. But all this remodeling and rewiring proceeds without turning off the main current of the wisdom and power of the eternal God. Indeed, the power is not in our hands.

In this way the Great Mystery really dissolves the incredible dilemma. The clear focus of it appears in another word from Paul. It immediately precedes his figure of earthen vessels. Paul affirms: "For it is the God who said, 'Let light shine out of darkness,' who has shone in our hearts to give the light of the knowledge of the glory of God in the face of Christ" (II Corinthians 4:6). To him Christ was the very likeness of God incarnated in human life. That same incarnation in the church is no less a mystery than God's actual presence in the life of Jesus Christ.

What can we say of the church in the future? Many people question its viability for the need of both the present and the future. In some quarters these questions are not merely critical, but quarrelsome. It is not an easy or optimistic situation in which to project an inspiring hope for the years ahead. Moreover, here we stand in a moment of convulsive change, an uncharted future that is making unimaginable demands upon us and all our ways. Can we honestly look out on the future with the bright faith that the church will so reform its institutional expression that it can speak the word the world needs to hear and can engage in the healing, reconciling acts necessary to redeem the future?

If we were to judge purely on the current scene, we might not be hopeful. But do not take your bearings from the existential circumstances that surround us. Begin with faith in God. The church sprang from his action, it has been saved and reformed over and over again by the action of his Spirit among living people. Our faith for the future should be a lively expectation that in unpredictable ways he will inspire, correct, and lead his people. In that faith we can find both standing ground for the present and a launching pad for risk-taking adventures of Christian action.

Without assuming that our decisions and actions here are universal, we must understand that we have the obligation to reach out toward the universal reality in which we, by faith, are rooted and seek to give it genuine expression at this moment in this place. Here we are gathered as a worshiping congregation. We are set in a community of great human potential and of great human needs. The congregation has gone through inspiring times of spiritual realization, and it is poignantly aware of its own shadowy side. Whatever happens elsewhere, we have the opportunity for a highly significant mission within the mandate of Christ and under the vision of the congregation as an expression of the pilgrim people of God.

In this faith, the worship and the work of the congregation can surely help each of us to change in such ways and to such an extent that we may all share in the transformation of the question, "What is the world coming to?" into the exclamation, "See what has come to the world!" *Amen*.

Forrest C. Weir
United Church of Christ, retired
Pacific Palisades, California

Sunday
August Twenty-first

Call to Worship: Jesus immediately reached out his hand and caught [Peter], saying to him, "O man of little faith, why did you doubt?" *Matthew 14:31*

Processional Hymn: "O Jesus, Thou Art Standing"

Invocation: Lord, how can we be sure that you are the true God and that you are with us to the end of time? We are filled with doubt until that still, small voice within us says, "Be still and know that I am God." Help our unbelief. *Amen.*

Sermon Scripture: John 20:24-29

Sermon Presentation: "Thomas"

Hymn of the Day: "Savior, Thy Dying Love"

Offertory Scripture: They gave according to their means, as I can testify, and beyond their means, of their own free will.
II Corinthians 8:3

Offertory Prayer: Give us this day and every day the reassurance we need that you are there. Accept these gifts as our thanks for your Lordship. *Amen.*

Prayer of the Day

Faith, Lord, faith. That's what it takes to be a follower of you. We find so many people in our world who claim to be realists, who live lives characterized by cynicism and pessimism. It is easy to be a faithful follower when all is going well. Everyone loves a winner. But life has its dark moments as well as light. It has peaks as well as valleys. There are moments of joy and times of bitter disappointment.

You call us to live by faith, but ours is not a blind faith. Instead, it is a faith that wrestles with doubt, struggles through hardships, endures confusion, and continues to trust in you even when all of the evidence seems to contradict your will.

Strengthen our faith so that we might stand firm against the winds of confusion and doubt that surround us. Guide us so that we may continually grow in our understanding and appreciation of your will and your truth. *Amen.*

Benediction: But let him ask in faith, with no doubting, for he who doubts is like a wave of the sea that is driven and tossed by the wind.
James 1:6

Recessional Hymn: "Rock of Ages, Cleft for Me"

Lectionary Lessons: The Thirteenth Sunday after Pentecost
Lesson 1—II Samuel 23:1-7; Psalm 67
Lesson 2—Ephesians 5:21-33
Gospel—John 6:55-69

History of the Hymn of the Day: "Savior, Thy Dying Love"
This hymn of consecration was written in 1862 by Dr. S. Dryden Phelps, an American Baptist minister. Published in Sankey's *Gospel Hymns* under the title "Something for Jesus," the music was written by another prominent American Baptist clergyman, Robert Lowry, in 1872. On his seventieth birthday Dr. Phelps received a telegram from Lowry which expressed the sentiment of all who knew him, "It is worth living seventy years, even if nothing comes of it but one such hymn as this one. Happy is the man who can produce one song which the world will keep on singing after its author shall have passed away."

Savior, thy dying love, thou gavest me;
Nor should I aught withhold,
Dear Lord, from thee;
In love my soul would bow,
My heart fulfill its vow,
Some off'ring bring thee now,
Something for thee.

Announcement for Next Week's Sermon: Did you ever fall asleep in church? Did the church ever fall asleep in you? Next Sunday, how to keep awake in church and how to keep the church awake in you.

Story of the Week: A man was asked to address a meeting of the Ladies' Literary Guild. The program chairman asked him to speak on the topic of China and Chinese art, religion and philosophy. He spent several long nights in research studying for his presentation. When he arrived at the meeting place on the great day, he said to the chairman, "I suppose you wanted me to speak about China because you are making a study of their early culture, is that right?"

"No," the chairman said, "we just wanted your topic to be

appropriate for today's luncheon. You see, we're going to serve Chop Suey."

THOMAS

Those of you who read the comic strip *Peanuts* are certainly aware of the character Lucy. She's the one who every fall persuades Charlie Brown to try to kick the football while she holds it. And every year she pulls the ball away just as Charlie Brown is about to kick it, and we see poor Charlie Brown go flying through the air. Lucy also offers psychiatric help for five cents a session from her lemonade-stand office; Charlie Brown usually needs this help, and she is usually the reason. Lucy also plays outfield on the Peanuts baseball team. She constantly tells Charlie Brown how bad the team is and that they have no chance whatsoever of winning a game.

Lucy is a realist. She has both feet firmly planted on the ground and deals in the hard, cold facts of everyday life. There is not much poetry in Lucy. Even her psychiatric advice is bluntly honest. Because she is such a realist, and because she is so bluntly honest, Lucy appears as a pessimist much of the time. Charlie Brown can poetically go on and on about the values of sportmanship, teamwork, and a positive attitude, but Lucy sees the team for what it is and bluntly maintains that it doesn't have a chance.

Thomas, a disciple of Jesus, is the same sort of person. Over the years he has gotten a bad name. He has been criticized in countless sermons as "old doubting Thomas," the guy who dared to put Jesus to the test. He would not take the word of the other disciples. Thomas was, like Lucy, a realist and a pessimist. Because this is the kind of person he was, the witness of his life and faith holds a special meaning for us.

We first meet Thomas in Jesus' telling the disciples that he would go again into Judea, where Lazarus lay dead. The disciples protested that there were many there who wanted to stone Jesus to death. But Jesus insisted that he must go. In the face of what must have appeared to him as certain death, Thomas said, "Let us also go, that we may die with him" (John 11:16). There is a message for us here. Even though Lucy was convinced that she was playing for a losing team, she played. She had cast her lot with good old Charlie Brown, and she was going to stick it out, game after losing game. We find her biblical counterpart doing the same thing. Thomas the realist, the pessimist, was convinced that Jesus was going to be killed, but in spite of this, and the danger it held for him as one of Jesus' followers, he was determined to go along. There is a place today for such a witness of loyalty and devotion and dedication to principles and causes. There is a place in the church for such a witness. It is easy to work in a growing and successful church that is already running like a well-oiled machine. It is something else to persist in spite of frustration, criticism, and our own fears that the plan, the committee, the dream might just fail in the end anyway. What action required the most faith? The following of the other disciples who were so taken with this wonderful Jesus that they would have followed him anywhere, or the following of Thomas, who clearly saw the dangers that were ahead, but said anyway, "Let us also go, that we may die with him."

Have you ever been in a group in which someone was explaining something, and you were missing the point completely? Have you ever been somewhere that you were so lost and out of it that you were ashamed to say so? Sometimes, in situations like these, some courageous individual will raise his or her hand and say, "Hey, wait a minute. I don't know what you are talking about." Doesn't it feel good when this happens? Someone else is as lost as you and has said so. Can't you just see Lucy Van Pelt raising her hand in school and saying just that kind of thing? Well, Thomas was that sort of person, too.

Jesus detailed the horrible events that awaited him and his disciples in Jerusalem. He told them not to be afraid, because he was going before them to his father to prepare a place for them. Jesus concluded, "And you know the way where I am going" (John 14:4). Imagine how confused and upset the disciples must have been. Jesus told them all of these way out things, and they did not, as the events of the next few days and weeks reveal, understand. Only Thomas, bluntly honest Thomas, dared to speak up. He said, "Lord, we do not know where you are going; how can we know the way?" (John 14:5). That must have been the question in all their hearts. If Thomas had not asked it, the disciples would not, and we would not, have Jesus' reply, a very famous, a very important reply indeed: "I am the way, and the truth, and the life; no one comes to the Father, but by me"

(John 14:6). Thank goodness Thomas was there and dared to ask for clarification on behalf of us all.

Finally, we find the disciples gathered together on Easter evening, when Jesus appeared to them as the risen Christ. Thomas was not there. Maybe if we knew why he was not there, the reason would make sense. When Thomas heard the disciples' story of Jesus' appearance to them, he did not believe. For this doubt, he has been labeled "doubting Thomas," a name that will probably always be remembered. But how else could he have reacted? This was Thomas the realist, the pessimist who persisted in spite of his worst fears. He had been there when his fellow disciples were ready to blindly follow Jesus into danger. He had been there when his fellow disciples had been too self-conscious to ask Jesus for clarification on his statements about the future. He had been there when Jesus had cried out and died. He knew these men; he knew that Jesus was dead. He must have felt compassion for them, but he was who he was, and he could not accept their version of what happened. He knew too much.

One week later, the disciples were gathered in the same place. This time Thomas was with them. Jesus appeared to them again. Why? His appearance among the disciples on Easter evening had convinced the others. Surely Christianity would have survived without Thomas. Why did Jesus come to them again? He came for Thomas' sake. After greeting them, he said to Thomas, "Put your finger here, and see my hands; and put out your hand, and place it in my side; do not be faithless, but believing" (John 20:27).

At this point we must discard the analogy between Lucy and Thomas. Lucy remains her lovable self to this day. Not so Thomas. Thomas was a man of courage, honesty, fierce loyalty, and determination. Yet he was a man of the real world. Thomas was concerned not with prophecies, dreams, poems, or sermons. He was concerned with things that made a real difference that he could see. Thomas could not swallow the testimony of the other disciples. He didn't have to; Jesus came and proved that to him. Into the midst of Thomas' life and way of looking at things came the risen Christ. When confronted with the risen Christ, what was Thomas' response? Not, "OK now I believe." Not some more of his probing questions, but the response of someone who has been confronted by something greater than the words of humankind, yet more real. What was the response of Thomas the realist, Thomas the pessimist, doubting Thomas? "My Lord and my God!" (John 20:28). Can you imagine the kind of witness for Christianity Thomas must have been from that moment forward? With his courage and determination, his realistic way of handling things, there must have been many people whose lives were better for Thomas having been with them.

Thank goodness for Thomas, because he stood where we stand. He stood in the midst of the world, seeing it for what it was, after the life of Jesus of Nazareth. He stood there having heard what had happened and having witnessed much of it, but still unable to believe, still unchanged. What happened? Thomas was confronted by the risen Christ and his life was changed. Christ came to Thomas in his faithlessness just as he comes to us in ours. The risen Christ still comes to everybody, individually, and presents himself as he is, "our Lord and our God." Christ comes because it is his nature to come, just as it is God's nature to send him. Christ comes because he knows the hardness of the human heart and knows that we, like Thomas, require personal assurance.

Christ is not our personal genie who will come and prove himself to us on demand, but Christ still comes. He still comes to people of little faith. He still comes to people of no faith. Christ still comes to people who need personal, individual, specialized attention—people like you and me. He comes, because he loves us and wants us to hear and understand the words that he spoke to our friend, doubting Thomas, so long ago, "I am the way, and the truth, and the life." He comes so that we, too, might be able to know new life in him, and one day testify, by calling to him and saying, as people whose lives will never be the same again, "My Lord, and my God!" *Amen.*

Michael L. Lyle
Braddock Street United Methodist Church
Winchester, Virginia

Sunday
August Twenty-eighth

Call to Worship: And we all, with unveiled face, beholding the glory of the Lord, are being changed into his likeness from one degree of glory to another; for this comes from the Lord who is the Spirit. *II Corinthians 3:18*

Processional Hymn: "Sing Them Over Again to Me"

Invocation: Lord, give us the courage to take chances for you. A church and a people who are afraid to risk are people without faith. Lead us to be fearless and faithful for you. *Amen.*

Sermon Scripture: Matthew 8:23-27

Sermon Presentation: "The Little Boat of the Church"

Hymn of the Day: "Savior, Like a Shepherd Lead Us"

Offertory Scripture: Now unto him that is able to do exceeding abundantly above all that we ask or think, according to the power that worketh in us. Unto him be glory in the church by Christ Jesus throughout all ages, world without end. *Amen.*

Ephesians 3:20-21 KJV

Offertory Prayer: Lord, don't let us drift; give us direction. Show us your way, beginning with a generous heart, to recognize our debt to you. *Amen.*

Prayer of the Day

Lord, it's a big wide sea out there, and our boat, your church, seems so very small. It would certainly be much easier to stay in the harbor and avoid all risks—to avoid the deep water—to avoid the possible storms.

But that's not what we're here for, is it, Lord? You've called us for a reason. You've given us a definite purpose. We are here to be your disciples, your representatives, your ambassadors.

In the midst of sin, you have called us to share the "good news" of your forgiveness, to tell others that they can be forgiven just as we are. In the storm of hatred in our world, you have called us to speak of love, not only of our friends, but of our enemies as well. Into depths of war, you send us to be peace-makers. Into the depths of despair and frustration, you have sent us to bring your message of hope. Into the midst of death, you have sent us with the words of eternal life.

It's tough sailing, Lord, but you have promised not only to show us the way, but also to be our shipmate, our captain, our anchor in the storms, and our rudder that keeps us on your course. *Amen.*

Benediction: Let us then with confidence draw near to the throne of grace, that we may receive mercy and find grace to help in time of need. *Hebrews 4:16*

Recessional Hymn: "Jesus, Lover of My Soul"

Lectionary Lessons: The Fourteenth Sunday after Pentecost
Lesson 1—I Kings 2:1-4, 10-12; Psalm 121
Lesson 2—Ephesians 6:10-20
Gospel—Mark 7:1-8, 14-15, 21-23

History of the Hymn of the Day: "Savior, Like a Shepherd Lead Us"

In 1859 William D. Bradbury gave the Christian world the great and peaceful hymn "Savior Like A Shepherd Lead Us." It is believed that this hymn poem had been written by the Reverend Henry F. Lyte, author of "Abide with Me," while others say it first appeared in a book by Dorothy Ann Thrupp. Bradbury was a protegé of the talented religious composer Lowell Mason and was instrumental in influencing and encouraging blind Fanny Crosby to turn her talents from writing secular songs to hymns for the church. Though poverty-stricken in his childhood, he was able to contribute great wealth through his immortal music.

Announcement for Next Week's Sermon: Do you have a heart condition? You say your heart is in good shape. God will be the judge of that. You may have a condition of the heart.

Story of the Week: The young junior high student was studying about politics. "Dad," he asked his father, the mayor, "what do you call a fellow who leaves your political party and goes over to the other side?"

"He's a traitor, son, a political traitor," the boy's father said.

"Well, what would you call someone who deserts the other party and comes over to your side?" the boy asked.

"I'd call him a man of rare judgment, a man who knows his own mind and a political convert," the boy's father said.

THE LITTLE BOAT OF THE CHURCH

Those of you who enjoy reading bumper stickers have probably seen the one that says, "I'd rather be sailing." Someone once spotted a sailboat in the San Francisco Bay that had a sticker that read, "I'd rather be driving my car."

A man went out on a sailboat, his first opportunity to be on a large boat on a large lake. There were a couple of times during which he felt he'd rather be driving his car; at least in a car he understood something about what to do, when, and why.

It was a glorious afternoon on the lake, with an adequate wind, abundant sunshine, and an experienced captain. The only time the man came close to feeling what the disciples must have felt in the stormy chaos of the eighth chapter of Matthew was when the tiller was turned over to him. The captain tightened the sail, and the man was perpendicular to the lake, hanging on for dear life!

In the midst of that little surprise, he was still able to feel confidence in his shipmate, since he knew the captain had to be experienced in what he was doing, having sailed for two or three decades. Not only did he learn to trust his partner, but he also learned a sailing phrase. After he managed to steer into the waves in such a way as to spray the captain, the captain told him, "a dry crew is a happy crew."

Believing that to be true, I'm sure we all realize that Jesus' disciples were not too happy on the little journey described in Matthew 8. Some of the disciples were sea-faring types. Peter, Andrew, James, and John were all fishermen. Some of the others were landlubbers, though. That day, when they were together in the boat heading for the other shore, something terrible happened; the reading from the Revised Standard Version of the Bible says that a great storm arose. The Greek New Testament, however, indicates that a great shaking occurred in the sea; that is, an earthquake shook the sea. It is frightening to be in any kind of earthquake, but at least on land you can be safe in an open field, or indoors by getting under a table or a door frame. But the disciples were in a sailboat on the water, and the waves began to heave and fall, literally swamping the board.

The poetry of Psalm 107 captures something of that experience: "They mounted up to heaven, they went down to the depths; their courage melted away in their evil plight; they reeled and staggered like drunken men, and were at their wit's end" (verses 26-27). That describes, doesn't it, the feeling of being in a sailboat in a storm!

For many people in the ancient world, water was a symbol of chaos. It is no wonder, because people would be caught at sea when a quick storm arose; people on land would be caught off guard by an earthquake-triggered tidal wave; men would lose their lives amid stories of great sea monsters.

Coupled with this understanding of the chaotic nature of water, however, was also a strong faith in God's deliverance. Psalm 46 captures this sense. It is a psalm often read during a funeral service, simply because it takes the chaos of our lives and affirms that somehow God is present in that experience: "God is our refuge and strength, a very present help in trouble. Therefore, we will not fear though the earth should change, though the mountains shake in the heart of the sea; though its waters roar and foam, though the mountains tremble with its tumult" (verses 1-3). The disciples found themselves caught in the fearful shaking sea. And Jesus, who got them into this predicament in the first place by having them follow him, was sound asleep.

Sometimes we read about similar experiences, when, for example, the driver of a car slumps over the wheel, and the passenger is in a scary predicament. Somehow, the passenger is able to reach over and bring the car to a safe stop and then seek help for the driver. The passenger does something. The disciples didn't. The disciples, in sheer panic for their lives, were not about to do anything but wake up Jesus. Their broken, stunted language mirrors their absolute fright: "Save, Lord, we are perishing" (Matthew 8:25). And awaking, Jesus asked "Why are you afraid, O men of little faith?" (verse 26).

Now, if you were one of those disciples, what would you say? "Why am I fainthearted? The sea is crashing into this boat, and you ask why my heart is in my throat?" But without waiting for a response from his disciples (Jesus believed that a dry crew is a happy crew), Jesus rebuked the winds and the sea, and there was a great calm.

New Testament scholars have long studied this passage, and several teach us that the boat which is enveloped by the waves is an image of the congregation, the church. It is a story that teaches us about the church. We often find ourselves afraid, buffeted about by the chaos of our lives and times. We don't know what to do. And like the disciples, we forget about Psalm 46, that tells us "God is our refuge and strength, a very present help in time of trouble."

Like the disciples, we follow Jesus; yet we lack the confidence that we will survive the worst hazards of storm and earthquake. We forget that the church will survive.

We have to remember that we have been called to follow Jesus. He calls us to respond, with him, to human needs. Our boat is not a pleasure craft. The boat of the church is not one of those lovely boats with two open bars and catered meals. No, our boat is a simple one, designed to get us from one shore to another. We move from shore to shore, because we are called to do so, to meet the needs of those lives that are adjacent to our waters.

Sometimes the seas get chaotic and fearful. Sometimes there is no wind for the sails—a lot of boat-rocking, nothing happening. Sometimes our leadership sleeps. Sometimes our sailors panic. Sometimes the trip runs smoothly, with everyone working together to assure a safe and productive mission.

The church is a boat upon the waters of life, transporting its members to the service of human needs. Sometimes, however, the church is more often like a boat on its trailer in the parking lot. It's nice to look at and to share stories about what it was like in the days when it sailed.

But when we do that, we deny the ship its true purpose. There is a poster that reads, "A ship in the harbor is safe, but that is not what ships are built for." We also deny the sailors the thrill of sailing, of holding the tiller firmly while pulling in the sails, tilting the boat at seventy degrees and sailing full speed ahead.

The risks are actually minimal when we decide to sail the boat instead of letting it sit idle. Sure, we might have to paint it sometime and fix its well-used places. Sure, we might be overeager in our sailing and capsize the boat—that could be the worst fate to befall our craft. But as sailing buffs know, in August of 1958, Buddy Melges and his crew capsized during a race—and they finished in second place by drifting over the finish line.

Think about it. What is your wish for the ship of the church, of this church? To have it covered and protected, resting on its trailer in the parking lot? To have it moored to a buoy, occasionally tossed and turned, tightly controlled by its short line of mooring, though in the water? To have it drifting in the lake, its crew sunbathing with sails down?

A church that doesn't enter the trials and struggles of life is safe, but that is not the purpose of the church.

We do gather to follow Jesus. May we enter his vessel, the church, in order to set upon the journey with him. May we leave the harbor, confident that he is with us. May we seek those shores upon which gather humanity's great and pressing needs. And may we go, prepared with the supplies necessary for a good and safe trip: a full measure of justice, an abundant supply of mercy, and the knowledge of going humbly with God.

Is Christ asleep in your heart? Is Christ asleep in this little boat of the church? Or is Christ awake in our hearts and in our church? Is our faith alive and alert, standing ready to face the chaos that seeks to upset our world and our lives?

God is our refuge and strength, a very present help in time of trouble. May we minister together in Christ's name, knowing this biblical truth. *Amen.*

Michael G. Bausch
United Church of Christ
Williams Bay, Wisconsin

Sunday
September Fourth

Call to Worship: But thanks be to God, that you who were once slaves of sin have become obedient from the heart to the standard of teaching to which you were committed.

Romans 6:17

Processional Hymn: "Thine Is the Glory"

Invocation: Lord, soften our hearts so that we hear your call to follow you. Soften our hearts to hear the cry for help from your children in need all over the world. Let us help in your name. *Amen.*

Sermon Scripture: Mark 7:1-8, 14-15, 21-23

Sermon Presentation: "A Condition of the Heart"

Hymn of the Day: "Breathe on Me, Breath of God"

Offertory Scripture: For where your treasure is, there will your heart be also. *Matthew 6:21*

Offertory Prayer: Open our hearts to your love and salvation. Open our purses to the needs of your people. *Amen.*

Prayer of the Day

Lord, what is religion? Is it just saying the right words at the right time? Is it a "gathering of the clan" at a special time and in a special place every week? Is it following a list of "thou shalt nots"? Is it going through certain rituals without really thinking about them?

As we read about our Lord's life, we see that our faith is more than words. It is more than actions. It truly is a way of life, a life involving more than tradition, more than ceremony, more than words, more than simply honoring God with our lips, but not with our hearts.

Help us to understand that you expect us to love you with all of our hearts, minds, and souls, and to love our neighbors as much as we love ourselves. Help us to truly trust Jesus as our Savior and to reach out with his love to those around us, working for peace and justice, forgiving and helping others, especially those in need.

Let ours be a genuine faith and religion. *Amen.*

Benediction: By this we shall know that we are of the truth, and reassure our hearts before him whenever our hearts condemn us; for God is greater than our hearts, and he knows everything. Beloved, if our hearts do not condemn us, we have confidence before God. *I John 3:19-21*

Recessional Hymn: "Immortal, Invisible, God Only Wise"

Lectionary Lessons: The Fifteenth Sunday after Pentecost

Lesson 1—Ecclesiasticus 5:8-15 *or* Proverbs 2:1-8; Psalm 119:129-136

Lesson 2—James 1:17-27

Gospel—Mark 7:31-37

History of the Hymn of the Day: "Breathe on Me, Breath of God"

The beauty of Edwin Hatch's hymn poem "Breathe on Me, Breath of God" was not discovered until after his death in 1889. His early years had been spent in Canada, first as professor of classics in Trinity College, Toronto, and then as Rector of the High School, Quebec. Even though later at Oxford, England, he received fame as church historian and theologian, it was while he was among the peaceful lakes and beautiful rivers of eastern Canada that he was moved to write this little gem of prayer to God.

Announcement for Next Week's Sermon: What is God really like? Each of us has his or her own concept. We could each draw a picture, and we would each be right. Next week: What is God Like?

Story of the Week: A kitten had strayed into the kindergarten class and the children were having great fun playing with it. After a while one of the little girls asked the teacher whether it was a girl cat or a boy cat.

The teacher didn't want to get into that subject with the little ones so she said, "I don't think I can tell."

"I know how we can tell," one little boy said. "We can vote on it."

A CONDITION OF THE HEART

Today we have the story of one of the classic confrontations between Jesus and the Pharisees. At stake was nothing less than the question of what constituted true religion: Was it the observation of various rituals and ordinances, or was it a condition of the heart? These are questions which continue to speak even more urgently for us here today.

Let us take a closer look at the background of this incident and the events immediately leading up to it. In the weeks and months preceding, Jesus' fame had been spreading throughout Galilee and Judea. His preaching had touched the hearts of many people and had set them on fire for God. His miracles were being talked about everywhere. There were reports that he had fed five thousand people from only five loaves of bread and two fish. And he could also heal the sick and cast out demons. It was reported that "wherever (Jesus) came, in villages, cities, or country, the people laid the sick in the marketplaces, and besought him that they might touch even the fringe of his garment; and as many as touched it were made well" (Mark 6:56).

Clearly, Jesus was not just any ordinary person! He talked about the kingdom of God in a way that any common person could understand. Jesus not only talked about God's kingdom to the people, but he also brought God's kingdom to the people through his miracles of feeding and healing. Through Jesus, many people experienced God's love in a way they had never before! Many people even started to believe that this man was the Christ, God's long-awaited Messiah!

Well, of course, it had to happen sooner or later that reports of all these goings on would come to the attention of the religious authorities in Jerusalem. And when they did, the authorities sent out an investigating committee of scribes to check out this Jesus, to ascertain whether he was truly a man of God or just another religious fraud.

So in cooperation with the local Pharisees, these Jerusalem scribes spent many days following Jesus around, gathering information on him with which to make their judgment. They listened to his teachings. They witnessed his miracles, and they saw how people's lives were changed through their association with him. But, incredibly, none of these things made that much of an impact upon them! What most caught their attention was the observation that some of Jesus' disciples ate with unwashed, defiled hands. The scribes and the Pharisees had so many great things to ponder about Jesus; yet they seemed to be concerned only about the fact that some of his disciples did not strictly observe the ceremonial handwashings before each and every meal!

This handwashing ritual had been invented by the Jewish elders of long ago as a way to symbolize one's cleanliness before God. Each time a person performed this ritual before a meal, he or she was supposed to remember and repent of the sins he or she had done since the last meal, and thus have them "washed away."

Even the scribes and the Pharisees would admit that these handwashings were not absolutely essential for salvation. But they did maintain that they were one of the marks of an especially holy person. A person who was truly religious would surely try faithfully to keep this, as well as other traditions, such as the washing of cups and pots and vessels of bronze.

We learn a great deal about those scribes and Pharisees when we hear that what they most noticed about Jesus was the fact that some of his disciples did not keep all of their traditions to the "nth" degree. They did not go up to Jesus and ask him to tell them more about the kingdom of God. They did not go up and ask him where he got the power and authority to perform his miracles. They did not ask him why he went about healing people, or what his teaching meant. The only question that this committee saw fit to ask Jesus was: "Why do your disciples not live according to the tradition of the elders, but eat with hands defiled?" (Mark 7:5).

These scribes and Pharisees were like the proverbial man who could not see the forest because of the trees. They saw only the little things, such as violations of their handwashing codes. Meanwhile, they were completely blind to the big things, such as people who were being healed of infirmities and delivered from demons. They never really saw the people who had been blessed by this man who went about doing good. Their eyes were blind to everything except what threatened their traditions, their vested interests, their authority, and their prestige.

Perhaps this has something to say to each of us today. What do our eyes pick up most readily? The big things or the little things? What are we most concerned about in religion?

The "big things" about Christianity are loving the Lord our God with all of our heart, mind, soul, and strength, and loving our neighbors as ourselves. Christianity is trusting in Jesus as our Savior and reaching out with his love to others by sharing the gospel in healing the sick, feeding the hungry, and working for peace and justice as well as forgiving and helping one another. These are the "big things," the important things about Christianity.

Far too often, many of us tend to be more concerned about the "little things," our traditions. Many of us are much more likely to get upset about a small change in church traditions than the fact that so many people do not know Jesus Christ in their hearts. Even here we often get upset when some small changes are made in the usual worship service. If only we could get as upset about the presence of hunger and injustice in the world, what a better world this would be!

Traditions are nice; they are often even valuable, but they are not essential. They must always be kept in their proper perspectives. Saying a certain version of the Lord's Prayer or singing the "right" kind of hymns is not what constitutes "true religion" any more than ceremonial handwashings did back in Jesus' time. The mistake of the scribes and Pharisees, and of many people today, is that they paid so much attention to their traditions they forgot to pay attention to loving God and their fellow man.

Jesus had some harsh words for these scribes and Pharisees when they charged him and his disciples with not being strict enough in their observance of rituals. He said to them, "Well did Isaiah prophesy of you hypocrites, as it is written, 'This people honors me with their lips, but their heart is far from me; in vain do they worship me, teaching as doctrines the precepts of men' " (Mark 7:6-7).

Jesus applied the words of Isaiah to the Pharisees, but they could also be spoken just as truly to many of us today. Many of us honor God with our lips, while our hearts stay far away. It is a very easy thing to do. We can honor God with our lips and say with approval, "seek ye first the kingdom of God, and his righteousness," while in our hearts we actually seek first our own kingdom, our own dominant position, and our own advancement. We can honor God with our lips and say with approval, "A day in thy courts is better than a thousand," while actually we may spend a hundred days outside of his courts to every one that we worship him there. We can honor God with our lips and say with approval. "Were the whole realm of nature mine, that were an offering far too small . . . love so amazing, so divine, demands my soul, my life, my all!" We say this while actually many of us do not see fit to give God anything of what we have, let alone a tithe or tenth portion of our earnings. And we can honor God with our lips and say with approval, "In Christ there is no male or female, Jew or Greek . . . we are all one body in him!" But in our hearts we draw rigid lines of separation, thinking, "Women should not be allowed to have the same responsibilities as men" or "Blacks should not be invited to worship in our church!"

How easy it is for us to say that this was true of the Pharisees and scribes! Yet how hard it is to say that it is true of us! And it is even harder still for each of us to confess, "This is true of me!" Perhaps each of us here needs to humbly ask, "Lord, is it I? Am I one of the guilty persons who honors you with lips, but not with the heart? Am I sometimes so stuck on my own traditions that I forget to love you and my neighbors as I should?"

Jesus told the scribes and the Pharisees, and us, that God has no regard for pious rituals and pious words unless they stem from a pious heart! May God help us to realize this and help us to earnestly desire a new heart that is washed clean of sin.

My friends, God has given us the power to become his children. Let us, therefore, now use this power to live as his children. I challenge and commission each and every one of you today to go out into the world and show your love for God and to show your love for your neighbors; for it is not the performance of rituals or the utterance of pious words that makes us Christians. It is the love in our hearts that is inspired by God, the Holy Spirit, that makes us Christians—God's children. This love must now become active through our words and deeds. So in the Name of Christ, let us now use God's power to really show our love for God and for one another. Let us begin now. Let us begin today! *Amen.*

George R. Karres
St. Peter's Lutheran Church
Fort Pierce, Florida

Sunday
September Eleventh

Call to Worship: Whoso offereth praise glorifieth me: and to him that ordereth his conversation aright will I show the salvation of God. *Psalm 50:23 KJV*

Processional Hymn: "Pass Me Not, O Gentle Savior"

Invocation: Lord, what are you really like? Show yourself to me so that I can know you as a friend. You are the true God, but I am only human. Help me in my search for you. *Amen.*

Sermon Scripture: Psalm 18:2; I Samuel 2:2; Psalm 32:2; Psalm 36:8; Revelation 22:1-2; Isaiah 48:18

Sermon Presentation: "Is God Like a Rock or a River?"

Hymn of the Day: "Eternal Father, Strong to Save"

Offertory Scripture: Worthy is the Lamb who was slain, to receive power and wealth and wisdom and might and honor and glory and blessing! *Revelation 5:12*

Offertory Prayer: I know who you are, Lord. My Lord, my God, my Savior, my Redeemer. How do I thank you for this great salvation? Take these my gifts as a down payment. *Amen.*

Prayer of the Day

Lord, in you, our God, we find the source of true strength and the strong, unmovable foundation for our faith. We find that your goodness and your mercy flow like a mighty river. Your peace is like a river, and your righteousness like the waves of the sea.

You, indeed, are like a river, constantly opening for us things that are new and possibilities that seem almost unimaginable. Yet you remain rock-like in your strength, in your will for our lives, and in your promise to share eternal life with us.

Help us come to grips with your direction and will for our lives. Help us to know when it is time to move along and when to stand fast. Lord, help us to realize that change and growth are dynamic parts of your creation. Every generation in its turn has more of the wonders and excitement of your creation revealed to them. Thank you for the truth that you have shared with us in our time and generation.

You have promised, Jesus, that as our Lord, you are the same yesterday, today, and tomorrow. As much as things change, we know that you are constant in your Word—in your grace—in your love for us. Our mighty river. Our strong rock. Jesus, our Lord and Savior. *Amen.*

Benediction: Behold, I stand at the door, and knock: if any man hear my voice, and open the door, I will come in to him, and will sup with him, and he with me. *Revelation 3:20 KJV*

Recessional Hymn: "For All the Saints"

Lectionary Lessons: The Sixteenth Sunday after Pentecost
Lesson 1—Proverbs 22:1-2, 8-9; Psalm 125
Lesson 2—James 2:1-5, 8-10, 14-17
Gospel—Mark 8:27-38

History of the Hymn of the Day: "Eternal Father, Strong to Save"

This hymn is the national hymn of the Navy and is used at the United States Naval Academy in Annapolis and on English ships. In addition a beautiful French translation is a standard part of the hymnbook of the French Navy.

Announcement for Next Week's Sermon: Love sure is strange. It can make you angry; it can make you giddy; it can make you act pretty silly. We can't live without love. Love sure is strange.

Story of the Week: A man who tried never to miss a boxing match on television had an important business meeting the night the championship bouts were going to be televised. He hated to miss seeing the fight but he did what he thought was the next best thing. He asked his wife to watch for him and tell him the result when he got home.

When the meeting was over and he came in the front door, he said, "Well, honey, how did the championship fight come out? Who won?"

"Nobody won," she said, "One of the men got hurt in the first round and fell down unconscious so they had to quit."

IS GOD LIKE A ROCK OR A RIVER?

Just to eliminate the suspense generated by the question posed in the sermon title—Is God like a rock or a river?—I am going to give you my conclusion first. The answer is both, and I have a hunch that you figured I was going to say that anyhow. What startled me was that when I began to follow either image, the rock or the river, the other popped up so regularly. When you start getting onto riverlike images about God, that rocklike God appears to bring you back on course. And when you connect with the sturdy, rocklike, unmoving God, the riverlike God washes over you. God may be like a rock in a river.

Here is a story that suggests both qualities of God: Originally, God did not give Moses just ten commandments, but something more like fifty. When Moses came down the mountain and started reading the commandments, the people went crazy. They were not about to put up with that many rules. Moses soon realized this was not going to work, so he went back up the mountain to talk it over with God. When Moses returned, he told the people, "I have some good news and some bad news. The good news is that I got God down to ten commandments. The bad news is that 'Thou shalt not commit adultery' is still on the list."

This is the first combination of images of God as both a river and a rock that I want to share. The joke suggests that God is changing and changeable, like a river. But then we run into the rocklike element of God—*Thou shalt not commit adultery* stays on the list as number seven. Perhaps a similar kind of negotiation is going on today. We have gone back up the mountain to work out a new sexual morality. The message we have found is that sex is no longer considered sinful and ugly. We have found the beauty of God's creation in the celebration of our bodies, in hugging, touching, dancing, and singing. But just as we were getting excited about the possibilities of a new sexual morality, we ran into an abiding, rocklike truth. We cannot have a sexual relationship with two partners. We cannot be married and also have a lover.

This is a word of God that we uncover through the struggles of human experience. I have listened to story after story of people who try to keep sexual relationships with two people. They invariably destroy the meaning of one, if not both, of these relationships. No one has ever told me that he or she was able to carry on both relationships with a love that was open, honest, and full of meaning.

God is like a river, opening us to the unfolding blessings of creation, even in our sexuality. God is like a rock, reminding us that *Thou shalt not commit adultery.*

Let's allow that example to go for a second. Consider the broader range of the river voice of God. This is the voice that calls us to be aware of what is new, to imagine the previously unimaginable. The riverlike God opens our eyes to see the injustices of sexism, the new possibilities for peace, the pain of our public schools that could be healed by the budget of just one extra military program, like the B-1 bomber or the MX missile.

The rock voice is a foundation that cannot be shaken. It is the unchanging power of the Ten Commandments, the strength of love, the gift of eternity, the miracle of the church, and the strength of prayer when everything else crumbles.

Yet now another voice of God is heard, a voice urging times of quiet, reflection, and nurture for our souls. We, a busy and often burned-out people, are looking for an anchor, a rock to hang onto. We will not give up the river, but we need the rock. Both are God's call in a different time.

We seek the rock; yet the cycle continues. As we move into the discovery of silence, the restoration of a lost sense of reverence and dignity in our worship, we come to the brink of illumination, and just then the toilet flushes, a door slams, or a child runs searching for a parent. We are brought back to earth, to this time and place. That, too, is God's Word, reminding us of all that is alive and moving around us. The river flows again.

Here is another image: How many of you are starting a new school year? Every year there are people of every age who park their faith in God, tie it to a rock, and never move it again. They have had enough moving, changing, and confusion. It is said that the optimum year for attaining new ideas about God is the sophomore year of high school. Probably the most important thing for every person in school this year is to keep in touch with the moving, changing riverlike God in all the changes of your life, realizing that God also remains a rock when change gets overwhelming. If you let your faith flow with the changes of life, you will also discover old memories of childhood faith that will appear like rocks of comfort and meaning.

It is interesting that the people who do just tie their faith to a rock, throw it overboard, quit believing in any God, and just let their faith sink like a rock are the ones who most want to keep the church from moving on. In England last spring, a new bishop was appointed in York. He stated that he had doubts about the virgin birth and the resurrection of the body. Two days later lightning hit his cathedral. The people who have been most critical of this bishop have suggested that the lightning was an act of God.

You can lose a sense of God by both drifting away from the rocklike foundations of faith and by standing still in belief or unbelief while God is moving.

You can go to the Bible and find a variety of notions of God; some of this is because different people understood God differently, but perhaps it is also because God is changing. Does God change and grow like us? I think so. The new truth you discover today—about life, love, a different future—does not mean that yesterday's word was not from God. The creation is moving, growing in blessing. This may even mean that one can change God's mind no matter how clumsy that language sounds. Remember that Jesus compared prayer to the pleading of a widow with a crooked judge or the friend banging on a neighbor's door at midnight to wake the godly part of you like a sleeping friend.

So let us move down the river of God's changing will, feel God's presence moving through us like a river, hear Jesus' words, "He who believes in me . . . 'Out of his heart shall flow rivers of living water' " (John 7:38), and believe God's Spirit is what it does, a river bringing forth lifegiving streams. Just as we get comfortable flowing like this river, we will run into the experiences of God that are like a rock, steady, eternal, something to stumble on if we are moving away too fast, but also a refuge, a shelter in the storm. Hear the words of the psalmist as we seek to center ourselves again, "Let the words of my mouth and the meditation of my heart be acceptable in thy sight, O Lord, my rock and my redeemer" (Psalm 19:14).

We prepare now to enter a time of meditation and music. One way to meditate is to picture certain parts of creation and feel their message. Take time to picture before you a river, and feel the Godlike presence of the river in your life. Then wait and watch, too, for the image of the rock to emerge, perhaps even in the river, and let its message come to you. Enter the images; let them blend; and let them enter you. If the door slams or the toilet flushes, welcome that, too, as part of a creation that always mixes the human and the divine, the rock and the river. All is wrapped in grace. *Amen.*

Larry Reimer
United Church of Gainesville
Gainesville, Florida

Sunday
September Eighteenth

Call to Worship: A new commandment I give to you, that you love one another; even as I have loved you, that you also love one another. By this all men will know that you are my disciples, if you have love for one another. *John 13:34-35*

Processional Hymn: "For the Beauty of the Earth"

Invocation: Love is what makes the world go round. The road to heaven is paved with love. Lord, fill this world with love so that there is room for nothing else. *Amen.*

Sermon Scripture: Luke 15:17-32

Sermon Presentation: "Love Never Gives Up"

Hymn of the Day: "God Be with You Till We Meet Again"

Offertory Scripture: Greater love has no man than this, that a man lay down his life for his friends. *John 15:13*

Offertory Prayer: Lord, we show our love in such little ways; yet those whom we love understand. Accept these gifts of love as one little way of saying, "I love you, Lord." *Amen.*

Prayer of the Day

Lord, there are two roads from which we must choose—one the low road of being defensive, of seeking revenge, of "doing it to others before they do it to us"; the other, the higher road, a road paved with forgiveness, with reconciliation, with love for other people, with compassion, with mercy, and with kindness.

It's a tough decision to make, Lord. The low road involves less risk, or so we think. Actually the low road leads us to greater misery and takes us farther away from you and the kingdom of heaven.

The high road has risks, too, Lord. But it is the way of love. It is your way. It is a road that is free of jealousy, free of conceit. It is a way that does not welcome pride, selfishness, or irritability. It is the way on which those who travel keep no record of wrongs.

You have already traveled the way. It leads to the cross. But that's not where it ended. Your way continued beyond the grave to eternal glory.

That's what you promise to all who follow where you have

led the way. Give us the strength, the patience, and the faith to travel the high road that bears your name. *Amen.*

Benediction: Love is patient and kind; love is not jealous or boastful; it is not arrogant or rude. Love does not insist on its own way; it is not irritable or resentful; it does not rejoice at wrong, but rejoices in the right. Love bears all things, believes all things, hopes all things, endures all things. So faith, hope, love abide, these three; but the greatest of these is love.

I Corinthians 13:4-7, 13

Recessional Hymn: "Lord Jesus, I Love Thee"

Lectionary Lessons: The Seventeenth Sunday after Pentecost
Lesson 1—Job 28:20-28; Psalm 27:1-6
Lesson 2—James 3:13-18
Gospel—Mark 9:30-37

History of the Hymn of the Day: "God Be with You Till We Meet Again"

An emotional hymn of prayer written in 1882 by Jeremiah Eames Rankin, a Congregational minister of New England. His purpose for writing the hymn was to find a way for the Christian to say good-bye which was not contradictory to his faith and belief. He finally settled for the phrase "God be with you," which he felt was the Christian way of saying "good-bye until we meet again." The story is told that Rankin invited two composers to write music for the words. One composer was well known, the other unknown. He chose the work of the unknown composer, William G. Tomer. He certainly must have been inspired in his choice for there is no finer example of the harmony of words and music than in this hymn. Without doubt, the popularity of "God Be with You Till We Meet Again" has been augmented considerably because of the melody.

Announcement for Next Week's Sermon: If someone gets something you feel isn't deserved, do you get angry? It just does not seem fair, but I guess that's life. It also happens to be God's way. How about that!

Story of the Week: Several kids were bragging about how tough they were.

The first little boy said, "I'm so tough that I can wear out a pair of shoes in six weeks."

"That's nothing," the second little boy said. "I'm so tough that I can wear out a pair of dungarees in six days."

But the little girl from next door had the best one. She said, "You two aren't so tough. I can wear out my grandmother in six minutes."

LOVE NEVER GIVES UP

Sometimes in a strange and unexpected way something good happens to us. We say this is our lucky day; good fortune smiles on us. We find an amazing grace touching us, and we are filled with peace and joy.

It was the third of the month, and, like many other residents of Pelham Parkway in the Bronx, a seventy-six-year-old retired shoe salesman had gone to the bank to cash his Social Security check and pay a few bills. As usual the line was long, and, as usual, a young woman at the teller's window asked him a question to verify his identity, this time his date of birth. The shoe salesman replied, and the young teller looked at him with a slight expression of surprise. "Please, wait a minute," she said and disappeared into the back of the bank.

Something was up. The salesman was certain of it. "I couldn't imagine why the delay," he recalled. "Things were running through my mind. Was I being accused of stealing somebody else's check? Was something wrong with my check? How was I going to pay my rent?"

As the salesman waited, imagining the eyes of everyone in the bank upon him, the young woman returned with two other tellers. His suspicions were confirmed; something was definitely up.

The three tellers faced him on the other side of the window. They threw their arms about one another's waists, opened their mouths, and sang:

Happy birthday to you,
Happy birthday to you,
Happy birthday, happy birthday,
Happy birthday to you!

What a bright surprise for him! He would never forget what happened on the third of the month in his bank in the Bronx.

This kind of "happening" does not occur very often. There are other times when bad things happen, when people behave in a mean and malicious way. There are times when people do not sing a "happy birthday" song—but give instead a nasty, scowling look, speak an angry word, close their hearts with hurt feelings, or behave in rude and sullen manners. And when this thing happens, we wonder what we should do. How should we deal with the mean blows life gives us? What should we say, when someone speaks the mean and spiteful word?

There are two things we can do, two ways to go, when this happens. First, when we are pushed, we can push right back. When someone curses us out, we can curse right back. When someone is mean and bitter, we can be mean and bitter, too, blow for blow, eye for eye, tooth for tooth.

The other way to go, and the other thing to do, is quite different. We can be patient and kind. We can refuse to be jealous, conceited, or proud. We can refuse to be ill-mannered, selfish, or irritable. We can refuse to keep a record of wrongs. We can think and feel and behave with faith and hope. We can live with the conviction that "love never gives up" (I Corinthians 13:7 TEV).

These two ways to go make a high road and a low road, and everyone can choose which way to go. The two ways represent two attitudes toward life. Each way is an interpretation and a philosophy of the meaning of life.

There is an old story, perhaps the greatest short story in all literature, that gives a picture of these two ways. Jesus told the story of a young man he called the prodigal son, the young man's father, and the young man's older brother (Luke 15:11-32).

In the story, the young son asks his father for his share of the family property, and on receiving it leaves home for a far country, where he wastes his money in reckless living. He is in a bad way. He is lonely and hungry; he will even eat the bean pods he throws on the ground for the pigs. But he comes to his senses. He decides to go back home, where he will take his chances with what he might find there.

The story shifts to the two persons back home—two persons with different attitudes toward the return of the prodigal son. The father has one philosophy; the older brother has another. The way each behaves when the young brother shows up tells the difference between their two philosophies of life. The father sees his young son coming back when the boy is still a long way down the road. The father's heart fills with pity, and without waiting a minute he runs toward the boy and throws his arms around his son. He calls the servants and asks them to bring the best robe, a ring for his son's finger, and shoes for his feet. He calls for a feast of celebration, all because his son is alive and home again. He was lost; now he is found.

What a crazy old father! He did not need to do all this. Why didn't he just stand on the porch, waiting for his son to walk up to the house by himself? Why didn't he stand there, arms folded across his chest, stern look in his eyes, with a few forthright questions for the boy? "Where do you think you've been? What do you mean showing up in that ragged coat and dirty feet? Go around back; wash up before you come in this house."

He could have said that. But he did not. He had a philosophy that would not let him talk that way. He had a kind heart; he was filled with compassion. Looking at his boy come home, the father knew only one thing: His son was lost, and now he is found. So he reached out with love.

What about the older brother? The story says he is out in the field, and with his working day over, he walks back, coming close to the house. He hears music and dancing, and calls a servant to ask, "What's going on?" He is told that his brother is back, safe and sound, and there's a celebration going on. But the brother is angry and refuses to go inside.

The father comes out to beg him to come in. But the older brother explodes. "Look, all these years I have worked like a slave for you! And what have you ever given me? Now this son of yours, who has wasted all your money—he comes back, and for him you make this celebration." The father says to this angry brother that everything he has is really his, but, "We have to celebrate, because your brother is back home."

That's how the story ends. Jesus told no more. I suppose the father goes back into the house. And I guess the older brother walks away, sullen and bitter, with his heart closed against the young man who had come home. He was all wrapped up in himself, this older brother, and because this was his attitude and philosophy, he did not and would not reach out with any kind of love.

Maybe this kind of attitude had encouraged the young son to leave home in the first place. If only the older brother had a different philosophy. If only he had walked into the house and held out his hand with a smile of welcome. If only he could have said, "I'm glad you're back. We've had an empty house all the time you have been away. I missed you. What happened? How are things with you?" But he did not say this. His way of thinking and feeling would not let him say it, because the older brother was jealous, conceited, and proud. He was ill-mannered, selfish, and irritable. He had given up on his younger brother a long time ago.

But "love never gives up." In the story Jesus told, the fact of love's never giving up is the great thing on which the life of the father is based. In the face of disappointment and reproach, in the face of anger and rejection, love never gives up. This is the nature of love. The father in Jesus' parable is the living representation of this meaning.

We can state the meaning of love in other ways. The apostle Paul, in his first letter to the Corinthians, gives an analysis of love. His words are familiar. He says that love is patient and kind, not jealous or boastful, not arrogant or rude. "Love does not insist on its own way; it is not irritable or resentful; it does not rejoice at wrong, but rejoices in the right" (I Corinthians 13:5*b*-6). Paul could have said as well that love is a spendthrift, that love gives and does not count the cost. Love gives and does not look for a return favor. Love does not worry about its gifts being tax deductible. Love gives to meet a need. Love does not care about the label of benefactor, patron, sponsor, supporting member.

Love has more than one definition. The English poet Shelley described love as "a going out of our own nature, and identification of ourselves with the good, true, and beautiful that exist in thought, action, or person not our own." Another definition, a bit more colorful, written on a t-shirt from the Philippines says, "LOVE is a basket with five loaves and two fishes; it's never enough until you start to give it away."

Love in its deep, full meaning is strong and powerful. The words of I Corinthians 13:7 put it like this, "There is nothing love cannot face" (NEB). "Love bears all things" (RSV). "Love knows no limit to its endurance" (JBP). "Love never gives up" (TEV). These words of Paul on the power of love find an echo in the beautiful words of Thomas à Kempis in the devotional classic, *The Imitation of Christ,* written more than five hundred years ago: "Though wearied [love] is not tired; though pressed, it is not straitened; though alarmed, it is not confounded; but as a lively flame and burning torch, it forceth its way upwards, and securely passeth through all."

Love can be defined and described in meaningful words; the

power of love can be given a beautiful statement. But the full wonder and strength of love is best seen in the living story of someone's life. Remember, for instance, how someone in time past entered Jericho and was just passing through, when he looked up and saw a little man in a sycamore tree, a man who had the reputation of being mean and miserable. The man looking up said, "Make haste and come down; for I must stay at your house today" (Luke 19:5). The man in the tree climbed down. And in the ensuing encounter his life was changed, because the eyes of love looked at him.

Or, again, in talking about the power of love, remember someone who once was asked by a number of persons to pass judgment on a woman who had done something wrong. He said the person without sin should throw the first stone. And after no stone was thrown, he said to the woman, "Neither do I condemn you; go, and do not sin again" (John 8:11). Love looks away from the past and opens the door to tomorrow.

Or, perhaps, think about someone who once stood before a high priest to answer charges against him in Jerusalem. His answer angered one of the guards standing near, and the guard struck him on the face. The man who was struck replied, "If I spoke amiss, state it in evidence; if I spoke well, why strike me?" (John 18:23 NEB). Love responds to arrogant provocation with calm compassion.

Without doubt the best description of love is told in the living story of someone who walks in the way of love. This kind of living definition we never forget. A group of tourist pilgrims in the Holy Land a few years ago visited the place in which Jesus began his walk to Calvary, carrying his heavy, wooden cross along what came to be called the Via Dolorosa. As the group of pilgrims started out to walk along this way, they noticed a small plaque hanging on the wall nearby at eye level. They stepped across the room and read the words on the plaque, written in English and German, at the entrance to this area of the original stones of the Via Dolorosa pavement.

> Jesus . . . looks at us with longing and asks us: Who will stand here at My side and share My Way, in which when men ill-treat us we respond with forgiving love? He who does thus is My true disciple.

A short quotation, "Charity endureth all things," completed the words on the plaque.

In the moment that they stood there, the pilgrims seemed to understand what it means to walk in the way of Jesus. And they understand now the full and deep truth of the words, "Love never gives up." *Amen.*

Henry M. Childs
First Congregational Church, former pastor
Rockaway Park, New York

Sunday
September Twenty-fifth

Call to Worship: He that hath my commandments, and keepeth them, he it is that loveth me: and he that loveth me shall be loved of my Father, and I will love him, and will manifest myself to him. *John 14:21 KJV*

Processional Hymn: "Savior, Teach Me, Day by Day"

Invocation: Lord, teach us to be a forgiving people. It is so easy for us to be judgmental and superior because we are Christian. That is not your way; let us follow your lesson of humility and love for all people. *Amen.*

Sermon Scripture: Matthew 20:1-16

Sermon Presentation: "Begrudging God's Grace"

Hymn of the Day: "How Great Thou Art"

Offertory Scripture: And now, Israel, what does the Lord your God require of you, but to fear the Lord your God, to walk in all his ways, to love him, to serve the Lord your God with all your heart and with all your soul. *Deuteronomy 10:12*

Offertory Prayer: Lord, we offer you first a contrite and humble heart. Now we offer you these gifts as an offering to show our love for you, not as we ought, but as we are able. *Amen.*

Prayer of the Day

Lord, you have said to us, "My thoughts are not your thoughts. My ways are not your ways." We forget so often that you are God, the Father, and we are your children. Like Adam and Eve, we would make decisions on our own, instead of seeking your guidance. We honestly believe that we know what is best for ourselves and for our world. We are quick to make judgments about the lives, the thoughts, the actions, the words, and the feelings of others. We truly see the speck in another's eye, but ignore the log in our own eye.

While seeking forgiveness, we are reluctant to forgive. While quick to condemn others, we want others to be patient and understanding in their dealings with us. We would try to hoard your grace, your forgiveness, your love for ourselves.

Remind us that you have created us to reflect your love, your goodness, and your grace and to share these things that you have given to us with those around us. *Amen.*

Benediction: You, who by God's power are guarded through faith for a salvation ready to be revealed in the last time.

I Peter 1:4-5

Recessional Hymn: "Jesus, with Thy Church Abide"

Lectionary Lessons: The Eighteenth Sunday after Pentecost
Lesson 1—Job 42:1-6; Psalm 27:7-14
Lesson 2—James 4:13-17, 5:7-11
Gospel—Mark 9:38-50

History of the Hymn of the Day: "How Great Thou Art"
Strangely enough, this truly impressive contemporary hymn received its present popular form through two different countries and two different translations. The original form was a Swedish poem "O Mighty God" by Carl Boberg written in 1886 and translated by Professor E. Gustav Johnson, of North Park College in 1925. The poem, based on the everlasting wonders and eternal powers of God had a metrical pattern that was easily identified with an old Swedish folk song and soon the words became a permanent part of that song. Before his death, Boberg had the joy of knowing his poem had become a cherished contribution to Swedish music. "O Mighty God" spread beyond Sweden and its native tongue. Soon it was popular in other countries, and sung in Russian, Polish, German, and other tongues. In 1923, the Reverend Stuart K. Hine, London missionary to the Ukraine, heard the song for the first time in Russia. Unaware of the fact that the song had originated in Sweden, Hine attributed it to a Russian prisoner and credited him with writing it in 1921. He was so impressed with the song that he made an English translation in 1948, which he called, "How Great Thou Art." The interesting fact of the story of this great hymn is that although two translations were made through three different languages, over thirty years apart, the might and grandeur of the hymn is preserved. "How Great Thou Art" inspires the human heart to the wonder and majesty of God.

Announcement for Next Week's Sermon: Did you ever wish you could sit down and have a good talk with God about just how bad his earth has become? We'll do just that next Sunday.

Story of the Week: The little fellow's father had been bragging about him. "Someday he's going to be a great politician," he said.

"He's only three years old," the man's friend said. "How do you know he's going to be a politician?"

"Because," the boy's father said, "he never stops talking. And even though the things he says don't make any sense, he sure can make them sound good."

BEGRUDGING GOD'S GRACE

Are you a person who holds grudges? Is there someone you may even be jealous of, or feel resentful toward because of some good fortune that has come his or her way? You know the reasons: You do all the work and someone else gets all the credit. How unfair! People like that do not deserve such honor! Other people seem to have all the luck. They are always in the spotlight, when it seems clear to you that they have not earned one bit of it. Where's the justice in all of that?

There are bound to be people around us that we just don't like very much. They may be those who disagree with us on politics, religion, or how to raise kids. Or they may be individuals who just seem lazy to us, unwilling to lift a finger to do any fair share of the work, but who rush to the front of the line for a paycheck or a handout. It is disgusting to us. We say that people like that don't deserve what they get.

In a very real way, we all would like to get something for nothing. But when it happens to someone else, we feel resentment, because someone got something for nothing! We are not feeling jealousy, but are begrudging. We begrudge someone because that person has received something that, in our view, is undeserved. It seems perfectly understandable that we would feel that way, in that kind of a situation. The concern is not about those who get what they don't deserve, but those who begrudge. Whether this emotion is understandable or reasonable makes little difference in the light of the fact that begrudging, for whatever reason, arises from the sin that is basic to us: the sin of wanting to be like God.

When we begrudge someone who receives that which we feel is not deserved, haven't we made a judgment about that person's worth? "They are the kind of people who don't deserve good fortune!" Anger and resentment build, but take comfort in the belief that people like that will get their just desserts in the end. We say to ourselves, "Someday those freeloaders and goldbrickers are going to get what they really deserve," and then our judgments will be vindicated. And so, beneath our resentment lies the belief that God agrees with us. In our begrudging moments, it's the only thing that makes sense to us. But can we be so sure?

> For my thoughts are not your thoughts, neither are your ways my ways, says the Lord. For as the heavens are higher than the earth, so are my ways higher than your ways, and my thoughts than your thoughts. (Isaiah 55:8-9)

In verses 6-7 of the above, the prophet Isaiah speaks about the wicked and unrighteous who need to turn and seek the Lord while he may be found. He is talking as much about the person who begrudges another human being as he is about the person who is begrudged for ungodly behavior. Both the judged and the judge stand on equal ground before the Creator. Anyone who thinks he or she knows God's thoughts, God's will, risks committing that most grievous sin of trying to be like God. Judging another person's worth before God is none of our business! That's God's business! His ways are not our ways; his thoughts are not our thoughts. No matter how sincere you may be, no matter how righteously indignant you may feel, it's the begrudging that clearly separates our ways and thoughts from God's.

Then it stands to reason that, if we could rid ourselves of those begrudging, graceless feelings, then we could do the will of God. Yes and no. If we could do such a thing, we would be well on our way to becoming more genuine children of God. But simply eliminating such resentment is not a matter of self-discipline or choice. That sin is not removed so easily.

It's more a matter of keeping it straight that God did not make us just like him, but rather in his image; there's a vast difference! We are not photocopies of the Creator; rather he has created us in such a way that, as we live, we strive to reflect his love and goodness, to be generous and forgiving, to be cheerful in our giving, and to be faithful to him.

However, we don't always strive so perfectly. We carry in our genes the formula for rebellion against God, a deep-seated resentment for being a creature instead of Creator. Because that first human being followed those instincts, we have lost that sense of love and goodness, that spirit of generosity and forgiveness (unless there are conditions). Where once grace abounded unquestioned and unconditional, it has been twisted into something one receives because one has earned it or has done something pleasing to God.

How easily we believe that grace is given because we earned it or deserve it. In our human way of thinking, distorted by sin, that's the only thing that makes sense. Unless, of course, we believe that grace is beyond all human sense. We can be told that, but words are cheap. What we really need is someone to show us.

Jesus could sense, among the highly religious folk of his day, that remnant of the old Adam coming through, a disbelief in a God, who could unconditionally be loving and gracious. The people of Jesus' time had clung for years to a more reasonable certainty: Do this for God and God will do that for you. But this belief is really based on a misconception of God: that God stands to gain something from his contact with us.

We think that if our sinfulness is offensive to God, then our attempts to lead a decent life ought to be pleasing to him, a fragrant offering. I'm sure God is delighted when we do right, but we are the ones who need his goodness around us, not God. Regardless of what we say or do, God remains changeless—whole and holy, perfect Love. God doesn't need us to complete his life. It is we who need him, which is why he made the first move, pouring his life into us in the form of Jesus Christ, because he saw our need.

Like the landowner in the parable from Matthew 20, God is generous. The Pharisees were like the laborers who worked all day and were angered when the owner of the vineyard issued the same paycheck to the ones who worked only an hour. To them, the generosity of the owner was baffling, and even disgusting. Was it cheap grace that those latecoming workers experienced? As Bonhoeffer used the term, cheap grace is not grace that is dispensed simply to people who, in our view, do not deserve it. Grace is cheapened when it becomes self-serving, when our only interest in God is what he can do for us now that we have done something wonderful for him. If we begrudge his generosity, his grace, what are we doing but trying to limit that grace, making it less than what it is?

Whenever we try to put a price on something priceless, we are the ones who cheapen!

God's ways and thoughts are not ours. He doesn't follow our patterns of logic, our legalisms, nor does he abide by our brand of justice. If so, then God would be in our image, just like us, dishing out grace and punishment as efficiently as we do.

God's grace is just what Jesus proclaimed it to be: First and foremost, it is the Father's to give as he chooses and to whom he chooses. It will baffle us and at times we will resent it. But finally, God's grace is such that it surrounds even those who resent that kind of unconditional, unbridled, illogical love. It's hard to believe, but it is far better for us to say that than to say it is not believable at all. Better that we struggle with it than deny it.

There is a play in which there is a scene depicting Judgment Day. All those who claim to be righteous stand eagerly before the Gates of Pearl, waiting for them to open wide. Suddenly, a rumor moves through the throng: "He's going to forgive those others, too!" Panic. Outrage. How unfair, they cry, as they raise their fists in angry protest and scream for justice. In the end, their complaining leads to their own condemnation, because they refused to believe in a God who is wholly and Holy Love.

May God grant us strength and wisdom to struggle with that which we are tempted to believe is not true: that God's grace is so boundless that is includes even those who we think don't deserve it. Perhaps we need to remember that it is not because we deserve grace and forgiveness that God so generously gives them. Maybe it's because we, who begrudge, may need it most of all. *Amen.*

Jon Lindekugel
Christ the King Lutheran Church
Hutchinson, Minnesota

Sunday
October Second

Call to Worship: Before the mountains were brought forth, or ever thou hadst formed the earth and the world, from everlasting to everlasting thou art God. *Psalm 90:2*

Processional Hymn: "Jesus, the Very Thought of Thee"

Invocation: Lord, every day of our lives we must have a close encounter with you. That is the staff of life that keeps our lives on course. Through daily prayer we keep in touch with you. Draw us closer every day to your side. *Amen.*

Sermon Scripture: Luke 19:39-44

Sermon Presentation: "Close Encounter"

Hymn of the Day: "Sweet Hour of Prayer"

Offertory Scripture: Know therefore that the Lord your God is God, the faithful God who keeps covenant and steadfast love with those who love him and keep his commandments, to a thousand generations. *Deuteronomy 7:9*

Offertory Prayer: O God, you are faithful in all things. You require that we also be faithful in the trusts that you give us. Here, Lord, is a demonstration of my stewardship of your trust. *Amen.*

Prayer of the Day

Lord, this morning I feel like a bug under glass or an amoeba under a microscope. So often we live our lives going where we want to go, doing what we want to do, with whomever we please and whenever we like. We treat the world as if it were our own private playground. We forget not only who created the world, but also who has given us the responsibility to care for everything and everyone in it. We act like the owners and not the caretakers. We forget that you are the creator and we are your created.

Lord, most of the time we think you aren't watching or listening to us and our world. We forget that you came into our world and lived among us as one of us. You are aware of our shortcomings and selfishness. We forget that you are painfully aware of our sinfulness. We assume that the pain of the cross is in the past. We forget that our sinfulness still causes you pain, perhaps not in your nail-pierced hands or feet or your side where the spear broke your flesh and made you bleed, but in your heart.

Make us aware of your presence in our world and in our lives. Let us follow your words and do your will. Help us to be the people you want us to be so that we can live in a world as you would have it. May each encounter with you be a joyful one. *Amen.*

Benediction: But by the grace of God I am what I am, and his grace toward me was not in vain. On the contrary, I worked harder than any of them, though it was not I, but the grace of God which is with me. *I Corinthians 15:10*

Recessional Hymn: "The King of Love My Shepherd Is"

Lectionary Lessons: The Nineteenth Sunday after Pentecost
Lesson 1—Genesis 2:18-24; Psalm 128
Lesson 2—Hebrews 1:1-4, 2:9-11
Gospel—Mark 10:2-16

History of the Hymn of the Day: "Sweet Hour of Prayer"
"Sweet Hour of Prayer," one of the world's most popular prayer hymns, was written by a man who could not see. In 1842, the Reverend William W. Walford, a blind English clergyman, dictated his inspirational poem of prayer to the Reverend Thomas Salmon, minister at the Congregational Church, Coleshill, England. Salmon took it with him on a journey to New York City, where it was pubished in September 1845. Without doubt, Walford's physical blindness gave him a spiritual sight to see, where many others could not see the tremendous significance of the power of illumination in prayer.

Announcement for Next Week's Sermon: "The devil made me do it." Do you really believe that happens? Next Sunday we will find out all about what the devil makes us do.

Story of the Week: The little second-grader's family had just moved and she was going to her new school for the first time. When she came home that afternoon she said to her mother, "What's sex?" Her mother had been expecting that question for some time and she was ready for her tiny daughter. So, for the next half hour she explained about the birds and the bees. Then she said to her, "Now, do you understand what I have been telling you?" "Yes," her daughter said, "I think I do." Then she showed her mother a school registration card that she had brought home from school and said, "But, how am I going to get all of that into this little square?"

CLOSE ENCOUNTER

Dear friends, I have just returned from Cloud Nine, where I had a conversation with—God! That sounds crazy, and I know where people go who talk like that. I'm on my way, but I thought I should stop here first and relate my story to you.

On first seeing God, I fell to my knees. *Stand up like a man,* he said. I told him I was a pastor, hoping to make some brownie points. It didn't faze him. I said I was one of his servants. He looked bemused. *Where are you from?* I told him I was from Earth. He looked at me quizzically, so I gave him an earful. "Earth is a planet between Venus and Mars, ninety-three million miles from the sun, 238,857 miles from the moon, spinning about a thousand miles an hour in space. It's an exciting place to live," I said. "Each morning the sun rises to warm our planet and give us light; we'd die without it. Warm and cool breezes blow. At night the moon appears, and we can count the stars. You'd love it down there.

"And we have four seasons: summer, when everything is green and glowing, colorful flowers of all shapes and fragrances that leave you breathless, birds of every kind and color, each singing its own song—you should see a cardinal—and insects of every size and shape—bees (have you tasted honey?)—and animals—dogs, cats, raccoons, horses, cows (we drink their milk).

"Then comes autumn and billions of leaves, no two alike and each in its own brilliant color and fishing in lakes and sailing in oceans and waterfalls and taking a hot shower on a cold day and a cool shower on a hot day . . . *Taking a shower?* Yes, don't you ever take a shower? Water, water, it's a miracle. You take two gases, hydrogen and oxygen, mix them together, two parts hydrogen, one part oxygen, and it becomes water. It just happens by itself. It's a marvel. We wash things in it, wash ourselves in it, drink it; we'd all die without it.

"Then comes winter and lots of water becomes flakes of snow, no two flakes alike, and covers plains and hills in a pure white mantle. Then comes Christmas. That's a big holiday during which we get a lot of presents if we believe in Santa Claus. He's a messenger, a jolly sort. Some think he's mother or father.

"Then comes spring, and you wouldn't believe this, but we have a flower called a crocus that actually blossoms out right through the snow. New life comes to the whole earth, and people feel like they have been born again. You know, like you've died and come alive again. And everyone has grown one year older and some a little wiser. Everybody loves spring. Good old mother earth, where would we be without her? She provides so many of our needs. It's great to be alive."

So you're living in paradise, just as I'd hoped.

"Well, not exactly. Some think we're running out of pure water, and if nothing is done, we may all die of thirst," I said.

And are you doing anything about it?"

"We're thinking about it. And then, too, some of the earth is poisoned—rivers, lakes, land."

Poisoned?

"We've been dumping toxic chemicals in thousands of places. One whole town had to be demolished and the people evacuated. Some think they are dying because of it."

You stopped dumping poison?

"We're working on it. And we're proud of our part of the earth and have a perfect right to be. We call it America, the land of the free and the home of the brave. Ever been to New York? You'd love New York. There's a lady there with a lamp held high; she's called the Statue of Liberty. Near her feet, there is a plaque that says something about 'give me your tired, your poor, your huddled masses yearning to breathe free,' and we've made that come true to thousands of boat people. They are people who have been forced from their land and homes, with no food, clothing, or money, and they struggle in rickety boats to reach our shores. Many of them drown. We welcome boat people, help them get places to live, jobs, food, and friends. And over the years we have sent thousands of tons of goods and food and billions of dollars to depressed peoples everywhere. We even help people in prisons. Some, perhaps, belong there, but thousands do not. Sometimes we write a thousand letters in protest to just one country appealing for freedom for just one person, and often he gets freed, and it's worth it. Some call us the 'good samaritan' of the whole world," I concluded.

World? That rings a bell. I sent one of my own down there a while back. He didn't stay long. They treated him rather shabbily. I brought him back. They called him Jesus, said God.

"Jesus!" I exclaimed. "We know him! We have a whole book about him! We gather in churches each Sunday to learn how to follow him. Churches are buildings with crosses on the steeples. He died on a cross. We crucified him and must never forget why. You know that. The story is in all of our songs during Lent."

What is Lent? God asked.

"It's a season of forty days when we walk what we call *the lonesome valley* and gain courage by walking close to Jesus. And we sing songs. Even slaves wrote some of them. A long time ago, we brought families over here in chains, auctioned them off, split them up, and made them our servants."

And you protested?

"I wasn't even born."

You would have protested?

"I think so. Anyway, one of the songs we sing is 'Sweet Little Jesus boy, we didn't know who you was.' The slaves were ignorant. Their grammar wasn't good, but their songs make us weep with both sorrow and joy. It seems as if they walked a valley more lonesome than ours. Yes, we know all about Jesus. Each week in church we sing, take a big offering, and listen to a crackerjack sermon. *Crackerjack* is just a saying. It means there is a surprise in every package. You'd be happy to know that Jesus is Lord and Master of all life. He's our Savior!"

He is? How?

"He keeps us from going astray, from worshiping other gods. He reveals to us the truth about our world and ourselves, shows us how love never fails."

And you believe and practice that?

"Some of the time, but we have trouble with love. It seems so idealistic, so impossible in the real world."

That's strange. I thought it was the only possible thing in the real world.

"Not for us, unless you have a different definition for love. Do you?"

No. Love is a deep, caring concern for the welfare of others. Why do you ask?

"Frankly, we're finding it difficult to practice loving others, and even wonder if it's possible. You see, America, where I live, is called a superpower, because when it comes to power, we are super. Another country that is called a superpower is Russia. Have you heard of it?"

Yes.

"Do you love them?"

Yes.

"Do they listen to you?"

About as much as Americans do.

"Well, anyway, we used to be friends, but not anymore. You see, some of us think they are out to get us or even to conquer the world, and they are building bombs in preparation for it. Bombs are big round things that when dropped explode and kill many people. Jesus sounds reasonable in church, but how can you love people who threaten you with bombs?"

Sounds sort of difficult. What are you doing about it?

"What can we do, except arm ourselves and half the world with bigger and better bombs?"

Better? You mean they make a bigger explosion and kill more people?

"No, no, no. We aren't planning to have them go bang and kill a lot of people. We feel we need them to defend our America, to feel safe and secure. Isn't that a part of love, a sort of deep, caring concern for the welfare of ourselves?"

Perhaps, if it really makes you feel safe and secure. Does it?

"No, but would you punish us for doing this?"

No, I punish no one. You punish yourselves. You're caught in a web you have built, and there seems no end in sight. Is that it?

"Well, yes and no, because there is an end in sight. Last week I heard a doctor telling a thousand people that there are now so many bombs that if they all exploded together they could destroy, decimate, incinerate, annihilate the whole world, every living thing—except cockroaches—and it made me very scared. Is it a sin to be scared? Would you be frightened if you were me?"

I think so.

"We feel that the church is called to be the conscience of America, and now my conscience is bothering me. It seems that things have gone so far that there's no love left to be an answer, or that we now are blind to the things that make for peace. I'd like to ask a final question: If, by chance, worse came to worse and mankind was on the verge of being almost totally destroyed, couldn't you, wouldn't you somehow step in and stop it?"

I'm not planning to. Remember Adam and Eve? The Holocaust? The world is yours to take care of, to be responsible. All of you are my family, slowly learning that there will be one world or none.

"But is there still time? What can we do to turn this thing around?"

Trust me. Seek guidance from this Christ you know all about. He can't be your Savior until he's your Lord. He can't be your master until you are his servant. Don't argue among yourselves. Listen to the still, small voice within the whirlwind. Be prepared to suffer, to love. The Spirit within you is greater than the spirit in the world.

"But what if things don't change?"

They will.

"But can you, I mean will you, help us?"

If you really ask. I always have. Amen.

Wally Cedarleaf
Chaplain, Port of Boston
Scituate, Massachusetts

Sunday
October Ninth

Call to Worship: Be sober, be watchful. Your adversary the devil prowls around like a roaring lion, seeking some one to devour. Resist him, firm in your faith, knowing that the same experience of suffering is required of your brotherhood throughout the world. *I Peter 5:8-9*

Processional Hymn: "Christian, Dost Thou See Them"

Invocation: Life is full of temptations. We get so tired of fighting evil that at times it seems as if God has given up on us. God will never tempt us beyond our endurance to resist. That is a promise. *Amen.*

Sermon Scripture: Mark 10:17-30

Sermon Presentation: "The Devil Made Me Do It!"

Hymn of the Day: "His Eye Is on the Sparrow"

Offertory Scripture: Watch and pray that you may not enter into temptation; the spirit indeed is willing, but the flesh is weak. *Matthew 26:41*

Offertory Prayer: Lord, we want to do your will, but we fail. As we return to you these our sacrificial gifts, let them be acceptable in your sight. *Amen.*

Prayer of the Day

A promise is broken! An act of disobedience is committed! A relationship is severed! A trust is shattered! Blame is shifted! We were created to be free. Instead we chose to be slaves of sin. Our world and the people in it feel broken—ashamed—cursed—alienated from one another and from you.

But you are a God not only of creation, but also of liberation. You have personally broken the chains of sin that held us in slavery. By your death you set us free to once again become children of God and heirs of your kingdom. You are also a God of reconciliation. You alone came into our world and gave totally of yourself. You are rich, but for our sakes you became poor. You are all powerful, but for our sakes you became weak—so weak that you could be killed on a cross.

You are the Lord of life, but for our sakes you died and rose again so that we could share eternal glory with you. We, your sinful children, thank you. *Amen.*

Benediction: For we have not a high priest who is unable to sympathize with our weaknesses, but one who in every respect has been tempted as we are, yet without sin. *Hebrews 4:15*

Recessional Hymn: "Rise Up, O Men of God"

Lectionary Lessons: The Twentieth Sunday after Pentecost
Lesson 1—Genesis 3:8-19; Psalm 90:1-12
Lesson 2—Hebrews 4:1-3, 9-13
Gospel—Mark 10:17-30

History of the Hymn of the Day: "His Eye Is on the Sparrow"
This beautiful gospel hymn was written because of the courage and faith of a woman bedridden for more than twenty years. Mrs. C. D. Martin and her husband were visiting Mr. and Mrs. Doolittle of Elmira, New York. Both of the Doolittles were "incurable cripples," but in spite of their handicaps carried on their business in a courageous manner. Greatly impressed by the faith of the saintly couple Dr. Martin commented upon the spirit and joy of his host and wife. Mrs. Doolittle's reaction was simple and direct, "His eye is on the sparrow and I know he watches me," she said. Mrs. Martin, who wrote many hymns and poems immediately recognized the potentiality of the phrase, and before the day ended she had arranged and incorporated it into one of the most touching hymns of all time.

Announcement for Next Week's Sermon: Does God really answer prayer? If you are not sure, you may not be able to get an answer to your prayers. You have got to believe.

Story of the Week: A man was talking to a friend and said, "My son's seventeenth birthday is next week, and if I give him everything he asked for, it's going to cost me a couple of hundred dollars."

His friend said, "That's one thing you can say for my boy. He was seventeen years old three months ago and the gift he asked for cost me only seventy-five cents."

"What in the world could you buy for only seventy-five cents that would satisfy any normal seventeen-year-old boy?" the man asked.

"Oh," his friend said. "That was easy. I gave him his own set of keys to the car."

THE DEVIL MADE ME DO IT!

It's an all too familiar story in Genesis, disrupted harmony in the Garden of Eden and the so called fall of humanity from peace and tranquility to an existence of hardship and dissonance. The snake has taken the blame for years—accompanied only by the woman—seducing, beguiling, letting all hell loose on earth and losing it all for us! There is a great deal of blaming being placed in this creation story.

A promise has been broken; an act of disobedience to the Creator God has supposedly occurred, as woman and man eat of the tree of which they were instructed not to eat. When God comes looking for them, they are ashamed and afraid. The man is confronted first. He is held accountable for his actions and is quick to blame the woman, the woman whom God gave to be with the man. The blame by implication is God's, also. Such an innocent man! Then God addresses the woman to get this story straight. She's innocent, too. That snake made her do it, is her reply. The implication here is that the snake was so crafty and powerful that no one could resist.

Can't you just hear the classic line, "The devil made me do it"? I am reminded of some girls and a few neighbor boys who were up to some mischief. The boys decided to pour water in an open basement window of a family they didn't like very much. They all went along on this adventure. Well, sure enough, not long after, the man of the house demanded punishment for those naughty kids. It seems the water landed right smack on the bed of his elderly father, who made his home in the basement. The girls were ashamed, but it was the boys who did it, they insisted! They were trying to hold on to their innocence; they were not responsible. It's not so very different from the Genesis story.

Humanity is created in freedom, and women and men are given responsibility for their actions. It's not good enough to put the blame on the snake, who has often been given almost equal power with God. The snake, in tradition, has come to bear resemblance to a personified devil. But the snake is a part of God's good creation, just as are man and woman. So don't scapegoat the snake or woman.

The patriarchal male-dominated society portrayed here in God's judgment, "I will greatly multiply your pain . . . and he shall rule over you" (Genesis 3:16), has ever made woman that devil or witch, the temptress and cause of evil. Woman, it appears, is to blame, but she's not any more to blame than the man. If anything, she claimed God's freedom and acted boldly—even if she, too, must accept responsibility for it.

This passage definitely needs liberation! We don't like what the punishment seems to be here. It describes not the way the world has to be, or what God intended it to be, but of course, how the writer experienced it—broken, alienated, feeling cursed. The vestiges of male patriarchal society are rooted in the fall, in the context of sin and brokenness. The relationship between man and woman has been cruelly distorted and broken. The relationship between humanity and creation—the earth, the animals—has also been alienated and barren. It is a devastating portrayal of life.

This story is not about the origin of sin, but the reality of sin. We are born into a world that knows sin and brokenness; it is environmental and relational. It is a fate for which we are not personally responsible; yet we can be guilty of committing sinful deeds. It is about relationships created in freedom, even with God, who is our Creator. It's about a broken covenant and accountability. It's about choices, the choices we make in our relationship to God and in our relationship with one another.

It was a good thing there were choices to be made in the Garden. The development of responsible human beings begins in having to make choices between good and evil. It's growing up, leaving the safety and structure of the womb or parental authority. It is taking responsibility for one's life in a complex and ambiguous world.

Statistics tell us that fundamentalist religious groups are gaining great momentum today. Why not? They restore the parent of the church. They take away personal responsibility and lay down rigid doctrines and rules that require little or no thinking or choosing. "The devil made me do it," or "You do it," provide a personal scapegoat. The world be damned as we rape the earth, crush the poor, and await nuclear holocaust and the second coming—there's nothing we can do but wait and be saved. It's no wonder the church seems threatening to people when it asks us to make decisions annually about our covenant, to think about our faith and actions as Christians without easily prescribed answers or a list of rules.

To make responsible, and sometimes difficult, choices is to care about oneself. A young woman in her early twenties, named Carrie, had a little baby she named Daniel. When she was in the hospital, she screened her visitors for fear of the appearance of the child's father, who was a major drug dealer and who abused her. She was a victim, dependent and scared. During this time, her family gave her a great deal of support; they gave her a home, worked to get her a job, provided child care, and helped her to find counseling and support services. This worked for awhile, but to their chagrin and dismay, she kept returning to the man she feared. She'd be abused and run home. She'd ask for help and then refuse help and later want it again. Carrie didn't love herself, nor did she believe anyone could really love her. She couldn't grow up, make her own decisions and live by them. Yes, she was a victim, a victim of a sexist society, subjugated by men. But she was also a victim of her own inability to live and act in freedom when she was offered it. We are all victims, but that's not an excuse. There are choices.

The disobedience in the Garden is not the eating of the forbidden fruit or gaining the knowledge of good and evil. Rather it is not being willing at some point in our lives to take responsibility for our lives and actions without blaming someone else. There are aspects of each of our lives that are too painful to confront, and when we meet God in those garden places we feel guilty, scared, and want to hide. We don't always want to grapple with the difficult questions and choices. That's when we lose what God offers us. The snake actually was leading the man and woman to a new maturity, to asking new questions, to reaching out.

When Roman Catholic Bishop Leroy Matthiesen of Amarillo, Texas, asked persons in his diocese to consider the moral implications of working at the Pantex plant, which is the final assembly point for United States nuclear weapons, he raised difficult questions of faith. He offered support and counseling to those workers as they searched their faith. If they decided that their relation to a God of love and justice called them to leave their jobs at Pantex, the bishop offered material support as well. He was saying that we have choices. We always have a choice. In covenant with God and one another, we find the support to make our choices and to take responsibility.

The lay leader of a congregation was angry when he heard the Matthiesen story in a sermon. The pastor raised the question of discipleship and accountability and was bold enough to suggest that there were decisions to be made. That was the first time the lay leader came to the pastor about a sermon. He felt the sermon had addressed him; in fact, he thought it was preached for him and singled him out. He worked for Sundstrand Corporation, which does defense work, and he negotiated contracts for the B-1 bomber. He heard a word spoken to him from his church in a personal way that he hadn't heard before. He didn't want to hear it; someone wanted to hold him accountable. What he did in his daily life might have implications for his relationship to God. His relationship with God might call for choices and decisions he didn't want to consider. It was painful. He was called to make choices, and he felt he couldn't do anything about it.

This situation reminds me of the rich young man who came to Jesus in Mark's Gospel, looking for something that seemed to be lacking in his life. He had everything a person could want—respect from his community, religious grounding, social status, material wealth—yet, something was missing. There was an emptiness, a searching. He came to Jesus looking for something spiritual to fulfill his need. Jesus has a great deal of courage in naming for this rich young man what he was afraid to name. The young man really didn't want to hear it. He, too, had his garden spots; he, too, hid from responsibility and accountability before God. Jesus asked him to do something with his life, to sell what he had (which was considerable), give the proceeds to the poor, and make a commitment to a covenant community. The young man couldn't do it, and he went away sorrowful. How hard it is to claim and enter the New Earth. By ourselves, it is impossible; we need God, who offers us the possibility to live in a covenant relationship.

God is not only a God of Creation—in the beginning—but also of liberation. Moving out of the garden only destroys us if we let it, if we refuse to live as responsible, moral people. God is not waiting in the safety of paradise for us to return, but the God of liberation and creation is with us here in the complexities, ambiguities, and fragmentation of life as we live it. God is here, calling us forward to respond when asked, "Where are you," to account for ourselves. Life and relationships do not have to be broken and alienated as Mark experiences and portrays them. God continues to act to restore the earth, the New Earth.

God depends on us to claim our part in creation, to take the covenant seriously, and to act in freedom, always knowing that God and the community offer forgiveness and grace. This God asks, "Where are you," in this community and the world as we hold one another accountable. *Amen.*

Betty Jo Birkhahn-Rommelfanger
Wheaton United Methodist Church
Evanston, Illinois

Sunday
October Sixteenth

Call to Worship: Likewise the Spirit helps us in our weakness; for we do not know how to pray as we ought, but the Spirit himself intercedes for us with sighs too deep for words.
Romans 8:26

Processional Hymn: "I Need Thee Every Hour"

Invocation: Lord, teach us to pray. Prayer is our conversation with our God. We need your constant encouragement just to go on day by day. When we pray, let us feel your very real presence in our lives. *Amen.*

Sermon Scripture: Matthew 7:7-11

Sermon Presentation: "God Answers Prayer"

Hymn of the Day: "Take My Life, and Let It Be Consecrated"

Offertory Scripture: So each of us shall give account of himself to God. *Romans 14:12*

Offertory Prayer: Lord, as you answer our prayers and supply our every need, let us respond to your kindness with these gifts to you and your church. *Amen.*

Prayer of the Day

Lord, it's so hard to pray sometimes. We think we need to say the right words and sound so holy and religious. Sometimes, we think that prayer is something that we use only for special occasions, like Thanksgiving dinner, when the whole family is gathered together and it is a tradition to pray. Or we use prayer in emergencies only. Prayer becomes our helpline. You only hear from some of us when we have a problem, need some advice, or have no where else to turn and come to you in desperation.

Help us to pray like the publican, admitting our rebellious nature and asking your forgiveness for our sins, thanking you for your love and your gifts of our time, talents, and treasures.

Help us to remember your promise that if we seek, we will find. If we knock, the door will be opened to us. If we ask, it shall be given to us. Lord, teach us to pray. Lord, help us to pray without ceasing and always with confidence. We pray in the name of the one whose prayer we call our "Lord's Prayer," our Lord Jesus Christ. *Amen.*

Benediction: Ask, and it will be given you; seek, and you will find; knock, and it will be opened to you. For every one who asks receives, and he who seeks finds, and to him who knocks it will be opened. *Matthew 7:7-8*

Recessional Hymn: "What a Friend We Have in Jesus"

Lectionary Lessons: The Twenty First Sunday after Pentecost
Lesson 1—Isaiah 53:7-12; Psalm 35:17-28
Lesson 2—Hebrews 4:14-16
Gospel—Mark 10:35-45

History of the Hymn of the Day: "Take My Life, and Let It Be Consecrated"

This challenging gospel hymn was written by Frances Ridley Havergal in 1874, four years before her death. The words were conceived while visiting the home of a friend where the author helped convert ten people. She was so happy and excited that she could not sleep until the words which were forming in her mind were written down. Throughout her life, Miss Havergall considered this hymn a measure of her own consecration to God and constantly reviewed the verses to renew her own spiritual life.

Take my life and let it be
Consecrated, Lord, to thee;
Take my moments and my days,
Let them flow in ceaseless praise.

Announcement for Next Week's Sermon: What do you see when you look at this world that God has given us? What you see will depend on your attitude, not your eye. Next Sunday, let's see what you see.

Story of the Week: Two housewives who were friends decided they would go back to work now that their children were grown. They went together to apply for employment at a large manufacturing plant.

They were sitting side by side as they filled in the long and detailed application forms. As one of the women came to the little box marked "age," she sat staring out of the window as though in deep thought.

Her friend leaned over and whispered, "Go ahead and put it down. The longer you wait, the worse it gets."

GOD ANSWERS PRAYER

It is not surprising that the disciples asked the Lord to teach them to pray. There is a story about two men who were talking about religion. They made a bet that neither could pray.

"I can," one announced. "I know the Lord's Prayer."

"Here's ten that says you don't," said the other.

The first one began, "Now I lay me down to sleep, I pray thee Lord, my soul to keep. . . ."

The other looked on in amazement and said, "Take the money, I didn't know you knew it." Let's explore together some expectations we might have as we pray.

What are you asking?

When we think of prayer, we imagine people with bowed heads, closed eyes, and possibly folded hands. But prayer is simply talking to God. We can pray while standing erect, sitting down, lying upon our pillows, driving our cars, or even washing windows (probably praying, "Lord, help me get through in time to watch the ball game").

The content of our prayers is often selfish: "Lord, I want. . . . Lord, do this . . . do that. . . ." Yes, we do manage to pray for others: "Lord, be with me and my family." The more devout prayers would include the poor sinners that live down the street. We pray for the Lord to bless us and ours, and the missionaries in Outer Mongolia. My, God is such a gracious Father to us! He still invites us, with all of our immature praying, to come before him with our needs. What are you praying for? For guidance from above? Strength for the journey? Comfort for your sorrow? Wisdom in the midst of a foolish world? Just what is it you really want? Are you persistent in your praying? Do you really know what you want, and are you praying in earnest about it?

Let's consider two ways of praying. The first is praying to be heard and known of men, the *pharisaical prayer*. "God, see what kind of man I am. Lord, thank you for endowing me with so many talents. Lord, I am just so thankful that I can be a blessing to old Sam across the street. Oh, yes, Lord, thank you that I don't have to live like that guy over there. Lord, I feel so good, I think I'll go out and play a round of golf today." It is little wonder that Jesus said that the Pharisees were blind leaders of the blind.

The other way of praying is with a sincere and contrite heart, the *publican's prayer*. The publican in Luke's Gospel knew how great a sinner he was; his bodily movements betrayed his sorrow. He would not even look up toward heaven as the Pharisee; rather, the publican bowed and knelt in humbleness before God. Weeping, he smote his chest crying, "Lord, be merciful to me a sinner." He probably went from the altar with an inner joy, a calm assurance, and a freer spirit. He prayed for help, and he received it.

If we are serious about what we are praying for, if we crave it, long for it, yearn after it, God will surely give us what is good. The story about the Canaanite woman who came to Jesus begging him to heal her daughter is an example of such prayer. Jesus did not answer her at first. The disciples, seeing that she cried all the more when Jesus hesitated, asked Jesus to send her away. Jesus told her that he was sent only to the lost sheep of Israel, but she came and knelt before him saying, "Lord, help me." Jesus then said, " 'It is not fair to take the children's bread and throw it to the dogs. She said, 'Yes, Lord; yet even the dogs eat the crumbs that fall from their masters' table.' Then Jesus answered her, 'O woman, great is your faith! Be it done for you as you desire' " (Matthew 15:21-28). She knew that Jesus could help her, and she would not be denied until she received. Her prayer was one of faith!

Then there are those who simply want a handout. John records how the people wanted to make Jesus their king, even by force if necessary, after the feeding of the five thousand. But Jesus knew their hearts as well as their motivations. When Jesus spoke about the true bread that came down from heaven, instead of recognizing Jesus as that Bread, the people said to him, "Lord, give us this bread always" (John 6:34). They wanted only what would satisfy their physical needs. Physical needs are important, because without food we would die. But Jesus reminds us as he did the Tempter, "Man shall not live by bread alone, but by every word that proceeds from the mouth of God" (Matthew 4:4). It really does matter what we pray for, because God wants to meet our needs by answering our prayers.

October Sixteenth

Who are you seeking?

"He who seeks, finds." Have you found what you have been looking for? It's possible that your source is not sufficient to meet your need. Have you ever lost or misplaced something of value? You search every nook and cranny but find nothing. Then one day you come upon it, remembering how it got there. Sometimes we try too hard and fail, when we should trace our steps and discover where they lead us. In our seeking for God, it is truer to say that God finds us before we find him. We would have never found God if we were not seeking after him. Paul says in Romans 3:11, "No one understands, no one seeks for God." Yet, when we look for God, the promise comes to us, as Paul states again, "That they should seek God, in the hope that they might feel after him and find him" (Acts 17:27). We need God!

Gliding sluggishly across the bosom of India like a great brown python is the Ganges River. Muddy and filthy, it is filled with the garbage and refuse of a hundred million people. But annually, thousands of devout pilgrims crawl on their bellies for miles, doing penance until they reach its slimy banks. Then they wade into the river up to their waists, lift their arms heavenward, and cry aloud. What are they doing? They are seeking to make atonement for their sins. They are trying to find God. As they know it, life is one day after another of hunger and meaninglessness within the structure of a primitive society. They are trying desperately to discover sense and meaning in it all. Through this ritual, they are hoping to become new persons. For those of us in Christ today, we have found meaning and purpose in our lives, because Christ was made an atonement for our sins. We pray in his name, we claim his promises, we know his assurances, that is why we can cry, "Abba, Father."

If we are not seeking God, we must be seeking the things of this world, which Jesus called *mammon.* Jesus says in Luke 17:33, "Whoever seeks to gain his life will lose it." This world holds nothing but false hopes and promises. The god of this world is the father of lies. He is big on demand, but short on supply. He seeks to destroy. Peter writes, "The devil prowls around like a roaring lion, seeking some one to devour" (I Peter 5:8). Those who follow the ways of the world may enjoy sin for a season, but the end thereof is the way of death. Listen to Paul as he writes to the saints at Philippi, speaking about the enemies of the cross, "Their end is destruction, their god is the belly, and they glory in their shame, with minds set on earthly things" (Philippians 3:19).

Too often we find powerless Christians, because their prayer life has fizzled out! This may be due, in part, to more worldly Christians in the church, than it is to godly Christians in the world. Let's guard against this spirit of the age and live in the Spirit of Christ who said, "Seek first his kingdom and his righteousness, and all these things shall be yours as well" (Matthew 6:33).

Why are you knocking?

Praying is the acceptable thing to do as a Christian. Jesus warned us about lengthy prayers with empty words. If our hearts are right with God, our prayers will be meaningful and full of purpose. We all have heard a dear Christian friend say, after being asked to do something for the Lord, "Let me pray about it first." That is well and good if one is praying for the right reasons: "Lord, will this glorify your name?" "Can I be of service to others?" "Lord, use me for your glory and the good of others!" If we are living out this prayerful attitude, I wonder why there is the delay; maybe time was needed to think about it further. Then this Christian thanks God after the decision has been made. It is giving God second thought that is such an affront to him. Rather than the merely acceptable, have we considered the exceptional? God knows our needs before we ask him. Taking God at his word, we come before him believing we shall receive, and we do. God never withholds from us what we need. The exceptional kind of prayer trusts our lives to God as he supplies all our needs, and we pray knowing that God hears and honors us when we pray in faith believing.

James says, "You do not have, because you do not ask" (James 4:2). Believe and you will receive! God says, "When you seek me with all your heart, I will be found" (Jeremiah 29:13). Believe, then receive! Jesus says, "Behold, I stand at the door and knock" (Revelation 3:20). Those who open the door of their hearts to Jesus believe to receive! Sometimes we do not know what or how to pray as we should; neither does anyone else know our hearts when we pray, save God alone. But we can be certain of this one thing: Purposeful prayer comes only by faith. In a little town in the French Pyrenees is a shrine celebrated for miracles of healing. One day shortly after World War II an amputee veteran visited there. As he hobbled up to the shrine, someone remarked, "That silly man, does he think that God will give him back his leg?" Overhearing, the veteran turned and replied, "Of course I do not expect God to give me back my leg. I am going to pray to God to help me live without it."

Those of us who know the reality of answered prayer can attest to the goodness of our Father who is in heaven. We have known through past experience that God answers prayer! What we may not have realized is that God wants us to learn through our praying that prayer changes us far more than that for which we have prayed. Getting to know God better through prayer enables us to pray intelligently for those things that are really needful in our lives and to think about others more than ourselves. *Amen.*

Nicholas Kobek
Chapel Heights Baptist Church
Decatur, Georgia

Sunday
October Twenty-third

Call to Worship: We know that in everything God works for good with those who love him, who are called according to his purpose. *Romans 8:28*

Processional Hymn: "We Give Thee But Thine Own"

Invocation: Lord, through all our lives we must choose between ugliness and beauty. Grant that we might surround our lives with beauty so that we may be closer to you. *Amen.*

Sermon Scripture: Philippians 4:4-9

Sermon Presentation: "Mud or Stars?"

Hymn of the Day: "I Love Thy Kingdom, Lord"

Offertory Scripture: He who exhorts, in his exhortation; he who contributes, in liberality; he who gives aid, with zeal; he who does acts of mercy, with cheerfulness. *Romans 12:8*

Offertory Prayer: Let my eyes keep looking up to heaven and the stars. Let me respond to this awesome sight with these my gifts. *Amen.*

Prayer of the Day

Lord, we hear that you bring good news to the poor and preach liberation to the captives. The problem is that all too often we don't realize how poor we truly are. We don't understand how captive we are by our human limitations, by our personal experiences, by our prejudices, and by our reluctance to change.

In our spiritual poverty and sinful bondage, we often doubt your goodness and your wisdom. We become mired in the mud and fail to appreciate the stars of your heaven. We see the clouds and forget that your Son is still shining. So often the "bad news" of the world, with its war, disease, hatred, and heartbreak come close to blocking out the "good news" of your gospel. But we know that, thanks to the cross and your glorious resurrection, the light will cast out the darkness, love will overcome hate, and life will overcome death.

Pull us out of the mud and help us to see your stars. *Amen.*

Benediction: Jesus then said to the Jews who had believed in him, "If you continue in my word, you are truly my disciples. . . . Truly, truly, I say to you, if any one keeps my word, he will never see death." *John 8:31, 51*

Recessional Hymn: "All Things Bright and Beautiful"

Lectionary Lessons: The Twenty-second Sunday after Pentecost
Lesson 1—Jeremiah 31:7-9; Psalm 126
Lesson 2—Hebrews 5:1-6
Gospel—Mark 10:46-52

History of the Hymn of the Day: "I Love Thy Kingdom, Lord"
Timothy Dwight, D. D., president of Yale College, wrote "I Love Thy Kingdom, Lord" just after the American Revolutionary War. Critics of early American hymnody say that the use of Watts' "Psalms and Hymns" did not become general throughout New England because of the reference to English characteristics. Something had to be added and changed to make it palatable to the newly liberated American patriots. Timothy Dwight was the one to do it, with alterations to Isaac Watts' hymnal and new versifications. "I Love Thy Kingdom, Lord" was part of the new arrangement.

I love Thy kingdom, Lord,
The house of Thine abode,
The Church our blest Redeemer saved
With His own precious blood.

Announcement for Next Week's Sermon: Free, something for free. That is a way to draw a crowd. If it is for free, we are always interested. Next Sunday, something for free, sort of.

Story of the Week: The minister was starting a new Sunday school class. "We are going to study the Bible in great depth," he said, "because I am sure there is much of it that we don't understand. And I am sure that you feel that is important or you wouldn't be in the class."

"Not exactly," one of the older men said, "I never worry much about the part I don't understand. It's the part that I do understand that bothers me."

MUD OR STARS?

Two men looked out from behind the bars
One saw mud, the other—stars!

Have you ever realized how much of our world is colored, governed by our own attitudes, frames of mind, seeing mud when we could see stars? There is a story of a man who brings his hungry child down to the kitchen one winter morning. He looks out the window and is thrilled to see the world blanketed by a foot of fresh snow. His wife comes down and makes breakfast. She brings it to the table. At the same time he sees a large black crow land on a branch and is entralled by the shower of whiteness. "Look, Clare, look," he shouts. She glances up for a second, then looks down saying, "Eat your egg."

For all of us there are days when nature and God have everything to offer, but we are not in an accepting mood. There are times when our closest friend has the "balm of Gilead" to share, but we are completely wrapped up, encrusted in our own mean selves. But, thank God, there are other times when, bereft of inspiration and purpose in life, the tiniest, most insignificant thing can expose rare beauty and a shout of joy.

All of us are prisoners, looking out from behind our bars, bound by our bodies, conditioned by our experiences, jaded by our prejudices, strapped by our blind spots. At times we feel as if the world is closing in on us, at other times, we are free and floating through the universe. For some, the sky is always falling, for others, never. When you look out, what do you see, mud or stars? Are you a mud raiser or a star gazer? Mud people aren't very hopeful, helpful, happy, or fun to be with. Star gazers are. Mud people read the wrong newspapers, books, and magazines. They watch the wrong television shows, pull the shades down, bark about the world going to the dogs—and theirs is. They doubt the goodness and wisdom of God. Star people see mud, but don't get mired in it. They realize that most everything is a blessing in disguise and turn seeming defeats into winged victories, banking on the goodness and guidance of God.

Jesus chose to see stars, to live above the clouds, with feet planted on the good earth. Hounded and harassed by mud people, he never lost heart. Facing a cross he shouted, "Be of good cheer, I have overcome the world" (John 16:33). And he did, and shows us how.

Mud people curse God and die. Star people praise their God, who permits nothing to come except that which makes them finally more tolerant, understanding, trusting, loving, and aware.

There are two attitudes that can take a load off our shoulders and help us sing a new song to the Lord, to ourselves, to our world, and may even help us to see stars: One—Don't criticize anything or anyone anytime. Don't judge anyone. Leave it to God. He has broader shoulders and does a better job. Start today, this minute. Don't criticize the weather; don't label people; don't quickly agree or disagree with what you hear or read. Let it float in and out of your consciousness, or let it simmer in your subconscious. What's valid will stick. What's not will be gone with the wind.

If there aren't enough birds around, whistle a happy tune yourself. If the sun isn't shining, smile. If you have no reason to smile, laugh out loud. Break the spell; put on a good show. God is watching. "But," you say, "what about the skunk in the back lot?" That's his home; you are the invader. Separate the pungent fragrance from the source, and inhale deeply. It will clear your sinuses and your brain. "But," you say, "what about the loud, late night music next door?" Simple. Tape record it and play it back the next morning at dawn.

Quit looking for typographical errors in the Sunday bulletin. Quit judging the orthodoxy of a sermon. Christ was crucified for less. Quit silently thanking God that you are better than someone else. The thought makes you worse, and God isn't listening anyway. "Judge not that you be not judged . . . the measure you give will be the measure you get" (Matthew 7:1-2). Simply put, that means you'll end up with mud in your eyes.

Two—Begin today, now, to throw overboard all thoughts of sickness, disease, and death. All of us live in a leaking boat. Cheer up, we'll never get out of the world alive. So let's live, live until that time.

Stop dwelling on cancer, multiple sclerosis, ulcers, headaches. For your own welfare, think only of wholeness and healing. Refuse to be sick. Take a deep breath every hour and say, "Right now, God is making me whole, right now." Then let his healing spirit inundate your body, mind, and heart. He wants to. Let him.

Stop reading about murders, rapes, and war. Forget about the headlines and the latest news, which is always old. Don't brag about how tired you are, making people sick. God tires of hearing it. Yet he waits and waits, with pockets full of healing ready to overflow your empty vessel. Empty your whole being of all your selfish anxieties about everything and nothing.

The percentage rises every year. Now the experts claim that 86 percent of all illnesses are triggered by mishandled stress. Does this mean that illness and disease may be self-chosen? Possibly. Illness results from the inability to cope with stress. All times are stressful times; so what can we do? Face it head on and defuse it with God. Who else? None who ever lived faced more stress than the apostle Paul. He was horsewhipped five times; beaten with rods three times; stoned and left for dead; shipwrecked three times; in danger from rivers, robbers, his own people, and the Gentiles; in hunger and thirst; in cold and exposure; concerned for the churches he founded; and living at his wit's end continuously. Yet, he wrote to the Philippians: "Have no anxiety about anything, but in everything by prayer and supplication with thanksgiving let your requests be made known to God. And the peace of God, which passes all understanding, will keep your hearts and your minds in Christ Jesus" (4:6-7).

You know, we were never meant to hack it alone. Whenever we try, we die. The good news is that God is alive, and Jesus is here. He waded through all kinds of mud in order that we might see the stars. Do you look for them in daily happenings? In your world? In others? In yourself? That's where it all begins.

> Two men looked out from behind the bars,
> One saw mud, the other—stars!

Christ the great physician tells us not to be anxious, to lift up our eyes and be healed. *Amen.*

Wally Cedarleaf
Chaplain, Port of Boston
Scituate, Massachusetts

Sunday
October Thirtieth

Call to Worship: Therefore, since we are justified by faith, we have peace with God through our Lord Jesus Christ.

Romans 5:1

Processional Hymn: "Blessed Assurance, Jesus Is Mine"

Invocation: On this Reformation Day may we take the opportunity to reform our lives, that they might be acceptable in the sight of God. We thank you for all the reformers who have delivered to us the true faith. *Amen.*

Sermon Scripture: Romans 3:19-28

Sermon Presentation: "True Freedom"

Hymn of the Day: "A Mighty Fortress Is Our God"

Offertory Scripture: Verily, verily, I say unto you, He that believeth on me, the works that I do shall he do also; and greater works than these shall he do; because I go unto my Father. And whatsoever ye shall ask in my name, that will I do, that the Father may be glorified in the Son. *John 14:12-13 KJV*

Offertory Prayer: Change is never easy. Change our lives and attitudes so that we may worship you with our lives and with our gifts. *Amen.*

Prayer of the Day

Lord, we live in a world that is constantly changing. It is a world that challenges us to find new ways of ministering in your name. As your church, we are constantly reforming and recreating this institution that you have given us. We thank you for the freedom of the gospel, which allows us to meet the needs of this modern world. No longer bound by laws and tradition that would restrict us, we have been given the freedom to take your truth and to express it in terms that make you meaningful to all people, of all times, and in all places. You allow us, by your grace, to renew your church and our lives so that in all we do and all we say we may reflect your love and your mercy.

Remove from us all fear, uncertainty, and ambiguity that would prevent us from being the people you would will us to be. Let us never forget that, while the world may change, you are the same yesterday, today, and tomorrow. *Amen.*

Benediction: Then as one man's trespass led to condemnation for all men, so one man's act of righteousness leads to acquittal and life for all men. *Romans 5:18*

Recessional Hymn: "Savior Like a Shepherd Lead Us"

Lectionary Lessons: The Twenty-third Sunday after Pentecost (Reformation)

Lesson 1—Deuteronomy 6:1-9; Psalm 119:33-48
Lesson 2—Hebrews 7:23-28
Gospel—Mark 12:28-34

History of the Hymn of the Day: "A Mighty Fortress Is Our God"

Martin Luther, one of the outstanding figures in the history of the Protestant Church, in no greater way served his fellow Christians than in the writing and composing of one of the world's best-loved hymns, "A Mighty Fortress Is Our God." It was written in the late summer of 1529. The famed German theologian, after a long period of deep depression, had found spiritual comfort in the strength of Psalm 46. He repeated over and over the words, "God is our refuge and strength, a very present help in trouble." With this thought in mind, he hurled his defiance at all his foes, physical and spiritual, the struggles of mind and body, the opposition of pope and people, and penned these words never to be forgotten by mortal men:

A mighty fortress is our God,
A bulwark never failing;
Our helper He, amid the flood,
Of mortal ills prevailing.
For still our ancient foe,
Doth seek to work us woe;
His craft and power are great,
And armed with cruel hate.
On earth is not his equal.

Announcement for Next Week's Sermon: Cheap is different from a bargain. God does not offer us cheap grace, but his grace is the biggest bargain we will ever get. Next week, there is nothing cheap about God.

Story of the Week: The candidate said to the voter, "Well, can I count on your vote next Tuesday?"

"Not this time," the voter said. "But, I've got you down as my second choice."

"Who's your first choice?" the candidate asked.

"Anybody else who is running," the voter said.

TRUE FREEDOM

It's just a four-letter word! Not a bad four letter word that would offend the listeners' ears, but a four letter word that catches the eye, the ear, a four-letter word that seems to leap from the printed page, a four-letter word that often sets people's hearts pounding, their feet running, their hands grabbing. The four letter word is *free!* There is something about that word that really moves us. Going through the food store, my kids can read that word on cereal boxes one hundred yards away. Take them to Burger King or McDonald's, and they can tell you what is free from drinking glasses to little plastic toys. If you're like me, you can talk to your kids until you're blue in the face, and they act deaf, but if Ronald McDonald comes on the television and tells them about his latest free offer, they are all ears.

Just look through the newspaper and see how many things you can get for free, such as one free candle if you purchase ten dollars worth of candles. My wife and I go around on those kinds of deals all the time. I keep claiming it's not really free. You can get a pumpkin with any purchase at some nurseries. The newspaper even has a whole column in its classified ads section of things you can get for free.

Yes, that word *free* certainly has quite an impact on us. We call our economic system one of free enterprise. We call our nation "The land of the free and the home of the brave."

Perhaps we would have the same reaction as did the people who heard Jesus say to them, "If you continue in my word, you are truly my disciples, and you will know the truth, and the truth will make you free" (John 8:32). Just like the people of his day, you might look at Jesus and say "You can't be talking to me, I'm already free."

But you know there is a great deal of truth in the word a wise man once spoke when he said, "Men rattle their chains to show that they are free." Most of us would claim to be free, while really feeling like a slave. I talked to a mother the other day. She told me about all the activities that her three children are involved in and how she has to run them here and there six, sometimes seven, days each week. There was band and choir, and sports and scouts. She looked tired and just plain worn out. While her children may be having the time of their young lives, this woman is a weary slave to the tight, overloaded schedule.

As Americans, we claim as our heritage the freedoms of speech, of assembly, and of religion. Yet just the other morning I met with a man who was issued a letter of reprimand by his company, because he wasn't able to come in to work when his name appeared on the call list on a Sunday morning. He works for a trucking outfit that doesn't want to give employees the right to go to church on a Sunday morning. Is there freedom of religion? Evidently not, if you work for this company.

On this Reformation Sunday, we, as Christians, know how easy it is to become slaves to tradition. As Christians, we hold dear the freedom that the gospel gives us in our relationship with God. This morning I'd like to talk to you about four areas of our lives in which our Lord offers us real freedom:

First of all, if we accept God's truth in our lives, if we truly seek to walk in his way, then we will know what it is to be free of fear. Think about how comforting that kind of freedom can be. Jesus doesn't promise us that we will never be afraid, but he does promise us the ability to overcome our fears with his help.

I can't think of anything scarier than death. I've been at the bedside of men and women who knew that the doctors and nurses could not do one more thing for them. They have looked me squarely in the eye and said, "Well, Pastor, I guess this is it." For some people, death can be a lonely experience. Even their own family members can't handle the situation. But as we pray with them, they realize that they are not alone. Like the psalmist, they can say, "Yea, though I walk through the valley of the shadow of death, I will fear no evil: for thou art with me" (Psalm 23:4 KJV). As we walk through this life, we realize that the Son of God walks by our side. No matter how bad things get, he is our bridge over troubled waters, and we can be free from lingering fear.

Second, Jesus can free us from ourselves. I met a man the other day who described himself by saying, "I am my own worse enemy. I try to change, but I can't. I can't help myself." Here was a man whose health was very poor. He has high blood pressure and a bad heart. He smokes two packs of cigarettes each day. Basically, his problem is that he sets very high standards for himself. He wants to be the very best that he can be at his job, at his hobby, and at sports, but he is miserable. He wants to change, but he can't; in his own words, "only God can help me." Be it the alcoholic, the dieter, the person who drives himself or herself unmercifully, Jesus gives the ability to be free and start over. But we need to ask for his help.

Third, Jesus can give us a freedom from other people. So often we're afraid of what other people will think of us or say about us. As we read scripture, we find that in the eyes of many people Jesus' actions were scandalous. It was the great statesman Adlai Stevenson who said, "A free society is one where it is safe to be unpopular." The people to whom Jesus spoke claimed to be free; yet they didn't allow him the freedom to talk with sinners. They didn't allow him the freedom to heal on the Sabbath. They didn't allow him the freedom to speak the Word of God, announcing that the kingdom of God had broken into their world. These people who were so free had shut him up by binding him to a tree and killing him. After all, if they didn't take care of him, "What would people say?" Jesus reminds us that it's more important what God says than what people say. Get your priorities straight.

Finally, he offers us a freedom that only he can give—a freedom from sin. I don't know about you, but I'm very critical of myself. If something doesn't go right, I ask myself, "Where did things go off the track?" If things go right, I analyze that, too, and say, "What did I do right?" I find it so very comforting to know that God isn't as critical of me as I am of myself. He really knows me; yet he goes right on loving me. He knows me better than I know myself, but his love keeps flowing toward me. Instead of condemning or just loving me when I do well, he promises to love and accept me more than I can love and accept myself. He takes my burdens upon himself and says, "Come to me and be free so that you can grow in my love."

There are many free things in this world, but until we come to know the freedom that Christ can give, then we will never know what it means to be free. Jesus says to me and to you "If the Son makes you free, you are free indeed" (John 8:36). That is what this Reformation Day is all about—freedom. Once we accept that freedom, then we can join Paul in his words to the Galatians: "For freedom Christ has set us free; stand fast therefore, and do not submit again to a yoke of slavery" (Galatians 5:1). *Amen*.

Thomas E. Richards, Jr.
St. Paul's Lutheran Church
Tannersville, Pennsylvania

Sunday
November Sixth

Call to Worship: For by grace are ye saved through faith; and that not of yourselves; it is the gift of God. *Ephesians 2:8 KJV*

Processional Hymn: "For All the Saints"

Invocation: Lord, we thank you for your many gifts to us, especially for the gift of your Son. We thank you for all the saints of this congregation who have given of themselves that we might worship you here in this place. *Amen.*

Sermon Scripture: Ephesians 5:1-10

Sermon Presentation: "Cheap Grace"

Hymn of the Day: "There's a Wideness in God's Mercy"

Offertory Scripture: Give unto the Lord the glory due unto his name: bring an offering, and come into his courts.

Psalm 96:8 KJV

Offertory Prayer: Lord, let us be part of that great congregation of saints who serve you. Let these gifts help your kingdom to come. *Amen.*

Prayer of the Day

Lord, really, the two words have nothing in common. In fact, the two words do not even belong in the same sentence, when it comes to our faith. The words are *cheap* and *grace.*

The cheapening of your grace is something we are all guilty of. We try to fit you into our lives without changing anything. We like to claim that we believe in you when it comes to discipleship, to "taking up our cross" and seeking the kingdom of God first. We do everything within our means to find some sort of compromise.

Help us to understand that there can be no forgiveness without true repentance, that our baptism calls us to responsible discipleship, that following you means that we will have to be willing to make sacrifices and even lay down our lives for your sake and for the sake of our brothers and sisters. But most of all, help us to understand that your grace is bestowed on us because you love us. Your love, your forgiveness, your grace are free gifts to us. But your grace cost Jesus his life. He died so that your love could overcome our hate. Your forgiveness is stronger than the power of our sin, and your life has shattered the bondage of death forever.

Your grace is free, but it is not cheap. *Amen.*

Benediction: But by the grace of God I am what I am, and his grace toward me was not in vain. On the contrary, I worked harder than any of them, though it was not I, but the grace of God which is with me. *I Corinthians 15:10*

Recessional Hymn: "Glorious Things of Thee Are Spoken

Lectionary Lessons: The Twenty-fourth Sunday after Pentecost (All Saints' Day)

Lesson 1—I Kings 17:8-16; Psalm 146
Lesson 2—Hebrews 9:24-28
Gospel—Mark 12:38-44

History of the Hymn of the Day: "There's a Wideness in God's Mercy"

It was said of Frederick William Faber, Anglican clergyman, the author of this hymn, that his vivid, unusual imagination was almost without comparison. "There's a Wideness in God's Mercy," written probably in 1846, is a good example of his remarkable talent. Comparing God's love to the wideness of the sea demonstrates not only an extraordinary ability to choose the right metaphor, but also a deep insight into the boundlessness of the mercy of the Almighty. This hymn was one of one hundred and fifty written by Faber, all of them composed after he was converted to Roman Catholicism in 1846. Protestants have used his hymns freely, however, finding in them a true expression of living faith.

There's a wideness in God's mercy
Like the wideness of the sea.

Announcement for Next Week's Sermon: If you break the law, you may be arrested. That is bad. Sometimes you break the law, you get arrested and put in jail, and that is good. Next week, we find out how bad can be good.

Story of the Week: The newspaper reporter was interviewing a celebrity, one of the world's most famous hotel owners. As a final question, he said to the great man, "Millions of travelers from all over the world have stayed in your hotels. I wonder if you have a word of advice that you would like to pass on to them?"

"Yes, I have," the great hotel man said. "Please keep the shower curtain *inside*."

CHEAP GRACE

I doubt that there is anyone here who does not know what a cheap shot is. Someone who plays tennis occasionally knows a cheap shot is one of those volleys that hits the top of the net, rolls along the top, and finally drops onto the other side, much to the disgust of the opponent. Golfers know what cheap shots are, too. They are those poorly hit balls that bounce off sprinkler heads, the sand trap rake, or some other fortuitously placed object and find them rolling toward the cup anyway.

Of course, you don't have to be a sports enthusiast to know what a cheap shot is. Surely, in conversation, we have all felt the sting of a derogatory remark at our weakest spot and spoken with a half grin and a chuckle, or worse, with deadly seriousness. Cheap shots—life is full of them.

Thanks to the German theologian Dietrich Bonhoeffer, we Christians are aware of a type of cheapness that is part of our lives in the church. Bonhoeffer calls it cheap grace. He says about it: "Cheap grace is the grace we bestow on ourselves. Cheap grace is the preaching of forgiveness without requiring repentance, baptism without church discipline, Communion without confession. Cheap grace is grace without discipleship, grace without the cross, grace without Jesus Christ, living and incarnate."

In the epistle to the Ephesians, Paul informs us that we are to be imitators of God as we know God in Christ Jesus. Paul straightforwardly tells us that the liar should stop lying, the wrathful should stop hating, the thief should stop stealing, the blasphemer should clean up his or her speech, and that all who know Jesus Christ should forgive and love one another. We have heard these and similar instructions many times. The question is: Is it obvious by the way in which we live that we have heard and responded?

If it is not, then we are purveyors of cheap grace. Every time we conduct ourselves as persons other than disciples of Jesus Christ, we cheapen what he did for us. Cheap grace is that kind of relationship with Jesus that finds us able to grasp what has been done for us with an easy joy. Cheap grace finds us able to fit Jesus into our lives without our having to change anything. Cheap grace finds us satisfied with just coming to church and understanding Jesus as he who absolves us of any real responsibility for changing our lives. This is what Bonhoeffer means by "grace without discipleship, grace without the cross, grace without Jesus Christ, living and incarnate." Cheap grace is grace without sacrifice, grace without suffering with and for somebody else, grace that finds itself always reduced to words and ideas and never finds itself translated into a tangible form that someone can feel and benefit from. Jesus suffered by being what he was. We will suffer when we truly strive to live lives like his; anything less is cheap grace.

By dwelling on cheap grace, we begin to see what costly grace, real grace, is, for grace is indeed costly. God's laws, found in the book of Leviticus, tell us not to harvest our fields to the very edges, but to leave something for the poor, the foreigners. The scripture speaks a message from ancient agricultural society that is not diminished for us today. We are not to harvest our checkbooks to their very depths for personal satisfaction. We are to leave something for those who have nothing, costly grace in the name of Jesus Christ. God asks us not to steal, cheat, or lie, not to gossip, humiliate, lead astray, seek revenge, or throw cheap shots. We are not allowed to do these things, then casually drop them in the lap of God in a moment of confession. Our lives were bought at far too dear a price for that. We are expected to surrender as much of ourselves in the pursuit of Christlike existence as was surrendered for us. We are to answer God with our lives. When we do, we will never again meet anyone or have another relationship in which Christ is not present.

Costly grace is the gospel message that must be sought again and again; the gift that must be asked for, the door at which we must knock. When seeking God and godliness, we dare not rely solely upon the preacher, or the Sunday school teacher, to do that seeking for us. There are aspects of seeking God that must be entered into alone. Jesus Christ, active and in control of our lives, is to be sought, both individually and collectively.

For too many of us, this seeking has been reduced to a Sunday morning routine, while those things that have nothing to do with God continue to consume most of our lives and our time.

When this is so, we are not the people of God. There is much more to Christianity than words and songs. Jesus taught that the Father forgives, and Jesus himself, forgave. Jesus taught that the kingdom is patient and gentle, and he, himself, was forebearing. Jesus taught that God is love, and he, himself, loved. Christ did not simply point to a reality or give a gift—he is the gift. The reality comes to expression through him.

The aging theologian, after a lifetime of study and reflection, is able to say that, in the shadow of God, all human learning is as nothing and humankind cannot really know anything. The lazy student who would quote the theologian's words as sufficient reason for not studying cannot be allowed this excuse, or the words of truth are cheapened. In the same way, we cannot live selfishly and as we please and still be Christians. Whenever we live this way and call ourselves God's people, we cheapen the words, but worse, we cheapen the action of God in Jesus Christ.

Grace is not cheap. It is free! It is a gift dearly bought and freely given, but it must always be sought with the knowledge that the highest possible price has been paid. Are we willing to pay a price ourselves? Are we willing, and do we truly search, knock, pray, read, give, listen, share, sacrifice, and suffer? That is what Jesus did. That is what he calls us to do.

The grace of God in Christ Jesus. By our lives, do we profess grace to be free, yet costly or cheap? When it comes right down to it, strictly in terms of expense, we cannot afford to cheapen the grace of God in Jesus Christ. Rather, by surrendering all that we are and have, we need strive for a glorious understanding of how costly, how infinitely precious, how truly sustaining and liberating is the grace of God. If you prefer the words of Paul: "Therefore be imitators of God, as beloved children. And walk in love, as Christ loved us and gave himself up for us, a fragrant offering and sacrifice to God" (Ephesians 5:1-2). In the name of Christ our Lord. *Amen.*

Michael L. Lyle
Braddock Street United Methodist Church
Winchester, Virginia

Sunday
November Thirteenth

Call to Worship: We know that in everything God works for good with those who love him, who are called according to his purpose. *Romans 8:28*

Processional Hymn: "Have Thine Own Way, Lord"

Invocation: Lord, we are a people united through prayer. We have a pastor and the many families that make up this church. We are truly a church when we are a people in prayer. *Amen.*

Sermon Scripture: Philippians 1:3-11

Sermon Presentation: "Pastor, People, and Prayer"

Hymn of the Day: "Now Thank We All Our God"

Offertory Scripture: Beloved, let us love one another; for love is of God, and he who loves is born of God and knows God. . . . Beloved, if God so loved us, we also ought to love one another . . . if we love one another, God abides in us and his love is perfected in us. *I John 4:7, 11-12*

Offertory Prayer: Lord, make us one in Spirit and in Truth. Take these our gifts and make them truly worthy of your sacrifice and love. *Amen.*

Prayer of the Day

O Lord, it has been said that your "gospel" does two things to those who hear it. "If afflicts the comfortable and comforts the afflicted." When we hear your *Word,* our lives will never be the same. Your Word brought the world into being. It rolled away the stone from the tomb on that first Easter morning. It is your Word that has calmed the fears, filled the hearts with hope, provided guidance for the lives, and given courage to your saints down through the ages.

You told your followers, "If the Son sets you free, you will be free indeed." Send your Word into our lives so that we might know the freedom that you promise each of us—the freedom from slavery to sin; the freedom from fear of death; the freedom that comes from serving you each day of our lives.

Allow us to hear your Word. Open our ears, our hearts, and our minds that we might hear and obey, that we might listen and live forever in your kingdom and in your service. *Amen.*

Benediction: As it is written, Eye hath not seen, nor ear heard, neither have entered into the heart of man, the things which God hath prepared for them that love him.

I Corinthians 2:9 KJV

Recessional Hymn: "We Gather Together"

Lectionary Lessons: The Twenty-fifth Sunday after Pentecost
Lesson 1—Daniel 7:9-14; Psalm 145:8-13
Lesson 2—Hebrews 10:11-18
Gospel—Mark 13:24-32

History of the Hymn of the Day: "Now Thank We All Our God"

This joyous Thanksgiving refrain was written by the Reverend Martin Rinkart, minister in the little town of Eilenburg, Saxony, at the close of the Thirty Years' War in 1648. Rinkart was the only surviving clergyman in the town, which was so crowded with refugees and so ravaged with plague and pestilence, famine and fury, that often fifty to one hundred funerals were held each day. When news finally arrived that the Peace of Westphalia had ended the great and terrible war, a decree was circulated ordering Thanksgiving services to be held in every church. Ministers were requested to preach on the text, "Now bless ye the Lord of all, who everywhere doeth great things." Martin Rinkart was so moved by the thought of this text that he sat down and wrote these words for his own Thanksgiving service:

Now thank we all our God,
With hearts, and hands, and voices,
Who wondrous things hath done,
In whom his world rejoices.

Announcement for Next Week's Sermon: If I asked you to pick the world's greatest preacher, who would you pick? I have made my choice. Next Sunday, the answer.

Story of the Week: An elderly man who thought he was a lady's man was flirting with the pretty waitress one morning at breakfast. He started out with the world's oldest cliché, "Darling, where have you been all my life?"

"Well," she said with a pretty smile, "for the first 45 years of it, I wasn't even born yet."

PASTOR, PEOPLE, AND PRAYER

In his letter to the Philippian church, Paul expressed a prayer of thanksgiving for what that congregation had meant to him. From a prison cell, Paul penned a letter of thanks for those fellow Christians in Philippi. He was thankful, though in a dirty dungeon. He prayed with joy in his heart, though he was a prisoner. Can you imagine yourself in prison, thankful for every remembrance of fellowship experienced in some certain congregation?

The first Christian congregation formed on European soil was at Philippi, a Roman colony in Macedonia. The organizer was the apostle Paul; you can read about his entry into Europe in the sixteenth chapter of the book of Acts. Paul, you will recall, was converted to Christ in Damascus, Syria, to the north of Jerusalem. He came to Jerusalem and sought the approval of the leaders of the Jerusalem church, and at first experienced rejection, because the people in power remembered how Paul (formerly Saul) had laid persecuting hands on the members of the infant church. Eventually Paul was accepted by the church, and from Jerusalem he moved northward up through Syria into what is known today as Turkey. Several churches were organized by Paul in Turkey. One day he was on the west coast of Turkey, at a place called Troas. He had a vision in which a man said to him, "Come over to Macedonia and help us." Paul regarded this as a legitimate call from God to proclaim the gospel to those in Greece and throughout Europe. So he crossed the Aegean Sea and landed in Macedonia (Greece), specifically at Philippi. There he established the first Christian congregation in Europe.

What was the setting, or context, of that pastor's prayer? Paul was in prison awaiting trial. His crime, officially, was that he had come preaching some new divinity. However, the issue was that this new divinity, this new God, claimed lordship over the emperor. The poets and philosophers taught that there were many gods throughout the Greco-Roman world. One more god did not make too much difference, providing that this new God did not enter into the affairs of human relationships, the affairs of daily life. As long as the gods were far removed from the arena of human experience, as long as the gods remained atop Mount Olympus, as long as the gods did not interfere in the activities of the people, as long as the gods did not dictate policy to the government, there was no problem. But along came this missionary, this apostle named Paul, teaching that the unknown divinity had been disclosed in Jesus of Nazareth, that this same Jesus had overcome death, that this Jesus was Lord of all life, that this Jesus was Lord over the emperor. That clearly was adventuresome preaching, and it was dangerous, especially for Paul, because it meant that the government, the state was not an absolute power. That was political preaching of the first order. That was the social gospel in its purest form. Paul was regarded by the government as a threat to the status quo; he was a Roman citizen, but definitely a subversive one. He was put into a prison cell.

Have you ever wondered why so many of the early proponents of the Christian gospel were imprisoned and even martyred? Perhaps it is because an authentic Christian proclamation is always political; that is, there are always some political overtones in authentic preaching of the gospel of the kingdom. Paul, for example, was not imprisoned for teaching "Jesus loves you; come and discover how pleasant and fun life can be with him," but for proclaiming that Christ is Lord of all of life, that God's will is primary for human relations and human institutions, and that all human relationships must reckon with the will of God as expressed in Jesus Christ.

Paul did not know about what is today called religious liberty. Political liberalism had not yet been devised or conceived. That would come much later in the revolutionary movements of America and France. But mark well that political liberalism came by way of revolution. However, there is a distinction between Christian freedom and religious liberty. One can live in a republic in which there is religious liberty and still not know Christian freedom. Conversely, one can live in a nation in which there is no guaranteed religious liberty and still know Christian freedom. When I say that, I am in no way making a case for totalitarian regimes (ancient or modern). But I am saying that the Christian faith can survive, even spread, when tyrants rule. When the church as an institution is persecuted, then the faith the church teaches becomes stronger. Faith dwells within temples not made with hands. Faith resides in minds and hearts. In early centuries, Christians were driven underground. What would we do were the church as an institution to fall on evil days? Would we be thankful for remembrances of Christian fellowship? Would we give thanks for the brothers and sisters praying for us? The church is people; the church is faith; the church is an experience. And Rome, with all her splendor, might, and claim to universal justice was tyrannical; yet Paul in prison was a free man in Christ.

Paul the missionary-pastor prayed with a purpose; he had an objective in mind. He was praying for Christian maturity within that congregation. Love must abound, expand, and develop. But love, without corresponding knowledge, may become impractical sentiment. For instance, we may want to do something for someone in need, but wanting to do so may be inadequate; we must know how and when. Love and knowledge go hand in hand. So it is that maturity is the ability to discern, the ability to avoid the mediocre, the ability to excel, to do one's best. Further, maturity is the ability to face those feelings of guilt that often plague us when our best may not be as good as we would have desired. Who of us has not needed some help in that department?

We believe in the possibility of maturity. Among other considerations, this surely means that we will be future-oriented people. That is the opposite of being filled with dismay and despair as we view the world scene; there is no such thing as a hopeless Christian. A Christian has hope and, therefore, a future. And when one ponders the grave, no, ponders oneself in that grave, one not only attains to earnestness, but also realizes that the future must be in the hands of God. Age does not chop away at the future, because Christ has given us eternal life. The best is yet to be. "Though we die, yet shall we live!" *Amen.*

John V. Strom
St. Mark's Lutheran Church
Indianapolis, Indiana

Sunday
November Twentieth

Call to Worship: Behold, the days are coming, says the Lord, when I will raise up for David a righteous Branch, and he shall reign as king and deal wisely, and shall execute justice and righteousness in the land. *Jeremiah 23:5*

Processional Hymn: "God of Our Fathers"

Invocation: On this day when we celebrate Christ as King of all worlds, we thank you for the mercy and forgiveness our King grants so generously. We worship and adore you forever and ever. *Amen.*

Sermon Scripture: Jonah 3:1-10

Sermon Presentation: "The World's Greatest Preacher"

Hymn of the Day: "Come, Ye Thankful People, Come"

Offertory Scripture: In every thing give thanks; for this is the will of God in Christ Jesus concerning you.
I Thessalonians 5:18 KJV

Offertory Prayer: Lord, let us give thanks at this special Thanksgiving season. Accept these our gifts of thanks to you. *Amen.*

Prayer of the Day

Lord, we are like little Jonahs, aren't we? We have been given the great responsibility of being your representatives to the world's people. We have been entrusted with your Holy Word, the "Good News" of God's grace, mercy, and love. This is a message that is so desperately needed.

Like Jonah, we are full of uncertainty and seek to shirk our God-given responsibility. We seek to hide among our busy schedules and family responsibilities. We are swallowed up and consumed by our own ambitions and desires for wealth, security, and glory.

Help us to be worthy of our calling. Guide us so that we can bring your word to all people and in all situations. May our words, spoken on your behalf, always be the right words for the right time, comfort to the troubled, peace to the disturbed, hope to the depressed, strength to the weak, and life to the dying.

Your Word is our source of truth, hope, and guidance. Let us be like salt, good salt that gives flavor. Let your Word shine like a bright light in an often dark world, guiding your people always toward you. *Amen.*

Benediction: Have no anxiety about anything, but in everything by prayer and supplication with thanksgiving let your requests be made known to God. *Philippians 4:6*

Recessional Hymn: "All People That on Earth Do Dwell"

Lectionary Lessons: The Last Sunday after Pentecost (Christ the King)

Lesson 1—Jeremiah 23:1-6; Psalm 93
Lesson 2—Revelation 1:4*b*-8
Gospel—John 18:33-37

History of the Hymn of the Day: "Come, Ye Thankful People, Come"

Of all the harvest hymns, "Come, Ye Thankful People, Come," written by the Reverend Henry Alford, dean of Canterbury Cathedral, is the most popular. It was first published in his "Psalms and Hymns" in 1844. To describe Alford as precocious as a child is an understatement. He started writing at the age of six, and by eleven had compiled a collection of hymns. At sixteen these were his words: "I do this day as in the presence of God and my own soul renew my covenant with God, and solemnly determine henceforth to become His, and do His work as far as in me lies." "Come, Ye Thankful People, Come" may not have been his most scholarly effort, but it will always remain the most popular writing of his career.

Announcement for Next Week's Sermon: Are you too comfortable in your life? There is a world out there and it is not always a pleasant place to be. I dare you to look around and see the real world.

Story of the Week: The author who was invited to speak at a Thanksgiving dinner opened his speech by saying, "For the past half-hour you have been giving your attention to a turkey stuffed with sage. Now I hope you will give your attention to a sage stuffed with turkey."

November Twentieth

THE WORLD'S GREATEST PREACHER

Who is the world's greatest preacher? Some names come rapidly to mind. Billy Graham, perhaps. Maybe Oral Roberts or Robert Schuller. For many it is the always-upbeat messenger, Norman Vincent Peale, with his message of the power of positive thinking. In any ranking of the world's greatest preachers, we would have to list Charles Spurgeon of the City Temple in London, John Wesley, John Knox, John Calvin, Martin Luther. Other names pop up from earlier ages, too—Augustine and Ambrose, Peter and Paul.

But the greatest preacher of all time is none of the above. It is Jonah. We know very little about him. He was a minor prophet of the time of King Jeroboam II. If we remember Jonah's story at all, we somehow get caught up in wondering how he could have been swallowed by a big fish and then live to tell about it. Yet the message of Jonah has nothing at all to do with fish. The miracle of Jonah is no fish story; it's about God's salvation of all who turn to him, even Gentiles, even sinners. The message is one we can hear and one that can help us to understand God's will for us.

The prophet was called to go to Nineveh, that great city, the capital of the wicked and horrible kingdom of Assyria. Jonah refused to go and instead boarded a ship bound for Tarshish (modern-day Spain), which was in the opposite direction. But God would not be stopped by Jonah. A great storm arose over the sea; the pagan sailors could recognize this storm as having been sent by the gods. They prayed while Jonah slept in the hold. Oh, he knew that the storm was God's handiwork, but that didn't matter. He would rather die than go to Nineveh and preach to those people. If he deserved to die for his disobedience, then so be it. The storm did not abate until, finally, the sailors, recognizing the role of Jonah in causing the tempest, threw him overboard.

Jonah couldn't thwart God's plan, and here came the fish into the story. God appointed a great fish to save Jonah from the sea and to bring him back to the land of Israel. God wouldn't let Jonah duck his plan to preach to the Ninevites. So spitting Jonah up on the shore, the great fish had done his part, and now Jonah recognized that to Nineveh he must go with God's message.

Jonah preached a very short sermon to the Ninevites, "Yet forty days, and Nineveh shall be overthrown" (Jonah 3:4). It wasn't a pleasant or a happy message. There was no such thing as positive thinking or possibility thinking. The sermon didn't have three points; law and gospel were not distinguished. The delivery was purposely brusque and rude. What set Jonah apart from so many golden-tongued orators of the pulpit was just this: It was God's Word for the people of Nineveh. Great preaching is always from the Word of God and not the newspaper. The greatest preaching is the Word of God to the situation of the people. Popular preachers give the people what they want to hear or deliver what the preacher wants them to hear; great preaching is from the Word of God.

Rather than the "fire and brimstone" sort we have a situation in which devil, hell, evil of any sort, sin, and the "dark night of soul" have been either abandoned or "psychologized" away. If there is sin, it is something that someone else is doing, be they liberals or secular humanists or evolutionists or fundamentalists or whatever. This isn't great preaching and it isn't even faithful preaching. We have no excuse to stand in the pulpit except to bear witness to what the scriptures say and not what we wish they said. Great preaching sets forth carefully and with diligence God's Word, which is law to judge sin and sinners, and gospel that offers repentant sinners the promise of God's complete and unqualified forgiveness. Great preaching is setting forth God's appropriate Word before his people.

Jonah's word from God was certainly appropriate. The Ninevites were a terribly wicked people. Their overriding sin was bloodthirstiness and extreme cruelty. The Bible tells us that the Assyrians carried off the ten northern tribes of Israel, who were never heard from again. The Ninevites were the Nazis of their day, and, of course, a Jewish prophet would want to see them duly punished and destroyed. Jonah went with his message from God into the great city of Nineveh, some three days' journey across. Jonah went one day's journey in and preached his five-word sermon. He preached it in a Hebrew language the people couldn't understand, and he preached it in such an obnoxious way that they wouldn't want to have heard it. But it was God's Word, and it had its effect.

Dr. Paul Scherer, a Lutheran clergyman, used to talk about a preacher who said he always prepared the first part of his sermon, because he wanted to get it going, but once he started he depended on the Holy Spirit. A parishioner said to this man one Sunday that his part was always better than the Holy Spirit's part. There's truth in that. Great preaching, or even good preaching, demands much hard work. The Word of God is an embodied word in the sentences and phrases of the sermon. It has often been said that one should spend an hour of preparation time for every minute spent preaching. That would mean that the average sermon should have twenty hours of preparation behind it.

Time must be spent translating the text from the original Greek or Hebrew. Certainly we possess fine English translations, but the preacher must also be able to understand the nuances that are found only in the original texts. Time is spent deciding the form of the text, the genre, literary and redactional insights, and reading the commentaries written by great theologians and biblical scholars. All this is needed to determine what the text meant in its original setting. The preacher must put the particular text in its scriptural context, its use in the preaching and worship of the church down through the ages. Then time must be set aside to decide what in the ancient text still remains God's clear Word for today.

Reading, contemplating, and praying are all part of preparation for preaching. Preparation is extremely important. There can never be any shortcut to good and faithful exposition of the Word of God. But preparation isn't the whole story. Jonah's message involved little preparation. His delivery did not involve getting a new hairdo or a fancy suit. He didn't choreograph his movements or back up his message with a massed choir or orchestra. Flowers were absent, and no fountains gurgled. No, Jonah's sermon wasn't polished, but it was enough to qualify as great preaching. Jonah became the world's greatest preacher by relying on the plain Word of God.

The text is contextual; the message is always delivered to a congregation in a particular time and place. The needs of one place are not always the needs of another; the preachments of one time are not always needed or heeded in another. God's Word needs to address specific and timely problems; it needs to be embodied in words for people today as in all the days of the past. In the midst of sin and corruption, it isn't appropriate to quote all the happy and undemanding passages of the Bible. When a person is burdened with sin and guilt, it isn't time to go back and talk about God's punishment and wrath. Nineveh didn't need a message about God's goodness and mercy—Nineveh needed to hear the message God had set forth for it: "Yet forty days, and Nineveh shall be overthrown." It was the right message at the right place at the right time. That kind of preaching is important, and it's heeded. Herman Melville wrote in his great *Moby Dick,* "The pulpit is ever this world's foremost part; all the rest comes in its rear; the pulpit leads the world. . . . Yes, the world is a ship on its passage out . . . and the pulpit is the prow." There is nothing so important as preaching. It is God's Word for his world. The preacher never need be ashamed to stand forth and proclaim the biblical message. C. F. W. Walther, in his magisterial study *Law and Gospel,* notes, "The preacher must not pray the Lord's Prayer after preaching—not 'forgive me my trespasses,' but rather 'I have proclaimed God's Word.' " Jonah went into the city of Nineveh going a day's journey. And he cried, "Yet forty days and Nineveh shall be overthrown." And the people of Nineveh believed God; they proclaimed a fast, and put on sackcloth, from the greatest of them to the least of them.

Jonah preached a sermon of five words in a foreign language, and look at his results! Everyone believed God and repented of his or her sins. The message reached the king, and he proclaimed a royal fast and, himself, put on sackcloth and ashes. He even ordered the animals to repent. Terence Fretheim of Luther Seminary noted in his book *The Message of Jonah* that St. Francis may have preached to the animals, but only Jonah, in the entire history of preaching, ever brought about the prayer and repentance of sheep and goats! Jonah's preaching made an impact. Lives were changed by the Word of God. The people responded to the Word with faith in God. The point of the story of Jonah is not so much that the wicked people of Nineveh repented, but that they repented and believed. Jonah is the greatest preacher of all time, because he was able to get the people of Nineveh to rend their garments and their hearts with a five-word sermon. He even got the animals to repent and believe. What power comes with the Word of God when it is rightly preached and proclaimed!

Yet the message of Jonah can be discouraging for preachers. They spend hours each week on their sermons and rarely see a response. We must trust that God can use even us, reluctant and unskilled, as expositors of his Word, that through us his Word might have the means to change lives and work faith even now. God has used Jonah, Chrysostom, Martin Luther, John Wesley, Charles Spurgeon, Billy Graham, Billy Sunday, Dwight L. Moody, Oral Roberts, and Norman Vincent Peale to bring people to faith in Christ and to build up that faith. In quieter and more humble ways God has used the message of countless preachers through the ages, the lives of faithful and godly men and women, and their Christian witness to bring his Word to his world. He promises that this Word does not return to him empty, but accomplishes that which he has purposed and prospers in that for which it is sent. This is God's promise to preachers.

But there is nothing wrong with great success. Jonah does give us a clue to how a church grows and prospers. Who is the great preacher in Nineveh? It really isn't Jonah. He has only "begun" to preach as the Bible says, and no five-word sermon can convince millions of hardened heathen to repent. No, the greatest preacher of all is the people themselves, who brought the message to one another and to their king. It is the people who proclaim the fast and repent. It is the work of committed people bearing witness to God that causes conversion and church growth. Growing churches are the result of good and faithful biblical preaching, which is heard and shared and acted upon by good and faithful people. We are all preachers of God's Word. Not all are called to be pastors in Christ's church, but all the baptized are called to be ministers and servants of Christ and preachers and witnesses of his Word. If we are all ministers and preachers, how much more effective can we be in changing the lives and minds of the people around us! Instead of one or two professional ministers and preachers, our churches can have hundreds, even thousands, bearing witness to Christ in our communities. The people of Nineveh were great preachers, who, together, made Jonah the greatest preacher of all time. What does it take for the Christian message to be heard? God's Word and God's people. The message of Jonah, the world's greatest preacher, comes down to us through three thousand years of human history. We, too, can witness to God's Word, and our world can be changed. *Amen.*

James D. Kegel
Doctoral Candidate
Evangelical Lutheran Church in America
Chicago, Illinois

Sunday
November Twenty-seventh

Call to Worship: And then they will see the Son of man coming in a cloud with power and great glory. Now when these things begin to take place, look up and raise your heads, because your redemption is drawing near. *Luke 21:27-28*

Processional Hymn: "O Come, O Come, Emmanuel"

Invocation: Lord, as we start this Advent season, let us truly prepare for your coming birth. Cleanse our hearts and change our lives so that we are ready to celebrate that Holy Christmas Day. *Amen.*

Sermon Scripture: Matthew 1:18-23

Sermon Presentation: "There's A World Out There!"

Hymn of the Day: "Angels, from the Realms of Glory"

Offertory Scripture: May the God of hope fill you with all joy and peace in believing, so that by the power of the Holy Spirit you may abound in hope. *Romans 15:13*

Offertory Prayer: God of hope, grant us your grace. As we look to your gift of Christmas, let us give our gifts with joy and satisfaction. *Amen.*

Prayer of the Day

Lord, there's a world out there, and what a world it is! We can hear it! We can touch it! We can see it! We can smell it! We can taste it!

It's the world that you created, and we corrupted. We lead people to believe that our purpose here on earth is to get wealthy, to gain glory, to be powerful. It's a world in which your love has been replaced by another law: "Do unto others before they do it unto you." It's a world that has gone off the course that you set. It's a world in which the forces of darkness do their best to snuff out your light. But you have shown us that yours truly is the power and the glory forever.

You sent your Son into the world to bring us your light and your truth. Instead of a warm welcome, we gave him a death on a cross and a cold tomb. But through the power of the resurrection, you have shown us that love, your love, will conquer our hate. Your light will outshine the darkness of our sin. You alone have the power to grant eternal life in a world full of death. *Amen.*

Benediction: Besides this you know what hour it is, how it is full time now for you to wake from sleep. For salvation is nearer to us now than when we first believed; the night is far gone, the day is at hand. *Romans 13:11*

Recessional Hymn: "Jesus, with Thy Church Abide"

Lectionary Lessons: First Sunday of Advent
Lesson 1—Jeremiah 33:14-16; Psalm 25:1-10
Lesson 2—I Thessalonians 3:9-13
Gospel—Luke 21:25-36

History of the Hymn of the Day: "Angels, from the Realms of Glory"

This Christmas hymn is one of James Montgomery's favorite compositions. Montgomery, one of the greatest of the Moravian hymn writers, wrote the hymn in 1816 and it is considered one of the most challenging hymns ever written. The tune going under the name "Regent Square" was written by Henry Smart, a blind composer of London, England. His physical vision may have been impaired, but Smart could see as few men are able to see. From the combined vision of these two men has come one of the immortal Christmas classics.

Angels, from the realms of glory,
Wing your flight o'er all the earth;
Ye who sang creation's story,
Now proclaim Messiah's birth:
Come and worship, Come and worship,
Worship Christ, the new-born King!

Announcement for Next Week's Sermon: Who are you? I know you by your name. Our name is very important to us. It is ours to honor or defame. What is in a name? Plenty, let's talk next Sunday.

Story of the Week: A couple of weeks before Christmas, when a businessman went to pick up his car in the building's parking garage, he found a card under the windshield wiper of his car. "Merry Christmas," it said, "from all the fellows in the parking garage."

Since he always parked his own car and picked it up himself, he saw no need to tip anyone. But, someone else felt differently about that. Because a week later another card on his windshield read, "Merry Christmas from all the fellows in the parking garage—second notice."

THERE'S A WORLD OUT THERE!

There's a world out there! Can you hear it? Can you hear the screams of children in the night? Children who have been beaten by their parents and by strangers.

There's a world out there! Can you hear it? Can you hear the silent screams of the homeless, the voiceless, who die in our city streets every night—die because they have no place to sleep other than an alley or a bench and nothing more for heat than the steam from an exhaust vent.

There's a world out there! Can you see it? A world in which the second leading cause of death among young people is suicide. What sort of malaise exists in a society whose young people find no hope or reason for living? What is the darkness existing in our world that causes a fourteen-year-old boy from a rich suburban community to hang himself from a tree in the front lawn? That boy left a note on the tree next to his limp and lifeless body: "This is the only thing here with roots."

There's a world out there! Can you see it? Can you see the hungry and homeless who live in your own community? Can you see the men, women, and families who gather daily in a shelter for a hot meal, for many the only food they will have all day?

There's a world out there! And it is a dark world, a world in which self-gratification has become the supreme goal for living. It is a dark world in which our joy comes from spending money. What do we do when we are depressed? We go shopping, of course! The accumulation of "stuff" has become our sole reason for existence.

It is a dark world playing a dark game. The game is quite simply to play—whoever dies with the most "stuff" wins! Naturally there are not many rules to this game. All we must do is acquire as much "stuff" as we can, and we will then be happy. At least, that is what we are told. From the time we awaken to the time we fall asleep, we are told that happiness is found in having the right car, toothpaste, mouthwash, brand of jeans, frozen dinner, floor cleaner, et cetera, et cetera ad nauseum. And yet, in those families who appear to be winning the game, those with the most "stuff," it is the children from those families who have no roots, no purpose, no hope, and who commit suicide.

There is a world out there! And it is very, very dark.

In this dark world, statistics inform us that in the average American household parents and children spend fourteen minutes a week talking. Fourteen minutes a week! In those same average households, there are three television sets that are on for more than thirty hours a week.

There is a world out there groping in the dark. It is as if our entire society is like a person who gets up in the middle of the night. Have you ever done this: You get out of bed in the dark of night and refuse to turn on a light. You say to yourself, "This is my house. I know where everything is! I don't need to turn on any lights." And just as you say that, you stub your toe on a chair you were certain was twelve inches to your right.

There is a world out there. A world in which the boundaries have all disappeared. Maybe it's just too dark and no one can see the boundaries anymore. Perhaps it is just easier to say yes to everyone and forget about boundaries. We desperately want to be liked; so we agree with everything. We affirm everybody's choice of life-style and ethics. Isn't it their right to do whatever they want? Isn't freedom the right of the individual to do whatever he or she wants, whatever makes him or her feel good? There are no boundaries anymore, and if there were, we couldn't see them because it is too dark.

Yes, it is a very dark world out there. We do not have to talk about El Salvador and Nicaragua to find darkness. We do not have to mention Ethiopia and South Africa to find darkness. The dark world exists right here outside and inside these walls.

There is a dark world out there, and it needs light! "Arise, shine; for your light has come, and the glory of the Lord has risen upon you" proclaims the prophet in Isaiah 60:1.

There is a light in this dark world. And that light has come. It has come to us. We must now take that light into the dark world, out there, and in here.

William Barclay, the famous Scottish preacher, tells the story of when he was in France in World War II. It was near the end of the war as he and his small patrol were engaged in "mopping-up" exercises. They were roaming the countryside looking for any straggling enemy personnel. As they were walking through the French countryside, their captain was shot and killed. The men were fond of their captain, so it was natural for them to see that he had a proper burial.

They went to the first church they found and asked the Catholic priest if they could bury their friend in the graveyard lying next to the stone church. The priest asked the soldiers if the dead Scotsman was Catholic. Naturally he was Anglican and not Roman Catholic. The priest explained to the soldiers that only Catholics could be buried in that graveyard. Seeing the sorrow in the soldiers' eyes, the priest thought of a compromise. He told those soldiers to bury their captain just outside the cemetery fence, and the priest would personally see that his grave site would be cared for. The soldiers agreed and buried their friend just beyond the old wire fence.

The next day, the soldiers were given some time off. So they decided to return to their friend's grave and place some flowers. When they arrived at that country church, they looked and looked and looked, but could not find their friend's grave. After they had given up on their search, they went to the rectory to ask the priest if he knew what had happened. The priest saw them coming up the walk and went out to meet them.

"You are probably looking for your friend's grave," the priest asked the soldiers. "Well, I must tell you what happened. Last night I lay in bed, but could not fall asleep. I kept thinking about your friend, and his grave resting outside the fence line. So I got up in the middle of the night, and I moved the fence."

A light shines in this dark world. And the contrast between the light and the darkness causes even a flickering candle to glow dazzlingly white.

We remember the Epiphany of our Lord and the visitation of the magi, those unknown foreigners who came with gifts to worship the Christ child. Those magi, too, lived in a dark world, a world in which people lived in fear and superstition, and hence created false gods. The false gods did not necessarily lighten their darkness, but made the darkness feel more comfortable.

There's a world out there. A world that embraces darkness rather than light. A world filled with false gods. A world seeking for some form of comfort and security in the darkness. Yet there is no succor to be found in the darkness.

There's a world out there, my friends. A world in which lies are called truth, and truth is called fantasy or myth. The real fantasy, though, is that everything is fine. The real fantasy in the darkness is that if we buy just a few more things, lose ourselves in enough alcohol, drugs, chemicals, or other forms of abuse which we call self-gratification, then we will be happy. That is the heart of the darkness.

But it is you and I who know where the light is. We have truth to speak to this dark world. The babe of Bethlehem, the child who was born in a cave, the infant whom magi traveled to worship—it is the baby who brings light. There is no other source of light for this dark world. The light, the truth we must offer the world, is the light of Christ.

The French Catholic priest worked in the dark of night to move a fence, so that when the morning light came, the light of day would find the situation righted. So, too, that story is a metaphor for Jesus' work in the world. Jesus has moved the fence so that all are included. We celebrate, because the light shines, and we see that the fence has been moved. The light shines, and everyone needs to hear that the light of Christ shines for all.

There's a world out there, and it is dark. Yet God has chosen you and me to spread the news of the light. We are to let the light of Christ shine in this dark world.

"Arise, shine, for your light has come!"

Let us go forth, to that dark world out there and tell them all that their light has come! *Amen.*

Scot E. Sorensen

Mt. Carmel Lutheran Church
San Luis Obispo, California

Sunday
December Fourth

Call to Worship: But the Counselor, the Holy Spirit, whom the Father will send in my name, he will teach you all things, and bring to your remembrance all that I have said to you.

John 14:26

Processional Hymn: "Come, Thou Long-Expected Jesus"

Invocation: O Lord, names are important to us. That is how we get to know each other, and that is also how we first got to know you. "Jesus loves me! This I know, for the Bible tells me so." That is how I first met you, the name above all other names. *Amen.*

Sermon Scripture: Matthew 1:18-23

Sermon Presentation: "What's in a Name?"

Hymn of the Day: "A Charge to Keep I Have"

Offertory Scripture: For ye know the grace of our Lord Jesus Christ, that, though he was rich, yet for your sakes he became poor, that ye through his poverty might be rich.

II Corinthians 8:9 KJV

Offertory Prayer: Lord, we call on your name in every time of need. You never fail us. Now, in your name, we present these gifts to you. *Amen.*

Prayer of the Day

Emmanuel, Jesus, Lord—we know you by many names, but most importantly, we know you as the one sent by God to save us from sin and Satan and to put an end to the hold that death has on our lives and the lives of our loved ones.

We are thankful that you know and care for each of us by name. We are thankful that you have honored us with the privilege of being known in all the world by your name and as your people, Christians. To be called a child of yours provides us with all of the prestige, all of the status, all of the glory we will ever need. We remember that you have given us the gift of life. When that life was distorted by our sinful thoughts, words, deeds, and even our failure to act, you did not forsake us. When our pride and disobedience disrupted your relationship with us, you continued to love us with a love that made you send your Son into our world to die on a cross so that we could have eternal life.

May we be worthy of our calling, and at the name of Jesus may every knee bow in respect, reverence, and obedience. *Amen.*

Benediction: Therefore God has highly exalted him and bestowed on him the name which is above every name, that at the name of Jesus every knee should bow, in heaven and on earth and under the earth.

Philippians 2:9-10

Recessional Hymn: "Come, Thou Almighty King"

Lectionary Lessons: The Second Sunday of Advent

Lesson 1—Baruch 5:1-9 *or* Malachi 3:1-4; Psalm 126
Lesson 2—Philippians 1:3-11
Gospel—Luke 3:1-6

History of the Hymn of the Day: "A Charge to Keep I Have"

An eighteenth-century hymn by Charles Wesley. Sung to the tune of "Old Kentucky" by Jeremiah Ingalls, this revival hymn could be heard swelling from tents and camp grounds all over America. About a hundred years after it was written, Lowell Mason composed the music which is used presently.

A charge to keep I have, A God to glorify,
A never-dying soul to save, And fit it for the sky.

Announcement for Next Week's Sermon: Do you get a little tired of the way Christmas is overdone in all the commercial ways? Maybe we should just ban Christmas. How about that? It all starts next Sunday.

Story of the Week: The teacher had asked the students in the history class to list the people they thought were the eleven greatest Americans. After half an hour, everyone had turned in their lists except one boy.

The teacher said to him, "What's the matter? Can't you think of eleven great Americans?"

"I've got all but one of them," he said. "I haven't been able to decide on the quarterback."

WHAT'S IN A NAME?

". . . and his name shall be called Emmanuel (which means God with us)." (Matthew 1:23)

Of the eight million people living in Sweden, one out of every fifteen is named Johansson. In the capital city of Stockholm, the Johanssons occupy sixty-two pages of the telephone directory. When a Swede makes a reservation at a restaurant, for example, that table may be mistakenly given to someone with that same name. Surgery has been performed on people who have absolutely nothing wrong with them, except that they share a common name.

Names are important! The first thing we teach a child is his or her name. A name gives identity. It tells us who we are. It distinguishes us from other people. Though we may share a common name, especially if our last name is Smith, Jones, or Miller, we can add a first or a middle name that gives us identity.

Our name tells us; it tells others that we are somebody. It used to be that we could have but a single name. David, the son of Jesse was all that distinguished the great king of Israel. As there were more and more people, it became increasingly difficult to distinguish among people with but a single name. So, occupations were added to that first name. John the miller, Sam the tailor, or Charles the weaver. People not only had a first name which gave meaning, but also there was added a second name to give further identification.

One of the great rituals that prospective parents go through is the process of selecting a name for the newborn. Usually we have something specific in mind. We want that name to convey something. Particular names are popular at certain times. A very popular girl's name is Debbie, but the earlier form of that name, of course, is Deborah, which means *bee* or *wasp*. Still a very common boy's name is David, which means *beloved*.

We change the forms of names as we grow older. A young boy is often called *Jimmy*. Then he comes into his teen years and sheds the name *Jimmy* in favor of *Jim*. A further progression takes place when he begins to sign his name *James*. Each time there is a change in his use of a particular form of his name, there is a corresponding (at least we hope so) change in his growth and maturity.

It is interesting to note that officials in Washington were a bit puzzled to know how to refer to President Carter. Some wanted to say James Earl Carter, Jr.; it appeared that the newly-elected president wanted to continue to use Jimmy, while some got around it by simply referring to him as Mr. President.

Names, how they are selected or how they are used, are meant to have meaning. When our Lord was born, Joseph, in a dream, was told "And his name shall be called Emmanuel (which means, God with us)" (Matthew 1:23). Luke records this naming thusly, "You will conceive in your womb and bear a son, and you shall call his name Jesus" (Luke 1:32).

God with us, and the Lord is salvation. His name is Emmanuel, Jesus, which had great meaning. Now and then we hear it said of someone, "He's trying to make a name for himself." We know that the person has been named, but we are saying, "He is trying to give that name greater meaning." He is trying to achieve prestige, status, position, recognition, or fame. In the future, when that name is said, the hearers will immediately think of that person in a more meaningful way.

". . . and you shall call his name Jesus—the name of one who did not try to make a name for himself. It is what he did that has forever given that name meaning and significance. It is little wonder that few parents have had the nerve to name their child Jesus, which is simply the Greek form of the Jewish name Yeshua.

Paul once wrote about this name to the Philippians: "Therefore God has highly exalted him and bestowed on him the name which is above every name, that at the name of Jesus every knee should bow . . . and every tongue confess that Jesus Christ is Lord" (Philippians 2:9-11).

Just as we change our names as we grow older, so the significance of the name of Jesus changed. It is a distinction Pilate made when he said, "Whom do you want me to release for you, Barabbas or Jesus who is called the Christ?" We no longer make that distinction, because we call him Jesus Christ. He is the one who God sent to live among us, truly Emmanuel. He is the man who lived among us, who demonstrated what it means to be human in the fullest sense of that word. He is the Christ, who revealed to us what God is truly like.

Paul took this name one step further and called him *Lord,* a name or title that underwent a change also. At first when the name *Lord* was used, it meant master or owner. It was always a title of respect. Later it became the official title of the Roman emperors—in Greek *kurios,* in Latin *dominus,* master and lord. When it came time to put these titles in writing, as the scriptures were being translated from the Hebrew into the Greek, the word *Jehovah* in Hebrew was transcribed into the Greek form *kurios,* lord. When Paul gave Jesus Christ the title of Lord, he was saying, "He is the Master and Owner of all life; he is the King of kings, and he is the Lord of lords."

So a name not only gives meaning, but also a name has power. It has been said that once you know a person's name, you have power over him or her. A teenage girl meets a boy, and the boy wants to know her name. As long as she refuses to divulge her name, he is powerless. A person was in a group in which the leader held control by using the names of the people within that group. Any time a person was not paying attention, the leader would say the person's name and it would almost snap the head around.

It isn't mere happenstance that, in the second chapter of Genesis when God is giving Adam dominion and control of this earth and the animals, we read, "The man gave names to all the cattle" (Genesis 2:20). The very naming of them gave him power over them. By giving a name to your dog, you control it whenever you pronounce that name. It is no casual matter, then, when we say, "Jesus Christ is Lord." Truly it is a confession that this child born in Bethlehem, who grew into manhood, is the very One to whom we submit and the very one who has authority. "That at the name of Jesus every knee shall bow . . . and every tongue confess that Jesus Christ is Lord."

Some have seen Jesus as One who stands over them in a power that breaks the human spirit, an authority that takes away our freedom and responsibility to be human, a divine coerciveness that will threaten us with disaster if we do not submit. How wrong we are! How far this is from the very truth and teaching of scripture. God's way has never been force, but love. It has never been coercion, but comes through a cross. It is because of what God has done in Jesus Christ, who came as a babe, lived among men, suffered and died on a cross, and then rose victorious—it is because of this that we give him our love and loyalty. It is not God's way to break down the door of our heart. It is his way to stand at the door knocking and awaiting our response. It is not God's way to make us knuckle under, but it is his way that we, like those lowly shepherds when we meet the Lord Christ, kneel in love and adoration. *Amen.*

James M. Logan
Catalina Baptist Church
Tucson, Arizona

Sunday
December Eleventh

Call to Worship: Without having seen him you love him; though you do not now see him you believe in him and rejoice with unutterable and exalted joy. *I Peter 1:8*

Processional Hymn: "O Little Town of Bethlehem"

Invocation: As we draw close to this Christmas season, grant us the true faith to see Christmas for what it is. This is the birthday of our Savior, the true God who came to us as a baby. Grant us a *Christ*mas this Christmas. *Amen.*

Sermon Scripture: Mark 1:1-8

Sermon Presentation: "Should Christmas Be Banned?"

Hymn of the Day: "Joy to the World"

Offertory Scripture: For God so loved the world, that he gave his only begotten Son, that whosoever believeth in him should not perish, but have everlasting life. *John 3:16 KJV*

Offertory Prayer: As the Spirit of Christmas grows in each one of us, let it be an occasion for great joy. Thank you, Lord, for this great gift. Accept this, my gift in return. *Amen.*

Prayer of the Day

Lord, this time of the year is so busy. As Christmas draws closer, we find our days full of preparations for this great holiday. We are busy planning family visits, buying gifts for family and friends, baking cookies and cakes, scheduling parties, wishing those around us a happy holiday. It wouldn't take much for us to crowd out the real meaning of Christmas.

In the midst of all of our preparations, make us mindful, first of all, of what began on that first Christmas, of how God put into motion his plan to reconcile the world unto himself by sending his Son into the world to die so that we might live, to be treated as a sinner so that we could be counted as righteous.

Remind us of who was born in that stable in Bethlehem two thousand years ago. Despite the humble surroundings, let us never forget that Jesus is the Son of God, the King of kings, the Lord of lords, the Prince of peace. And let us never forget why

God sent his Son into our world—not to judge us, but to save us, not to condemn us, but to declare our sins forgiven.

Guide us in our celebration of the birth of our Lord, Jesus Christ. May the true meaning and importance of this day be evident in all we do and say. *Amen.*

Benediction: So whatever you wish that men would do to you, do so to them; for this is the law and the prophets.

Matthew 7:12

Recessional Hymn: "Go, Tell It on the Mountain"

Lectionary Lessons: The Third Sunday of Advent

Lesson 1—Zephaniah 3:14-20; Isaiah 12:2-6
Lesson 2—Philippians 4:4-9
Gospel—Luke 3:7-18

History of the Hymn of the Day: "Joy to the World"

There could be no hymn which can boast of such famous parenthood as this two-hundred-fifty-year-old Christmas carol. The words were penned by that master of English hymns, that giant of sacred verse, that most famous of hymn writers, Isaac Watts. The music was composed by that wonder of divine sound, that leader of choral interpretation, that most famous of song writers George Frederick Handel (an adaptation from *Messiah*). Who can say which one has been more responsible for the continued popularity of "Joy to the World"? Contemporaries, Handel died (1759) some eleven years after Watts. But what they created together has never died—and probably never will!

Announcement for Next Week's Sermon: Are you fit to inherit the church? If Christ left you in charge of the church, could you handle it? He did leave you in charge. Now what are you going to do?

Story of the Week: A young fellow about twelve years old went into the bank to deposit $75 in his savings account. The banker, being friendly and interested in the boy, said, "That's a pretty big deposit. How did you earn the money?"

"Selling Christmas cards," the little boy said.

"You did real well," the banker said. "You must have sold cards to a lot of people in your neighborhood."

"No, sir," the boy said. "One family bought all of them. Their dog bit me."

SHOULD CHRISTMAS BE BANNED?

The beginning of the gospel of Jesus Christ, the Son of God. (Mark 1:1)

Among the changes that have taken place in American society during recent years is the fact that many products, customs, and practices have been banned or abolished. There was a time when DDT was the world's most widely used insecticide, but DDT was banned by the Federal Government several years ago. Once upon a time, parents could take their children to movies without being concerned that they would be exposed to sex, violence, profanity, and smut, but then Hollywood decided that good taste and morality didn't make money and thus should be banned. A group of concerned Christians have tried to persuade merchants to ban the sale of such sleazy sex magazines as *Playboy*, *Penthouse*, and *Hustler*. It now appears that their efforts have met with some success, but their opponents feel that if those magazines are banned, their constitutionally-guaranteed right of freedom of choice might also be banned.

In this age of "enlightened abolishment," maybe we Christians ought to ask ourselves, "Should Christmas be banned?" If such a proposal passed, it would not be for the first time. In seventeenth-century England, when the Puritans were in charge, Parliament passed a law banning Christmas. People were forbidden to light candles, exchange gifts, decorate their homes, sing carols, and make plum puddings or mince pies. The Puritans believed that the celebration of Christmas was spiritually degrading, that gift giving and feasting detracted from the true meaning of the Incarnation.

Strangely enough, it might seem that Mark, the author of the earliest Gospel, agreed with the Puritans. Of the four Gospels, Mark is the only one that has absolutely nothing to say about the birth of Jesus. Matthew tells of the virgin birth and of the wise men who came bearing gifts. Luke describes the shepherds abiding in the fields as the angels sang. Even John says that "the Word became flesh and dwelt among us" (John 1:14). Mark, however, begins his Gospel with a stark declaration: "The beginning of the gospel of Jesus Christ, the Son of God."

Should Christmas be banned? Absolutely not—as long as we remember what began on that first Christmas. Christmas is "the beginning of the gospel of Jesus Christ," as Mark succinctly reminds us. That is *what* Christmas is all about: the beginning of the gospel. *Gospel* is a word that means "good news" or "glad tidings." When Jesus was born in Bethlehem of Judea, the world of that day had very little good news. The Romans ruled all of the civilized Western world with an iron hand. They were harsh conquerors, and the people they ruled often suffered greatly. Human life was cheap. There was no such thing as human rights, the E.R.A., or freedom. Slavery was the dominant institution, with more than sixty million people held in bondage. Girl babies often were slain at birth or were raised to be sold into prostitution; women were considered to be inferior in all ways. Anyone who was not a Roman citizen could be taxed for 100 percent of his or her earnings. The world into which Jesus was born was a world without hope, a world in which love was rarer than diamonds or gold.

But then Jesus was born, and the gospel began. A baby boy was born to a Jewish carpenter and his teenaged bride, and people began to hear some good news for a change. Where there had been darkness, now there was light. Where there had been nothing but despair, now some people began to hope. In a world that seldom heard music outside of a Roman banquet hall, ordinary shepherds heard angels singing the "Hallelujah Chorus." Three foreign astrologers—men not known for their generosity—gladly gave that baby precious gifts. An old man named Simeon, who had just about given up hope for himself and his nation, saw that baby and sang with hilarious joy, "Lord, now lettest thou thy servant depart in peace . . . for mine eyes have seen thy salvation" (Luke 2:29-30). No matter where we read about Jesus' birth in the Bible, there good news begins.

Maybe that is how we should begin our Christmas also, by telling people about the good news that came in Jesus Christ. Instead of spending so much money for gifts, maybe we should spend more time in sharing the good news of God's love for humankind. One example will suffice: One Sunday afternoon, we went to a nursing home to provide a worship service for the residents there. It was a simple service—three familiar hymns, a prayer, and a brief meditation. After the service, we spent some time talking with each of those elderly people. One little lady held my hand and wouldn't let go. "Stay a little longer and laugh again for me!"

The beginning of the gospel of Jesus Christ for some folks, like the little lady, is to hear Christian laughter. For others, it is to be hugged and told that God loves them and that you do, too. For still others, it may be a daily phone call or a note once a week or a smile or simply visiting and listening to them. For a young person, it may be a word of encouragement. For a young mother, it might be volunteering to take care of her baby once in a while so she can get out of the house. For a tired worker, the beginning of the gospel of Jesus Christ might come as a sacramental cup of coffee (your treat) at the corner drug store. Like the world into which Jesus was born, there is a famine of good news in our world as well. The beginning of the gospel of Jesus Christ, for some folks this Christmas, just may have to begin with your telling them.

Should Christmas be banned? Absolutely not—as long as we remember *who* was born on that first Christmas. Mark began his Gospel with the words, "The beginning of the gospel of Jesus Christ, the Son of God." The reason good news began on that first Christmas day is that the Son of God was born in Bethlehem of Judea. That is the *who* of Christmas! For more than four hundred years, the Jews had heard no word from the Lord. All they had were memories of a God who had spoken through their prophets long ago. Even those memories were of a God who often seemed stern, judgmental, and remote. Now, at least a few of them knew that God had come to earth as a tiny, adorable baby. Instead of being afraid of God, now they had an image of God who was loving and lovable. No wonder Mark said that the good news began when the Son of God came into the world.

Of course, we modern Christians have known all of our lives that Jesus is the Son of God. We regularly affirm that we believe in God the Father Almighty, maker of heaven and earth, and in Jesus Christ his only Son, our Lord. From our earliest years in Sunday school, we have been taught that Jesus is God's Son. We have heard countless sermons about Jesus and have sung innumerable hymns about him as the Son of God. That may be our greatest problem—the good news that Jesus is God's Son is still good, but it really isn't news for us any more. So Jesus is the Son of God. So what else is new? What's exciting and thrilling and life-changing about that?

People today are in much the same situation as Peter and James and John when Jesus led them up the Mount of

Transfiguration. Those men had lived with Jesus for almost three years. They had eaten with him, had been taught by him, and had seen him perform miracles, but still they didn't know who he really was. They thought they knew, but in reality, they did not. Six days before, Jesus had asked them who they thought he was. One said he was John the Baptist, another said Elijah, another said Jeremiah, and so on. Peter even said that Jesus was "the Christ, the Son of the living God" (Matthew 16:16). That was correct, but Jesus pointed out that Peter did not say that for himself, but because God gave him the answer. In spite of being with Jesus all of that time, his three closest friends really had no good news to tell about him. Then on that mountain, Jesus was transfigured by the glory of God. His clothes became white, and his face shone like the sun. Two holy figures, Moses and Elijah, appeared and talked with him. Then God's voice thundered from the heavens, "This is my beloved Son, with whom I am well pleased; listen to him" (Matthew 17:5). Then they knew! Then they believed! Then they had some good news to share with the rest of the world!

If Christmas really is to make a difference in our lives, if we really want to share some good news for a change, we must really believe that Jesus is the Son of God. This will happen only when we allow Jesus to take over our lives. In a cathedral in Europe, an organist was practicing one day when a rather disreputable chap came up and asked if he could play the organ for a while. The stranger looked so much like a bum that the organist was hesitant, but at last agreed to let him play. The tramp's fingers danced over the keyboard, and glorious music filled the cathedral. When he finished, the organist asked who he was. The stranger replied, "Felix Mendelssohn." After the great artist departed, the organist said to himself, "Just think! I almost did not let the master play." If people like you and I will let our Master Jesus, the Son of God, take over the console of our lives, we, too, will have some good news to share with the world.

Should Christmas be banned? Absolutely not—as long as we remember *why* Jesus was born on that first Christmas. Mark knew why—because that first Christmas was "the beginning of the gospel of Jesus Christ." *Christ* is not Jesus' name, but his title. *Christ* means "Messiah" or "Savior." The reason *why* Jesus was born was so that he could be our Savior. Joseph was told by an angel of God that Mary was pregnant by the Holy Spirit, and that Joseph "shall call his name Jesus, for he will save his people from their sins" (Matthew 1:21). Jesus, the Son of God, was born as a baby on that first Christmas for one reason and one reason only: to be the Christ, our Savior. That is the *why* of Christmas, the best news of the gospel.

When Jimmy Carter was inaugurated as the President of the United States, the inaugural prayer was given by United Methodist Bishop William R. Cannon. At the conclusion of that prayer—which was broadcast on national television and radio—Bishop Cannon said, "All this we ask in the name of Jesus Christ, thy Son and our Savior. Amen." Later, Bishop Cannon was criticized by some reporters, because they said Jesus Christ is not recognized as the Son of God and their Savior of all of the people of the United States. When Bishop Cannon heard about this criticism, he replied, "Jesus may not be the Savior of all of the people of the United States, but he wants to be!"

If that isn't good news for sharing at Christmas time, then I don't know what good news is! That is the gospel that Christians like you and I are asked to share, not only on Christmas day, but on every day of our lives. Jesus is our Christ, our Messiah, our Savior, and there are literally millions of people who have never heard that good news.

Several years ago, when "All In the Family" was the leading program on television, Archie Bunker told his wife, Edith, that he wanted to be on the bowling team so bad he could taste it! He described the bowling shirts that the Cannonballers wore: All yellow silk, with bright red piping on the collar and sleeves. And on the back, there's a picture of a cannon firing a bowling ball at the set of pins. He said, "When you got something like that on your back, Edith, you know you're somebody!"

When you have Jesus Christ as your Savior, you not only know that you are somebody; you are somebody! When Jesus is your Savior, you are a whole person again, just the way God intended you to be. When Jesus is your Savior, you are free from the dominion of sin, because Jesus takes all of your sins away and makes you as clean as new-fallen snow. When Jesus is your Savior, you never have to worry about dying, because Jesus himself said, "Whoever lives and believes in me shall never die" (John 11:26). How can we know these claims are true? Ask Mary Magdalene! Ask Zacchaeus! Ask Paul! Ask Augustine or Francis of Assisi or Martin Luther or John Wesley or Billy Graham or

Mother Teresa! Ask your born-again Christian neighbor next to you in the pew! Ask any real Christian what it means to have Jesus Christ as your Savior; accept Jesus as your Savior, too. Share that good news gently and lovingly with others who do not know him, and then you will understand *why* Christmas is "the beginning of the gospel of Jesus Christ, the Son of God."

Should Christmas be banned? In the opinion of Saint Mark, the answer is a resounding no!—as long as Christians remember what began on that first Christmas and who was born on that first Christmas and why.

That is my opinion as well. Now, both Saint Mark and I would like to ask, "What is your opinion?" *Amen.*

Raymond W. Gibson
Kentucky Conference—United Methodist Church
Lexington, Kentucky

Sunday
December Eighteenth

Call to Worship: Therefore, if any one is in Christ, he is a new creation; the old has passed away, behold, the new has come. *II Corinthians 5:17*

Processional Hymn: "What Child Is This"

Invocation: Lord, we take this Advent season to celebrate the birthday of the church. Make us loyal members, always ready to serve both you and your church. Bless the people of this congregation and all those who have gone before so that we might have this church today. *Amen.*

Sermon Scripture: Colossians 1:3-12

Sermon Presentation: "Fit to Share the Heritage"

Hymn of the Day: "Hark! the Herald Angels Sing"

Offertory Scripture: We receive from him whatever we ask, because we keep his commandments and do what pleases him. *I John 3:22*

Offertory Prayer: You have given of yourself; you have given us the church. Now let us give to you to strengthen your kingdom here on earth. *Amen.*

Prayer of the Day

Lord, like the hymn says, "I am the church. You are the church. We are the church together." We are called the body of Christ and like any body, we are called to action. We are called to speak your words, to touch people's lives and give them comfort in their moments of pain, reassurance in their moments of doubt, guidance in their times of uncertainty, life in the midst of death.

We are thankful for the dedication of the saints of the past who have made our congregation the strong Christ-centered church that it is today. Make us ready, willing, and able to carry on the faithful work begun by our forebears. Remind us that the church of tomorrow is dependent on how faithful we are to our God-given task today.

When we become lazy, move us. When we become indecisive, guide us. When we become weak, strengthen us. We are the church. To you, our Lord, we say, "Thank God." *Amen.*

Benediction: God our Savior . . . saved us, not because of deeds done by us in righteousness, but in virtue of his own mercy, by the washing of regeneration and renewal in the Holy Spirit. *Titus 3:4-5*

Recessional Hymn: "The Church's One Foundation"

Lectionary Lessons: The Fourth Sunday of Advent
Lesson 1—Micah 5:2-5*a* (5:1-4*a*); Psalm 80:1-7
Lesson 2—Hebrews 10:5-10
Gospel—Luke 1:39-55

History of the Hymn of the Day: "Hark! the Herald Angels Sing"
Charles Wesley of England is without doubt one of the two most productive hymn writers of all time—the other being Isaac Watts. Yet, strangely enough, Wesley was able to get only one hymn poem into the Church of England's Book of Common Prayer—and that one by error! An eighteenth-century printer didn't know that the "established Church" of England frowned with disapproval on Wesley's hymns. He needed to fill an empty space in the Book of Common Prayer and took it upon himself to insert a Christmas poem called "Hark, How All the Welkin Rings!" by an Anglican clergyman names Charles Wesley. When the error was discovered attempts were made to have it removed, but it proved so popular that it was allowed to remain. This is not the end of the story. "Hark! the Herald Angels Sing" still might not have reached its tremendous Christmas popularity if it hadn't been for other twists of fate. Wesley had called his poem "Hymn for Christmas Day" and it was sung with mild enthusiasm for over a hundred years. It might have slipped gradually into the mist of oblivion if it had not been for a tenor, William Haymen Cummings. When vocalizing on a bit of Felix Mendelssohn's "The Festgesang," he noticed how the arrangement was perfect for Wesley's "Hymn for Christmas Day." Retitled "Hark! the Herald Angels Sing" and strengthened by the powerful music of Mendelssohn, Wesley's hymn became one of the greatest Nativity songs ever composed. Written in 1738, one of the first of Wesley's hymns became one of his greatest.

Announcement for Next Week's Sermon: Something big will happen next Sunday. It is a very special day. We will be celebrating a birthday. I won't tell you whose birthday, you will have to guess.

Story of the Week: Once at a banquet when half a dozen speakers had said "a few words" and the golf trophies had been passed out and the clock was ready to strike 11:00 o'clock, the master of ceremonies said, "Now ladies and gentlemen, here is the moment we have been waiting all evening for. Mr. Gene Murphy will now give us his address."

Mr. Murphy walked to the lectern and said, "Thank you Mr. Chairman. My address is 6320 Pat Avenue, Canoga Park, California 91303. Please write to me sometime."

FIT TO SHARE THE HERITAGE

A minister, interviewing a person who was applying for a church staff position, read over the application and said: "I see your birthday is April 12. What year?" The simple reply was: "Every year!"

Likewise, we celebrate the birthday of this church every year. I want to challenge you to be the church, the church Christ would have you be. But you have to keep plugging away, dig a little deeper. Do you have any idea how many churches closed their doors and gave up because people quit too soon?

Henry Comstock was a miner back in the middle 1800s. He staked his claim and dug until he found gold. He was digging out a little ore, but he knew there was more. So he worked and dug, always convinced that somewhere there had to be the mother lode. The days turned into weeks, into months, the months into years. Finally, he gave up in 1859, when someone offered him $11,000 for his claim. Henry Comstock probably looked at the buyer and said, "You've got yourself a deal. You've got yourself a mine." And the person who bought it dug a little deeper—just a few feet—and the Comstock mine produced $340 million in gold. The same attitude is reflected in many churches. Congregations who should have dug a little deeper didn't. They got discouraged. They didn't dig deep enough.

Our lives are filled with so many things that we tend to take the church for granted. A Concorde plane that takes only three and a half hours to fly to Europe doesn't cause much wonder any more. People on the moon? Computers that think? Robots that do our work? We yawn and ask, "What's next?" We regard it all as commonplace, and we regard our church as just one thing more in a "too filled life." We give up and don't bother to dig deeper. We forget that Jesus said, "The kingdom of heaven is at hand" (Matthew 10:7).

When we look back over the years to those men and women who founded this church, we say, "They had what it takes." Today I ask this church to look to its past. I urge you to consider the present, and I challenge you to face the future in the Spirit of Christ. Or, to put it in other terms, like a piano, you may not be grand, but you can be upright!

There is a story of a young man who was determined that his first automobile would be a wonder and a joy. He worked and saved until the great day arrived, when he could buy his dream machine. It was a van, and it was beautiful, loaded with all the extras money could buy! He drove the van off the lot with the pride of a man who knows destiny has smiled on him. The next day, however, the new van was towed, bent and battered, back to the dealer. An angry and disillusioned owner stormed into the salesman's office, demanding a complete refund.

"What happened?" asked the startled salesman.

"I bought your van," the young man sputtered. "I drove it out to the interstate to give it a test run. I set the automatic cruise control, went to the back to fix myself a cup of coffee, and the darn thing ran off the road!"

I suspect there is a hunger in each of us to put our lives on cruise control, to avoid responsibility. How often do we as church members sit back, hoping the church will run by itself as we, figuratively, enjoy our cup of coffee?

If this church is to have a great future in the coming years, every one of us must make an effort to let the church be the church—the true Body of Christ in this community, reaching all across the world.

In this vein, the Apostle Paul could write to the Philippian church: "Not that I have already obtained this or am already perfect; but I press on to make it my own, because Christ Jesus has made me his own. Brethren, I do not consider that I have made it my own; but one thing I do, forgetting what lies behind and straining forward to what lies ahead, I press on toward the goal" (Philippians 3:12-14). Paul felt that when Jesus stopped him on the Damascus road, Christ had a dream, a purpose, and a vision for which he had grasped Paul. The rest of his life, Paul devoted to fulfilling that dream. Christ calls your church to press on to fulfill that dream that the founders had long ago, the dream that Christ has for this church in this community for the rest of this century and on into the twenty-first century.

Religion is a commodity which, the more you give away, the more you have remaining. I ask this church to take this idea to heart as it looks to the future. As a challenge, I offer you five elements that must be present for the church to grow:

First, the church must have a clear understanding of what it is about. When Jesus began his ministry, the first thing he did was to announce his mission: "The Spirit of the Lord is upon me, because he has anointed me to preach good news to the poor. He has sent me to proclaim release to the captives and recovering of sight to the blind, to set at liberty those who are oppressed, to proclaim the acceptable year of the Lord (Luke 4:18-19). Jesus understood what he was here for. The question is, do we?

Second, we must turn our attention to the world outside. If the church is to grow, it must reach out to the old, to the young, to families, to singles, to those who are like us, and to those who are different from us. What can we do for them in Jesus' name?

And what about those beyond our doors, beyond our borders? By the end of this century, over half of the world's Christians will be in Asia, Africa, and Latin America, where most of them will be dreadfully poor. How shall we treat these people, as our enemies or as our brothers and sisters in Christ?

In the Soviet Union, there are eighteen and a half million members of the Communist Party, while there are fifty million Christian church members. Are these the people we should hate? Are these the people on whom we should drop our nuclear bombs? Think of what war does to people. A girl in Beirut, Lebanon, had seen war rage as long as she had lived. Since she was born, she has been hearing bombs and seeing red and white colors. . . . Why was she born? Are children in other countries like this? She has seen happy children playing in gardens—but only in magazines.

What are we as Christians doing to help? The average single American working mother with three children and a salary of $10,500 paid more taxes last year than Boeing, General Electric,

DuPont, Texaco, Mobil Oil, and AT&T combined. Does this stir us Christians to anger, to take action in the name of Christ?

Third, a growing church must use the Bible. We are people of the Book, and we must meet the hunger in people for the Word of God.

Fourth, a growing church is also a praying church. Each of us must spend time in prayer, and as a congregation we need to pray each week for guidance from the Lord for the days ahead.

Fifth, in a growing church fit for the future, each of us has a ministry to fulfill. This ministry requires much of our time, and of course this means sharing our money. Dean Fenton Morley of Salisbury Cathedral in England once said, "There has been a relation between money and religion ever since Noah. He was the only man able to float a company when the rest of the world was in liquidation." In Oliver Goldsmith's *The Man in Black,* one of the characters makes the statement that after he had resided at college for seven years, his father died and left him his blessing! What did our forebears in this church leave us that will challenge us to make this church great in the years ahead?

A woman was having trouble with her car, so she took it to the garage, where she asked for an estimate of the cost of fixing it. When she acted surprised at the high cost, the manager told her, "But that price includes parts and labor."

"Well," she asked "what would it cost without parts and labor?"

Is this church fit to share the heritage without your parts and your labor?

There is a story about a minister who arrived at a little country church for the service. He noticed a collection box near the door. Thinking it was for mission work, he slipped in a twenty dollar bill. After the service, one of the deacons approached, thanked him, and said, "You'll understand that we are not able to pay you a fee for this service, but we have a box in the back so that any who have been helped by the service, and feel grateful, may put something in. Whatever is in the box, we ask the minister to accept toward his travel expenses. I am delighted to be able to tell you that there were twenty dollars. Here it is with our thanks."

The minister smiled and took it and went his way. When he got home, he told his family the story at the dinner table. His son remarked, "Well, you know, Dad, if you had put more in, you would have gotten more out!"

G. K. Chesterton once wrote: "The really great man is the man who makes every man feel great." This church should be filled with men and women who make every man and woman and child in this community feel great; then this church will become a really great church!

May God grant you the will and the courage to become a church fit to share the heritage of God's people. May God bless you all! *Amen.*

Carl A. Viehe
St. Stephen's-Bethlemen United Church of Christ
Buffalo, New York

Sunday
December Twenty-fifth

Call to Worship: He is the image of the invisible God, the first-born of all creation; for in him all things were created, in heaven and on earth, visible and invisible, whether thrones or dominions or principalities or authorities—all things were created through him and for him. He is before all things, and in him all things hold together. He is the head of the body, the church; he is the beginning, the first-born from the dead, that in everything he might be pre-eminent. For in him all the fulness of God was pleased to dwell. *Colossians 1:15-19*

Processional Hymn: "O Come, All Ye Faithful"

Invocation: On this Holy and happy day, we call on you to be our God and let us be your people. As we worship the baby of Bethlehem, let us find a new humility and know you are the perfector of our faith. Love us now and forever. *Amen.*

Sermon Scripture: Luke 2:1-20

Sermon Presentation: "Someday, Something Big"

Hymn of the Day: "Silent Night, Holy Night"

Offertory Scripture: But when the time had fully come, God sent forth his Son, born of woman, born under the law, to redeem those who were under the law. *Galatians 4:4*

Offertory Prayer: With the birth of your Son, we come out from under the law of death into the new life of love and forgiveness. Make us thankful for this great gift. *Amen.*

Prayer of the Day

Lord, we live in a world of "hype." We are barraged with descriptions that use the words *tremendous, greatest, spectacular, extraordinary,* and *wonderful* to describe everything from a sale on soap to the latest hit song. Ours is a world in which all fame and glory are short-lived. Humility is not a trait we understand or appreciate.

Cure us of our spiritual blindness that makes us unwilling and unable to see the Messiah born in a corner of a stable and dying on a cross on a hillside. Cure us of our spiritual deafness, that blocks our hearing of the "good news" in which we are told that you seek out the lost, care about the poor and the sinful, and welcome all who seek your forgiveness, your truth, and your love.

Let us see, hear, and know on this holiest of days that "unto us is born a Savior who is Christ the King." *Amen.*

Benediction: So we are ambassadors for Christ, God making his appeal through us. We beseech you on behalf of Christ, be reconciled to God. For our sake he made him to be sin who knew no sin, so that in him we might become the righteousness of God. *II Corinthians 5:20-21*

Recessional Hymn: "Away in a Manger"

Lectionary Lessons: Christmas Day

Lesson 1—Isaiah 52:7-10; Psalm 98

Lesson 2—Hebrews 1:1-12

Gospel—John 1:1-14

History of the Hymn of the Day: "Silent Night, Holy Night"

This most beautiful of Christmas hymns was written on the night before Christmas in 1818 at the little village of Oberndorf, Austria, by Joseph Mohr, the vicar of the Church of St. Nicholas. Mohr gave the words of the simple poem to his organist Franz Gruber, who composed the music in time for the Christmas Eve service. The drama of the first rendition of "Silent Night, Holy Night" was augmented by the fact that the organ broke down, and the first public presentation of Christmas' most famous hymn was a simple duet between the author and the composer with voice and plain guitar accompaniment. The breaking down of the organ was instrumental in popularizing the new hymn. Later when the organ was being repaired, Gruber played the new carol on it as a means of testing the tone of the instrument. The repairman was fascinated and enchanted. He requested a copy and took it back with him to his own village of Zillerthal where it was received joyously. Four daughters of a Zillerthal glove maker named Strasse used this song in concerts from town to town and village to village while their father sold gloves. Soon everyone was singing "Silent Night, Holy Night," and so they have through the generations up to now, and so they will as long as Christmas is a part of the human life.

Announcement for Next Week's Sermon: It is a new year. We start the new year with resolutions. Make your first resolution to be here in church next Sunday.

Story of the Week: A little girl had been sent to her room as punishment. After a while she reappeared in a happy mood.

"Well, Mamma," she said, "I've thought things over and I prayed."

"That's fine," said her mother. "Now that should help you be a good little girl."

"Oh, I didn't pray to be good," she said. "I asked God to help you put up with me."

SOMEDAY, SOMETHING BIG

What a night, the old newspaperman growled to himself as he forced himself out of bed and felt his feet tighten as they hit the cold floor. Here it was, 5:00 o'clock on a Jerusalem morning, and sleep had completely eluded him. He reached for a cigarette, glad that the hour of the day at least spared him a lecture about his habits. But he was aggravated over what had kept him awake. *Curses,* he thought, *it wasn't even important!* That thought made him choke and start coughing on the smoke. All he'd done the whole night long was chase thoughts about an experience he'd had thirty years ago. Half his lifetime, he sighed cynically. Thirty years ago, he had been a novice reporter assigned to get a story out of Bethlehem. He knew when he received the assignment it was like trying to get wool from a camel; he also knew he had no choice. If he wanted to work in Jerusalem someday, it meant beginning in Bethlehem. Someday, he had told himself, something big would come his way. Strange twist of life, wasn't it, that he was still looking for something big, still envying those home office boys with the big cigars and tailored suits.

But why, in Caesar's name, did Bethlehem keep him awake? Why couldn't he think his nostalgic thoughts and then sleep? Now he'd probably muff today's job—not that it mattered so much anymore. Awake over Bethlehem! Population still three hundred! Real excitement for a one-time rarin'-to-go reporter bent on being the next Woodward or Bernstein! And about the only thing that had been happening was a census, ordered by Caesar so that he could collect his taxes. So get a story on taxes, he had been told. Well, he had gone, reconciled to listening to the perennial griping of people about taxes, taxes, taxes.

Good thing he arrived when he did, and lucky he worked for the *Jerusalem Times*, or he wouldn't have jostled loose that room. All sold out, the innkeeper had told him, until his calling card and a couple of gold coins found their way to the fellow's eager hand. Sometimes, he had to admit, being on the *Times* staff had its advantages. But a story . . . where on the streets of Bethlehem does anyone find a story, even the next Bernstein of Judea?

He talked to soldiers. He talked to census-takers. And Caesar only knows he spoke to at last half the people in this God-forsaken, easily forgotten place. Yet it kept him awake all night! Strangely, it was the thoughts of a few people among the many that haunted him, thoughts he hadn't had for years. He remembered that the inkeeper had told him of a couple he'd turned away late that same night he'd rented a room. Maybe, suggested the innkeeper (probably wanting to be helpful in his small town way) he could do a story on this couple—you know the kind, human interest, isn't that what you call it? The woman was very pregnant, he continued, and they'd come all the way from Nazareth. *Wonderful,* he'd replied sarcastically to himself, *that will really be news in Jerusalem!* Only when he was told that the innkeeper had sent them to a corner in the stable did he pause. *Just a twinge of old-fashioned guilt,* he'd rationalized as he remembered how he had obtained his own room. Peasants wouldn't know what to do with a decent place anyhow, and if the kid was born in that barn, at least he'd have no illusions about the world.

Yet, he recalled that later that night he'd looked for the couple. Well, actually, he'd just arranged to happen into them outside the stable. Maybe, here would be a story after all. But he'd learned that she was practically a girl and that the man with her was not yet her husband. The poor people were probably having a horrible time already because of those circumstances. Who was he to make things worse for them! If he wanted scandal, he'd rather go digging in Augustus Caesar's backyard and leave these poor folk alone. Too bad the world couldn't believe he had a sense of decency! Anyway, no sense digging around in these people's lives. Nothing big here.

On the other hand, with all the messiah-talk going around, he hoped that he would be around if this ever came to pass—especially if this "savior" could set the Romans in their place, as folks were hoping! That would be the day to be on the scene. If only he could work his way up the news business ladder quickly enough to be in Jerusalem when it happened. Now, here it was, Jerusalem thirty years later and no messiah.

Oh, yes, Bethlehem. What really made it a strange place was those shepherds. The old newsman took another puff on his cigarette and admitted he'd never have seen that simple couple again had it not been for shepherds. Toward morning of that same blandly ordinary night, word began circulating among townsfolk that there had been angels on the hills outside Bethlehem, angels announcing a messiah. *Rumors of angels,* he corrected himself. With nothing better to do, he remembered that he had tried to follow up on that rumor. Maybe there was substance to it. Maybe a great religious man had had a powerful experience of the Jewish God. Maybe this God was ready to send his heavenly armies to make war. Maybe here was his messiah story sooner than he thought.

Yes, he had traced down the tale, all right, and he had found that some shepherds had started it. Shepherds! Who on earth trusts shepherds? They not only smelled like their sheep, but also they were spooked easily; they were superstitious; they . . . well, forget it. But he recalled he didn't forget it, because . . . because those silly shepherds risked their sheep, their livelihood, to the wild dogs and other animals just to come to Bethlehem. He shuddered to himself, and this time not because of the cigarette smoke. He shuddered, because he had found himself at that stable again. He found himself looking at that couple (he thought he heard the man call her Mary). Only this time there was with them a baby. In those incredible surroundings, a child had been born. And his parents were so taken with the wonder of this birth, so radiant, that you'd have thought they were in a suite at the Jerusalem Hilton! He saw that mother but for an instant as a chill passed through him: *She believes,* he thought. *She believes what those shepherds were saying about his being a savior! She trusts shepherds!*

He would have left right then in incomprehension if he could have, but something about that woman compelled him to glance at the child. Over her shoulder he looked, trying to be casual, trying to be as indifferent as the census-takers glad to have one more Jew to exact a few coins from. Over her shoulder he looked, and from between rough-cut clothes, two eyes caught his. Beautiful, dark, and so piercing were they that he felt as if he were standing there naked—yes, with even his very soul exposed! A few moments later he remembered stumbling out into the night air, catching his breath, and reminding himself of his need for objectivity.

Was there a story here? If so, what was it? And if he could say what it was, would anyone believe him? In the end, it was just a baby, wasn't it? A baby born in an unusual place, one must admit, but that was nothing big. Someday, something big would come his way. In the meantime, he'd recalled, he couldn't let himself get excited over a few coincidences. Too many loose ends, he had told himself, far too many loose ends. Nevertheless, for a long time he wondered, wondered about shepherds risking sheep, about shepherds being believable, about eyes that kept piercing him all over again. For a long time he wondered: *What if it were true?* Some days he had the almost unearthly feeling he'd missed the obvious. Then at last he forgot. For years he forgot.

Until last night, he muttered as he crushed his cigarette. Why remember now!? Jesus. He remembered the young woman had called him that. Jesus. *Half the kids in Palestine were called Jesus,* he swore to himself. *Wonder if any of them have ever amounted to anything.* He reached for his pencil and paper in the early morning light, and remembered that it was a Jesus he was to investigate today. Jesus of Nazareth, his notes said. He sighed to himself. He'd wanted to cover the John the Baptizer story, and who does he get? Jesus of Nazareth—about as important as Jesus of Bethlehem. Maybe someday, someday, something worthy will come his way. He thrust his notes into his pocket and paused as the morning light filled up his room. Someday. Would that it were today.

It is indeed as John writes:

> The true light that enlightens every man was coming into the world. He was in the world, and the world was made through him, yet the world knew him not. He came to his own home, and his own people received him not. But to all who received him, who believed in his name, he gave power to become children of God. (John 1:9-12)

Glenn L. Borreson
First Lutheran Church
Decorah, Iowa

SECTION II:

SPECIAL SEASONS, SPECIAL SERMONS, SPECIAL SERIES

SPECIAL SEASONS

WHERE IS YOUR GOD?

(Ash Wednesday)

When terrible things happen, rational people seek rational explanations. This, that, or the other circumstance was, they will say, responsible, and so the terrible thing can be understood. And religious people, of course, have their religious explanations. The event, by their accounting, was the will of God or the fault of human evil and must, therefore, be accepted on those terms.

To a degree, most of us buy a bit of both for the terrible things that happen to us. Slip on the ice and break a leg—that's nothing more than the adverse effects of the law of gravity, to be rational about it. But it is also, we usually suspect, somehow related to God and his purposes for our lives. He knew that ice would be there on the street and that it would do us harm, but he did nothing to cause us to change our direction and miss the injury, because he figures it's good for us to suffer now and then.

Yet the terrible times also come when neither common sense nor the resources of faith are enough. The Hebrew people, for example, to whom the prophet Joel addressed his message, had had a rough going, first with a plague of locusts that destroyed their crops, then with a devastating drought. When food is scarce in marginal economies, people die by the thousands, and it's difficult for anyone to have hope for the future. And to rub the trouble in, they were the Chosen People, but this was happening to them anyway, to the grim delight of their neighbors in other nations with other gods, who said to them, again and again, "If this is happening to you Hebrews, then where is your God?"

While we no longer worry over the smart remarks of rival religionists, we ask much the same kind of question when our terrible things are terrible enough. Where are you, God? You say you love us and care about us. Then how come this happened, this whatever-it-is that is so impossible to understand and so difficult to reconcile to your good and gracious will? Where are you, God? Where are you?

Now, then, the testimony of the gospel, the good news about Jesus Christ, is very simply that that question is answered.

Where is your God? Look at that terrible thing happening to Jesus Christ as he is rejected and arrested and condemned on trumped-up charges and beaten and scorned and then executed by the people he came to save. See that happening and know where God is when anything even remotely like it happens to you, because he is there with you, feeling your hurt and your pain, knowing what you are going through fully as much as you know yourself. God was in Jesus Christ, Paul wrote, reconciling the world to himself, taking upon himself all the outrageous misfortune, the incomprehensible accidents, the hopelessness and despair, the injustice and cruelty, all the anguished mystery of this life in which people do not live happily ever after. God knows that about us, because he has been there, too. He is, of course, a God of majesty and glory, beyond our imagining. But he is also the God who became one with us to die for us, that ever after we might know he understands.

Where is your God? Especially when terrible things happen, where is your God? With you, as one who has been down that road before, that you might know his comfort and his peace and his strength. With you, that you might testify to his love and minister in his name to others who under adversity wonder about him. And should they ask, you can tell them that God so loved the world that he sent his Son and that he then sent you. We clasp each other's hands; we share our sorrows and our joys; we speak a word of comfort to each other; and we know where to find our God. *Amen.*

Carl T. Uehling
Evangelical Lutheran Church in America
Wyndmoor, Pennsylvania

A MEDITATION

(Maundy Thursday)

"On the night in which he was betrayed. . . ." It is a terrible thing to be betrayed, to have our goodwill exploited for another's advantage, to suffer the treachery of one in whom we have confidence. It is a soul-devastating experience. It violates our trust, our sense of justice, and it destroys that mutual confidence which is the basis of all human relations. Yet, it is one of the most persistent problems of our human existence.

In one form or another we all have experienced it—when a contract we made was violated, when a covenant was one-sidedly broken, or a man or woman in whom we put our faith turned against us and was our undoing. It happens to all of us in our daily lives.

What arouses and hurts us is the way in which goodness is constantly betrayed by the turn of events that often denies all justice and seems to obliterate any evidence of God's action to conquer or crush evil. Betrayal strikes at our faith. This is where we come closest to the problem, for the force of all other betrayals is born of the deep sense of injustice that comes into focus in the crisis of Jesus' encounter with both, in his life and on the cross. If anyone ever felt the force of betrayal, it was Jesus.

Much has been written and spoken about Jesus' sufferings and almost without exception we, who are now observing Maundy Thursday according to a centuries-old tradition, are identifying ourselves with Jesus, his sufferings, spiritual disappointments, and pains. In doing so, we again become aware of the many setbacks, disappointments, and sad experiences we have been exposed to by other people in our own lives.

But we are wrong when we, in compassion and love for Jesus, our Lord, keep forgetting who we are, that in fact we, too, just like the unfaithful disciples over whom we sit in righteous judgment, are poor, fallible, sinful, and forgetful human beings. Like them, we are only too often liable to stumble and to fall, to commit errors, mistakes, and deceit, even treachery.

We read in the Gospels that on the night of the Passover meal Jesus sat at table with his disciples and said to them: "One of you will betray me." On hearing this, the disciples sprang from their seats and turning to the Master asked him, "Lord, is it I?"

In this brief moment, in this short outcry, we find the expression of a guilty conscience, of feeble, frail humanity. These men who asked, "Is it I?" were not casual acquaintances or friends. No, they were handpicked, trusted followers and disciples of Jesus. They had pledged their allegiance to him, had even offered to lay down their lives for him; yet they were so unsure of themselves that at this crucial moment they asked the question: "Lord, is it I?"

Not one, but all asked that question. With all their loyalty, doubts had been in their minds at one time or other. Sometimes they had been uncertain that they had done the right thing in following the man Jesus, who had asked them to share his poverty and deprivations, who had set before them the image of the kingdom to come, but who so often led them into personal exposure and danger saying "Blessed are ye when men shall persecute you and betray you and bring you before magistrates and accuse you falsely for my sake." Where was their reward?

At that particular moment their doubts came back to their minds, and they felt they had been in thoughts disloyal to their Master, that they had somehow betrayed him. They were sorrowful, it says in the scriptures, sorrowful that they had doubted and in their minds had betrayed him whom they really loved. We know that the one whom Jesus singled out, unknown to all others, had already committed that terrible sin of betrayal. It was Judas Iscariot who had sold out his Master and friend for the paltry sum of thirty pieces of silver, the price of a slave. But we also know that this was not the only betrayal during that night, because before the night was over and the rooster had crowed three times, the most devoted friend and disciple of Jesus had denied three times all knowledge of him, and at the time of Jesus' arrest on the Mount of Olives, all the disciples fled in terror and abject fright that they might also be arrested.

Maundy Thursday, the night on which Jesus was betrayed, is a time of sadness and of critical self-examination for all Christian people. It is a time when we must look into our innermost hearts and ask ourselves, "Is it I, Lord?" We must question our innermost thoughts and feelings, our faith, our loyalty, and our behavior not only toward Jesus Christ, our Savior and Redeemer, our friend to whom we have pledged our unswerving discipleship, but also toward our fellow human beings, whom we must respect and even love. Have we been true to the trust our Lord Jesus has set in us? How often have we betrayed his love for us and sold out our faith and loyalty for worldly profits and material advantages?

On a night like this, we must ask ourselves how much pain and deepest disappointment have we caused to loved ones through disloyalty and betrayal? Who can say, "Lord, not I." "I have never deserted you or betrayed you. I am free of any guilt!"?

There is an incident in the Gospels in which Jesus was called upon to pass judgment on an adulteress. He said, "He who is free from guilt himself, let him throw the first stone" and all accusers faded away like snow in the sun . . .

So, now, not one of us is free from the guilt of disloyalty, of betrayal. This is the night when we must ponder on this, when we must ask God for forgiveness for what we have done in human blindness, frailty, and foolishness.

Jesus forgave his betrayers, but to those betrayed and to all who suffer in this world, to all who would follow him, he says: "Life cannot break you, it cannot wholly betray you, it cannot frustrate God's purposes in you, if you will let God's purposes be fulfilled in your suffering, betrayed experiences. Take into your hands life's suffering and defeat, born of loyalty to me." And then he also said: "What you suffer in loyalty to me will become a source of God's power for you and for the world. Accept it and let God use it in you and your life."

As a token of a new covenant that he made on this night of betrayal between God his Father and all humankind, he then took bread and broke it and gave it to his disciples saying, "Eat of this bread which is a symbol of my body, which is broken for you, and drink of this cup of wine, which is a symbol of my blood that is shed for you. Whenever you do this hereafter, remember this night and remember me" (see Matthew 26:26-30).

Redemption for the betrayer and redemption for the betrayed, forgiveness for the sinner and assurance of God's lasting grace for the sufferers of this world—surely this is the message that comes to us through the experiences of Maundy Thursday and through the table in the Upper Room. *Amen.*

Walter P. Brock
Congregational Church, retired
Diamond Springs, California

THE NEED TO FORGIVE

(Good Friday)

In Munkacsy's painting *Christ on Calvary* a momentary burst of sunlight so irradiates the figure on the cross that all the light in the picture seems to proceed from him. The others stand in the shadows. This redemptive drama localized its scene on Golgotha; its burst of light, however, illumines both the shadows of history and the deep divine purpose at the heart of things.

Each word the Master spoke during his ordeal is like a window opened to his very heart. Characteristically, his first word was a prayer not for himself, desolate in pain, not for his disciples, frightened and heartbroken, not for his mother, stricken with soul-wracking grief—it was a prayer for his cruel murderers, those swarthy Roman soldiers, the Scribes, the Pharisees, Herod, Pilate, the whole pitiable lot who through the long night had not known what they were doing. "Father, forgive them, for they know not what they do" (Luke 23:34).

His second word likewise centered on his compassionate forgiveness to the sinner dying by his side. You remember the familiar account:

> And one of the malefactors which were hanged railed on him saying, If thou be Christ, save thyself and us. But the other answering rebuking him, saying, Dost not thou fear God, seeing thou art in the same condemnation? And we indeed justly; for we receive the due reward of our deeds: but this man hath done nothing amiss. And he said unto Jesus, Lord, remember me when thou comest into thy kingdom. And Jesus said unto him, Verily I say unto thee, today shalt thou be with me in paradise. (Luke 23:39-43 KJV)

Had Jesus followed what some persons call the natural disposition, how easy it would have been in his agony simply to have ignored them, or to have said with the one that justice was being done to them, especially since the other had railed on him personally. His compassionate word of mercy, however, was like a long beam of light that stretched down through his whole life, catching up all his words and deeds, revealing clearly a line running through all of them up to this crowning word. He had told Peter that when one is wronged, one should forgive even seventy times seven times. He had pictured the disposition of God in the story of the prodigal son, making the father go down the road to meet the returning prodigal with a redemptive and restoring outreach, seeking to find that which had been lost and to restore to life that which had been dead. He had even spoken the word of forgiveness for the immoral woman. He had received with quiet serenity the taunts of the Scribes and the Pharisees. He had said that the merciful are blessed because they shall obtain mercy. But now all of these incidents and words took on heightened significance, for in the supreme test of his life, the Master's gracious spirit lifted all his words into one picture that made an impression so strong that in both life and death he became the very incarnation of the world's finest conception of God. The event there at Calvary thus revealed the unconquerable strategy of love.

No one can look upon it, catch its significance, and let it become the fixed star by which one steers one's life without seeing it in some very definite clues for the kind of human attitude and behavior necessary to achieve reconciliation among all people. Consider the disposition of Jesus toward the two men crucified with him. It was not as though he had to overlook something, push down a normal revulsion, or suppress a natural antagonism. He saw a wrong, whether done to him or to others, as being a signal flung out from the heart of the offender, expressing a need, and it was to that need that the Master responded. Not even to Judas did he speak sharp condemnation. Judas had his own condemnation. Jesus saw in him only a pitiable failure. To the one malefactor who pled for forgiveness, he could speak a word of welcome for the life that was to follow. But was this criminal's need any greater than that of the other, who railed on Jesus? He, too, was in as much poverty of spirit as the other, and the only barrier between him and the Master was his own attitude. The grace of forgiveness in us, as in Jesus, springs in part from a recognition of a need in others. It was said of Henry Ward Beecher that "no one ever felt the full force of his kindness until he did Beecher an injury."

But again consider the interior need Jesus felt to forgive. To be the kind of person he was, to exhibit the character of his Father, it was essential that he act in this manner. Vindictiveness in persons is a virus as potent in both the realm of the physical and of the spiritual life as the most deadly disease known to medicine. Hate toward others is the great poison. It so hardens the walls of personality that it insulates the inner life, making impossible the healing flow of goodwill between persons.

Beyond this, it insulates one against spiritual communion with God. In Shakespeare's *Macbeth*, when the murderers tried to pray, their prayers stuck in their throats. Jesus long before, knowing the impossibility of communion with God through the attitude of vindictiveness, had said: "First be reconciled to thy brother, and then come and offer thy gift" (Matthew 5:24 KJV). If, then, we would be healthy persons, we need as much to cultivate the disposition of merciful compassion as others need our forgiveness.

This, in fact, is a road on which two meet but do not pass. One must let down the bars first and so begin the process of reconciliation. But the moment the two meet and are reconciled, they are joined by the third, the Master himself. *Amen*.

Forrest C. Weir
United Church of Christ, Retired
Pacific Palisades, California

THE SECRET OF THANKSGIVING

(Thanksgiving)

Thanksgiving is the consummate American holiday. Other nations may have celebrations related to the harvest, but they are not specifically "thanksgiving" events; celebration best describes them. In fact, our American Thanksgiving does not have its roots in the cycle of seed time and harvest at all. Its beginnings are in a thanksgiving for which there was no bounty of earth. Really, it was to show gratitude for survival after a bitter and harsh winter—and in anticipation of a repetition of that cruel winter that had taken nearly half the colony of Puritans.

Thanksgiving is American. We share it only with our sister nation to the north—Canada—which observes its Thanksgiving Day in October, before the snows fall.

In another sense, it is best celebrated of all our holidays and the most faithfully observed. It can hardly be said that we celebrate our other patriotic holidays at all. Independence Day and Memorial Day and all the others have scant attention paid to their true meanings. And when "Presidents' Day" comes in February, many people may be wondering which president is being honored. All of these "holidays" are just excuses to get away for a weekend. Even making a holiday of the birthday of Martin Luther King, Jr., may be the kiss of death to his memory. Most people will bless him now only for an extra day off from work, instead of remembering the influence and teaching of his life. But Americans do celebrate Thanksgiving. And in the overwhelming majority, they celebrate it close to its true intent.

However, we cannot be so naive as to believe they celebrate in church. Only a few churches are even open today. Instead, some families will make the excuse that they were having a big dinner at their house, and they just couldn't get to church. That is as much as saying that those who are at worship have little or nothing to get ready for. And besides, it can be done. There are many busy women who will somehow manage to have time to give thanks in God's house.

But this has become a day when huge numbers of our people draw aside to think of their blessings. In some way, at some moment in the great day, they will pause. Their prayer may be only a murmur of the heart, maybe only a breath they can't find a way to put into words, but a few will stretch the capacity of their hearts to realize the blessings they share with those they love.

Let us remember Luke 17:17-20, an incident from the life of Jesus, which illustrates the power thanksgiving brings to us.

Considering all that has been said about Thanksgiving in America, this may seem an odd choice to read. At first glance, it seems even contradictory. It seems to emphasize the ungrateful—and the shame that only one gave thanks.

But the point is not in the ratio of grateful versus ungrateful. The point is in what Jesus saw in one man's gratitude—the presence and the strength of his faith. The other nine were also made well, and we can't rightly say they weren't grateful. They surely must have been, but this man saw his healing as a gift from God. And the blessing of that gift caused his once depressed and miserable heart to break out into a doxology of thanksgiving.

America is a thankful nation today. Our land flows with milk and honey. The way most of us live would have seemed like science-fiction to our grandparents. We have opportunities at the touch of a dial that William Bradford in Plymouth Colony would never have dreamed of, if he had, he would surely have thought it all very sinful.

There are two lessons that can enhance our gratitude and can also deepen our appreciation of those blessings. The first is to see the grace of God. That tenth leper in Luke 17 saw the difference between simply being healed and being blessed by God's grace. Because he was so sensitive to the gift he had been given, he recognized the mercy it was.

No one is really defeated or impoverished until he or she begins to say that his or her troubles are not deserved, that instead blessings are deserved. The one who surveys personal misery and asks "Why me" will also be the one who forgets that he or she doesn't deserve to be blessed either.

A woman once went to a beauty parlor to be all fixed up for an important event. She told the operator how important it was that she look her very best.

The operator said, "Don't worry, Madam. I'll do you justice."

The woman said, "I don't want justice. I want mercy." Gratitude really translates our achievements into blessings when we remember the loving mercy of God.

Like that tenth leper, we come to God today simply to give thanks. We don't comprehend why he has chosen to give us gifts, to fill our lives with good things. We only know that he has and does. The second lesson that a gratitude like that of the man in the story helps us to understand is that there is a giver. Maybe the other nine men thanked their lucky stars that they happened to be on the road the day Jesus came along. Not that tenth man. He saw the hand of God in his healing.

And so do we. Why have we been so blessed? We know ourselves well enough to know that it's not because we are worthy of it. Even when what we have comes through our own hard work or skill or whatever we do to achieve a scale of affluence, even then we know that the talent, and even the ambition, came from God.

We are not masters of all we survey; we are recipients. We receive, and we give thanks.

It's the thankful heart that puts joy into this day. Even if we choose the strange liturgies and ceremonies of football and enormous dinners, the joy and the excitement come when we remember that there is a Giver. There is One who gives and gives and gives.

He gives us freedom of body and soul. He gives us the family that upholds us and fills us with love. He gives peace and satisfaction in the midst of the turmoil and pressures of life. He gives us a sense of accomplishment that says our labor and our love are worthy contributions to society. He permits us to serve in his kingdom, and even says that the gifts we bring will help someone else be grateful to him.

Most of all, he permits us to live out our gratitude in lives of faithful service. He says that our gratitude can change the lives of others and enable them to share his love.

There is one idea that we Christians cannot easily shake from our minds: If life is given to us, if blessings are shown to us, then the secret of life's meaning and value are more in the Giver than in the gift itself. The gift inspires the song of thanks. And maybe that's why the other nine did not return. They knew that thankfulness demanded too much.

A long time ago on a tiny island in the Mediterranean, a man sat in lonely exile, banished to a desolate place because of his faith in Christ, far from those with whom he yearned to share the glory of God. With nothing to make his life rich, nothing to bring joy, nothing but the threat of life-long loneliness, he wrote a letter that was somehow smuggled off that island. In that letter, he wrote a song of thanksgiving. It ends this way: "Hallelujah! For the Lord our God the Almighty reigns" (Revelation 19:6).

That may be the secret of Thanksgiving, not that we are blessed, but that even in our blessedness the Lord God omnipotent reigns. *Amen.*

Kenneth E. Hartzheim
St. Paul's Lutheran Church in Sunny Hills
Fullerton, California

GOD—IN A BABY?

(Christmas Eve)

Joseph went from Nazareth to the city of David, Bethlehem. Mary, pregnant, went with him, and while they were there, Mary gave birth to a son, her firstborn, and laid him in a manger, because there was no room for them in the house.

That's it!! That's all there is to it! That's what we've come here tonight to celebrate—an amazingly simply story of a birth. And we make so much out of it. We literally overdo it. We hang lights, decorate trees, make beautiful our churches with garlands and flowers and ribbons and banners. And in the midst of the glamour and glitter sits a simple crib full of straw, reminding us of the simplicity of the event. Perhaps we overdo it out of a healthy agnosticism—because we can't really believe it! Peace, hope, wholeness, and fulfillment for the life of the world, for my life, all that in a baby born in a cattle shed? The real presence of the Holy Power responsible for all that exists in our universe was present in a child held in the arms of its mother? Can it be?

There is something very difficult to understand, that the power of the universe, creator of life and love and joy and hope, was born in a baby. We have heard the story read, and we are to proclaim the good news that Christ is born. God is with us! Emmanuel—in a babe, in a crib. Can you believe it?

Martin Luther wrestled within his mind to believe it. In his *Christmas Book* he wrote that God puts a babe in a crib. Our common sense revolts and says, "Could not God have saved the world some other way?" The Christian faith is foolishness. It says that God can do anything, and yet makes him so weak that either his Son had no power and wisdom or else the whole story is made up.

God—in a baby. We mention God with fear and trembling, for what do we mean when we use the word *god* in our day? If anyone thinks more than once about the word *god,* or uses it as more than a colloquial expression, the questions swirl. Is there any reality behind those three letters G—O—D? Or is it just a sound we make, especially at Christmas time, a sound with no reality behind it?

The Bible speaks of the reality of God only in terms of experiences people had with this reality. For some, God was seen as far off, unapproachable, mysterious. They saw God in a burning bush, a pillar of fire, or a cloud, in lightning and thunder on a mountaintop. Others knew God as being near to them, close to them, in an intense personal experience. They saw God in another person, in an angel coming near with a burning coal, in a vision, or in an all-night wrestling match. Christianity is at its best when it can keep the tension between a God who is far off, unknowable, and mysterious in his working and a God who is also close at hand, within us, in our midst. The wonder of Christmas is the wonder of a God who is beyond our comprehension and experience becoming as near to us as a baby drawn close to its mother's breast to nurse. God—in a baby.

A baby represents newness and potential. We have a hope for a new life, that this new life might be spared all that is hurtful and sad in our lives. There is a sense that we who give birth to a baby have somehow an extension of our own lives, a claim to immortality, to reincarnation because, in a certain way, we do go on. In our children there is something more to our identities than just us. There's the enthusiasm and spontaneity of a young life, when all is fresh and new and experienced for the first time. Oh, how we all delight to see it! As the popular Christmas song, "O Holy Night," puts it in pointing us toward the baby of Bethlehem, "A thrill of hope, the weary world rejoices. For yonder breaks a new and glorious morn."

At Christmas we are awakened again to the potential of life, the possibilities for our lives, the potential for peace in our world and in ourselves, and the possibility of renewal of all that is old and tired and wornout. We try to say it by giving presents and hanging lights and singing carols and doing gestures of goodwill. And God said it with a baby, Jesus.

Joseph went with Mary to Bethlehem, and there she gave birth to a son, her firstborn, and she laid him in a manger. There are three perspectives from which we can speak of this birth.

1. *A view from within.* As participants in the faith that God became flesh and blood in Jesus the Christ, we can speak of an outer nativity in Bethlehem nearly two thousand years ago becoming an inner nativity in our hearts as we know a new birth. An incarnation back there and then has created a strangely wonderful new person here and now in you and in me. It's real for us, and we're sure of it.

2. *A view from without*. This is a perspective of, perhaps, some who are here and certainly of many who are not here or in any church. They are the analytical, detached products of Western rational thinking, who see Christianity and religion in general as phenomena to be studied. This perspective would see the faith in a God who became man in a baby as an interesting religious concept to be considered alongside other religious claims.

There is a third perspective of many of us who fall somewhere in between the other two views. Many of us, like Martin Luther, are not always sure that we ought to call ourselves Christians, but would feel sad if we felt outside the Christian community. And so we, at times, feel half in and half out. Those of us who share this perspective are spiritual people and sense that we know God, but don't feel we possess completely all the gifts God has promised to his people. We stay connected and somewhat loyal to the faith, because we have been shaped by it and it is a part of us. But we don't always know all the peace and joy, the wholeness and fulfillment that is promised. Our lives are not all that we wish them to be. But we hope, and we affirm this peace and fulfillment as being a possibility of God for the world and for ourselves. We envision for ourselves what we cannot always confirm. So we look to that baby born of Mary in Bethlehem, and we hope for ourselves and for our world. The miracle of Christmas is that the desire to have may become a strange kind of having.

Joseph went with Mary to Bethlehem, and there she gave birth to a son, her firstborn, and she laid him in a manger. Glory to God in the highest! *Amen*.

William K. Harman

Bethlehem Lutheran Church
Encinitas, California

SPECIAL SERMONS

A CHIP OFF THE OLD BLOCK

(Confirmation)

Years had passed since the kid had been home. In fact, he was no longer a kid. He'd grown up, moved to the city, and worked in a towering building at a job nobody back home could understand. But today? Today he was back home, walking down the main street. Storekeepers nodded to themselves as he meandered by their businesses. "Must be George's kid home for a visit," they agreed. "Look at those big steps, would you, and the way he swings his arms just like his old man. Sure enough, it's George's kid. A regular chip off the old block!" And so it was—the kid who's no longer a kid comes home. And in spite of three-piece suits, a sophisticated life-style, and a job nobody understands, in spite of it all, there's a basic identity that remains: He's still George's kid, a chip off the old block. He's someone's son, and that family resemblance runs deep, ah, so very deep.

Among Christians, there's always been the question of a family resemblance with Jesus. We're part of his family, but take away the choir robes and confirmation gowns and liturgy and then put us on Main Street, who'll know the difference? How can you tell if someone's a follower of Jesus, a disciple of the Master? What is the telltale mark? Is it a certain look on the face, an aura of "holiness," a somber piety, or an eternal smile? Is the mark of a disciple being able to name the date you were converted or to pull your baptismal certificate out of the file? Is it knowing all the right answers when the pastor descends on you with a question the night of confirmation catechization?

Whenever the church has invented its own signs for identifying true Christians, it has often been unfaithful to its master. It has often been unloving when, in fact, the center of our identity as followers of Jesus is our love for one another. We don't know how Jesus swung his arms when he walked. We don't know whether his face had some kind of eternal glow. But we do know that he loved. And this is the telltale sign for our lives: When we love like he loved, there's no mistake; the family resemblance comes through and it comes through in three ways.

First, you can see it in the stories we tell. Have you ever noticed how much you can tell about people by the stories they bring with them? Some are always telling jokes, others sad stories. Some use stories to laugh at themselves; others use them to ridicule. A high school kid working on house construction with his grandfather remembered that whenever a particular electrician joined them on the job, they were going to hear the latest dirty joke. In fact, it is difficult thinking of him at all apart from those stories!

At the center of every one of us, I might add, are the stories we tell. They are a part of who we are. And if we're Christians, there's one story that keeps going in and out of our lives all our days: the story of Jesus and his love. If we stop telling that one, we'll lose our identity as Christians. We need to tell it, and we need to hear it in order to get out of bed on a day we feel like the most rotten creature ever made and in order to get out of ourselves when we are as brimful of smug self-satisfaction as Garfield the Cat. Oh, I know the story of Jesus is familiar. It was familiar to a pastor friend of mine, too. There, during one of his children's sermons, the assistant pastor asked the kids gathered around him, "What is gray, has a bushy tail, and gathers nuts in the fall?" One brave little five-year-old raised his hand, "I know the answer should be Jesus," he began, "but it sounds like a squirrel to me."

Sometimes "Jesus" isn't the answer to the question, but whatever else was happening between that little five-year-old and his pastor, the boy knew that at the center of life is the story of Jesus—which is to be told and retold. And if we do it often enough and well enough, it'll influence the other stories we tell. Maybe that grandfather's electrician would have been able to tell funny stories that didn't ridicule people. Maybe the complainer can find a story with hope, and we all can learn to laugh with instead of at others. Whoever we are, as Christians the story of Jesus cannot be allowed to die; it is a part of us!

The second part of our identity as Jesus' people is in the acts we do. It was in their love for one another, Jesus said, that the world would know people were his disciples. He was really wise, this Jesus. He must have understood well how we all are judged by our actions. Look around and see how it happens all the time: One of your classmates in school clowns around all the time—you call him a goof-off! A neighbor is always complaining—you find yourself calling him a complainer. A friend always remembers your family's birthdays with cards and gifts—you decide that's the most thoughtful person you know. Our actions are indeed the way people judge us! Right or wrong, it is so.

Love is, for Jesus, an action word. It's doing what's best for another person, no matter how we feel. We might not even like that other person, but love is still possible. It is an action, a caring before it is a feeling. Please hear that! Christian love is not a squishy, smoochy feeling that makes eight-year-old boys want to croak! It is not some emotional high you get listening to Barbara Mandrell or Engelbert Humperdinck! It is action, doing what is best for your neighbor even though it may be hard for you. It is like going to the cross. It is congratulating the person who got the part you wanted in the school play with all your heart and soul. *Action.* It is visiting your friend in the nursing home, even when she asks, "Who was that?" as you walk out the door. *Action.* It means being fair-and-square in your business dealings with that character you know would cheat you just to have even the smallest chance of succeeding. *Action.* It is our acts by which we are known; as Christians, our lives and loves are to bear the marks of the one who gave his life for us.

Now don't tell me how difficult this is sometimes. I know that perfectly well—and just as personally as you do. That's why we need to remember that the third part of our identity as Jesus' people is in the hope we hold. Mark Twain said that he could live months off the glory of a compliment, but I'll put before you this morning that you can live a lifetime hanging onto the hope God gives. It is the hope that no matter where you are, no matter where you've come from, no matter how dismally you choose to paint your past, God makes this very day the first one of the rest of your life. Our hope is not found in perfectly telling the story of Jesus. Our hope is not found in doing acts of love as he did. Our hope is in him, in that special love that inspires us, in being raised from the dead just as he was!

Why does a person walk into this church after years of absence? Because of a hope that burns deep within, burning low, but burning. Because of a hope that there is a love deeper and truer than any other known, a love that would even die for that person.

Why do we pray for you young persons about to celebrate the Rite of Confirmation? Exactly because we know you are so much like us: full of good intentions and promises that we may try to get out of doing tomorrow, like a coat which doesn't fit. Why pray for you? Exactly because we want you to keep hoping and trusting in the power of God when you doubt yourself. In many ways, we are all children hoping to grow up into disciples!

These stories we tell, these acts we do, these hopes we hold—these are never proofs of our own perfection. Not at all! At their very best, they are witnesses to a world that needs to know what love really is, and where it's found—in Jesus! We are his. So, let's live like members of his family. Be a chip off the old block, so to speak, and let the world nod its head, saying as it sees you in action: "Yup, must be one of Jesus' people again." *Amen.*

Glenn L. Borreson
First Lutheran Church
Decorah, Iowa

BREAD FOR THE WILDERNESS

(Communion)

Legend and history mix in the mysterious figure of Elijah, prophet of God around 850 B.C., opponent of Ahab and Jezebel. Jezebel, you remember, was a strong woman, and Ahab's marriage to her was probably a sharp diplomatic move. But when Ahab built a shrine for her god Melkart, it wasn't enough. She imported hundreds of prophets of that god and of other Baals. In fact, she seems to have tried to convert the religious loyalties of the whole northern kingdom. Elijah alone seems to have stood against her.

Elijah won a decisive and famous challenge to the priests of Baal, and Jezebel vowed vengeance, and we have the wonderful story of his exhausting flight for safety. Hunted down, he threw in the towel. He had no drink and no food and little enough shade from desert scrub. "It is enough, Lord. Take away my life," Elijah pleaded. He lay down to die, but what he found in his collapse was not death. It was mercy. An angel touched him: " 'Arise and eat.' And he . . . went in the strength of that food forty days and forty nights to Horeb the mount of God" (I Kings 19:5, 8).

The story articulates an age old cry of despair, one we all feel in one way and at one time or another. Everyone of us has a wilderness inside, wilderness to endure, wilderness to travel through. And we need bread, sustenance, food for the journey.

That wilderness may be the kind of despair that is born of a long and seemingly fruitless struggle to find joy or a meaning for our lives, and everything seems instead to be flat. It may be the impossibility of trying to be a super mom—successful in career, parenting, homemaking, and entertaining, matching the slick pictures in the magazines. It may be a chronic habit of biting off more than we can chew, commitments to study and to friends and to courses and causes that finally tear us apart. It may be an inner ambivalence that prevents us, in our indecisive self-doubt and lack of trust, from taking any definite path, from making any commitments at all.

It may be the teenager's frantic distractedness, that of someone whose whole life has been spent under the threat of nuclear annihilation, whose parents seem like aliens, whose culture, best expressed in the plaintive MTV video images, seems only to suggest a hopeless surrender to drugs for a high, or even the final insanity of suicide.

Wilderness. It may be in the Vietnam vet, who went proudly to war for his country and his flag, and then found that the atrocities were not all on the other side. His country was killing women and children in those villages, and there was no end that he could see. He now asks, reading of the Contras in Nicaragua: What are we doing this time? Can the world not get any better? The wilderness may be that of the vigorous sixty-year-old man who is afraid of growing old without something more dramatic to show for his life than a decent marriage, two kids, and a middle class income, who still yearns for something more. "Is this all?" he asks. It may be an unforgiven guilt, a rootless and misguided set of values, a sense of worthlessness because of unemployment. It may be chronic pain or chronic illness in yourself or someone close to you. But whatever, in your wilderness or mine, we wonder where the sustenance will come from. "It is enough, Lord. Take away my life."

Often our wilderness arises from a belief that life consists in accomplishments, so when accomplishments are no longer possible, there is only the void. A man once described an invalid aunt, who, he said, couldn't do anything any more. She might as well have died. His measurement of worth was all in doing. Someone answered him with a verb of doing, but it was a verb with a twist, and it expressed the truth that there was a God to live for, if not human notoriety. The answer was: "I think she can still *pray.*"

We live in a fast-paced culture, with daily promises being made, false promises, about sustenance for the life-way along which each of us by birth has been privileged and called to walk. In a department store there was a massive wall of what must have been over one hundred television sets, all turned on, all evidently different models and brands. The whole store was like that, with racks of clothes, counters of perfume, sections of dishes, furniture, bedding, draperies, appliances. Each somehow, advertising itself—"Take me and make your life new again." And like those television sets, all the items were tuned to the same channel, the same picture, and that promise was false. We need a richer bread for the journey.

You and I can be proud of much in our culture, our productivity, our technology, the arts, the ordinary friendliness of folks we meet. But there are enough skeletons, griefs, and twisted values to make it also a wilderness. The culture's assumptive world, as we might call it, often stresses the very opposite of what will truly nurture and reconcile, the things, as Scripture says, "that make for peace." Over and over, it offers us junk food instead of bread, as different from true soul food as junk mail is different from a personal, handwritten, first-class letter.

"Why" asked Isaiah, "do you spend your money for that which is not bread?" (Isaiah 55:2). Even in this comfortable life of ours, we know the truth of the angel's words to Elijah: "Arise and eat, else the journey will be too great for you" (I Kings 19:7).

The story has clues in it about the deeper assumptive world of our religious parents in the faith. The most fundamental perspective, we have already cited. Elijah was at his wit's end, and his energy's end, perhaps even at the end of his faith. "It is enough." The alcoholic begins healing with the admission that he or she can't manage alone. Elijah's help here came at the end of his rope, and he wasn't told to get up for worship or to follow some five or ten rules for creating in him a new level of courage or hope.. He was accepted for the miserable and despairing person that he was. And right there in that condition, he heard the words, *Look around you.* "Behold, there was at his head a cake baked on hot stones and a jar of water" (I Kings 19:6).

Bread for the wilderness. The gift of divine mercy, of course, does not necessarily come in the dramatic and miraculous, as in this Elijah story. It simply seems like a miracle when it comes.

The gift is in seeing it, often enough in the most pedestrian of places. A cup of cold water, a listening ear, a word of comfort, a bag of wheat in Ethiopia, someone of integrity when all others seem ready to cheat—in such mundane ways does the grace of God insert itself into the world's desert trails.

Elijah, of course, wasn't without God, even in his own mind, as he lay down to die. He spoke to God in his despair. He was like Job, who rebelled, but addressed God in his rebellion. One of the virtues, if there are any, of being in our last straits is that we usually turn to God, even if in complaint, in our despair. And that, of course, is an act of faith. Instead of seeing a godless world as the given and then trying to find God in it, we turn to

God in our extremity as the most real and ask: What now we are to make of this world?

What is bread for this journey? The enduring food. The New Testament with one voice answers: the grace of the God we know in Jesus Christ. John doesn't even tell us the story of the Lord's Supper, with bread and wine, but he wrote a discourse on that very Christian meal, that center of our Christian life and feeding: "I am the bread of life; he who comes to me shall not hunger" (John 6:35).

We don't begin with rules of faith or theological instructions. We place ourselves where there is living bread, in the midst of the community of faith. Rise and eat.

The ancient story of Elijah continues immediately with another picture of the quiet sustenance of God's grace, and with it we close. Elijah came to a cave and lodged there. And the word of the Lord came to him: "What are you doing here?" (I Kings 19:9). Why do you still hide away? And Elijah stood at the mouth of the cave.

The Lord passed by, and a great wind rent the mountains, breaking the rocks, but the Lord was not in the wind. And after the wind came an earthquake, but the Lord was not in the earthquake. Then a fire, but the Lord was not in the fire. After the fire came a still, small voice. And in that voice, Elijah heard the Word of the Lord, and he wrapped his face in his mantle.

Turn us, O God, toward the sunlight when we are preoccupied with the darkness, that we may receive your grace. Feed our souls with food that lasts and nourishes when we are tempted to fill our lives with so much that does not matter. Speak to us amid the cacophony of our time in your still, small voice, that we may be sent again on the journey and sustained there in Jesus Christ our Lord. *Amen.*

Gaylord B. Noyce
Yale University Divinity School
New Haven, Connecticut

WHAT THEN SHALL WE SAY TO THIS?

(Funeral)

This meditation was offered at the funeral of a man who died as a result of a self-inflicted gunshot wound.

We are here to worship God, a God who is Christlike! We are not here this day to offer explanations. Rather we are here to make affirmations! We are not here to deny our questions nor to suppress our feelings of grief, which are manifested in many ways. Rather, we are here to entrust our questions and our sorrow to the Christlike God, the God who holds onto us and does not intend to let us go.

We are not here as people without hope. Rather, we are here to witness to our faith. And in that faith we are going to make three affirmations found throughout Scripture. The first is found in the eighth chapter of Romans.

> What then shall we say to this? If God is for us, who is against us? He who did not spare his own Son but gave him up for us all, will he not also give us all things with him? Who shall bring any charge against God's elect? It is God who justifies; who is to condemn? Is it Christ Jesus, who died, yes, who was raised from the dead, who is at the right hand of God, who indeed intercedes for us? Who shall separate us from the love of Christ? Shall tribulation, or distress, or persecution, or famine, or nakedness, or peril, or sword? As it is written,
>
> > "For thy sake we are being killed all the day long;
> > we are regarded as sheep to be slaughtered."
>
> No, in all these things we are more than conquerors through him who loved us. For I am sure that neither death, nor life, nor angels, nor principalities, nor things present, nor things to come, nor powers, nor height, nor depth, nor anything else in all creation, will be able to separate us from the love of God in Christ Jesus our Lord. (Romans 8:31-39)

The first affirmation is that God has made us to be ultimately indestructible. There is more to life than death. In the Christlike

God, life, not death, is the final word. Life does not end; rather life changes and continues. Death is not a terminal, but a gateway; it is not a closed door, but an open window; it is not an exit, but an entrance. There is no being, no conflict, no power that can finally separate us from the Christlike God. As one child so wonderfully affirmed, "No, nothing can ever keep God from keeping me."

A small girl would walk through a cemetery on the way home from school. A classmate asked her, "Aren't you afraid?" She answered, "Why should I be? That is the best way that leads home!"

In Christ we are ultimately indestructible!

The second affirmation is that we are allowed to grieve. Sorrow does not deny faith. Just the opposite—grief affirms the very essence of faith. Sorrow is a consequence of our loving and of our caring for people, and love is the *sine qua non* of our betting our all on the Christlike God.

More than this, God is with us in our sorrow. Such is demonstrated on the cross of Jesus Christ. Paul wrote, "If God is for us, who is against us? He who did not spare his own Son but gave him up for us all, will he not also give us all things with him?" (Romans 8:31*b*-32).

God lost a part of himself, just as we have lost. There was sorrow in the heart of God on the day we now call Good Friday. God knows what it is like to love and then to lose. God in Christ is one for us, one with us, one of us. God suffers for us, and God suffers with us.

In God's scheme of things, we do not avoid difficulty, but we are seen through difficulty. Life is not easy, but we can be made great enough for life. We will not escape sorrow and stress, but we are given strength and solace in tempestuous and trying times. God has sorrow with us, and God will see us through.

Clark Poling was a chaplain in World War II. When he left for overseas duty, he said to his father, "Dad, I don't want you to pray for my return. Dad, just pray that I shall be adequate."

Clark Poling was one of the four chaplains to go down on the U.S.S. *Dorchester*, which sank at 1:15 A.M. on February 5, 1943. His actions in saving the lives of men and in giving away his own lifebelt made him one of the war's greatest heroes of courage and Christian witness. Yet the only prayer he wanted prayed on his behalf was: "God make me adequate." God did.

May you know that you are allowed to grieve. More than this, may you know a deep and perplexing loss be made adequate through the Christlike God.

The final affirmation is that we have no right to make final judgments on anyone at any time. Paul wrote to the church at Rome, "Who shall bring any charge against God's elect? It is God who justifies, who is to condemn?" (Romans 8:33). Only God knows those he will ultimately bring home.

Only those without fault, only those who are wholly merciful can judge. Therefore, we are permanently disqualified from having permanent opinions concerning anyone. We see in parts; God sees in whole. We see in time; God sees in eternity. We see only actions. God sees the deepest longings of the heart. We see only what appears to be. God sees what really is.

More than this, the God who does judge is far more merciful and gracious than we could ever dare to imagine, even in our wildest of imaginings. The hymnist wrote:

> There is a wideness in God's mercy,
> Like the wideness of the sea;
> There's a kindness of His justice,
> Which is more than liberty.
>
> There is no place where earth's sorrows
> Are more felt than up in heaven;
> There is no place where earth's failings
> Have such kindly judgment given.
>
> For the love of God is broader
> Then the measure of man's mind;
> And the heart of the Eternal
> Is most wonderfully kind.
>
> —Frederick W. Faber

In Christ we are forever people. Forever people do sorrow because forever people love. More than this, forever people leave judgment to the eternal and Christlike God. *Amen*

Edward C. Wilson
Indian Trail Presbyterian Church
Indian Trail, North Carolina

Obituary for Charles Johnson*

All of us here today share so many memories of Charles.

We remember:

hunting trips, wading through marshes and bogs, silent times waiting for a bird, a sound, a movement in the grass—times when you feel close to a person without having to use words.

There are memories of:

fishing trips with buddies,

the great pickles he canned, and the meals he cooked, Charles as an Uncle and Grandpa, always there to help, to play,

the yard Charles loved, and all of the out-of-doors,

his family whom he loved, both those near and far away, Charles the sharer—of money, possessions, himself.

Yes, hundreds of memories crowd our thoughts, waiting to be triggered by a word, a place, an event.

You will ever be a part of our lives. All the good you have done will live on in our hearts.

Blessed be Charles' memory.

Usually I write my own obituaries, which augment the ones printed by the family. They are always short and read before the sermon proper. It seems to serve two purposes: making the event "personal" while allowing the funeral sermon to be what it needs to be—not an extended eulogy, but a strong attempt to proclaim the gospel in the midst of grief and loss.

*An assumed name.

MEDITATION

(Funeral)

Dear family and friends:

There are times when we look out from our lives and things make sense. We grow up, find someone to love, work at a job, go on vacation, plant some flowers, mow the lawn. There is a rhythm to it all, whether it be hectic and fast-paced or slower.

Then, there are other times when we look out from our lives and nothing makes sense, not our lives, not our places in things, not events. Almost without warning, like a thief in the night, death snatched our friend. That event knocked the air out of us worse than any blow to the stomach could have done. It seemed for a while as if life were a frenzy of events, and then later—time seemed to stop and every moment of grief was like a year. Why?

Many who were close to __________ were scalded by the news of (his/her) death. Old wounds break open from other pains and set-backs, and it is a great weight. We remember the words of the psalmist: "Call upon me in the day of trouble; I will deliver you, and you shall glorify me" (Psalm 50:15).

We are calling, Lord. Are you here? Are you really strong enough to bear our grief? It seems too great. Perhaps you are strong enough for this moment, this day . . . but will you be there, God, in the middle of a lonely night? Will you be there at that odd moment when a memory seems to cut to the quick and the longing is a painful ache?

If our God is strong enough, we can bear our grief, go on, and even find some happiness in living. It is at times of great trial that we discover God's strength.

There was a man who was dying of cancer. He was a tough old character who had met the rejections of his life with a good brawl and untold kegs of beer and fifths of whiskey. This colorful old story-teller was a wild card who rarely darkened the church door. A pastor visited in his home and gave him Holy Communion. A couple of hours passed as he told the funny and bitter stories of his life—his father's rejection, his family's refusal to speak to him because he had married out of his faith. As he sat there and looked at the little plastic glasses of wine and the wafers that stuck to the roof of his mouth, the pastor cried inside, *Is this the best you can do? This measly little meal? Is this all there is for a man who's dying? This, God, this is supposed to heal eighty years of burned bridges and broken family ties?*

Then it came, the strength of this sacrament. Without apologies, in bread and wine was the power of our crucified Lord raised up by God. "Yes," said Jesus in the bread and wine. "I am enough. Here is life. Real life. Full life. Whole life. Life begun anew. A really fresh start with no questions asked. Here it is for you and for a dying man. What more can be offered than that?"

The pain didn't go away, but the anxiety, the fear, and the desperation did. Burdens were born by the One who said, "Come to me, for my burden is light."

So it is today with our burdens. How paltry the words of Scripture and hope seem compared to our pain. Yet, God can hold us. God can bear us up in this minute and the next and tonight and tomorrow and the days to come.

God's strength has many hands, many faces. See it come in the fruit salad brought by a friend, in the embrace of a family member, in the tears we share, in the hymns we sing, in the comforting breeze, in a gentle day, in an early morning, in the inexplicable peace of mind that comes at times to the grieving.

See how God comes today, wounded as you have been, no stranger to suffering. You can trust him. If you have suffered hardship or loss, you know that you can trust the ones who have been through it. They don't give easy answers. They don't run away from your pain. We can trust this One, our strong God, because he has been there in the bleak night when his Son died for us. How true the obituary verse is, "God hath not promised skies always blue."

Yet God comes, our hope comes, in words strong and sure: "Lo, I am with you always, to the close of the age" (Matthew 28:20). God comes promising that this death is not an end but the beginning of life.

Our God comes. Our God is here. Our God is strong enough to bear this and every burden of our lives. This is the hope we celebrate. *Amen.*

Norene A. Smith
Christ Lutheran Church
Slayton, Minnesota

THE INCARNATION

(Incarnation)

The Incarnation, an event which is central to all Christian thought, is viewed by the Roman Catholic Church as one of the Holy Mysteries and by Catholics and Protestants alike as the foundation of all subsequent Christian doctrine. In its simplest terms, the doctrine of the Incarnation avers that in Jesus, God was actually present in the flesh. Thus Jesus, as the Christ, was both human and divine. But in this simple statement are implied complex theological developments, both before and after the event.

During his lifetime, Jesus was hardly recognized as the Messiah. Only a meager few among the Jews saw in him the "Anointed One" who was to redeem Israel. And as he hung upon the cross, even those who had believed were disillusioned, fearful for their own safety, and actually fled. But as suddenly as their confidence had given way to despair, that confidence was renewed and strengthened by the reappearance of Jesus to his disciples. Now they knew that their faith was justified, that the Messiah had truly lived among them, that he had conquered death, and that he would soon return to establish the kingdom for which the Jews had long waited.

So the church, in its formative years, reached back into Hebrew history and drew from it the prophecies that foretold the coming of one who would bring the Jewish nation out of travail and suffering into a new and glorious day. This was the Messiah, the "Anointed One" (the Greek term *Christos* means the same). He was to be a king, a glorious ruler, a son of God (many Hebrew kings had held this title because of their faithfulness), a descendant of David (all the kings of Judah, from the tenth century to the sixth B.C., were descendants of that great king), and a savior of the Hebrew people. Reflecting the prophecies of Daniel and of Enoch, they pictured him as the "Son of man," a supernatural being whose divine mission was to be fulfilled on earth. In the Christian experience of the risen Lord, Christians believed they saw these prophecies fulfilled. They drew the inference that Isaiah, the Judean prophet of the eighth century, foresaw his coming:

Behold, a virgin shall conceive and bear a son, and his name shall be called Emmanuel. (Matthew 1:23)

For to us a child is born, to us a son is given; and the government will be upon his shoulder, and his name will be called "Wonderful, Counselor, Mighty God, Everlasting Father, Prince of Peace." (Isaiah 9:6)

But how do we account for his suffering? How do we explain his rejection at the hands of the Jews? Why—if he was the Messiah? And they found the answer in the prophet of the Exile as he described the "Suffering Servant," Israel. Never had the Suffering Servant been equated with the Messiah, but by combining the two, the church found meaning and divine purpose in the martyrdom of Christ:

> He was despised and rejected by men;
>   a man of sorrows, and acquainted with grief;
> and as one from whom men hide their faces
>   he was despised, and we esteemed him not.
> Surely he has borne our griefs
>   and carried our sorrows . . .
> he was wounded for our transgressions,
>   he was bruised for our iniquities;
> upon him was the chastisement that made us whole,
>   and with his stripes we are healed.
> All we like sheep have gone astray;
>   we have turned every one to his own way;
> and the Lord has laid on him
>   the iniquity of us all. (Isaiah 53:3-6)

Thus for the Christian community, breaking at this point with Jewish tradition, the suffering of Christ is viewed as the very instrument through which he fulfills the messianic function. And the message of the early church became the kerygma: "He died for our sins." He was the sacrificial lamb whose blood was shed for our transgressions.

How did the human Jesus become the Son of God? Many in the early church held that he came to be so by "adoption." Some interpreted the event of Jesus' baptism (the descent of the Holy Spirit as a dove) as the moment in which sonship was established. Some early manuscripts, in describing this event, read: "Thou art my Son; today I have begotten thee." The Gospels of Matthew and Luke, on the other hand, attribute Jesus' divinity to his miraculous birth. Still others (Paul and the author of John's Gospel, for instance) held that Christ was pre-existent and was with God before the beginning of time.

But the concept of pre-existence is a story in itself; it is rooted more in Greek than in Hebrew thought. Let us go back, then, to Ephesus in the early fifth century B.C., to a Greek philosopher known as Heraclitus. In his day, there was no concept of "natural law" as it is conceived today; in a very real sense, he foreshadowed this scientific view. Everything in the physical world is in constant flux, he said, constantly changing; nothing abides; only change is real, and all things are in the process of passing away. Except, he said—and this is significant—all is in flux except one unchanging element, namely the law of orderly process, the principle whereby this change takes place. This is eternal and unchanging. He called this principle *logos*.

Two hundred years later (Socrates, Plato, and Aristotle had lived and died in the intervening period), Stoicism arose as a school of thought in which all personal deities were cast aside. The *logos* of Heraclitus—the principle of universal natural law, "Nature," "Universal Reason"—was given the status of deity. The Logos was God, and for the Stoic to do the will of God was simply to seek to know the laws of Nature and to live according to those laws.

Now let us skip another two or three hundred years. A contemporary of Jesus (although there is no reason to believe that either knew of the existence of the other) was an Alexandrian philosopher named Philo. He was a Jew who was well-grounded in the Jewish faith and in Greek thought. He sought to bring together the religious insights of these two thought streams. With the God of Judaism as his supreme deity, Philo conceived the Logos as a "Second God" *(deutero-deus)*, as the creative agent through whom the Supreme Deity brought the world into being. It appears that he also equated the Logos with "Wisdom" as it is portrayed in certain Jewish literature; in this literature, Wisdom seems also at times to be personified and to serve as God's creative agent. Thus Hebrew "Wisdom" and Greek "Reason" become identical. Both are pre-existent before the beginning of time.

Now let us look at the introduction to John's Gospel:

> In the beginning was the Word [*logos*], and the Word was with God, and the Word was God. He was in the beginning with God; all things were made through him, and without him was not anything made that was made. In him was life, and the life was the light of men. (John 1:1-4)

The author of John's Gospel has followed Philo's pattern in viewing the Logos as God's creative agent. He also appears to equate the Logos with Hebrew "Wisdom," because the entire introduction to John's Gospel (verses 1-18, excepting 6-8) is in direct parallel to excerpts from Hebrew wisdom literature, substituting the term Logos for Wisdom. And we suddenly discover that in John's Gospel the Logos is Jesus Christ! Thus Christ is the creative agent of God, a pre-existent being, the Son of God: "The [Logos] became flesh and dwelt among us" (John 1:14)!

Yet another element enters the picture as we find the Apostle Paul going beyond the bounds of Judaism to carry the message of redemption to non-Jews. To these people, the Jewish concept of the Messiah had no meaning. Throughout Asia Minor, Macedonia, and Greece, Paul preached to people who were principally influenced by the mystery religions of their day, religions which promised personal salvation based on the power of mythical deities who had experienced various forms of death and resurrection—redeemer gods, gods of fertility who were thus responsible for life. Many were the deities, usually male and female associated together, and many were the religions (Isis and Serapis in Egypt, Cybele and Attis in Phrygia, Demeter and Persephone in Greece, Ashtart and Baal in Syria). The mysteries were the dominant religions of the day, and the Jewish Messiah had no appeal. Yet, as Paul went about among the Gentiles, he rightly pointed to his religion as "the mystery of the mysteries," a religion in which Christ is truly *kyrios*, "Lord of Life," superior to all the mythical deities, One who "in our generation" lived and died and rose again, a victor over sin and death. He is the true redeemer God.

So in the context of Hebrew prophecy, Greek philosophy, and the mystery religions, the early church came to know Jesus as the Christ, the Son of the living God, the Messiah, the Anointed One, the Logos, God's creative agent, Kyrios, the Lord of life—and with it all, as the Suffering Servant "who has borne our grief and was wounded for our transgressions"—the Savior of the World. This is the Incarnation. Paul sums it all up: "In Christ God was reconciling the world to himself" (II Corinthians 5:19). This is the Incarnation—God in Christ.

That is the doctrine which is the heritage of the Christian church from its early beginnings. In those early days there was no attempt to explain this mystery. Later generations raised doubts as to how this could be. The doctrine of the Trinity developed, giving status to Father, Son, and Holy Spirit as three "Persons," each of whom is God; this, too, was held to be a mystery.

How can there be threeness in oneness? Arius, an Alexandrian priest, had the temerity to teach that the Son must be inferior to the Father, because the Son was created by the Father. Subsequently, Arius was brought before the Council of Nicea in A.D. 325, and was condemned as a heretic. Yet, it was necessary for the church to clarify the relationship between God the Father and God the Son. Hence, the Creed developed by the Council of Nicea:

> [We] believe in one God: the Father Almighty, maker of heaven and earth, and of all things visible and invisible; And in One Lord Jesus Christ, the only begotten Son of God: begotten of the Father before all worlds, God of God, Light of Light, God of very God, begotten, not made, being of one substance with the Father.

Here, of course, is the clarifying principle: Although Father and Son are distinct, they are one in essence, of one nature!

But the Christians in Syria feared that this interpretation did not do justice to the humanness of Jesus. Surely he was God; yet he was also truly man! The church saw the importance of maintaining this distinction, but it was not until the Council of Chalcedon in A.D. 451 that it was established in a definition of faith:

> We, then, following the holy Fathers, all with one consent, teach men to confess one and the same Son, our Lord Jesus Christ, the same perfect in Godhead and also perfect in manhood; truly God and truly man, of a reasonable soul and body; consubstantial (of the same essence) with the Father according to the Godhead, and consubstantial with us according to the manhood, in all things like unto us, without sin; begotten before all ages of the Father according to the Godhead, and in these latter days, for us and our salvation, born of the Virgin Mary, the Mother of God, according to the manhood; one and the same Christ, Son, Lord, Only-begotten, in two natures, inconfusedly, unchangeably, indivisibly, inseparably, the distinction of natures being by no means taken away by the union, but rather the property of each nature being preserved, and concurring in one person and one subsistence, not parted or divided into two persons, but one and the same Son and Only-begotten, God the Word (Logos), the Lord Jesus Christ.

But now the questions prod us: How can one person have two natures? How can one person be truly human and truly divine? How can one be both finite and infinite? It is a holy mystery, says the Catholic church; some Protestant scholars agree.

But if we study John's Gospel with these questions in mind, we come up with some rather clarifying insights: God is a spirit. God is love. Now the historical Jesus was fully human, with mind, soul, and body, "in all things like unto us, without sin"; his spirit also was human. But if his spirit was wholly one of love, then his spirit was actually God's spirit—it was both human and divine! It was human in that it was his spirit; it was divine in that God is love. Thus the spirit of Jesus is the spirit of God; the historical Jesus was truly human and (in spirit or essence) truly divine, finite as an individual human being and infinite as God's universal spirit of love. Now we can see clearly what Jesus at the Last Supper is saying to his disciples, as reported in John's Gospel:

> If you had known me, you would have known my Father also; henceforth you know him and have seen him. . . . He who has seen me has seen the Father. . . . Do you not believe that I am in the Father and the Father in me? The words that I say to you I do not speak on my own authority; but the Father who dwells in me does his works. (John 14:7, 9-10)

Obviously, Jesus is not saying here that he is the Father; yet, he is saying, "I and the Father are one (in spirit)." This, then, is the clear meaning of the Incarnation and the basis for the Nicene Creed and the Definition of Chalcedon: God, as the spirit of love, is manifested in a man who being human, is also (in spirit) divine, "of one essence with the Father."

But Jesus goes beyond this expression of his relation to the Father. He proceeds to extend the concept of incarnation to the presence of God-Christ in people's hearts: "I am in my Father, and you in me, and I in you. . . . If a man loves me, he will keep my word, and my Father will love him, and we will come to him and make our home with him" (John 14:20, 23).

In his epistles the author of John's Gospel is equally explicit:

> All who keep his commandments abide in him, and he in them. . . . Beloved, let us love one another; for love is of God, and he who loves is born of God and knows God. He who does not love does not know God; for God is love . . . he has given us

> of his own Spirit . . . and he who abides in love abides in God, and God abides in him. (I John 3:24; 4:7, 13, 16)

Thus the incarnation of God in Christ is extended to the incarnation of God (and Christ) in man and, therefore, in the words of Paul, through love man becomes "a new creature in Christ!"

In the same manner also, Jesus says to Nicodemus: "Unless one is born of water and the Spirit, he cannot enter the kingdom of God . . . that which is born of the Spirit is spirit" (John 3:5-6).

This rebirth, as pictured in John's Gospel and in the writings of the apostle Paul, is salvation. It is the kingdom of God. Some years ago, I ran across an old translation of the Bible. It was difficult to read, but one very familiar verse was quite understandable, and quite surprising. Instead of translating Matthew 6:33 as, "Seek ye first the kingdom of God and his righteousness," it read "Seek ye first the reign of God!" This opened up to me a whole new meaning! So often we have interpreted this teaching to mean that we should make the primary purpose of our lives and of our religion that of getting into heaven when we die, but it doesn't mean this at all! Rather, it means that we should seek, above all things, to bring about the reign of God in our own hearts and in the hearts of all people; all other things will take care of themselves! Where is God's kingdom? Where is anyone's kingdom? It's where he reigns. If God reigns in your heart and in mine, then Jesus' words are most meaningful: The kingdom of God is within you!

God is love, and the reign of God is the reign of love in the hearts of men. Thus one is "reborn"; thus one becomes "a new creature in Christ." This is salvation; this is the kingdom of God. "God was in Christ, reconciling the world to himself." This is the Incarnation. *Amen.*

Daniel J. Bowden
United Church of Christ
Indianola, Washington

RESPONSIBLE STEWARDSHIP

(Stewardship)

He also said to the disciples, "There was a rich man who had a steward, and charges were brought to him that this man was wasting his goods. And he called him and said to him, 'What is this that I hear about you? Turn in the account of your stewardship, for you can no longer be steward.' And the steward said to himself, 'What shall I do, since my master is taking the stewardship away from me? I am not strong enough to dig, and I am ashamed to beg. I have decided what to do, so that people may receive me into their houses when I am put out of the stewardship.' So, summoning his master's debtors one by one, he said to the first, 'How much do you owe my master?' He said, 'A hundred measures of oil.' And he said to him, 'Take your bill, and sit down quickly and write fifty.' Then he said to another, 'And how much do you owe?' He said, 'A hundred measures of wheat.' He said to him, 'Take your bill and write eighty.' The master commended the dishonest steward for his shrewdness; for the sons of this world are more shrewd in dealing with their own generation than the sons of light. And I tell you, make friends for yourselves by means of unrighteous mammon, so that when it fails they may receive you into the eternal habitations. . . . You cannot serve God and mammon." (Luke 16:1-9, 13)

Here is one of the most intriguing stories told by our Lord. If this story is regarded as a parable and the lord who called his steward to account represents God, it is difficult to explain why God should commend a dishonest man and place his approval upon a clever piece of cheating. The difficulty is removed when we see the story not as a parable but as an incident from real life, showing how smart, but godless, businessmen have gone about their business in all ages. But just as a bee extracts honey even from a poisonous flower, so our Lord draws perennially important lessons from the sinful conduct of the worldly-wise.

The story deals with stewardship and concentrates on the central thing in stewardship, namely, responsibility. The specific emphases, as applied to ourselves, are four: (1) we are responsible; (2) we have acted irresponsibly; (3) we face a day of reckoning; and (4) we must be intelligent enough to insure our future.

First, we are responsible. Like the dishonest steward, we do not own anything. All that he had belonged to his master and was entrusted to him to use for the realization of the owner's purpose in regard to it. We are in exactly the same position. What we have, our material possessions, our mental talents and abilities, our time and energy, our potentialities and opportunities, all these have been given to us as a trust for which we are accountable to God. Luther states it simply but strongly in the closing words of his explanation of the first article of the Creed: "For all of which I am in duty bound to thank, praise, serve, and obey him." A correct understanding of the doctrine of creation thus culminates in a heightened sense of responsibility. Stewardship is a constant reminder that God created human existence to be responsible existence. Life is a gift from the hand of God, but "to whom much is given, of him will much be required." Stewardship is thus a philosophy of life that determines not only religious activity in the narrow sense, but also all of life's orders—home, citizenship, business and industry, science, and art. Everything God has created has a meaning and a purpose based on his will. We have been entrusted with a life created by God and redeemed by Christ. We can use it selfishly and foolishly or as honest and faithful stewards. In either case, we are responsible.

It is this sense of responsibility which more than anything else distinguishes a human being from other creatures. Paul describes it as the law of conscience written during creation in the hearts of all. Conscience is not a separate human faculty or capacity. It is the human being as a whole standing in a relationship of personal responsibility to his Creator. In conscience God speaks to people and makes each a responsible "you" to the Maker. Thus the gospel is not directed primarily to intellect or feelings but to conscience. "By the open statement of the truth," says the apostle, "we would commend ourselves to every man's conscience in the sight of God" (II Corinthians 4:2). This is what gives stewardship its meaning as the Christian life-attitude.

Second, we have acted irresponsibly. The report given to the master was that his steward had wasted the owner's goods. He had appropriated the property that was not his and had used it for his own purposes. The same report is true of you and of me and of our whole nation, a nation that spends more for gambling than for the church, more for advertising cigarettes than for missions, is guilty of grave embezzlement of the Lord's resources. It is so also with our personal stewardship. Have we not wasted the Lord's goods by placing material gain and selfish pleasure at the top of our priorities? Danish author J. Anker Larsen, in *The Philosopher's Stone*, tells the story of a talented young man with a highly promising future, who, like the prodigal of the gospel story, squandered what he had in loose and irresponsible living. At the end an awakened conscience drove him to despair and suicide. He left behind him a note which said, "I made God's vineyard my playground. Now I can no longer work there." Such is the epitaph of an irresponsible life.

Third, we face a day of reckoning. The dishonest steward thought that he could get away with his deception. He was too clever to be caught. Any talk of responsibility was, to him, mere childish prattle. But the day came when he heard the grim summons, "Turn in the account of your stewardship. You can no longer be steward." We confront not a mere principle of retribution, but the judgment throne of God, himself. In a universe in which the bedrock of reality is the righteous will of God, we cannot cheat him with impunity; "God is not mocked, for whatever a man sows, that he will also reap" (Galatians 6:7). "He who spits at heaven," says a Spanish proverb, "spits in his own face." Running through the entire Bible is the solemn truth of inescapable judgment. Sooner or later we face a day of reckoning.

Fourth, and here lies the main point of the story, we must be intelligent enough to ensure our future. Facing the day of reckoning, the dishonest steward was spurred into action. He called his master's debtors, one by one, and by arbitrarily changing their notes and lowering their indebtedness he made them his partners in crime. He obligated them to himself in such a way that he could count on them when he was deposed from office. He was dishonest, but, in the light of his own low standards, he was wise. The master does not commend the steward for his dishonesty but for his shrewdness. The man acted intelligently on his own low level. Jesus adds, "The sons of this world are more shrewd in dealing with their own generation than the sons of light." He wants the sons of light, the people of God's kingdom, to be as wise in acting according to the high standards of the kingdom as the worldly wise are in acting according to their low standards.

Our Lord stresses again and again not responsibility, but *intelligent* responsibility. The man who built his house on the sand was not a wicked man, but a stupid man who forgot about storms. The rich farmer who tore down his old barn and built a bigger one so that he could store all his rich harvest and be secure for many years was short-sighted, because he left God out of his calculations. The virgins whose lamps flickered out were not bad girls—they, too, were virgins—but they were foolish virgins who did not make provision for enough oil. Jesus tells us to be not only as innocent as doves, but also as wise as serpents. High ideals that soar above the earth are not enough. You must also have the realistic wisdom that hugs the contours of the earth with a serpentine sinuosity.

The wisdom of the dishonest steward was to make friends who would help him in his hour of need. He thus insured his temporary earthly future. True wisdom, according to Jesus, is to be in a relation of friendship with God, who alone can ensure our eternal future. We, ourselves, however, can never build that relationship. Conscience is not the bridge to heaven; it only reveals that the bridge is out. When we realize this, we learn to appreciate the gospel, which assures us that while it is not in our power to make friends with God, God has done everything in his power to make friends with us. He, himself, through the saving work of Christ, has repaired the broken relationship and enables us to fulfill the destiny for which we were created and redeemed.

Our Lord concludes his lesson on stewardship with the words, "You cannot serve God and mammon." Mammon is money, and money can become a dangerous rival to God. In contrast to the dishonest steward's wrong use of money, which Jesus calls "unrighteous mammon," Jesus seeks to point out the right use, with eternal habitations in mind. Money, in itself, is neither righteous nor unrighteous, because it has only instrumental, not intrinsic, value and has no moral qualities. It becomes righteous or unrighteous depending on how we acquire it and how we use it. But in stating that even in using it for righteous purposes, we must handle "unrighteous mammon," our Lord points to the human predicament that not even a good steward can escape. Jesus, the supreme realist, sees that in a sin-cursed world our stewardship must be carried out through sin-tainted decisions and with sin-tainted instruments. Indeed, as Luther observed, the steward, himself, is sinner and saint, righteous and unrighteous, at the same time. But living by the grace of forgiveness, by which our judge is also our Savior, we fulfill our calling according to the wisdom and the strength he gives us.

Ministers tend to be sensitive to the criticism that they talk about money when they should be talking about God. Some years ago, an American preacher visited in a church in Finland. Since the story of the dishonest steward was the gospel lesson appointed for the day, his sermon dealt with the right use of money. After the service, the senior pastor of the church remarked to him, "It seems strange to me that you Americans can speak so freely about money while preaching a sermon. Of course, I understand that your churches are dependent on voluntary contributions while ours are tax-supported. But when occasionally I must announce an offering for some special cause, such as missions, I feel embarrassed to have to refer to such a mundane matter as money after having preached God's Word." The American replied, "Our Lord felt no such embarrassment. And when Paul, in the fifteenth chapter of First Corinthians presented his magnificent vision of the consummation of history, he was not embarrassed in beginning the next chapter with the words, 'Now as to the offering.' "

God's sovereignty and man's responsibility—this is what stewardship is about. The sovereignty of God extends over every aspect of a person's life, including his pocketbook, and stewardship concerns not only money but also a person's whole existence in responsibility to God. "Present your bodies," says Paul, your whole selves, not just your opinions, "as a living sacrifice" (Romans 12:1). Why? Because Christ gave his body, his whole self, as a sacrifice for you. If, as God's children, we share in his purpose, then what we do is determined by what he does. Our management of his household is patterned on the way he manages it. God's relation to the world is revealed in the heart of the gospel, "God so loved the world that he gave his only Son" (John 3:16). The nature of our actions is derived from God's own nature and from our relationship to him. Thus the apostle can say, "With eyes wide open to the mercies of God, I beg you to give yourselves to him." To give and to keep on giving is the nature of a God who is love. Love can never be close-lipped or tight-fisted. It is compelled from within to share, to sacrifice, and to give. Christian giving can, therefore, never be an occasional performance or a special ceremony. When, as the apostle says, our minds are remolded by God from within, then Christian giving is the normal, steady, increasing outflow of our life in God. Thus the main problem in the financial support of the church is not getting into people's pocketbooks, but getting Christ into people's hearts.

The way to responsible stewardship is contained in the apostolic word, "For the love of Christ controls us, because we are convinced that one has died for all . . . that those who live might live no longer for themselves but for him" (II Corinthians 5:14-15). *Amen.*

T. A. Kantonen
Professor Emeritus of Systematic Theology
Trinity Lutheran Seminary
Columbus, Ohio

TWO LOVE SONGS

(Wedding)

On this happy day, I want to call your attention to the fact that a Christian marriage ought to elevate and celebrate two kinds of love. To put it another way, the music of a marriage in Christ contains the melodies of two love songs. One is the universal, natural, physical, and sexual love that is widely described in the love poetry and music of the whole world. This is the love that knows the great joy of a man and a woman cherishing each other above any other human.

The other kind of love is that which makes of Christian marriage something that does not despise the physical, sexual, and emotional union of husband and wife; it is a love that goes far beyond. This is the love that is God's own love, that comes as a gift from him and is intended to govern all our human relationships.

We can rejoice that a triumphant affirmation of both kinds of love is found in the Scriptures. The celebration of sexual love between a woman and a man is found most vividly and literally in a part of the Old Testament that is seldom, if ever, read or preached about in public worship these days. I refer to the Song of Solomon. I have never heard a sermon preached on any part of this book and can find no printed sermon on it in my library! That is probably because the passionate, sexual love therein described is so very explicit. The old rabbis found it so explicit that they forbade its being read by young boys. In the Christian era, it became a prescribed reading for part of the Passover season, but was to be read only privately and individually, and not publicly. Even then, it was spiritualized to refer to the relationship between Yahweh and Israel, rather than to a man and a woman. In fact, there was only one other Hebrew writing which had a harder time getting into the Old Testament canon of approved writings: Ecclesiastes.

The happy and lyrical description of the joys of erotic love in the Song of Solomon were simply too much for our more ascetic forebears! Not only the rabbis, but early Christian writers as well, tended to interpret it as an allegory. For Christians, it was an allegory of the relationship between Christ and the church. To take it literally was dangerous and risked immorality.

Yet, one of its most beautiful verses stands firmly as a true description of the lasting quality and power of this highest of human loves:

> Many waters cannot quench love,
> neither can floods drown it.
> If a man offered for love
> all the wealth of his house,
> it would be utterly scorned. (Song of Solomon 8:7)

That is certainly a high view of what this love is all about. It is not sheer "Pollyanna romanticism." The Song of Solomon also speaks of the tensions and disappointments of this love. It is certainly not the kind of love in which either the man or the woman constantly uses the other for selfish ends. There is a mutuality of loving respect here that puts to shame much of what the modern world sees, writes about, and advertises, using sex as the vehicle! There is uninhibited appreciation of both the outer and the inner beauties of each. But this love is like the oasis of Engedi, west of the Dead Sea—a wild and desolate spot. Here, as in other Old Testament passages mentioning Engedi, it is an isolated refuge and beauty spot in the midst of a dreary desert. So, sang the writer of the Song of Solomon, is the deep and abiding love of one man and one woman, in the deserts of society and in the midst of so much brokenness in human relationships.

And yet, the greatest weakness of this natural, universal, erotic love is that it is not permanent. We cannot say of this form of love, as beautiful and desirable as it is, that it never fails. It does fail, because the two human beings who feel and experience it uniquely toward each other, reach moments when that feeling is diminished or ruptured. Times come in every marriage built on erotic love alone when it is not enough to overcome disappointments, to bridge misunderstandings, or to guarantee the continuation of a satisfying relationship.

That is why every Christian marriage needs to be celebrated with not one, but two love songs! The Song of Solomon is good, as far as it goes. But it is the love song of I Corinthians 13 that must become the most meaningful melody for a Christian marriage. The climactic theme of the superiority of God's own love to all others sounds in these familiar verses: "Love bears all things, believes all things, hopes all things, endures all things.

Love never ends. . . . So faith, hope, love abide, these three; but the greatest of these is love" (13:7-8, 13).

Natural, erotic love between the sexes does not bear, believe, hope, and endure all things. So many little things can throw it off track, because that love has in it the subtle need for self-gratification or self-justification at the expense of the other. A marriage built only on the decency, common sense, and sexual morality of our human peers or societal practices seems only pale and deathlike alongside the Christlike geniality of God's own love. There is nothing abstract or visionary in Luther's urging that in Christ we are called to be "little Christs to one another." That advice certainly applies to the marriage relationship as well as to all others. The poet of the Song of Solomon was correct when he wrote, "Many waters cannot quench love, neither can floods drown it."

But Paul, the apostle of Christ, took that love to its ultimate meaning when he hymned it to the music of God's own endless, perfect love, demonstrated in the life and example of Jesus Christ, to the members of the Corinthian church.

I hope and pray for your marriage that it will always be lightened in time of heaviness, believed in time of doubt, and endured when trials may seem beyond endurance. And may you always let these two biblical love songs sing in your hearts and lives, throughout your whole life together! *Amen*.

Harold G. Deal
Luther Place Memorial Church
Washington, D.C.

RESPONSIBLE FREEDOM

(World Day of Prayer)

Jesus taught his disciples to pray. What does this mean? It means that prayer is by no means an obvious or natural activity. It is the expression of the fact that the disciples were permitted to pray because Jesus told them they might—and he knows the Father. He promised that God would hear them.

The disciples prayed only because they were followers of Christ and had fellowship with him. Only those who like to adhere to Jesus have access to the Father through him. Christian prayer is directed to God through a Mediator; not even prayer affords direct access to the Father. Only through Jesus Christ can we find the Father in prayer.

Christian prayer presupposes faith: that is, adherence to Jesus Christ. He is the one and only Mediator of our prayers. We pray at his command, and to that word Christian prayer is always bound. We pray to God because we believe in him through Jesus Christ. We are privileged to know that he knows our needs before we ask him. This is what gives Christian prayer its boundless confidence and its joyous certainty.

It matters little what form of prayer we adopt or how many words we use. What matters is the faith that lays a hold on God and touches the heart of the Father who knew us long before we came to him. Genuine prayer is never good works, an exercise, or a pious attitude, but it is always the prayer of a child to a father. It is never self-display, whether before God, ourselves, or other people. If God were ignorant of our needs, we should have to determine beforehand how we should tell him about them, what we should tell him, and whether we should tell him. So faith, which is the mainspring of Christian prayer, excludes all reflection and premeditation.

Prayer is the supreme instance of the hidden character of the Christian life. It is the antithesis of self-display. When men and women pray, they have ceased to know themselves and know only God, whom they call upon. Prayer does not aim at any direct effect upon the world—it is only directed to God.

Jesus told his disciples not only how to pray, but also what to pray. The Lord's Prayer is not merely the pattern prayer; it is the way Christians must pray!

God's name. God's will. God's kingdom. God must be the primary object not only of our praying, but also of our daily lives.

Once we have made the decision to become a child of God, through our baptism and the gifts that God gives to us from it, we are called to become a follower, or disciple, of the Word. The bearers of Jesus' Word are called to go out and spread the good news of Jesus Christ. The bearers of Jesus' Word receive a final word of promise for their work. They are now Christ's fellow workers and will be like him in all things. They are to meet those to whom they are sent as if they were Christ himself. They become bearers of his presence.

They bring with them the most precious gift in the world—the gift of Jesus Christ. And with him, they bring God the Father, and that means indeed forgiveness and salvation, life, and eternal bliss. This is the reward and fruit of toil and suffering.

But as great and tremendous as these words really sound to us, we still have another responsibility to ourselves, this being the freedom to do as we want, the freedom to think, the freedom to make decisions on our own. We have to decide for ourselves issues that involve us and threaten our very existence. The issue at hand is the question: Will I, as a Christian, become disloyal to God? A whole new ballgame is opening up in front of our eyes, and many times we do not want to be a part of it. But we cannot back away from the problems or issues that sit right in front of us, and we know that all questions must have answers. This is our freedom.

Faith, loyalty, love, trust. The constant cries are heard. Whom do I follow the most? The church, Jesus, God, my pastor, my family, my job, my home, my wife or husband, my children or grandchildren, my friends, my neighbors, my parishioners—whom can I keep serving the right way? This is a really tough question to answer and, more importantly, to answer truthfully. All of these things constantly threaten our decisions. Yet there are more groups threatening our decision-making—social or service organizations, local or national politics, school or church groups, the economy, or your family budget. There may be so much pressure and tension that you just feel like giving up or letting someone else handle your affairs, or better yet, you just want to go on a far away vacation and leave your problems behind. There are still other problems facing you—the threat of medical or physical illness, alcohol or drug addiction, unwanted pregnancy, the problem of loneliness, the high rate of felonies, rape, and other crimes that make one afraid to walk the streets at night or to go shopping at the mall or downtown. Or what about that close friend or relative who is dying and you just cannot face the fact that there is something wrong that cannot be cured by medical science?

Loyalty and trust. These are words that sometimes just don't work. Yet if we search the Scriptures, we may find that Jesus probably encountered the same awful and sometimes heartbreaking situations that you and I have to face daily. A follower, a disciple of Christ, listens to him. He is everywhere in truth and in love. Call upon him as he expects you to call and help others in his name. He is everywhere one and the same.

Where today do we hear the call of Jesus to discipleship and responsible freedom? There is no other answer than this: Hear the Word and receive the sacrament faithfully; in it, hear him, and you will hear the call. You will find the courage to tackle and confront the problems that trouble and burden you so—love, faith, grace, forgiveness, salvation.

Listen to God's will. May his loving kindness and mercy keep you strong in your belief and the faith that sustains you daily. Jesus has freed us from our sins. May we walk in his ways, sure and true in the light of the resurrection and the overcoming of death on the cross.

He lives. You live. You are free. *Amen.*

Gene A. Parker
Prince of Peace Lutheran Church
Stuart, Florida

SPECIAL SERIES

RECEIVING THE HOLY SPIRIT

Come, Holy Spirit, heavenly Dove,
With all thy quickening powers;
Kindle a flame of sacred love
In these cold hearts of ours.

The working of the Holy Spirit fills the pages of the New Testament. The Spirit descended on Jesus at the time of his baptism. The Spirit was promised by Jesus. The Spirit came in power at Pentecost. The power of the Holy Spirit has extended down through the centuries through a variety of religious traditions. It was the Holy Spirit who brought a heart-warming experience into the life of the early church. It was the Holy Spirit who started the Pentecostal movement in America through a revival in Los Angeles, at the turn of the century, that lasted three years. The Spirit's power has moved into our own day with the charismatic movement, which recognizes the many gifts of the Spirit given for the common good.

The Holy Spirit—powerful, mysterious, God present with us. How can we receive that flame in these cold hearts of ours?

The first step in receiving the Holy Spirit is found in John 14:15: love Christ! There are some things that the world cannot understand about our faith. The cross is one example. The Holy Spirit is another. The world cannot receive him or know him or see him, suggested Jesus in John 14. But the person who loves Jesus Christ will know the Spirit, because the Spirit remains with and is in that person.

One of the gifts I received for my birthday was small, but very special. To outsiders, the gift might have seemed silly, but I knew the giver, and the giver knew me; therefore, the gift meant something. When we have a relationship with Jesus Christ, the Spirit, given by him, makes sense; that Spirit touches us at our point of greatest need because we know the giver!

Says Paul in Romans 10:9, "If you confess with your lips that Jesus is Lord and believe in your heart that God raised him from the dead, you will be saved." It is in accepting Christ that we make ourselves available to receive the Holy Spirit.

The Spirit is received at Baptism. In speaking to the crowd at Pentecost, in Acts 2:38, Peter said, "Each one of you must turn away from his sins and be baptized in the name of Jesus Christ, so that your sins will be forgiven; and you will receive God's gift, the Holy Spirit" (TEV). When baptism is offered in the name of the Father, and the Son, and the Holy Spirit, the Spirit is also given at that time.

When one receives the Holy Spirit, the presence and power of the Spirit causes one to be filled to overflowing. The young Christian grows under the guidance of the church and loving Christian parents and gradually comes to the place where he or she confirms a faith and can sense the work of the Holy Spirit within.

The Spirit is received at the time we confess our faith in Jesus Christ. In helping the early Christians to identify the Holy Spirit among them, the writer of I John said that anyone who acknowledges that Jesus Christ came as a human being has the Spirit who comes from God. Receiving the Holy Spirit means loving Christ.

Receiving the Holy Spirit means to obey. John 14:15 also mentions obedience. Sprinkled throughout this chapter are references to obedience, closely connected with loving Christ. John 14:21 says "Whoever accepts my commandments and obeys them is the one who loves me."

The sailboat is a symbol of our faith. To be obedient means to set the rudder of our will to follow God's direction in our lives and to trim our sails so that we will catch the full force of the wind of the Holy Spirit. All of this takes human effort, planning, and obedience. No sailor ever just sat in the boat without navigating and arrived at a planned destination. The Mayflower didn't arrive in America all by itself while the crew played cards in their quarters. Rather the crew of the sailboat must set the rudder, trim the sail, catch the wind; then, as a result of their obedience, they will find that the Holy Spirit will move the boat ahead.

Catherine Marshall, in her book *The Helper*, suggests that receiving the Holy Spirit means being willing to be put to work, to witness to the world, and to reach for the towel and basin to wash the feet of those in need. Obedience is facing in the right direction and allowing the Holy Spirit to fill us and move us.

Receiving the Holy Spirit means being open to the fresh winds of the Spirit day by day. Even though the Spirit may be within us as a result of our baptism, confirmation, and personal acknowledgement of Jesus Christ, there are times when we lose our awareness of the Spirit or push the Spirit out of our daily lives. We, at that point, need a fresh Spirit; we need to be open! We need to be open to what the Spirit wants, not what we want.

In I Corinthians 12, a well known chapter on the gifts of the Spirit, Paul notes that the Spirit gives the gifts. He gives a different gift to each person!

The initiative is with the Spirit. It is our job to be open. Oh, I wish that receiving the Spirit would occur when a certain prayer is prayed or by coming forward when a certain hymn is sung. But there is no set formula. These opportunities only help us to be open. The Spirit sets the place and the time.

In some cases in the Bible, the coming of the Holy Spirit takes place at a time other than baptism. In Acts 8, Peter and John traveled to Samaria, and there they prayed for the believers that they might receive the Holy Spirit, "For the Holy Spirit had not yet come down on any of them; they had only been baptized in the name of the Lord Jesus. Then Peter and John placed their hands on them and they received the Holy Spirit" (18:16-17 TEV).

The Spirit may come to individuals and to groups as a way of building up the whole body of believers. His coming might be sudden, or there might be a gradual unfolding of the Spirit in a person's life from the time of baptism. The work of the Spirit is always fresh. We need it to fill our sails, which need to be constantly refilled with new wind to propel us in our Christian life. Otherwise, we become a drifting boat on a windless day, or we become like the balloon that is out of air—limp and lifeless.

> The wind blows wherever it wishes; you hear the sound it makes, but you do not know where it comes from or where it is going. It is like that with everyone who is born of the Spirit. (John 3:8 TEV)

We need to be open to the Holy Spirit. Some of us may have lives that are like a fogged-in airport. We've closed down the runways and shut down the terminal with our resistance to the gospel and our heavy secular schedules. Some of us have very thick skin, and the Spirit has a difficult time showing itself from within or even getting in! So—be open!

God is near to each of us. We can receive the Holy Spirit. Certainly, the coming of the Spirit into each of our lives is not intended by God to be a complicated matter. God does not desire to confuse us or to lead us into arguments about how the Spirit is received.

The Holy Spirit is God with us. The Holy Spirit gives comfort and strength for our daily living, at home, on the job, or at leisure. In these moments, I hope that God has been able to use this message and that you have been considering the place of the Spirit in your life. Although I can offer no magical formula, in conclusion, let me suggest three guidelines by which the Spirit can come into our lives and into the life of our church:

1. Love Jesus Christ;
2. Obey Christ's commandments;
3. Be open.

Amen.

EXPERIENCING THE HOLY SPIRIT

How do you know that the Holy Spirit is a part of your life? You and God need to examine your life and the presence or absence of his Spirit. There is always the temptation to make judgments about the place of the Holy Spirit in other people's lives. But now the focus is on your own life and the Holy Spirit within you. To help you, offered here are several scriptural yardsticks.

First, anyone who acknowledges that Jesus Christ is Lord can do so only by the guidance of the Holy Spirit! It seems that this takes most of the mystery out of the gift of the Holy Spirit and may well remove the lingering doubt in your mind whether God's Holy Spirit is a part of your life. Can you say that Jesus Christ is Lord? If you are able to make that faith statement, then the Holy Spirit is a part of your life, because you cannot make that profession of faith unless you are guided by the Spirit.

This verse establishes the ground rule for being guided by the Holy Spirit. When you feel the nudging of the Spirit, always ask yourself: Is this thought or action in keeping with my belief that Jesus Christ is Lord? You see, there are other spirits; Paul calls them "lying spirits" in I Timothy 4:1.

It's not always easy to tell whether you are being directed by the Holy Spirit or a lying spirit. The lying spirits can be very convincing. There once was a man who thought that the Holy Spirit was directing him to have prayer with a woman, including what he called "the laying on of hands." This laying on of hands ended up to be more like pawing. He had to be confronted with his behavior and was made aware that it was unacceptable. Was the Holy Spirit guiding him? Was this action in keeping with Jesus as Lord? If a Jim Jones tells all the members of his church to drink a poison, is that in keeping with Jesus as Lord? Keep that question before you. But, above all, remember that if you can say that Jesus is Lord, the Holy Spirit is a part of your life!

Second, when the Holy Spirit is a part of your life you will find him to be a helper and counselor. A pastor was called to a hospital where a person had died. The family was upset and unwilling to leave. The pastor prayed to God and asked for help while riding the elevator. (Some of the most sincere prayers are offered on hospital elevators.) Within thirty minutes after the pastor's arrival, the family was calm and ready to leave. That was the work of the Holy Spirit—God present with us for guidance, comfort, and strength!

The direction of the Spirit is often called for: Should I buy a house now? Should I agree to serve as a Sunday school teacher? Should I cheat, do drugs, or have sex outside of marriage? Careful and persistent prayer, centering on Jesus as Lord, will help you to open yourself to the Spirit's leading in these personal decisions. But in the end we are not puppets or robots, pushed and pulled by the Spirit, with decisions made for us. Rather, with our God-given human freedom, we must decide. It is the Spirit's guidance that will make the final decision, pleasing to God and in accordance with the Holy Spirit. To be a counselor means to provide guidance and to help the clients to identify their internal resources so that they can make the right decisions. The Spirit promised by Jesus in John 14 is referred to as the helper or counselor, because under the Spirit's guidance, all things will work together for good.

Third, your experience of the Holy Spirit will be confirmed by the presence of gifts and fruits in your life. It is clear in I Corinthians 12 that there are different kinds of spiritual gifts, different ways of serving, and different abilities to perform service. How is the presence of the Spirit shown in you? Wisdom, knowledge, faith, the power to heal, to proclaim God's message, to work miracles, to tell the difference between gifts, to speak in strange tongues—what gift of the Spirit do you have? He gives a different gift to each person.

A different gift . . . all the more reason in these moments to focus on your gift and not to worry about, but simply celebrate, the gifts of others.

"But," someone is thinking, "don't I have to speak in tongues?" It's unfortunate that some Christians equate the gift of the Holy Spirit with the gift of tongues alone. When the apostles were filled with the Holy Spirit at Pentecost, one of the signs of the Spirit's presence and power was that those present began to speak in other languages, which they had never studied or heard, but everyone was able to understand what was being said, words describing the wonderful works of God (Acts 2:4-11). The gift of tongues developed from that experience and apparently became a troublesome gift; it was unintelligible and disrupted worship services like a noisy gong or a clanging bell.

Today some Christians receive the gift of speaking in tongues. I would not question the gift or the sincerity of those who use it, but I would dispute any claim that speaking in tongues is the evidence that one has received the Holy Spirit. Many, many Christians are filled with the Holy Spirit and do not speak in tongues. If there is a greater gift, it is love. What is your gift?

The fruit of the Spirit, as recorded in Galatians 5:22, is another way of examining the place of the Spirit in your life. Unlike the gifts, the fruits come more as a package deal; they represent the way in which the Spirit controls us internally, as opposed to the external control of the law. Will you measure your life today against these fruits of love, joy, peace, patience, kindness, goodness, faithfulness, humility, and self-control?

Finally, the experience of the Holy Spirit in our lives is marked by our concern for others.

> The Spirit of the Lord is upon me, because he has chosen me to bring good news to the poor. He has sent me to proclaim liberty to the captives and recovery of sight to the blind, to set free the oppressed and announce that the time has come when the Lord will save his people. (Luke 4:18-19 TEV)

It is when the Spirit of the Lord is upon me that I care for the poor, the captives, the blind, the oppressed, and all of those brothers and sisters in the world under similar situations.

The work of the Spirit in the life of Jesus should also be the work of the Spirit in ours. The experience of the Holy Spirit in my life reminds me to look beyond myself, my family, and my church to the needs of all of humanity. It is a call to action: Action verbs punctuate the above verses: *bring, proclaim, set free, announce.* This was Jesus' first sermon, his first public act following baptism. The Spirit set the tone for his ministry and for ours.

It is helpful to hear the Spirit's call for liberty of captives, when people are being held hostage in our world. This is not a call for vengeance or military power, but, as in Jesus' own ministry, for a releasing of the Holy Spirit in people's lives, even the terrorists, so that love will prevail and peace will come.

Experiencing the Holy Spirit in our individual lives means bringing foodstuffs to the church for the poor, participating, as physically able, in Christian works, and ministering to others with the gifts and fruits of the Spirit as you experience them in your life.

Someone recently said, "I think I can see one of the major thrusts of your ministry here. You want us to be involved outside of our church, in mission, in helping others." This is not my agenda; it is the work of the Holy Spirit in our lives.

Now it's time for each of us to pray for the experience of the Holy Spirit in our lives, not in the lives of others, but in my life, in your life.

I have suggested that you have the Holy Spirit in your life when you acknowledge that Jesus Christ is Lord, when you experience God with you as the helper and counselor, when you are able to identify the presence of gifts and fruits in your life, and when you have a deep concern for others. I suspect that many here will have a reason to celebrate this morning, because the Holy Spirit is already with you. Our journey is not complete; we still need to grow and mature so that we are completely filled with his presence. Some of you have been doubtful about the Holy Spirit's presence in your life, and now you sense his presence more fully. Others may still be searching for that filling. I encourage you to love Christ, to obey him, and to be open to hear his word: "As bad as you are, you know how to give good things to your children. How much more, then, will the Father in heaven give the Holy Spirit to those who ask him!" (Luke 11:13 TEV). *Amen.*

LIVING THE HOLY SPIRIT

Have you ever thought about starting your own religious group? There are several new ones popping up these days. How would you go about it? Perhaps you would read a book on new parish development. Maybe you would call together a committee to discuss the need for a new group and establish task groups—a building committee, a budget commitee, and an evangelism committee. Or you might simply rent a hall, advertise, and begin the perfect church, leaving behind all the faults that you have seen or heard of in other local churches.

Chapter two of the Acts of the Apostles gives a careful and stirring description of the formation of the first church group. Peter lined up three thousand people along the river, stirred their hearts with a sermon calling them to repentance and baptism, and then added them to the church rolls.

Back up just a little in chapter two, and you will read of the coming of the Holy Spirit. The wind, fire, and power of God had come upon Peter and the other disciples, and that living Spirit took the form of the church!

The drama of Christ's death and resurrection had finally begun to sink in, and Peter offered his pointed witness. "What shall we do?" asked those who heard. Peter's response was not "Set up a committee" or "Let's raise some money," but "Repent, and be baptized" (Acts 2:38). The church began in response to that message given to Peter by the Holy Spirit, and what follows describes the marks of that church.

"They spent their time in learning from the apostles" (Acts 2:42 TEV). The followers of Jesus were drawn together by the things they believed in common. This gave them a bond of strength. In order to live that Spirit as the body of believers, they had to know what they believed. They studied the scriptures and listened to the apostles teach. Good for them! This is one point at which we have sometimes let God's Spirit down. Many of us would reword Paul's thirteenth chapter to the Corinthians to read: "When I was a child, I spoke like a child, I thought like a child, I reasoned like a child, and I studied and learned of God's ways in Sunday school. But now that I am grown, I have given up Sunday school and scripture study all together." These early believers knew that a part of living the Spirit is studying and learning to discover what we really believe and gaining insight into the natures of God, Christ, and our call to discipleship.

Many need to become as little children again and return to small groups and Scripture study. It is a sincere hope that the return to the study of the Bible will help us to reclaim this part of being the church of the Holy Spirit; a fresh touch of the Spirit may well drive us back into Bible study and help the Bible come alive. To live the Spirit meant that those early followers of Christ, now formed into the church, wanted to learn and study, following their Spirit-filled experiences and baptism. This was a mark of the church. *O Lord, make us hungry once again for the Book of Life!*

They took part "in the fellowship and shared in the fellowship meals, maintaining good fellowship." The Greek word for fellowship is *koinonia,* meaning a kind of bonding together in love and friendship. Those believers found themselves together around the table, sharing meals. These fellowship meals may well have been the forerunner of the organized church picnic! The meals of the early church and of our day have a deeper meaning: Every time we break bread together as brothers and sisters, we remember the body and blood of Christ. We have given certain liturgy to the Lord's Supper and have separated it from the fellowship meal. In the early church the common meal and the sacrament were a unit.

There were prayers. The early church involved itself in prayer and praise. No doubt the members remembered others in prayer and in their prayers were unified against those who would persecute them. No doubt they prayed for counsel and help from the Holy Spirit, so that their group would grow stronger in the Lord. Every congregation should be a praying one. We need one another, and others need our intercessions.

Many churches place prayer cards in the pews and announce that a prayer group will pray for requests, without any publicity. On most Sundays, worshipers are given the opportunity to pray aloud or to offer prayer requests aloud, but I suspect that not every worshiper is comfortable in speaking out or sharing personal concerns openly. However, prayer is another mark of the church.

Finally, there was a sharing and caring spirit among this body of believers. There was a sharing of property and possessions with those in need. The gift of the Holy Spirit evidently brought a new commitment to the lives of the people. They believed in one another, prayed for one another, loved one another. They took Jesus' teaching about loving your neighbor as yourself seriously. Their fellowship no doubt became the center of community life in which the lonely could find friends, the sinner could find understanding and forgiveness, and the believers could find support. Here again, we find a significant mark of the church and as with these other marks, our church is called to measure itself against this kind of life. Do the lonely find friends here? Do sinners find understanding and forgiveness? Do believers find support? Do we share our belongings and sell possessions and distribute them to those in need?

There is another word here about this church. The final verse says that "the Lord added to their group those who were being saved" (Acts 2:47). *They* didn't add to the number daily, the Lord did. But I suspect that the addition of these persons came, in part, because of the faithfulness of the people to the work of the Holy Spirit among them. The way the Lord adds to our number is both a challenge and a liberation.

Evangelism is not one of my greatest strengths, and so I am glad that it is the risen Lord who transforms persons and adds to our members. These persons are not coming because of me or you, even though the Lord certainly uses us in the work. I hope that these new members have come because they find here a church permeated by the Holy Spirit and alive with teaching and learning, fellowship and meals, prayers, and helping those in need. It is into the church that is living the Spirit that the Lord adds persons.

Is this an odd way to start a church? Yes, because here we are today, hundreds of years later. Be careful, though, in your joy, for these verses from the Acts of the Apostles tend to paint a picture that is too neat. Everybody seems too happy. Of course, we know it doesn't stay that pleasant. Paul's letters attest to that, and the church today is not perfect. Perhaps in Acts, Luke is describing the ideal church, the way it should be, the best it can become with the help of God's Spirit. Seen in that light, it makes for a pretty good model for all of us—that is, for those of us who have been baptized in the name of Jesus Christ, have had our sins forgiven, and have received God's gift—the Holy Spirit. *Amen.*

David A. Highfield
Hunt's Memorial United Methodist Church
Riderwood, Maryland

SECTION III:

APPENDIXES

A. INFORMATION YOU CAN USE

Highlight Dates of the Church Year

	1988	1989	1990
Epiphany	Jan. 6	Jan. 6	Jan. 6
Ash Wednesday	Feb. 17	Feb. 8	Feb. 28
Palm Sunday	March 27	March 19	April 8
Good Friday	April 1	March 24	April 13
Easter	April 3	March 26	April 15
Ascension Day	May 12	May 4	May 24
Pentecost	May 22	May 14	June 3
Trinity Sunday	May 29	May 21	June 10
Thanksgiving	Nov. 24	Nov. 23	Nov. 22
Advent Sunday	Nov. 27	Dec. 3	Dec. 2

Colors of the Church Seasons

White:	Christmas and Easter Seasons; Ascension Day; Trinity Sunday; All Saints' Day; Weddings
Red:	Day of Pentecost
Purple:	Seasons of Advent and Lent
Green:	Season after Epiphany; Thanksgiving
Black:	Good Friday; Funerals (Funerals optional White or Green)

Bible Selections

Faithfulness

Know therefore that the Lord your God is God, the faithful God who keps covenant and steadfast love with those who love him and keep his commandments, to a thousand generations.

Deuteronomy 7:9

Many a man proclaims his own loyalty, but a faithful man who can find?

Proverbs 20:6

The steadfast love of the Lord never ceases, his mercies never come to an end; they are new every morning; great is thy faithfulness.

Lamentations 3:22-23

Who then is the faithful and wise servant, whom his master has set over his household, to give them their food at the proper time? Matthew 24:45

God is faithful, and he will not let you be tempted beyond your strength, but with the temptation will also provide the way of escape, that you may be able to endure it.

I Corinthians 10:13

But the fruit of the Spirit is . . . faithfulness.

Galatians 5:22

What you have heard from me before many witnesses entrust to faithful men who will be able to teach others also.

II Timothy 2:2

If we are faithless, he remains faithful—for he cannot deny himself. II Timothy 2:13

He who is faithful in a very little is faithful also in much; and he who is dishonest in a very little is dishonest also in much. Luke 16:10

B. *IDEAS YOU CAN USE**

*Taken from *40 Proven Ways to a Successful Church* by Al Stauderman and Jim Morentz (Nashville: Abingdon Press, 1980).

Your Church Building Talks!

Does your church have a "Do Not Enter" sign in front of it? Here's what puts a "Do Not Enter" sign in front of your church: the grass isn't cut, the shrubs are overgrown, the building needs painting, the front walk is cracked, a windowpane is broken, nobody has swept the walk, some letters are missing on your sign. When this is the case, your church is saying to everyone who passes by, "Nobody cares!" And when you have a church that says nobody cares, you might as well put up a big "Do Not Enter" sign out in front.

But suppose the outside is perfect. The visitor walks past well-groomed lawns and shrubs and up neatly swept steps and into the narthex, foyer, lobby, or whatever you call your entrance hall. What's there? Is it clean and orderly, with friendly greeters or ushers? Or is there a table messed up with old pamphlets, bulletins, and papers? Does it smell musty, as if the church were closed up 99 percent of the time?

And then the visitor finally gets to the pew. Does the visitor get the feeling that the seat ought to be dusted off before it can be occupied? And then what does the visitor do? Sit there feeling like an intruder? Or like a welcome guest?

The attitude of your ushers can make a big difference in whether or not people come back for a second time—a pleasant greeting, not too effusive, and some indication of help with the service! If you have a printed order of service in the bulletin or elsewhere, make sure that your visitor knows about it. It's greatly helpful if the usher or some regular worshiper will open the hymnal or service book to the right page and hand it to the visitor. Maybe the order of service begins on page 57, and it might take the visitor the whole hour of worship to find the right place.

The printed bulletin tells a tale, too. If it's a third-rate mimeograph job or a confused jumble of announcements and lists of hymns, it doesn't help the visitor, and instead says to him, "You're on your own, bud, in this church!"

The atmosphere has a message, too. If people visit back and forth before the service, talking in stage whispers and socializing, the visitor may feel like a fish out of water. Everybody is having a good time except him. They're saying, "Don't come back."

When the minister enters, his demeanor as well as his dress says a great deal. As he walks up the aisle, if his pants are too short, his robe's on crooked, his shoes aren't shined, and his hair rumpled and unkempt, he's part of that sign that says "Do Not Enter"!

It can't be emphasized too much that your building broadcasts a message. It should say, "This congregation is proud of its church. It's God's house and we keep it that way, not like some neglected shack."

It's the job of everybody in the congregation to help maintain the church's property. If they don't have the money to engage competent caretakers and repair people, they ought to have the time to devote to doing the work themselves. Nobody is too poor to give a few hours to a clean-up, fix-up, paint-up program. Just cutting the lawn and trimming the shrubs regularly can be somebody's major contribution to the congregation. It helps create a neat look that says to the world, "This is our church, and we care about it."

Even if your building is newly painted and glistening white, the lawns carefully manicured and the walkways swept, it may still say "Do Not Enter." Is there a sign telling the hours of services? And if the congregation generally uses a side entrance or a back door, does the visitor know about this? How many times have visitors wrestled with the locked front door of a church only to learn, finally, that for some reason a side door is used as the main entrance. A simple, small sign can convey this information. Without it, you may be telling visitors, "Do Not Enter!"

Most difficult is to find the church office or pastor's study. People who have some reason to come to the church during the week may have to circle the whole building, trying every door, before they find out where the pastor or secretary can be found.

Everything says to the visitor, "You're not welcome here. Regular members know their way around, we'll let you be embarrassed"!

Stand out in front of your church and listen. Is it saying "Welcome," or is it saying "Do Not Enter"?

How to Wake Up Your Sunday School

Most major denominations have in recent years reported a sharp decline in enrollment in religious education programs, especially Sunday schools. Many churches no longer have a thriving adult Bible or discussion class, or a complete educational program for adult members. While there are still some good-sized Sunday schools, they don't begin to reach all the potential Sunday school pupils in the community. Millions of children are not receiving religious education in any form.

Are you satisfied with the number of adults in learning situations in your church? And is your educational program for children reaching its goals?

At First Lutheran, a downtown city church in Los Angeles, we had all the problems. The Sunday school program was faltering, and teachers were becoming discouraged. Our members attended worship services faithfully, but seemed to overlook the educational opportunities. And when the adults failed to attend, the children often had no means of getting to the church.

To draw attention to the fact that Sunday school is important, the congregational leaders decided to try to engender some excitement about the educational program and to try to stir up the notion that something big was happening or about to happen. So they closed the Sunday school for July and August!

Of course, a lot of Sunday schools are closed during July and August anyway, so that hardly was a noteworthy event. But in their case the school had normally been open every Sunday of the year. This time they turned July and August into a four-week leadership training course, mandatory for all teachers, but with identical programs for each month, so that teachers could choose which one to attend and thus avoid conflict with their own vacation programs.

During this time they laid out the curriculum for the entire year. Each teacher was thus able to see the teaching plan and contents for all the grade levels. All departments used a regular thirteen-week cycle, including the adult segments. For the adult classes three courses were to be offered during each thirteen-week period, enabling adults to choose the topics likely to be of most interest to them. The approach to the adult group was, "There's got to be something here that you are interested in." With three thirteen-week cycles, each containing three courses, there were nine courses offered for adults during the year. They felt at least one of these courses would have enough appeal to each adult to get him or her out for at least one thirteen-week period. If adults were unwilling to commit themselves for the entire year, they could at least come for one of the cycles. Many adults did commit themselves to just one of the thirteen-week cycles, but once they got into the courses it wasn't too difficult to keep them coming back.

The entire teaching program was then laid out in a little catalog, rather similar to college or school catalogs. . . . It listed the courses for all age groups, with a short description of each course. This made a rather elaborate sixteen-page booklet, but the same result can probably be achieved on a more modest scale by a mimeographed outline of the courses.

The booklet was called "Invitation to Learn." In addition to the outlines of the courses, it carried a message from the pastor urging all members to regard the educational opportunities as much a part of their church commitment as the worship services. The concluding paragraphs said,

> You will note that the courses have been stressed and not the teachers. A list of teachers will be made available before each series of courses is offered. All teachers have been trained in an intensive preparatory course. Excellent leadership is therefore offered.
>
> Now it is up to you. Like the farmer who must thin out the seed so that a mature crop may be realized, so the church member must cut out lesser interests and put worship and study together as the first requirement on Sunday morning. Give yourself and the members of your family the opportunity to learn by accepting this invitation to learn! On Sunday, let us go to the house of the Lord and learn together how rightly to handle the word of truth.

The program was all-inclusive. It included pastor's classes for future members, the teen-age groups, and went all the way down to the tiniest tots in the nursery. It was intended to show that education is a continuing process and one that deserves high priority in the parish. For this reason, a great deal of time was put into preparing the program and the brochure. It also revealed to the congregation that teachers were willing to attend training sessions and to prepare for their classes. Through regular promotion it tried to prepare people for the novel process of making a personal commitment to an educational program in which they would know in advance the theme of the classes and the dates for the courses.

It was a great success. When the Sunday school closed for the summer previous to this program, it had seven persons attending the adult class regularly, one of those typical classes. . . . When sessions resumed in the fall, one hundred fifty-five persons were enrolled in the adult education section in the three different classes. During the year it slowed down a little, but even for the third thirteen-week series the adult group had dropped only from 155 to 130, which is not bad! If you want your Sunday school to wake up, you must invest some time, money, and imagination, and you've got to deliver a good program.

SECTION IV:

INDEXES

INDEX OF SCRIPTURE REFERENCES

Old Testament

New Testament

INDEX OF NAMES, TITLES, AND HYMNS

The page numbers in boldface type following hymn titles indicate a historical sketch of that hymn.

INDEX OF SERMON TOPICS